URBAN
AMERICA

URBAN AMERICA
GROWTH, CRISIS, AND REBIRTH

JOHN F. McDONALD

M.E.Sharpe
Armonk, New York
London, England

Library of Congress Cataloging-in-Publication Data

McDonald, John F., 1943–
  Urban America : growth, crisis, and rebirth / John F. McDonald.
    p. cm.
  Includes bibliographical references and index.
  ISBN 978-0-7656-1806-1 (cloth : alk. paper)—ISBN 978-0-7656-1807-8 (pbk : alk. paper)
    1. Cities and towns—United States—History. 2. Urban renewal—United States—History.
  3. United States—Race relations—History. 4. Sociology, Urban—United States—History.
  I. Title.

HT123.M213 2007
307.76′40973—dc22   2006101368

Printed in the United States of America

The paper used in this publication meets the minimum requirements of
American National Standard for Information Sciences
Permanence of Paper for Printed Library Materials,
ANSI Z 39.48-1984.

∞

BM (c)   10   9   8   7   6   5   4   3   2   1
BM (p)   10   9   8   7   6   5   4   3   2   1

For Glena

Contents

Part IV. The Rebirth of Urban America After 1990

List of Tables

Preface

This book is an expression of hope—hope for America's cities and the people who live in them. It is also a call for others to follow this lead in their thinking and action. As the book demonstrates, this call to be hopeful about the cities is firmly based on evidence. It is not a vain hope. At the same time, hope must be backed by careful study and effective action. This book is thus a call to understand why it is reasonable to be hopeful, and a call for further effort to achieve positive results. As such, the intent is that the book reach a wide audience beyond the scholarly community, including public officials, journalists, and citizens in general. It is written in nontechnical terms.

Within this book I attempt to bring historical perspective to the urban crisis that gripped most of America's major cities for roughly two decades. The historical perspective includes the legacy of slavery, as amply documented by Gunnar Myrdal in *An American Dilemma* (1944). The period of rapid urban growth and Great Migration from the South after World War II substantially improved the lives of most Americans, but also produced the tensions and frustrations that led to violent outbursts in the 1960s. A period of urban crisis followed, and that crisis was visited primarily upon black Americans in the cities. The descent of the cities during this time gave many people cause to lose hope for the cities, and many still are in this frame of mind.

The period of descent came to an end sometime around 1990 in many urban areas. The most important part of this book is the study of the urban rebirth that has occurred. This study also shows that urban rebirth is far from complete and may be fragile. Some of the data for the first five years of the twenty-first century are worrisome—all the more reason to be hopeful and vigilant.

This book is partly based a long career of studying America's cities that began when I attended Professor Kenneth B. Clark's course at Harvard Summer School in 1965. Consequently, there are many people who could be thanked. However, I shall mention only three. First, I thank the people of M.E. Sharpe who encouraged and promptly agreed to this book. Thanks are also due to Stan Wakefield, who helped develop the book proposal and then marketed it skillfully. But mainly I thank my wife, Glena McDonald. She has served as initial reader and proofreader for the book, and as inspiration.

Introduction

This book is a chronicle of the dramatic events that took place in urban America in the second half of the twentieth century. A drama in the real world is a series of events that are fascinating and memorable enough to resemble those in a play. The thesis in this book is that the drama of urban America since 1950 has three acts. After a brief transition to peacetime, urban America experienced robust growth up to the early 1970s. The end of this first act was announced a few years in advance by rioters in the Watts section of Los Angeles in August 1965. The Watts riot came just four days after President Lyndon B. Johnson signed the Voting Rights Act on August 10, 1965. The Voting Rights Act was a signal achievement of the civil rights movement, and it came in the same year as President Johnson's Great Society programs. There were plenty of signs of trouble brewing in urban areas, and the blizzard of programs that was the Great Society was partly in response to those problems. But the urban riots of the 1960s made it clear that a new period for urban America was beginning. The second act began with a bang.

The urban crisis that began in the late 1960s lasted until approximately 1990. That crisis had many dimensions that are discussed in this book. One useful characterization—the vicious circle—was put forth by Gunnar Myrdal in his classic study, *An American Dilemma* (1944). The decline of the major cities and the attendant social problems were all related and reinforced one another. Those problems included racial segregation, central-city fiscal problems, inner-city joblessness, dependence on welfare, teenage pregnancies, births out of wedlock, serious crime, drug addiction, poor education, and general hopelessness. The urban crisis was visited primarily upon black Americans in the inner cities. Black Americans play pivotal roles in the urban drama, and the book concentrates on them in several chapters. Act 2 was a bad time for cities and the people who lived in them, but Act 2 did end.

No one announced the end of Act 2, but sometime shortly after 1990 the downward spiral that had gripped America's cities stopped. The argument in this book is that urban decline halted and, in many urban areas, a "virtuous circle" began in which improvements in several dimensions became mutually reinforcing. I also argue that many observers of the urban scene failed to see that Act 3 had begun. There are at least three reasons for this failure. First, the beginning of Act 3 was unexpected. Urban analysts were used to Act 2 and its themes and did not think that a basic alteration of theme was possible. Second, the beginning of Act 3 was not easy to discern. The opposite of rioting did not break out, and the data in the early years were their usual messy and puzzling selves. But third, I think that some analysts, journalists, and advocates are invested in the theme of urban decline. "Isn't it terrible? America needs to pay more attention to its cities. More programs and money are needed. Don't confuse me with the facts." To be sure, urban America still suffers from many problems. The point is, however, that many of those problems have been getting better, not worse. The murder rate in this country has dropped by 50 percent since the early 1990s to levels that have not been seen since before the start of the urban crisis in the mid-1960s. We still have far too many murders—especially compared to every other advanced nation—but real progress has occurred. The time is well past due for the nation to focus on how to keep the momentum of social and economic progress going.

The basic purpose of this book is to back up and work through all three acts. Just as Act 1 contained signs of the trouble ahead in Act 2, there were indicators during Act 2 that suggested things might change. One period does lead to the next, but I am no economic determinist.[1] The reversal of the vicious circle into a virtuous circle was indeed unexpected. However, a great and largely unexpected event took place at the same time as the rebirth of urban America—the end of the Cold War. As eminent Cold War historian John Gaddis (2005) recounts, the sickness of the Soviet society and economy was becoming increasingly obvious in the 1980s.[2] But Gaddis argues that the end of the Cold War in 1989–91 was brought about by a small group of important actors—Pope John Paul II, Ronald Reagan (an actual actor, after all), Margaret Thatcher, Lech Walesa, Mikhail Gorbachev, Boris Yeltsin, and Chairman Deng Xiaoping in China. No such cast of characters can be identified in the rebirth of urban America; Act 3 was not, I would argue, the result of the heroic efforts of a few "great men and women." Rather, the efforts of literally millions of individuals were involved. Millions of welfare mothers found employment after "welfare as we knew it" ended in 1996. Millions of immigrants came to America's cities with the hope of a better life and stayed to revitalize neighborhoods too. Some of those efforts were purposeful, and some were mistakes that had unexpected consequences. For example, the boom in the construction of downtown office buildings at the end of the 1980s created both financial havoc and a supply of office space that was available at low rents. Other important factors just happened. The AIDS epidemic convinced most people that having unprotected sex is not a good idea. And, as Steven Levitt and Stephen Dubner (2005) have pointed out, the 1973 Supreme Court decision in the case of *Roe v. Wade*, which established a woman's right to an abortion in the first two trimesters of pregnancy, was followed by a reduction in the crime rate eighteen years later. Is this a coincidence? Levitt and Dubner think not.

The story in outline form can be told using population figures for the three main regions of the nation. Table A.1 shows the population for the nation (excluding Alaska and Hawaii) and for the Northeast, the South, and the West by decade from 1950 to 2000. Total population and black population data are displayed. We see that the nation entered the 1950s with a population of 150.7 million, of whom 58.0 percent (87.4 million) lived in the Northeast, 29.0 percent (43.7 million) resided in the South, and only 13.0 percent (19.6 million) in the West. The South had 63.3 percent (9.5 million) out of a national total of 15.0 million black residents. In 2000 the population for the nation (excluding Alaska and Hawaii) was 279.6 million, with 44.6 percent (124.6 million) in the Northeast, 33.5 percent (93.6 million) in the South, and 22.0 percent (61.4 million) in the West. The share of the population in the Northeast dropped by 13.6 percentage points, with the West picking up most of that share. The regional distribution of the black population changed dramatically over the half-century. In 2000 the South was home to 49.1 percent of the black population of 34.6 million. The share of the black population living in the Northeast had increased from 33.0 percent to 42.1 percent, and the West increased its share of the black population from 3.8 percent to 8.8 percent.

The basic story of growth, crisis, and rebirth of America's major urban areas can be seen in Table A.2, which shows percentage changes in population for 1950 to 1970, 1970 to 1990, and 1990 to 2000. With the exceptions of Los Angeles and San Francisco–Oakland, all of the major urban areas in 1950 were located in the Northeast. A critical part of the overall story is the emergence of major urban areas in the South and West after 1950, but for now we presume that major urban areas are primarily located in the Northeast.

Table A.2 shows that the population of the nation (excluding Alaska and Hawaii) increased by 34.1 percent from 1950 to 1970. Population growth in the Northeast of 26.8 percent fell short of the national total, but the difference in growth is a relatively modest 7.3 percent (3.65 percent per decade). Population growth in the South was 31.6 percent over this same period, and the West was booming with population growth of 72.5 percent. The Great Migration of blacks from the South is clearly in evidence. The total black

Table A.1

Population of the Contiguous Forty-eight States plus the District of Columbia (1,000s)

	1950	1960	1970	1980	1990	2000
USA total	150,696	178,464	202,143	225,179	247,052	279,583
USA black	15,043	18,860	22,564	26,464	29,937	34,614
Northeast total	87,401	100,607	110,839	113,449	116,532	124,640
Northeast black	4,957	7,465	10,231	11,690	13,031	14,569
South total	43,734	50,663	57,568	69,923	79,392	93,584
South black	9,516	10,321	10,654	12,545	14,127	17,012
West total	19,586	27,194	33,734	41,806	51,128	61,359
West black	570	1,074	1,678	2,231	2,779	3,033

Note: Northeast includes New England, Mid-Atlantic region, East–North–Central region, West–North–Central region, Delaware, Maryland, and the District of Columbia. South includes the eleven states of the Confederacy plus Kentucky, Oklahoma, and West Virginia. West includes the Mountain and Pacific regions (excluding Alaska and Hawaii).

Source: Census of Population.

Table A.2

Percentage Changes in Population

	1950–1970	1970–1990	1990–2000	1950–2000
USA total	34.1	22.2	13.2	85.5
USA black	50.0	32.7	15.6	130.1
Northeast total	26.8	5.1	7.0	42.6
Northeast black	106.4	27.4	11.8	193.9
South total	31.6	37.9	17.9	114.0
South black	12.0	32.6	20.4	78.8
West total	72.5	51.6	20.0	213.7
West black	194.4	158.8	9.1	432.1

Source: Table A.1.

population increased by 50.0 percent over those twenty years, but the black population of the Northeast increased by 106.4 percent—from 4.97 million to 10.23 million. The black population of the South increased by only 12.0 percent during this period. The small black population in the West increased by 194 percent, reaching 1.68 million. The migration of the black population from the South to the Northeast was a factor in the overall population growth of the northern region. The growth in the black population accounts for 22.5 percent of the population growth of the Northeast in the 1950s and 1960s. Clearly the Northeast was seen as the region of economic and social opportunity.

The twenty years from 1970 to 1990 stand in sharp contrast to the previous twenty years. During this twenty-year period, national population growth slowed to 22.2 percent, but population in the Northeast increased by only 5.1 percent! The difference between the national and regional growth figures has widened to 17.1 percent (8.55 percent per decade), compared to 7.3 percent during the 1950–70 period. Population growth of 5.1 percent is far below the natural rate of population growth (births minus deaths) of 15 percent. Just as the Great Migration of blacks to the Northeast was indicative of relative economic and social opportunity, the migration of people from the Northeast during the 1970s and 1980s is indicative of declining economic opportunity compared to the rest of the nation. The black population of the Northeast increased by 27.4 percent during this period, but this figure is in strong contrast to the 106.4 percent growth recorded in the previous twenty years. Since the black population of the nation increased by 32.7 percent in the 1970s and 1980s, it is fair to say that the Great Migration to the Northeast was over. The urban riots of the 1960s, which could be watched on television, may well have played a role in convincing people not to migrate to the great northeastern urban areas. Population growth in the South was a robust 37.9 percent, and the West continued to boom with population growth of 51.8 percent over these twenty years. The term "Sunbelt" appeared during this period.

Now consider the data for the 1990s. Yet another demographic shift is in evidence. The change is not as dramatic as the one that took place in the 1970s and 1980s, but it is noticeable. The population of the nation increased by 13.2 percent, and the Northeast came back with population growth of 7.0 percent, a difference of 6.2 percent over the decade. More importantly, perhaps, the population growth in the 1990s exceeded the growth over the previous twenty years of 5.1 percent. As we shall see, this population growth in the Northeast translated into population growth in some of the major central cities such as New York, Chicago, Boston, Columbus, Kansas City, Indianapolis, and Min-neapolis–St. Paul. Black population growth in the Northeast of 11.8 percent fell short of national growth by a modest 3.8 percent. Population growth in the South of 17.9 percent kept up its pace from the 1970s and 1980s, but the growth of the West slowed to a relatively sedate (for it) figure of 20.0 percent. The locus of black population growth shifted to the South with an increase of 20.4 percent, compared to 11.8 percent in the Northeast and only 9.1 percent in the West.

This short excursion into population figures has shown that the first twenty years of the period examined in this book were a time of growth in the Northeast, the home of nearly all of the nation's major urban areas. While population in the other two regions grew more rapidly than in the Northeast, the Northeast is by far the nation's most mature region, and a somewhat slower growth rate is to be expected in a mature region. The Great Migration of the black population to the Northeast was in full swing. The next twenty years, 1970 to 1990, are roughly the years of urban crisis. Population growth in the Northeast was a minuscule 5.1 percent over these twenty years. The Great Migration ended. People were "voting with their feet." The Northeast simply was not providing economic opportunity as it had before. The move to the Sunbelt—both the South and the West—is clear in these data. As we shall see, very slow population growth in the Northeast was associated with sizable population declines in major central cities (even as many suburban areas prospered). Indeed, some of those population losses were devastating. But there is evidence of a comeback in the Northeast in the 1990s. Popula-tion growth in the 1990s of 7.0 percent exceeded the growth for the entire 1970–90 period. As we shall see, population increased in some major central cities. The task of this book is to describe more fully and uncover the reasons for the outcomes shown in Tables A.1 and A.2.

The figures on poverty in the United States are another telling set of in-

Table A.3

Poverty in the United States: 1949–2000 (in percent)

	1949	1960	1970	1980	1990	2000
All persons	39.5	22.3	12.6	13.0	13.5	11.3
Blacks	76.7	55.1*	33.5	32.5	31.9	22.5
Hispanics	65.3	n.a.	22.8**	25.7	28.1	21.5
Persons in female-headed households	62.4	48.9	38.1	36.7	37.2	28.5
Blacks in female-headed households	n.a.	70.6	58.7	53.4	50.6	38.6

*Figure for 1959.
**Figure for 1972, not available for 1960 or 1970.
Sources: U.S. Bureau of the Census (various years) and Iceland (2006).

troductory data. The official poverty rate figures begin with 1959, but John Iceland (2006) used data from the 1950 census to estimate poverty rates in 1949 using the official definition of poverty (which varies by household size). Poverty rates for the entire population and for certain population subgroups are shown in Table A.3. The national poverty rate as estimated by Iceland (2006) for 1949 was 39.5 percent. Poverty declined dramatically in the 1950s and 1960s to 22.2 percent in 1960 and 12.6 percent in 1970, a record that is consistent with the economic growth and prosperity of this period. But, after a decline to 11.1 percent in 1973 (the all-time low point), the poverty rate fell no further for the next twenty years. The national poverty rate had inched up to 13.0 percent in 1980 and 13.5 percent in 1990. The 1990s are a different story. Poverty increased in the recession of the early 1990s to 15.1 percent in 1993, and then fell steadily to 11.3 percent in 2000—coming very close to the all-time low. The poverty rate increased somewhat during the next five years because of the recession of 2001 and the slow recovery in employment, but remained relatively low at 12.6 percent in 2005.

The trends in the overall poverty rate thus correspond to the periods of growth, crisis, and rebirth in the nation's urban areas. However, the data on poverty for black persons, Hispanic persons, persons in female-headed households, and persons in households headed by black females illustrate the three periods more clearly. As shown in Table A.3, the poverty rate for blacks started at an astonishing 76.7 percent in 1949 and dropped to 33.5 percent in 1970 as blacks moved from the rural South to urban areas, especially urban areas of the Northeast. However, black poverty made no further significant declines for the next twenty years. Blacks entered the decade of the 1990s with a poverty rate of 31.9 percent. But see what happened next. After the recession of the early 1990s, black poverty began to drop, and it reached its all-time low point of 22.5 percent in 2000. The story for the Hispanic population is broadly similar to that for blacks. Hispanic poverty was 65.3 percent in 1949, and it had dropped to 22.8 percent in 1972. From this point, poverty increased to 25.7 percent in 1980 and 28.1 percent in 1990. Again, after the recession of the early 1990s, poverty among Hispanics fell to 21.5 percent in 2000, the lowest level on record. The periods of growth, crisis, and rebirth are illustrated clearly by the poverty rates of the nation's two largest minority groups.

Next, we turn to the poverty rates for persons in female-headed families. The poverty rate for these persons fell from 62.4 percent in 1949 to 38.1 percent in 1970, but then improved very little for the next twenty years. Then poverty dropped from 37.2 percent in 1990 to 28.5 percent in 2000. The data for persons in households headed by black females show continuous improvement, but that improvement was more rapid before 1970 and after 1990. The poverty rate for 1949 is not available, but it stood at 70.6 percent in 1959. Poverty fell to 58.7 percent in 1970 and 50.6 percent in 1990, and then dropped to 38.6 percent in 2000—a record for the lowest rate for this group. A member of a household headed by a black female had a better than 50–50 chance of being poor until 1995. In summary, the data in Table A.3 show that America made great progress at reducing poverty from 1949 to the early 1970s, but made little progress for the next twenty years. The decade of the 1990s brought further progress in the fight against poverty. A primary task of this book is to study the major urban areas to understand why all of this happened.

The method I followed in this book was to identify seventeen urban areas in the Northeast and a dozen urban areas in the Sunbelt (six in the South and six in the West), and to study these urban areas from 1950 to 2005. Most of the chapters contain detailed examinations of either the northeastern urban areas, the urban areas in the Sunbelt, or both, during one of the time periods labeled Growth, Crisis, or Rebirth.

As one who lived through the urban crisis from age twenty-one to age forty-eight (and who lived through the entire Cold War as well), I am struggling with the question of where we go from here. International terrorists have supplied the answer on the foreign policy side for now, but my expertise does not include fighting the "war on terror." I hope that this book will help stimulate the thinking that we need to recognize the rebirth of urban America and to nurture and enhance the positive forces that are at work.

Notes

1. Indeed, the urban crisis referred to in the title of this book was a crisis visited primarily upon the urban black population in the northern cities. But this crisis, and especially its

racial dimension, could have turned out differently. For example, the South could have won the Civil War, kept slavery for many more years, and as a separate nation prevented much of the Great Migration of blacks to the cities of the North in the twentieth century. How could the South have won? Military historian Bevin Alexander (1993) argues that Robert E. Lee missed a real opportunity to create a situation in which Britain might have recognized the Confederacy and the North might well have negotiated a peace. Lee's invasion of the North in 1863 was potentially a master stroke, but Lee violated what Alexander has called the first rule of winning wars by mounting a frontal attack on July 3, 1863, at Gettysburg. Instead he could have skirted the Union army, moved to the East, and simultaneously threatened Philadelphia, Baltimore, and Washington, D.C. Furthermore, a major portion of his army—the left flank—was out of position and therefore unable to be useful during the crucial parts of the battle. The eminent historian James McPherson (1988) observed in *Battle Cry of Freedom* that the vice president of the Confederacy, Alexander Stephens, was on route under a flag of truce to the Union lines at Norfolk. President of the Confederacy Jefferson Davis had hoped that Stephens would arrive in Washington at the same time the victorious Lee would be marching on the northern capital. The reports of the Stephens mission and the outcome of the battle reached President Abraham Lincoln at the same time, and he curtly refused to permit Stephens to pass through the lines. As Alexander (1993) argues, Lee might never have made these mistakes if the strategic genius Thomas "Stonewell" Jackson had not been killed on May 2, 1863, at Chancellorsville. Jackson was in the process of sweeping around the flank of the Union army, attacking from the rear, and cutting off its retreat when he was killed by what was probably "friendly fire." Jackson repeatedly had tried to persuade Lee that such a maneuver was their best strategy, and at last had won the authority to go ahead. Upon Jackson's death, Lee reverted to his direct method of battle and destroyed the offensive power of the southern army. This exercise in hypothetical history should not lead anyone to conclude that the northern victory was not the better outcome.

2. Gaddis (2005) recounts the story that the opening of the Berlin Wall in November 1989 was a mistake. The East German Politburo had intended only to relax somewhat the rules for travel to West Berlin, but the official who held the press conference got confused and announced that citizens of East Germany were free to leave permanently through any of the border crossings, effective immediately. The border guards had not been informed of the new "policy," but when a large crowd gathered at one of the gates, the guards took it upon themselves to open the wall—rather than fire on their countrymen. Great historical forces were indeed at work, but there was an idiosyncratic element at work on that day as well.

Part I

Urban America in 1950

1
Urban Areas of the Northeast

The American Economy in 1950

In 1950 there was really only one major league sport—baseball. Major league baseball was played in only ten cities: Boston (2 teams), New York (3 teams), Philadelphia (2 teams), Chicago (2 teams), St. Louis (2 teams), Washington, D.C., Pittsburgh, Cleveland, Cincinnati, and Detroit. Half of the sixteen teams were located on the East Coast in the Boston–New York–Philadelphia–Washington axis. This configuration for major league baseball was set in 1903 with the founding of the American League and was doubtless based partly on how far one could travel overnight by train at the turn of the twentieth century. In 1947 the Brooklyn Dodgers had hired the first black player in the major leagues since the nineteenth century, Jackie Robinson, and in 1950 there were only five black players. The Negro League was still active, with teams in many of the major league cities. All of this was about to change. One major league team, the St. Louis Browns, moved to Baltimore in 1953 and took the name Baltimore Orioles, and the New York Giants and the Brooklyn Dodgers moved to the West Coast in 1957. Teams started to travel by airplane. The numbers of black players and players from Latin America would increase dramatically. The Negro League folded. But in 1950 all of that was in the future.

The United States had come through World War II and the immediate postwar years as by far the most powerful and economically advanced nation in the world. The nation's major cities had been the "arsenals of democracy" during the war, and after the war had switched successfully to the production of consumer goods. The fear that the economy would enter a postwar depression proved unfounded. Both the Cold War and the hot war in Korea had begun, but Americans were poised to enter a period of unprecedented prosperity. James T. Patterson (1996), in his marvelous contribution to the *Oxford History of the United States* series, calls it the period of "Grand Expectations."

The United States had a population of 151 million in 1950. The nation's population is now over 300 million, so one basic fact about our urban areas is that they have had to grow to accommodate a doubling of the population. (No new urban areas have been founded. They all existed in 1950.) Life was different in 1950. The median annual household income in the nation in 1950 was $2,599 (including families and unrelated individuals). Median income for families in urban areas was $3,673. There were 40.2 million registered passenger cars (and taxis). There were very few four-lane highways. Only 10 percent of households owned television sets, and 38 percent of the population had never seen a television program (although all of the Los Angeles Rams football games were televised in 1950). Agricultural employment was still 7 million in 1950, and nonagricultural employment as reported in the 1950 census was 49.23 million—broken down as follows:

Mining and construction	4.36 million
Manufacturing	14.58 million
Transportation, communication, and utilities	4.37 million
Wholesale and retail trade	10.55 million
Finance, insurance, and real estate (FIRE)	1.92 million
Business and repair services	1.41 million
Other services	9.55 million
Public sector	2.49 million
Total	49.23 million

Manufacturing was 29.6 percent of nonagricultural employment in 1950, and mining and construction and distribution (transportation, communication, utilities, and trade) made up 19.3 percent of the total. Services of all kinds (including FIRE) made up 26.2 percent of nonagricultural employment. The economy was dominated by the production and distribution of goods.

This author was seven years old in 1950. My parents and I lived in Decatur, Illinois (an industrial urban area of 99,000 in central Illinois farm country—the Soybean Capital of the World), in a new four-room house with about 900 square feet of living space and a basement. Much of the basement was taken up by the coal furnace and the coal bin. During the winter my father shoveled coal into the furnace at regular intervals. Air conditioning was unknown (at least to us). We had an electric refrigerator, but everyone called it an icebox. There was no television station in Illinois outside of Chicago. It is likely true that I had never heard of television, let alone seen it. My parents did own a car; my recollection is that it was a Nash. My father worked as a grain inspector for the federal government in downtown Decatur. My mother also worked, something that was quite unusual for a mother in those days. She was the receptionist and assistant for a physician whose specialization was eye, ear, nose, and throat. This is, of course, a specialty that no longer exists. My mother was trained as a Red Cross first-aid instructor but had no medical training beyond that. Much later she told me stories of the patients who appeared at the doctor's office in dire straits—usually with eye injuries. I walked three blocks to my school and attended the second grade. We had lived in another house when I was in kindergarten, and I had taken the city bus to school. I would walk to a close neighbor's house, and the mother saw to it that her son and I got on the bus. I presume that the bus driver made sure that we got off at the right place. We never locked our house in those days.

So life was different in 1950. We shall begin this history with a systematic look at the urban areas of the Northeast in that year. The purpose of this chapter is to give a snapshot in 1950 of the top seventeen urban areas in the Northeast, which is assumed to extend from Washington, D.C., west to Kansas City and north to Minneapolis–St. Paul. The next chapter is a quick look at the twelve largest urban areas of the Sunbelt. Chapter 3 is a short update on race in urban America—in the context of Gunnar Myrdal's 1944 book, *An American Dilemma*.

Principles of Business Location in 1950

We have seen that the production and distribution of goods dominated the U.S. economy in 1950. The northeastern portion of the nation dominated the production of goods, and most of that production was located inside the cities of the Northeast. An understanding of the history of urban America first requires knowledge of the principles of business location that were at work in 1950. Businesses must assemble inputs and distribute output to customers. Choosing a location that will save on transportation costs can be a very complex problem that must take into account the costs of transporting the inputs and outputs and the relative weights attached to those costs.

The urban areas of the Northeast all began as what are called transshipment points—breaks in the national or regional transportation system where freight must be moved from one mode of transportation to another (or from one carrier to another if there is no change in mode). In particular, the urban areas of the East Coast began life as ports where agricultural products were brought in by boat or wagon and moved out on ships. Goods also arrived on ships and were transferred to wagons or boats for distribution to customers. The major urban areas of the Midwest began as ports on the Great Lakes (Chicago, Cleveland, Detroit, Milwaukee) or as river ports (St. Louis, Cincinnati, Kansas City, Minneapolis–St. Paul). Their first function was to transport agricultural products to the consumers in the East, but soon entrepreneurs realized that transshipment points for agricultural products could be centers of production as well.

During the first half of the nineteenth century, two factors combined to create America's first group of real cities. Those two factors were the invention of large-scale production methods (for that time) and what economic historians call the transportation revolution. Factories with economies of scale were developed in several industries—textiles, apparel, iron, tools, ordnance, wagons, lumber, food products such as flour, and so on. The transportation revolution was based first on the steamboat and, a few years later, on the railroad. Production to build the railroads and companies to run them became major parts of the economy. These two factors made it economical to house large manufacturing enterprises at the transshipment points. For example, Cyrus McCormick invented the mechanical reaper in his home state of Virginia in 1831. He started production of the reaper in Cincinnati in 1845, but he realized that Chicago, the rapidly growing city that was to become the focus of the transportation system of the Midwest, was the place to produce his reapers. He moved his factory to Chicago in 1847, even before there was one railroad serving the city. He produced 700 reapers in 1848, and by 1850 production had doubled. McCormick had made a good decision because Chicago became the central point for a vast railroad system that serves the Midwest and the nation. The McCormick Reaper Works became International Harvester. Thanks to many other entrepreneurs like McCormick, Chicago became the nation's number two center of production and distribution (second to New York).

Business location within the city was based on access to transportation, which in the nineteenth and early twentieth centuries meant access to water and rail. McCormick's first Chicago reaper plant was located at the mouth of the Chicago River, which was also home to the enormous grain elevators from which the agricultural products of the Midwest were shipped east. Later, McCormick factories were placed on both the north and south branches of this river. The Union Stockyards, which consolidated Chicago's various stockyards and meat packers into one location in 1865, was located at a rail junction and on a tributary of the Chicago River. Cattle and hogs arrived by rail from Midwestern farms, and packed meat was sent to customers by rail. (The tributary of the Chicago River, called Bubbly Creek because of the horrible pollution, was used as a sewer.) The iron and steel industry and other heavy industry were located on the south side of the city where the Calumet River empties into Lake Michigan. A new generation of steel plants was located across the state line in Indiana—again on Lake Michigan. Inland Steel, located in the southern suburb of Chicago Heights, took its name from the remarkable fact that it was not located on Lake Michigan. It was, however, located near a bevy of rail lines that extend in all four directions. Steel plants needed to locate where inputs could be assembled at the least cost. In the case of the steel industry of Chicago and northwest Indiana, ore came by ship from Duluth, and coal and limestone were brought by rail from southern Illinois, southern Indiana, and Kentucky. Other Chicago industries that produced goods for the farmers and artisans of the Midwest (and sold them by catalog through Sears, Roebuck and Montgomery Ward) were located within easy reach of the many rail lines that delivered the goods to the customers.

In general, the allocation of land to various uses is based on the amount those various users are willing to pay. Land-use zoning—municipal laws that allocate land to the various uses—did not exist until the 1920s. "Downtown" locations were dominated by retailers and people who needed office space—lawyers, accountants, bankers, and the like. Manufacturers might have liked being located downtown (and some were), but they could not normally outbid these users for downtown sites. Manufacturing firms that established themselves on the outskirts of downtown or on the rivers, canals, and rail lines did so because they outbid others for those sites. Housing was constructed outside downtown and near the manufacturing plants. By the end of the nineteenth century, major cities had rail systems in place that permitted workers to commute to their jobs in and near the downtown area. In fact, anyone who has eaten at the Subway chain of sandwich shops knows that one John McDonald is credited with being the father of the New York subway system. As far as is known, this important figure in urban history is not related to the author of this book.

The era of the automobile began in earnest in the 1920s, but the introduction of the truck on a large scale initially had a larger impact on industrial location than did the automobile. Trucks were used primarily to transport physical inputs and outputs within cities in the period of 1920 to 1950. Few modern highways existed in those days, so rail transportation still dominated long-haul freight. Trucking freed lighter industry to form a more dispersed location pattern within cities and nearby suburbs because cities had decent internal street systems. Industry also benefited from a complex network of rail lines and rail yards within cities. Chicago led the way in this regard, and its system still exists. Heavy industry (steel and other primary metals, oil refining, and chemicals) was still tied to sites with rail and water transportation, but lighter industry (machinery, apparel, instruments, and so on) could locate at many sites within the city, with its good streets and internal rail network. Real estate development firms established large industrial parks for industry. This was how things stood in 1950. As we shall see, massive changes in the composition of the economy and the nature of the transportation system undermined the economic base of the city as it existed in 1950.

Urban Areas of the Northeast: Population, Employment, and Earnings

Population data for the top seventeen urban areas in the Northeast (and their central cities) are shown in Table 1.1. Washington, D.C. (always a special case), Baltimore, and Kansas City are included in the Northeast. The urban areas are ranked by the population of the metropolitan area, which consists of one or more counties. To continue with the baseball story, the top nine urban areas were nine of the ten with major league teams in 1950. Cincinnati was the smallest urban area with a team—smaller than Baltimore, Minneapolis–St. Paul, and Buffalo. Baseball franchises were subsequently awarded to all urban areas in the top fifteen, except for Buffalo. It is also clear why it made sense to move the St. Louis Browns to Baltimore, the largest urban area in the Northeast without a team. St. Louis was attempting to support two teams with a population of only 1.68 million, and Baltimore had no team and a population of 1.34 million.

It is obvious that New York (the Big Apple) and Chicago (the Second City) are in classes by themselves.

New York

New York occupies a spectacular site. Its harbor is huge and is protected by Long Island, and the Hudson River extends far inland. It is difficult to imagine a better setup for a nineteenth-century port city to engage in commerce and trade. Philadelphia outpaced New York in the eighteenth century, but by 1810 New York (i.e., Manhattan), together with its small neighbor Brooklyn, had a population of almost 100,000—which surpassed Philadelphia for the first time. From this point on, New York participated robustly in the twin revolutions in transportation and large-scale production that created the first great American cities. The Erie Canal opened in 1826 and connected New York to the growing Great Lakes region, but many other canals were constructed in those days that expanded New York's market area. By 1850, New York was connected to the West (Chicago and St. Louis) by rail. It had emerged as the nation's leading port as well as the focus of an internal transportation system that served the entire Northeast.

Trade and commerce required financial services. New York became the nation's banking, finance, and insurance capital in the mid-nineteenth century. Foreign investment in America, especially in railroads, flowed through New York. New York also participated in industrial growth, becoming the greatest manufacturing city in the nation. Its early industrial concentrations were in apparel, iron, and printing and publishing. Manufacturing has never dominated

Table 1.1

Urban Areas of the Northeast: Population in 1950 (1,000s)

Urban area	Urban area population	Black population in urban area (percent)	Central city population	Black population in central city (percent)
New York	13,318	1,020 (7.7)	7,892	748 (9.5)
Chicago	5,495	587 (10.7)	3,621	492 (13.6)
Philadelphia	3,671	480 (13.1)	2,072	376 (18.1)
Detroit	3,016	358 (11.9)	1,850	300 (16.2)
Boston	2,370	52 (2.2)	801	40 (5.0)
Pittsburgh	2,213	136 (6.1)	677	82 (12.1)
St. Louis	1,681	215 (12.8)	857	154 (18.0)
Cleveland	1,466	152 (10.5)	915	148 (16.2)
Washington, D.C.	1,464	334 (22.8)	802	281 (35.0)
Baltimore	1,337	265 (19.8)	950	222 (23.4)
Minneapolis–St. Paul	1,117	13 (1.2)	833	13 (1.6)
Buffalo	1,089	124 (11.4)	580	37 (6.4)
Cincinnati	904	95 (10.5)	504	88 (17.5)
Milwaukee	871	22 (2.5)	637	22 (3.5)
Kansas City	814	87 (10.7)	457	56 (12.3)
Indianapolis	552	65 (11.8)	427	64 (14.0)
Columbus	503	52 (10.3)	376	47 (12.5)
Mean		10.4%		13.8%

Source: Census of Population and Housing.

New York's economy as it has those of other urban areas such as Detroit, Pittsburgh, Cleveland, and Chicago, but the sheer size of New York made its manufacturing sector the largest in the nation. Individual manufacturing firms in New York tended to be relatively small, and they tended to cluster together to benefit from economies of agglomeration—sharing of a labor pool, having access to specialized products and services, and so on.

New York also emerged as the gateway to the nation. Immigrants came to New York and, while many moved on, many stayed to work in the city's booming economy. The foreign-born numbered 384,000 and were 47 percent of the New York population in 1860. This huge migration was a potentially volatile mix that produced several urban riots in the nineteenth century.

As urban sociologist Janet Abu-Lughod (1999) puts it, New York solidified its character in the period of 1870 to 1929. The first twenty years of this period were dominated by massive migration from Europe. Most of that growth took place on Manhattan, where industry expanded and densities increased. The Lower East Side became the famous port of entry for immigrants. The next phase of growth, from the 1890s to World War I, saw more immigration and growth as well as refinement of the financial sector into modern Wall Street with its stock market, investment banking, insurance, and legal and accounting services. The construction of the subway system got under way in the 1890s. The modern city of New York was created in 1898 when the five boroughs were united under one municipal administration. As Manhattan became increasingly crowded, manufacturing was pushed to the other boroughs and to New Jersey. Apparel and printing and publishing remained in Manhattan, but industrial activities such as iron foundries, stone and marble cutters, boot and shoe firms, and electronics firms moved to Brooklyn, Newark, and other locations away from downtown.

Immigration from abroad ceased to be a major driving force behind the New York economy during World War I and was cut off sharply by the restrictive immigration law of 1924. Instead, internal migration became the source of population growth. Black migration from the South started in large numbers during the war and continued in the 1920s, but white people who moved from the farms and small towns of the South and the East were greater in number. Abu-Lughod (1999, p. 71) points to "a new burst of explosive construction that pushed the envelope of development well beyond the city's limits, as fast-growing suburban communities began to dot the adjacent counties of Nassau, Westchester, and even Suffolk." This was the first period of "white flight" to the suburbs. Population density of the Lower East Side declined to a more sensible level, and as whites moved out of Harlem and blacks moved in, Harlem became the largest concentration of black people in the nation during the 1920s. Manhattan solidified its position as the nation's capital of finance, publishing, and entertainment—including the new industry of broadcasting. Manhattan also assumed its modern appearance: both the Empire State Building and the Chrysler Building were opened on the eve of the stock market crash of 1929.

The financial and commercial sectors of New York were hit very hard by the Great Depression as international trade dwindled and industrial employment dropped, too. But Harlem was hardest hit by the Depression, and a study headed by the sociologist E. Franklin Frazier (1937) found poverty, poor and crowded housing, lack of medical care, poor education, and high crime (and sometimes overzealous police). The Harlem Riot of 1935 was the first instance of an outburst of urban blacks against racial discrimination and poverty. Another riot took place in Harlem in August 1943. This time the precipitating event was an altercation between a policeman and a female client at a hotel. A black soldier intervened, and false rumors spread that a white policeman had killed a black soldier. Soon after, windows were broken, stores looted, and fires set in Harlem. Dominic Capeci (1977), a scholar of the Harlem Riot of 1943, believes that the underlying causes included inflation in rents and prices, segregation in the military, and racial discrimination in defense jobs. Federal rent control was implemented in New York City before the end of the year. Overall, World War II gave the New York economy a big boost. War production included aircraft manufacturing, which was located at plants in the suburbs on Long Island.

Conversion to the peacetime economy brings us to 1950. Table 1.2 shows that the population of the New York–New Jersey urban area was 13.06 million, and 1.02 million (7.7 percent) of that population was black. New York City had a population of 7.89 million, with a black population of 748,000 (9.5 percent). The sheer size of the New York–New Jersey urban area must be kept in mind as the discussion of urban areas proceeds. Its black population exceeded the entire population of the Cincinnati urban area. Table 1.2 shows that total employment in the urban area was 5.31 million, of which 30.5 percent (1.62 million) was in manufacturing. As Table 1.2 shows, this is not a particularly high concentration in manufacturing, especially compared to Detroit, Cleveland, and Milwaukee—all over 40 percent. Only 56.4 percent of the manufacturing jobs were located in New York City at this time. As Table 1.2 shows, manufacturing employment was more heavily concentrated in the central city in most of the major northeastern urban areas. Women held 31.7 percent of the jobs in the urban area, which is a pretty typical percentage for northeastern urban areas. The urban area was home to 463,000 employees in finance, insurance, and real estate (FIRE) and business services. This amounts to only 8.7 percent of total employment, but this sector alone employed more people than the total at work in the Cleveland urban area! Average earnings for men of $3,012 per year in the urban area, also shown in Table 1.2, were similar to earnings in other major urban areas. On the other hand, with the exception of Washington, D.C., average earnings for women of $1,708 were the highest in the nation. Earnings for women probably reflect the higher skills required by employers in New York's office towers. However, the median years of education for adults (age twenty-five and over) in the urban area were not particularly high—only 9.6 years for men and 9.4 years for women.[1] Remember that half of the adults had *fewer* years of education.

Chicago

Chicago was still the second city and second urban area in 1950. It lost the first of these distinctions to Los Angeles sometime in the 1980s, but the Los Angeles urban area jumped ahead of the Chicago urban area in the 1950s. Chicago did not exist before the 1830s. In 1829 the state of Illinois announced that it would build a canal at the village of Chicago to connect Lake Michigan

12

Table 1.2

Urban Areas of the Northeast: Employment and Earnings in 1950 (employment in 1,000s)

Urban area	Employment (percent female)	Manufacturing (percent)	Manufacturing in city: 1947 (percent)	FIRE, business services (percent)	Male earnings (median $)	Female earnings (median $)	Median years education M/F
New York	5,314 (31.7)	1,623 (30.5)	58.6	463 (8.7)	3,012	1,708	9.6/9.4
Chicago	2,362 (30.8)	885 (37.5)	78.3	145 (6.1)	3,201	1,610	9.9/9.9
Philadelphia	1,438 (30.9)	527 (36.6)	61.8	77 (5.3)	2,841	1,479	9.5/9.5
Detroit	1,193 (25.8)	560 (46.9)	60.8	52 (4.4)	3,277	1,483	9.9/10.3
Boston	915 (33.1)	262 (28.6)	37.6	64 (7.0)	2,771	1,414	11.7/12.0
Pittsburgh	809 (24.7)	307 (37.9)	24.0	33 (4.1)	2,787	1,154	9.0/9.3
St. Louis	677 (30.6)	229 (33.8)	70.6	35 (5.1)	2,852	1,354	8.8/8.8
Cleveland	616 (29.8)	250 (40.5)	83.3	30 (4.9)	3,167	1,400	10.4/10.5
Washington, D.C.	621 (38.5)	45 (7.2)	NA	35 (5.6)	3,005	2,004	12.1/12.2
Baltimore	528 (30.3)	158 (29.8)	71.2	26 (4.9)	2,708	1,204	8.8/8.8
Minneapolis–St. Paul	461 (33.4)	116 (25.2)	86.6	33 (7.1)	3,020	1,341	10.8/11.6
Buffalo	424 (26.9)	171 (40.3)	47.3	16 (3.8)	3,004	1,270	9.5/9.6
Cincinnati	357 (30.5)	118 (33.1)	72.1	20 (5.5)	2,812	1,,243	9.1/9.2
Milwaukee	375 (30.4)	161 (42.8)	75.1	18 (4.7)	3,201	1,369	9.6/9.6
Kansas City	340 (31.5)	81 (23.9)	59.4	22 (6.4)	2,886	1,372	10.7/11.3
Indianapolis	234 (32.1)	77 (32.9)	86.2	14 (5.9)	3,038	1,436	10.6/10.9
Columbus	200 (32.4)	50 (25.0)	75.4	13 (6.3)	2,832	1,415	11.0/11.6

Source: Census of Population and Housing.

to the Illinois River (and thus to the Mississippi River). This announcement set off a land boom that has few rivals in world history. The canal would make Chicago *the* transshipment point between the Great Lakes and the Mississippi River system. At that time, water transportation ruled both the freight and passenger markets. While the Midwest (the old Northwest) was only sparsely settled then, people knew that the region was about to be settled and that both agricultural and urban economic activity would go hand-in-hand. Because of the national depression of the 1830s, the Illinois and Michigan Canal was not completed until 1848, the same year in which the first railroad steamed west ten miles from Chicago to the Des Plaines River. Soon the Galena and Chicago Union railway stretched over 100 miles west to Galena. The 1850s saw the first boom in railroad construction, and Chicago became the central point for railroads in every direction. Chief among these railroads was the Illinois Central, the Rock Island, the Chicago and Northwestern, the Michigan Central, and the Chicago, Burlington, and Quincy.

Chicago's position at the center of the rail network made it into a transportation and manufacturing powerhouse in the last decades of the nineteenth century. The rail network was focused on downtown Chicago, which was located at the mouth of the Chicago River. Commercial development became concentrated in Chicago's Loop, an area of a little more than a square mile bounded by Lake Michigan on the east and by the Chicago River on the north and west. However, many businesses soon outgrew their original downtown locations and moved outward. Emblematic of this trend was the founding, as mentioned above, of the Union Stockyards in 1865 five miles south of downtown at a point of access to both water and rail transportation.[2] The movement of business to the "suburbs" is nothing new. Chicago was the fastest-growing urban area in the world in the 1880s and 1890s, and reached a population of 1.37 million in 1890, 2.67 million in 1910, and 4.41 million in 1930. The population growth was largely the result of migration from Europe before that migration was cut off in 1924. Population growth resumed after the Depression of the 1930s; in 1950, the population of the urban area was 5.5 million and the city of Chicago reached its all-time high of 3.62 million.

Chicago had been a major destination in the Great Migration of blacks from the South since the beginning of this movement during World War I. A black-owned newspaper, the *Chicago Defender*, was delivered by the Illinois Central railroad to people in the South, and it ran advertisements for jobs in Chicago and advice on how to get there. By 1950, the black population of the Chicago urban area (the city of Chicago and its suburbs) had reached 587,000 (10.7 percent of the urban area). The black population of the city of Chicago was 492,000, which was 13.6 percent of the city's population.[3]

The Chicago economy of 1950 had a diversified manufacturing base that provided an amazing 885,000 jobs (37.5 percent of total employment—well above the national figure of 29.6 percent). Manufacturing was heavily concentrated in primary metals, fabricated metals, and machinery. These industries employed 419,000 workers, which was 47.3 percent of manufacturing employment. The machinery industries (electrical and nonelectrical) employed 210,000 people, including 59,000 women. The Chicago urban area contained 6.1 percent of all the manufacturing jobs in the nation. The Census of Manufactures reported that there were 852,000 jobs in manufacturing in the urban area in 1947, and that 667,000 (78.3 percent) of these were located within the city of Chicago. The dominance of the central city by wholesale and retail trade can also be documented. Wholesale trade employed 155,000 in the urban area in 1948, and 138,000 (89 percent) of those jobs were located in the city. Retail trade employment in the urban area was 354,000 in that same year, and 249,000 (70 percent) of the jobs were located in the city. As shown in Table 1.2, women held 30.8 percent of the jobs, which was quite typical for major urban areas in the Northeast. Median earnings for men (at $3,201) and for women (at $1,610) were relatively high, even though the median education level of 9.9 years was not especially high. In fact, earnings for men were greater only in Detroit, and women's earnings were higher only in New York and Washington, D.C.

Philadelphia and Detroit

The next two urban areas—Philadelphia and Detroit—were similar in size. Both had metropolitan populations in excess of 3 million and central cities of about 2 million. Both central cities had reached their historic population peaks in 1950. And each urban area had sizable black populations of 12 to 13 percent that were the result of the waves of the Great Migration from the South in the 1920s and 1940s. The two cities are, of course, quite different in both their histories and economic functions.

The Philadelphia urban area was big, diverse, and old. As shown in Table 1.2, its economy was similar to Chicago's in some basic measures. About 37 percent of employment was in manufacturing, and no particular manufacturing industry was dominant. As researchers with the Philadelphia Economic Monitoring project showed, all sectors of manufacturing were well represented in Philadelphia. Durable goods provided 48 percent, and nondurable goods accounted for 52 percent of manufacturing employment. The top durable goods industry was electrical machinery and equipment, while apparel was the leading nondurable industry. Some 61.8 percent of manufacturing employment was located in the central city. As in Chicago, about 31 percent of jobs were held by women, but median earnings for both men and women were about 10 percent lower in Philadelphia than in Chicago.

Detroit was and is our most industrial large urban area. Manufacturing provided 668,000 jobs, 47 percent of employment in the Detroit urban area in 1950, by far the highest percentage among all large urban areas. The city of Detroit was home to 60.8 percent of the manufacturing jobs, and another 12.8 percent (mainly Ford Motor Company) were located in Dearborn, adjacent to Detroit. The "transportation equipment" (i.e., auto industry) employed 339,000 people, which was 61 percent of manufacturing employment and 28 percent of total employment. Detroit's fate has been tied to the auto industry since the turn of the twentieth century.

The first American automobile producer was not located in Detroit. The Duryea Company of Springfield, Massachusetts, was the first to begin production of a gasoline-powered car in the United States in 1896. Olds, the first Detroit producer, began in 1899, but by 1904, 42 percent of American automobiles were being produced in the Detroit area. By 1914, Detroit was making 78 percent of the vastly expanded auto industry output. Why was Detroit so successful in this new business? One critical antecedent was the ship and boat industry. It was here that the internal combustion gasoline engine was developed into a practical engine for powering boats. Several early Detroit auto entrepreneurs had backgrounds in the boat engine business. Olds produced them, Leland made parts for them, and Dodge and Ford repaired them. Other industries that were present in Michigan supported the auto industry, examples being the carriage industry, steel, wheelwrights, and machine tools. The firms and workers in these industries had the skills to produce the components needed for the auto. Financing was available from investors who had made fortunes in lumber, mining, food processing, and other industries. What is more, the investors in Detroit were willing to learn about the potential of the auto industry. All of this created an innovative contagion in which the development of ideas, products, and markets acquired its own momentum. Economists call this phenomenon *agglomeration economies*. Firms locate together to be where the action is. Several other urban areas have benefited from this phenomenon—most notably the San Francisco Bay area with its Silicon Valley.

Henry Ford's first car company had failed, but in 1903 he was ready to join the dozens of other car companies in Detroit with another venture. At this point he was forty years old and knew just about everything there was to know about the car business. Furthermore, he had the vision that the future of the business was to build a car that was cheap enough to be marketed on a massive scale to the farmers and artisans of the day. In 1903 cars were expensive, and only the well-to-do bought them. There were only about 800 cars in Detroit at the time. Ford's timing was good; his new company was successful and he was able to plow money back into design work. The year 1908 stands as a landmark year in industrial and urban history. In that year, Henry Ford introduced the Model T Ford, a reliable, durable, and compact car. It benefited from recent improvements in steel technology that permitted steel parts to be both lighter and stronger. The Model T was successful from the beginning. But then the story changed. Up until then, Ford had been only one part of the Detroit auto industry and its agglomeration economies.

Henry Ford had visited the Union Stockyards in Chicago and seen the conveyer belt system used by meatpackers to "disassemble" cattle into cuts of beef. Inspired, Ford invented the assembly line. At first, assembly lines were developed for various parts of the Model T—motors, transmissions, and so on. Then, in 1914, the first moving assembly line was introduced in which the chassis of the Model T was pulled along by conveyer belt. These improvements in production methods permitted Ford to cut the price of the Model T from $780 in 1910 to $360 in 1914. David Halberstam's 1986 book *The Reckoning* informs us that in 1914 Ford produced 268,000 cars with 13,000 employees while the other 299 U.S. car makers produced 287,000 cars with 66,000 employees. Ford's share of the market (in terms of cars produced) had increased from 9.4 percent in 1908 to 48 percent in 1914. The chief source of this tremendous growth in the Ford Motor Company was the economy of scale provided for the firm through assembly-line production. As Mr. Ford himself once modestly put it, "I invented the modern age."

Ford did not stop with the Model T assembly line. Beginning in 1918 he created his River Rouge complex, located on the Detroit River in Dearborn at southwestern edge of the city of Detroit. River Rouge eventually became a fully integrated manufacturing facility that took iron ore in at one end and shipped cars out the other end. "The Rouge" began as a boat factory in 1918, added a pig iron plant in 1920, branched out to tractors, auto engines, and a steel plant in 1925, and then became the plant for the Model A Ford that was introduced in 1925. The Rouge was 1.5 miles long by 0.75 miles wide, had 23 major buildings and 93 miles of railroad track, and employed as many as 75,000 workers. At the Rouge it took four days to produce a completed car from raw materials.

First place in the auto industry was taken over by General Motors in the 1920s under the leadership of Alfred Sloan, who emphasized a more diverse product line using a divisional structure and clever marketing. The Cadillac, Fisher Body, and other General Motors plants were located in the city of Detroit. Chrysler emerged as the number three auto company. The Chrysler auto body plant and "Dodge Main" were its largest plants in the city of Detroit, and Plymouth and Chrysler assembly plants were located there as well.

(Actually, Dodge Main was located in Hamtramck, a separate town located within the boundaries of the city of Detroit.) The industry recovered from the Depression of the 1930s by converting to war production in the 1940s, but by 1950 the auto companies were running on all cylinders, producing cars and trucks for the American public. The auto industry was also a leader in industrial unionism. The United Auto Workers (UAW) had organized the "big three" by the late 1930s after a bitter struggle—especially with Ford. The impact of the UAW is seen in the median earnings of men shown in Table 1.2. These earnings of $3,277 were the highest in the nation, even though the median years of education for adult men were an unexceptional 9.9 years. Median earnings of women in Detroit were exceeded only by those in New York, Chicago, and Washington, D.C.

Boston and Pittsburgh

The next group of urban areas includes Boston and Pittsburgh. Each had populations of 2.2 to 2.4 million in 1950 and relatively small central cities. The population of the city of Boston of 801,000 was 33.8 percent of the urban area, and the city of Pittsburgh's population of 677,000 was only 30.6 percent of its urban total. Also, both had relatively small black populations. The black population of the Boston urban area was only 52,000 (2.2 percent), while the black population in the Pittsburgh area of 136,000 was 6.1 percent of the total.

The economy of the Boston urban area was less concentrated in manufacturing than were most of the other major urban areas. Boston is the state capital of Massachusetts and home to a large concentration of colleges and universities. As shown in Table 1.2, in 1950 manufacturing provided 28.6 percent of employment, and only 37.6 percent of manufacturing was located in the city of Boston. Compared to the other urban areas, a higher proportion of jobs in the Boston urban area—33 percent—were held by women. The relatively low concentration of employment in manufacturing meant that the median earnings of men were a relatively low $2,771, while the median earnings of $1,414 for women were well above average. The men and women of the Boston urban area were among the most highly educated in the nation with 11.7 and 12.0 years of education, respectively, on average.

The Pittsburgh economy presents a sharp contrast to Boston. With 307,000 jobs, the concentration in manufacturing was heavy, and almost half (48.3 percent) of those jobs were in primary metals (i.e., the iron and steel industry). Primary metals employed 148,000 workers, which was 18.3 percent of all workers in the Pittsburgh urban area in 1950. This concentration in one industry was not nearly as great as autos in Detroit, but clearly the economy of Pittsburgh was tied to the fortunes of the iron and steel industry. However, manufacturing was not primarily located in the city of Pittsburgh. Only 24.0 percent of the manufacturing jobs were located in the central city. In particular, much of the iron and steel industry was along the Monongahela River in Homestead and the other industrial towns of the Steel Valley. Recall that the central city contains a relatively small portion of the population of the urban area as well. While the iron and steel industry had been unionized by the United Steel Workers, the median earnings in Pittsburgh were not relatively high. Median earnings for men of $2,787 were close to men's earnings in the Boston urban area, and women in Pittsburgh earned a relatively low $1,154. Both men and women in the Pittsburgh urban area had relatively low levels of education—9.0 years for men and 9.3 years for women.

St. Louis, Cleveland, Washington, D.C., and Baltimore

The next size category for metropolitan areas includes St. Louis, Cleveland, Washington, D.C., and Baltimore. These urban areas had 1.3 to 1.7 million people, and each central city contained 800,000 to 950,000 people. Not surprisingly, Baltimore and Washington, D.C., had the largest percentages of black population of any of the Snowbelt urban areas—19.8 percent and 22.8 percent, respectively. The population of the District of Columbia (the central city) was 35 percent black, by far the largest percentage in the Snowbelt. The legacy of the Civil War years and the employment opportunities afforded by the federal government would appear to account for this. Both urban areas are often classified as southern, but they are regarded as part of the Snowbelt here. However, both St. Louis, 12.8 percent black, and Cleveland, 10.4 percent black, also had relatively large black populations at this time.

St. Louis, the smallest urban area attempting to support two baseball teams, had an economy with a pretty typical concentration in manufacturing of 33.8 percent (with fully 70.6 percent of those jobs located in the city). Some of the industry in St. Louis was directly related to the agricultural economy of the Midwest—beer in St. Louis, stockyards in East St. Louis, Illinois, and so on. Women held 30.6 percent of the jobs. Median earnings were also pretty typical at $2,852 for men and $1,354 for women. The median education level of 8.8 years in the St. Louis urban area was the lowest among the major urban areas in the Northeast (tied with Baltimore).

The Cleveland economy was heavily concentrated in manufacturing, with 390,000 jobs (40.5 percent of employment), and 83.3 percent of those jobs were located in the city of Cleveland. In fact, only the Detroit, Buffalo, and Milwaukee urban areas were more heavily concentrated in manufacturing. Cleveland had large fabricated metals and nonelectrical machinery industries (employment of 40,000 in each). Median earnings and education levels for both men and women in Cleveland were also relatively high: $3,167 and 10.4 years for men and $1,400 and 10.5 years for women.

Washington, D.C., is the atypical major urban area because of the dominance of the federal government. Government employed 189,000 workers in 1950, which was 30.4 percent of total employment. Government employment is also reflected in the number of women workers—38.5 percent of employees, by far the highest for any major urban area in the nation. Also, while median male earnings were a typical $3,005, female median earnings of $2,004 were the highest in the nation by a wide margin. The residents of the Washington, D.C., urban area were, on average, the most highly educated in the nation: 12.1 years of education for men and 12.2 years for women. Many civil service government jobs required a high school diploma.

Baltimore, an East Coast city about the same size as St. Louis in the Midwest, had a lower concentration in manufacturing than did St. Louis (29.8 percent versus 33.8 percent), although those jobs (71.2 percent) were heavily concentrated in the city. Both men and women in Baltimore had lower median earnings than those in St. Louis, but slightly over 30 percent of the jobs in both urban areas were held by women. The median education level in Baltimore was low—only 8.8 years for both men and women. Only a few miles away in Washington, the median person had over three more years of education than did residents of Baltimore.

Five More Urban Areas

The next group of five urban areas includes Minneapolis–St. Paul, Buffalo, Cincinnati, Milwaukee, and Kansas City, Missouri. Population in this rather diverse group ranges from 814,000 to 1.12 million, and central city population was smallest at 457,000 in Kansas City and largest at 833,000 in Minneapolis–St. Paul. These twin cities are lumped together because they are adjacent—separated by only a street. The black populations of Buffalo, Cincinnati, and Kansas City ranged from 10.5 to 11.4 percent, reflecting their roles as recipients in the Great Migration. However, Minneapolis–St. Paul and Milwaukee had hardly been affected by the migration of black people from the South, probably because they are farther to the North than other urban areas such as St. Louis and Chicago.

These five urban areas represented a diverse group of local economies. Buffalo and Milwaukee had very high concentrations in manufacturing (both over 40 percent of employment), and Minneapolis–St. Paul and Kansas City had very low manufacturing concentrations—25.2 percent and 23.9 percent, respectively. Cincinnati had a more typical 33.1 percent of employment in manufacturing. Both Minneapolis–St. Paul and Kansas City faced west toward the vast agricultural areas of the Great Plains, serving as transportation centers and transshipment points and, to a lesser extent, centers of manufacturing production. Manufacturing was very heavily concentrated in the twin central cities (86.6 percent) of Minneapolis and St. Paul, but not in the central city, Kansas City (59.4 percent). St. Paul is the state capital, and Minneapolis is the home of Minnesota's great state university, so government was a major employer there. The concentration of manufacturing in the central city was relatively high for Milwaukee (75.1 percent) and Cincinnati (72.1 percent), but a low 47.3 percent in Buffalo. Women held only 26.9 percent of the jobs in Buffalo, but they held over 30 percent of the jobs in Milwaukee (and in the other three urban areas as well). Median earnings for both men and women were highest in the manufacturing city of Milwaukee and lowest in Cincinnati, the major urban area of the Northeast adjacent to Appalachia.

Indianapolis and Columbus

The last two urban areas on the list are Indianapolis and Columbus. Each had only something over 500,000 people in 1950, but they are included because they grew to prominence in later years. The omission of Indianapolis and Columbus would mean that an important part of the story would be omitted as well.

Indianapolis is both the political and economic capital of Indiana, and it was a typical northeastern urban area in 1950. Blacks made up 11.8 percent of the population of the urban area, manufacturing was 32.9 percent of total employment, and the earnings of men ($3,038) and women ($1,436) were better than average. Women held 32.1 percent of the jobs. Manufacturing employment was highly concentrated in the central city at 86.2 percent.

Columbus is also a state capital, located between Cleveland and Cincinnati. With a 10.3 percent black population in 1950, its racial composition matched other northeastern urban areas. However, manufacturing employment in Columbus was a relatively low 25.0 percent. State government (including Ohio State University) had a sizable presence in the local economy with 7.4 percent of employment. Earnings in Columbus for men were lower than in Indianapolis ($2,832 versus $3,038), probably because of the relatively low concentration of manufacturing in Columbus. Earnings for women were $1,415, which matches Indianapolis. The education level in Columbus ranked third among the seventeen urban areas listed in Table 1.2, behind Washington, D.C., and Boston. The median education level for men was 11.0 years and for women 11.6 years.

Housing and Housing Programs

The state of the nation's housing left much to be desired in 1950. Vacancy rates were very low by historic standards, and much of the housing stock was old and substandard in quality. These points are illustrated in Table 1.3 for the major urban areas of the Northeast. The vacancy rate in the Milwaukee urban housing market was a minuscule 1.58 percent. Vacancy rates varied from this low up to 5.87 percent in the Baltimore urban area, and most of the vacancy rates in Table 1.3 are well below 3.5 percent. As a comparison, the vacancy rate in metropolitan areas in 1991 was 8.0 percent. Rates of home ownership varied from a low in New York of 31.7 percent up to 61.8 percent in Detroit and 61.9 percent in Philadelphia. Most of the ownership percentages were in the high 40s to 50s. The percentage of units occupied by nonwhites followed the population percentages shown in Table 1.1.

Perhaps the most telling information in Table 1.3 is the percentage of housing that was regarded as substandard by the Census Bureau. Housing was substandard if it lacked hot running water, or if it did not have private toilet and bath, or if it was dilapidated. Some units failed on all three counts, but it took only one to be considered substandard. In New York and Boston the percentage of substandard units was a relatively low 12.2 percent, but St. Louis recorded a shocking 34.1 percent. Nine of the seventeen major urban areas in the Northeast had substandard units in excess of 20 percent, and this group included Chicago with 21.8 percent substandard. As for my hometown of Decatur, Illinois, 37.9 percent of the units in the urban area were substandard in 1950 (although surely the percentage was substantially lower within the city limits). I can recall the outhouses that were used by neighbor families, and the burning of same in celebration of the installation of indoor plumbing.

The quality of the housing stock was negatively affected by the lack of housing construction in the 1930s and early 1940s. Nonfarm housing starts in the United States averaged only 348,000 for the ten years from 1935 to 1944. Housing starts jumped up to 1.08 million per year during 1945 to 1949, and increased further to 1.54 million per year in the first five years of the 1950s. Table 1.3 shows the percentage of new units—the ones that had been built between 1940 and 1950. Washington, D.C., led with 38.2 percent, which no doubt reflects the huge increase in federal employment that took place during World War II. Three urban areas—Detroit, Baltimore, and Columbus—had percentages of new units in excess of 20 percent. Otherwise, most of the urban areas had less than 15 percent new units. Philadelphia was a typical case with 13.4 percent new units.

The Philadelphia housing stock was described by the Philadelphia Economic Monitoring Project researchers (Stull and Stull 1991) as antiquated

Table 1.3

Housing in 1950

Urban area	Vacancy rate (percent)	Owner occupied (percent)	Occupied by nonwhite (percent)	Substandard (percent)*	Built after 1940 (percent)	Public housing units	Percent public housing
New York	4.55	31.7	6.8	12.2	12.2	16,882	0.43
Chicago	2.60	41.8	9.5	21.8	11.5	8,483	0.51
Philadelphia	3.32	61.9	12.1	17.0	13.4	3,248	0.31
Detroit	3.38	61.8	9.2	13.1	25.9	4,879	0.57
Boston	3.15	44.5	2.2	12.2	8.2	5,102	0.76
Pittsburgh	2.07	54.8	5.4	32.1	14.5	4,463	0.71
St. Louis	2.56	51.4	11.5	34.1	14.9	1,315	0.26
Cleveland	2.51	53.5	8.3	11.3	16.2	5,179	1.18
Washington, D.C.	3.57	42.6	18.2	12.9	38.2	3,147	0.75
Baltimore	5.87	55.0	16.2	21.3	22.8	5,021	1.28
Minneapolis–St. Paul	2.96	60.3	1.3	24.8	16.9	464	0.14
Buffalo	3.47	53.8	3.4	14.5	13.8	2,571	0.81
Cincinnati	2.82	49.1	10.2	27.9	13.0	3,818	1.34
Milwaukee	1.58	49.8	1.9	18.5	14.3	651	0.26
Kansas City	3.03	58.3	10.4	29.7	15.7	0	0.00
Indianapolis	2.33	58.5	10.5	31.0	18.9	748	0.43
Columbus	1.72	53.7	8.9	22.0	20.3	1,352	0.91

*Substandard units lack hot running water, or lack private toilet and bath, or are dilapidated.

Source: Census of Population and Housing, 1950.

and inadequate.[4] Units were concentrated near the centers of manufacturing in the urban area, and more than 60 percent had been built before 1920. Little housing construction had taken place in the 1930s and 1940s; Stull and Stull (1991) found that the vacancy rate in 1950 was a very low 2.7 percent (2.4 percent in the central city and 3.2 percent in the suburbs). The vacancy rate recorded by the U.S. Census was 3.23 percent, which is only slightly different. Remember the original *Rocky* movie? Much of the housing stock consisted of small row houses that were no longer considered acceptable by the middle class. The Census recorded that 17.0 percent of the housing stock was substandard, and many households with lower incomes lived in crowded rental units in poor condition.

The federal government had begun to recognize that the nation had a housing problem, and declared in the Housing Act of 1949 the goal "to provide a decent home and suitable living environment to all Americans." One might question the feasibility of this goal and whether it should be the responsibility of the federal government, but this statement remains in place to this day. Federal housing policy in 1950 consisted of three programs and federal income tax deductions for mortgage interest and local property taxes. The three programs are mortgage insurance, public housing, and slum clearance. The three programs are examined first in chronological order, and then the income tax deductions are illustrated.

The first major federal housing program was created by the National Housing Act of 1934. This act created the Federal Housing Administration (FHA) and provided for mortgage loan insurance to buyers who could qualify. The FHA mortgage insurance program was created during the Depression as part of the effort to have a banking and financial system that would not collapse as in the early 1930s. The borrower paid an insurance premium that was 0.5 percent of the outstanding loan balance so that the lender could be protected from the borrower's possible default. The FHA program has a maximum loan amount, which started at $16,000 in 1935 and was lowered to $14,000 in 1950. The maximum maturity permitted started at twenty years in 1935, and this was raised to twenty-five years in 1938. The interest rate was regulated; a maximum of 5.00 percent was permitted in 1935, and this was lowered to 4.5 percent in 1940 and 4.25 percent in 1950. The maximum allowable loan-to-value ratio was 80 percent in 1935, and this was raised to 90 percent in 1938. Prior to the creation of the FHA program, mortgage loans normally were of short duration (e.g., seven to ten years) and had low loan-to-value ratios (typically 65 percent). Buyers would have to obtain a new loan after a few years because the typical mortgage required only interest payments with a "balloon" payment at the end. The FHA program essentially created the mortgage loan as we know it—low down payment, lengthy maturity, and full amortization (i.e., the level monthly payments paid the interest and paid off the loan). The FHA insurance meant that lenders—banks and savings and loans—could offer such terms. In 1950 a qualified buyer could obtain a twenty-five-year loan of up to $14,000 with a 10 percent down payment at an interest rate of no more than 4.25 percent (plus the FHA insurance premium). The FHA mortgage insurance program is also available for apartment buildings with "reasonable" rents.

A similar program of mortgage insurance was instituted in 1944 for veterans under the Servicemen's Readjustment Act, popularly known as the GI Bill. Qualified veterans could borrow up to 100 percent of the value of the home. The Veterans Administration (VA) loan guarantee covered up to 60 percent of the loan, and the veteran paid virtually nothing for this guarantee. A maximum interest rate of 5 percent was in place during 1944–50.

The FHA and VA programs had a major impact on the housing market, especially on new single-family units. In 1950 there was a total of $45.2 billion in outstanding mortgage debt on family houses with one to four units. The FHA program insured $8.5 billion of that total (18.8 percent), and the VA program insured $10.3 billion (22.8 percent of the total). The FHA and VA programs had been successful in making mortgage loans available to middle-class families and veterans, but the FHA was subject to criticism after only a few years of operation. The intent of the FHA program was to insure mortgages on "sound" business principles; consequently an underwriting manual was written to ensure that FHA loans were sound. Gunnar Myrdal (1944), in *An American Dilemma*, pointed out that the FHA underwriting manual of 1938 included the statement that FHA property valuators were urged to consider whether the area or property to be insured was subject to "adverse influences," which included business and industrial uses, lower-class occupancy, and inharmonious racial groups. The manual advocated use of restrictive covenants for tracts to be developed with new housing. As Myrdal stated, these restrictive covenants were meant to include the "prohibition of the occupancy of properties except by the race for which they are intended" (1944, p. 349). Racial restrictive covenants were commonly used in real estate at that time but were declared unconstitutional by the Supreme Court in 1948 in the case of *Shelley v. Kraemer*. The effect of these underwriting standards was to concentrate the FHA program on newer, suburban housing. FHA underwriters tended to avoid inner city areas that appeared to be subject to adverse influences. Chapter 3 is a general update on Myrdal's massive study to 1950, and more will be said about the FHA throughout the book.

The second major federal program, the public housing program, was created by the Housing Act of 1937. The sponsor of the original bill was Senator Robert Wagner of New York, and it met with a favorable reception from Congress and President Franklin D. Roosevelt, the former governor of New

York. The act set up the U.S. Housing Authority and authorized it to make loans to local public housing agencies for up to 90 percent of the development cost of a project. Local agencies would issue bonds for the remaining 10 percent of the development cost. The Authority sold tax-exempt bonds to raise the funds for the loans, and the secretary of the Treasury was authorized to purchase the bonds. Several provisions of the 1937 act ensured that public housing would aid low-income families. The Authority could also contract to make annual contributions to the local public housing agency in amounts not greater than the going federal rate of interest plus 1 percent on the development cost. Annual contributions were conditional on local or state contributions in the form of cash or tax remissions. Local agencies were required to meet current operating costs out of rents collected from tenants and to remit any excess to the federal government to offset the federal annual contribution. In the late 1940s nearly all of the annual federal contribution was offset by such remissions (but this was to change dramatically). The public housing program thus relied on the initiative of local authorities to plan and execute public housing projects. The federal government would not be directly in the business of constructing and managing public housing. One other feature of the program was important. The law required that the number of new units be matched by the removal or rehabilitation of an equivalent number of unsafe or unsanitary units. This was called the principle of "equivalent elimination," which meant that the intent of the public housing program was to improve the quality of housing within a fixed supply. Slum clearance was to be combined with public housing.

The construction of public housing began in 1939, and by 1950 172,000 units had been completed nationwide. The bulk of those units were built between 1940 and 1943, by which time a total of 161,000 units had been completed. During 1944 to 1950 only an additional 11,000 units were added. Table 1.3 shows the number of public housing units in the major northeastern cities. New York had 14,171 units and Chicago had 8,483. Most of the other cities had a few thousand units. The seventeen cities listed in Table 1.3 had a total of 64,612 units, which was 38 percent of the national total. Only in Cleveland, Baltimore, and Cincinnati did public housing constitute more than 1 percent of the housing stock. It is fair to say that the public housing program had not yet produced enough units to make a major impact on urban housing markets.

The Housing Act of 1949 was landmark legislation. As noted above, the act declared as its goal "to provide a decent home and suitable living environment to all Americans." The act adopted the dual approach of public housing and slum clearance. Congress authorized the construction of 135,000 units of public housing per year for six years, a total of 810,000 units to be added to the existing stock of 172,000 units. The idea was to have almost 1 million units of public housing by 1955. To accomplish this goal, the act added to the ability of local public housing agencies to sell bonds by increasing the federal annual contribution. The slum clearance part of the act came to be known as urban renewal, but the original title in the act was "Slum Clearance and Community Development and Redevelopment." The program authorized federal officials to provide two-thirds of the net cost of a slum clearance project that was initiated by a local agency. The local agency planned a project and used its power of eminent domain to purchase the property. The net cost of the project is the cost of property acquisition plus demolition and site improvement costs plus the cost of supporting public facilities minus the price realized from the resale of the land. It was the intent of the act that the land would be resold to private real estate developers as well as to local public housing agencies. Congress wanted to get private enterprise involved in community development and redevelopment, and used the power of eminent domain combined with federal funds to do the job. As in the case of public housing, the onus was on local officials to plan and propose projects to the federal government. Since this major policy shift had only been enacted in 1949, there were no material effects on cities in 1950. The operation of the urban renewal program will be discussed later in the book.

The federal income tax provides deductions of mortgage interest and local property taxes to homeowners. These deductions were built into the income tax when it was adopted in 1913. The effect is to reduce the cost of housing for the homeowner compared to the cost of renting. Here is how it works. Suppose you are a homeowner in 1950. You have purchased a home for $10,000 and obtained a mortgage of $9,000 with FHA mortgage insurance at an interest rate of 4.25 percent. Suppose you pay a local property tax equal to 2 percent of the value of the house. The real economic cost of the house per year is the sum of mortgage interest, maintenance and depreciation (typically about 2.5 percent of the value of the house), and property taxes, and these are:

Mortgage interest	$382.50
Maintenance and depreciation	250.00
Property taxes	200.00
FHA mortgage insurance	45.00
Total	877.50

As a homeowner you get to take deductions equal to $582.50. In 1950 the typical household faced the minimum federal income tax rate of 17.4 percent at the margin, so the deductions reduced the federal tax bill by $101.36. The cost of the house has thus been reduced by $101.36 to $776.14, a reduction of 11.6 percent. In 1950 the top income tax rate was 90 percent on incomes in excess of $400,000, so the value of the homeowner deductions was greater the larger was one's income. These deductions have come under attack over the years, but remain in place.

Conclusion

The major urban areas of the Northeast formed a distinct hierarchy in 1950. Atop the nation's urban areas was the New York–New Jersey urban area with a population of 13.3 million. There is an old "fun fact" called the rank-size rule for urban areas. The idea is that the size of an urban area times its rank is equal to a constant. In the case of New York the calculation is 13.3 times 1. The next urban area in the northeastern hierarchy was Chicago, and the calculation is 5.5 times 2, which equals 11—pretty close. Next in line is Philadelphia with 3.7 x 3 = 11.1. After that there is Detroit; 3.0 x 4 = 12; then Boston with 2.4 x 5 = 12; and then Pittsburgh with 2.2 x 6 = 13.2. We may be on to something here, but what does this mean? The basic idea is that urban areas form a hierarchy not only by size, but by function as well. The largest urban area performs all of the functions performed by the other urban areas, but it also is home of some industries that exist nowhere else. These industries have a market area as large as the entire region. What was unique about New York? Well, we have already noted some of it: the New York Stock Exchange, investment banking, publishing, entertainment, broadcasting. These activities existed to some extent in Chicago and Philadelphia, too, but New York was the dominant player. As we move down the hierarchy, we encounter urban areas that served as regional centers. Chicago was economic headquarters of a very large region, while St. Louis, Kansas City, Milwaukee, Indianapolis, and Minneapolis–St. Paul covered regions that were part of the Chicago market area. Other urban areas were primarily centers of production. Detroit, Cleveland, Buffalo, and Pittsburgh fit this model. The region covered by Philadelphia extended west and south to include Pittsburgh, Baltimore, and other parts of the East Coast. Boston is the capital of the New England region.

In 1950 the urban areas of the Northeast had converted back to a peacetime economy and were poised to participate in the coming prosperity. Most of them (twelve out of seventeen) contained heavy concentrations of manufacturing (above the national average of 29 percent), and much of that manufacturing was located in the central city. However, some urban areas were never heavily invested in manufacturing: Washington, D.C., Boston, Kansas City, and Minneapolis–St. Paul. And manufacturing was not heavily concentrated in the central city in a few: Boston, Pittsburgh, and Buffalo. Median education levels for adults (age twenty-five and over) in 1950 were low by contemporary standards. The median education level for men was less than eleven years in fourteen out of the seventeen urban areas, and less than ten years in ten of them.

Housing in the northeastern urban areas was not a pretty picture. There had been very little housing construction since the 1920s (except in Washington, D.C.); vacancy rates were very low, housing was old and crowded, and many, many units lacked basic features such as running hot water, toilets, and bathtubs. Some suburban housing had been constructed previously, mainly in the New York urban area, but the suburban boom was almost entirely in the future. The federal government had recognized the nation's housing problem, but had not done much about it as of 1950 other than to offer the FHA and VA mortgage insurance programs.

But before we turn to that future, we need to take a look at the urban areas in the rest of the nation, specifically the South and the West. And we need to take a careful look at the status of the black population as of 1950. This group will have a critical impact on urban America.

Notes

1. Median earnings for men in the northeastern urban areas depended upon their years of education and the proportion of their jobs that were in manufacturing. The estimated equation is

$$MENEARN = 1444 + 106 \text{ EDYRS} + 12.71 \text{ PCTMANUF}$$

The coefficients are highly statistically significant, and the R-square is 0.39. The equation says that an additional year of education added $106 to men's median earnings, and that men earned $127 more if living in a place where the proportion of their jobs in manufacturing was 10 percent larger. These findings provide some confirmation of the idea that pay was better in manufacturing cities at that time. Median female earnings in the northeastern urban areas were statistically unrelated to both education and proportion of jobs in manufacturing.

2. The name Union Stockyards was not based on victory in the Civil War, but on the fact that several firms consolidated their stockyards and meat-packing establishments in one location. The Union Stockyards closed for good in 1971.

3. The black population of the nation, 15.04 million, was 10.0 percent of the total population in 1950. As shown in Table 1.1, the population was distributed as follows: 4.96 million in the Northeast, 9.52 million in the South, and 0.57 million in the West. The population of the Northeast was 5.7 percent black, while the South's population was 21.8 percent black. The population of the West was only 2.9 percent black.

4. Volumes from the Philadelphia Economic Monitoring Project include Summers and Luce (1985) and Madden and Stull (1991).

2

Urban Areas of the Sunbelt, Before Air Conditioning

The name "Sunbelt" was invented sometime in the 1960s. In 1950 the nation outside the Northeast was sharply divided into the South and the West. The South here is defined as the eleven states of the Confederacy plus Kentucky and Oklahoma. The West is defined as the mountain and Pacific regions. Since the South and the West were so different in 1950, they are examined separately. It is helpful first to recall the breakdown in Table A.1 (p. xviii) of the nation's population into the three broad regions identified in this book. The Northeast was home to 58.0 percent of the nation's population in 1950, and the West contained only 13.0 percent of the people. The South still contained 63.3 percent of the black population, while the West had a black population of only 570,000, 2.9 percent of its total and 3.8 percent of the nation's black population. As we shall see, the South had a population of almost 44 million people, but had no urban area with a population of 1 million or more. In contrast, the West had only 19.6 million people and two large urban areas—Los Angeles with 4.65 million and San Francisco–Oakland with 2.24 million. The Northeast had a population double that of the South and had twelve urban areas with populations in excess of 1 million (and four with populations over 3 million).

The South

The South had been a distinctly different region throughout American history and, indeed, had made a serious effort to set itself up as a separate nation based on slavery and the production of primary agricultural products. The first wave of urbanization and industrialization in the period of 1830 to 1860 produced nine cities with populations over 100,000. Only one, New Orleans, was located in the South.[1] Slavery was abolished with the 13th Amendment in 1865, but the South continued to be an economy devoted to the production of primary products, mainly cotton. A fundamental fact about the post–Civil War era is that the ownership of land remained with the old planter class. The large plantations were preserved as entities, but the nature of their operation changed. As Gavin Wright (1986), the eminent economic historian of the South, observed, sharecropping and tenant farming emerged as the solutions to the problem. Planters wished to maintain ownership and lacked credit from banks. Former slaves wanted to have autonomy and to live in separate households. Furthermore, sharecropping was more productive and manageable than an alternative that was tried early on—a centralized system of gang wage labor. The white population of the South was also largely an agricultural population of small farmers, tenant farmers, and sharecroppers.

Industrialization in the South had a late start and was confined to basic industries that relied on southern resources and low-wage labor. Industrial employment was concentrated in cotton goods and lumber and timber products. Other industries included apparel, tobacco products, furniture, turpentine and resin, cottonseed oil, and iron and steel (in the Birmingham area). As Wright shows, industrial employment was highly racially segregated. Employment in cotton textiles was reserved almost exclusively for whites, and jobs in saw and planing mills went primarily to blacks. Low wages meant that there was little or no incentive to turn southern industry into a modern, progressive sector. Indeed, the basic idea was not to do so.

Wright (1986) argues that the analogy to a colonial economy is apt. The economy of the South up to the 1940s was based on primary products, low-wage labor, and an associated cultural isolation. Political power was used to maintain an economy based on low-wage labor and a society based on segregation and denial of basic civil rights to blacks. The abolition of slavery had not eliminated the historical legacy of separateness, which continued up to modern times. But in 1950 all of this had begun to change. In Wright's view, the critical economic event was the imposition of national wage and labor standards beginning in the 1930s. Because the South lost the Civil War and could not set up its own national government, during the twentieth century it increasingly came under the political jurisdiction of the nation. It became subject to the laws and policies of the New Deal of the 1930s as well as the market forces and technologies of the nation. These forces eventually eliminated the stake that southern property owners had in keeping a separate labor market. Decisions were made to invite in flows of capital and labor, and the distinct "southern economy" began to disappear.

The process of change in the South was hastened by World War II. Labor shortages caused by the size of the wartime military production and migration

Table 2.1

Urban Areas of the Sunbelt: Population in 1950 (1,000s)

Urban area	Urban area population	Black population in urban area (percent)	Central city population	Black population in central city (percent)
Dallas–	976		434	57 (13.1)
Fort Worth		123 (12.6)	279	37 (13.3)
Houston	808	149 (18.4)	596	125 (25.0)
New Orleans	685	201 (29.3)	570	182 (31.9)
Atlanta	672	166 (24.7)	331	121 (36.6)
Birmingham	559	208 (37.2)	326	130 (40.0)
Miami	495	65 (13.1)	249	40 (16.1)
Los Angeles	4,650	226 (4.9)	1,970	171 (8.7)
San Francisco–	2,241	147 (6.6)	775	43 (5.5)
Oakland			385	47 (12.2)
Seattle	734	16 (2.2)	468	16 (3.4)
Denver	564	16 (2.8)	416	15 (3.6)
San Diego	557	17 (3.1)	334	15 (4.5)
Phoenix	332	14 (4.2)	107	5 (4.7)

Source: Census of Population and Housing.

to the North produced a significant increase in wages on the farm. Now an incentive existed to adopt the new technology of mechanical cotton harvesting. International Harvester began to produce mechanical cotton harvesters in 1941, but the machines were costly and unreliable. Gilbert Fite (1950, p. 28), an authority on agriculture in the South, wrote that there was "little likelihood that mechanization will shortly sweep the entire cotton belt." But, as Wright (1986, p. 242) argues, the increase in unskilled wages brought about by changes at the national level created great pressure to unblock the "harvest bottleneck." In 1950 the mechanization of southern agriculture had just begun; only 8 percent of cotton was mechanically harvested in 1950. By 1960 this figure had grown to 51 percent, and reached 100 percent in 1972 (Wright 1986, p. 244). There are many people still walking around who remember picking cotton by hand, but that has been only a memory for over thirty years. The story of the modernization and urbanization of the South came after 1950.

Given this background, the urban areas of the South in 1950 can be described fairly briefly. As shown in Table 2.1, the South had only six urban areas with populations over one-half million. The top two were Dallas–Fort Worth and Houston in Texas. (Dallas–Fort Worth is listed as a single urban area here, although the Census Bureau considered these cities to be separate urban areas in 1950.) They were emerging in the 1940s as modern urban areas in the rapidly growing state of Texas. The economy of Texas had been stimulated by World War II and its demand for oil and petroleum products. Population growth in Texas was 20.2 percent in the 1940s, compared to 14.4 percent for the nation, and Dallas–Fort Worth had grown by 59.0 percent and Houston by 52.6 percent. The black population of the Dallas–Fort Worth urban areas was only 12.6 percent of the total; the black population in Houston was somewhat greater at 18.4 percent.

Manufacturing employment in both Texas urban areas was well below the national average of 29 percent; Table 2.2 shows 20.9 percent in Dallas–Fort Worth and 22.3 percent in Houston. Employment in Dallas–Fort Worth included a sizable wholesale trade sector with 24,000 jobs (5.9 percent of total employment). Both transportation and wholesale trade were important parts of the Houston economy, with 7.6 percent and 5.5 percent of the jobs. Median earnings for men in Dallas–Fort Worth were $2,696, which was lower than in any of the seventeen major urban areas of the Northeast (although only a few dollars below the $2,708 in Baltimore). Men in Houston had median earnings of $2,904, which was comparable to earnings for men in northeastern urban areas. Women in both Dallas–Fort Worth and Houston had median earnings that were low compared to the Northeast: $1,171 and $1,115 respectively. Women in Pittsburgh made $1,154 on average, which was the least of any major northeastern urban area. Median education levels for both men and women in the two Texas urban areas were all above ten years, and comparable to those in the northeastern urban areas.

The other urban areas of the South included three in the Deep South—New Orleans, Birmingham, and Atlanta—and Miami, the new urban area in Florida. The three urban areas of the Deep South had all experienced population growth in excess of 20 percent in the 1940s: 24 percent in New Orleans, 21 percent in Birmingham, and 30 percent in Atlanta. But as we see in Table 2.1, all three were still relatively small, with populations of less than 700,000 in each case. The migration of the black population from the farms and small towns of the South noted by Myrdal (1944) can be seen in Table 2.1. These three urban areas all had relatively high concentrations of black population of well over the 21.8 percent for the South as a whole. The Birmingham urban area had the highest concentration of any major urban area in the nation, with 37.2 percent.

The three urban areas of the Deep South were three different urban economies. New Orleans was a center of transportation and commerce, as it always had been. Little manufacturing was being done in New Orleans; as shown in Table 2.2, 15.6 percent of employment was engaged in manufacturing.

Table 2.2

Urban Areas of the Sunbelt: Employment and Earnings in 1950 (employment in 1,000s)

Urban area	Employment	Manufacturing employment (percent)	Manufacturing in city: 1947 (percent)	FIRE and business services (percent)	Male earnings (median $)	Female earnings (median $)	Median years education M/F
Dallas–Fort Worth	415	87 (20.9)	91.3	30 (7.2)	2,696	1,171	10.9/11.4
Houston	325	73 (22.3)	69.3	18 (5.6)	2,904	1,115	10.2/10.5
New Orleans	255	40 (15.6)	77.8	14 (5.6)	2,206	909	8.5/8.6
Atlanta	272	53 (19.5)	73.9	18 (6.5)	2,308	1,122	9.5/9.9
Birmingham	202	52 (26.0)	49.7	9 (4.6)	2,292	742	8.8/9.3
Miami	200	15 (7.4)	71.0	12.5 (6.2)	2,510	1,163	11.0/11.4
Los Angeles	1,782	436 (24.5)	46.5	117 (6.6)	2,997	1,224	11.9/12.0
San Francisco–Oakland	865	172 (19.9)	57.3	68 (7.9)	3,131	1,529	11.7/12.1
Seattle	282	57 (20.4)	91.6	18 (6.4)	3,103	1,269	11.8/12.2
Denver	218	36 (16.6)	90.4	14 (6.3)	2,741	1,151	11.8/12.1
San Diego	133	21 (15.7)	89.4	8 (5.9)	2,610	1,031	11.8/12.1
Phoenix	108	10 (9.3)	40.5	6 (5.4)	2,271	923	10.1/11.1

Source: Census of Population and Housing.

Transportation and wholesale trade employed 17.9 percent of workers in the New Orleans urban area. Atlanta was an inland center of transportation and commerce, with relatively little manufacturing as well. Transportation and wholesale trade employed 12.2 percent of the workers in the Atlanta urban area, and manufacturing employed 19.4 percent. Atlanta is also the state capital, and government provided 6.3 percent of the jobs. "Southern wages" prevailed. Median earnings in both New Orleans and Atlanta were quite low; $2,206 for men and only $909 for women in New Orleans, and $2,308 for men and $1,122 for women in Atlanta. Median education levels were low in both urban areas: 9.5 years and 9.9 years for men and women in Atlanta, and only 8.5 and 8.6 years for men and women in New Orleans. The education levels for New Orleans were the lowest of any major urban area in the nation in 1950. The median earnings in New Orleans were the lowest of any major urban area in the nation in 1950 as well. In contrast, Birmingham was the manufacturing town of the South. Manufacturing provided 26.1 percent of the jobs in Birmingham, which was below the overall national average but was larger than any other major urban area in the South (or the West, for that matter). The primary metals industry (i.e., iron and steel) employed 29,000 workers out of a total of 52,000 in manufacturing. However, the education level of adults in Birmingham was low; 8.8 years for men and 9.3 years for women. Median earnings were also low, at $2,292 for men and only $742 for women.

The Miami urban area was in the process of taking off in 1950. Its population of only 268,000 in 1940 made it comparable in size to Grand Rapids, Michigan, Hartford, Connecticut, Harrisburg, Pennsylvania, and other such lower-level urban areas. Then the population shot ahead by 85 percent in the 1940s to reach 495,000 in 1950. Only 13.1 percent of that population was black. The economy of Miami was based on commerce and trade, construction, and providing a place for recreation and retirement. A minuscule 7.4 percent of employment was engaged in manufacturing. Transportation and wholesale trade provided 13.0 percent of the jobs, and the construction industry employed 10.6 percent. Southern wages were paid in Miami; median earnings were $2,510 for men and $1,163 for women even though education levels were high—11.0 years for men and 11.4 years for women.

Now let us take a quick look at the state of the housing in the urban areas of the South. In general, vacancy rates were low (except in Miami), although not as low as in the northeastern urban areas, and much of the housing was substandard—lacking hot running water, or toilet and bath, or in dilapidated condition. The details are shown in Table 2.3. The two Texas urban areas presented similar conditions. Both Dallas–Fort Worth and Houston had proportions of substandard units under 30 percent, and over 40 percent of the

Table 2.3

Housing in 1950

Urban area	Vacancy rate (percent)	Owner occupied (percent)	Occupied by non-whites (percent)	Substan-dard (percent)*	Built after 1940 (percent)	Public housing units	Public housing (percent)
Dallas–Fort Worth	4.96	58.5	11.7	28.3	41.0	2,243	0.74
Houston	6.61	55.5	17.5	26.8	42.7	2,251	0.88
New Orleans	4.73	38.3	27.7	40.0	23.8	5,381	2.60
Atlanta	3.63	50.6	21.9	38.1	29.1	5,188	2.67
Birmingham	3.70	50.7	34.3	51.8	24.6	2,768	1.74
Miami	14.50	53.9	9.7	17.4	48.2	1,318	0.73
Los Angeles	5.39	54.1	5.0	9.0	33.9	3,468	0.23
San Francisco–Oakland	4.77	49.1	7.5	9.5	29.9	2,663	0.36
Seattle	6.38	63.2	3.5	13.1	31.0	1,068	0.43
Denver	5.13	55.5	2.9	15.6	27.2	770	0.43
San Diego	6.84	52.7	3.4	11.2	44.5	n.a.	n.a.
Phoenix	10.74	57.0	5.8	30.0	52.6	604	0.56

*Substandard defined as lacking running hot water, or lacking toilet and bathtub, or dilapidated.
Source: Census of Population and Housing.

units in both urban areas had been built since 1940. Neither urban area had constructed very many public housing units.

The three urban areas of the Deep South were in contrast to their Texas neighbors. New Orleans, Atlanta, and Birmingham all had very high percentages of substandard units, ranging from 38.1 percent in Atlanta to 51.8 percent in Birmingham. Indeed, it may be shocking for the modern reader to learn that a majority of the housing units in a major American urban area were substandard in 1950. Many rural areas of the South did not have electricity or indoor plumbing in 1950, but one might have different expectations of housing in a major urban area. Twenty-four to 29 percent of the housing units had been constructed since 1940 in these three urban areas. Some of that new construction was public housing. And all three had made more extensive use of the public housing program than had most urban areas; public housing as a percentage of all units was 2.60 in New Orleans, 2.67 in Atlanta, and 1.74 in Birmingham.

Miami was a special case of a southern urban area, and this shows up in housing. The vacancy rate was a very high 14.5 percent. The Census survey was done in March 1950, so this high vacancy rate may reflect the return of winter occupants to the North. Recall also that the construction industry was a major employer of Miami workers. Almost half of the units had been built since 1940 (48.2 percent), and only 17.4 percent were rated as substandard. Miami had very few public housing units at this time.

To summarize, the South was not highly urbanized in 1950. The population of the South was half that of the Northeast, but the region contained no urban area with a population over 1 million. The economy of the South clearly was in transition, but in 1950 it was still an economy dominated by primary products and low wages. The two major urban areas in Texas had begun to grow rapidly as the Texas oil economy was taking off, and Miami was starting to boom as a center of commerce and recreation and retirement. But the three "major" urban areas of the Deep South—New Orleans, Atlanta, and Birmingham—were places of low education levels and wages, high percentages of black population, and bad housing conditions.

The West

The San Francisco–Oakland urban area was the first, and for many years the only, urban area in the West. The United States claimed the small town of San Francisco on January 30, 1847, during the war with Mexico. A year later gold was discovered, and the California Gold Rush brought a wave of immigration that increased the population of the town from 1,000 to 25,000 by December 1849. Oakland was founded across the bay in 1852. While the Gold Rush had created the urban area, a second and more permanent source of growth was the completion of the transcontinental railroad in 1869. Prominent San Franciscans were behind the effort to build the railroad, and to choose the northern route in preference to a route that would have run through the southwest to Los Angeles. Those leaders included the men who are known as the "big four" of California—Leland Stanford, Collis Huntington, Charles Crocker, and Mark Hopkins. These men were the founders of the Central Pacific Railroad, which became the western portion of the transcontinental railroad. The most prominent supporter of the southern route was Secretary of War Jefferson Davis of Mississippi, who had been ordered by Congress in 1853 to conduct a survey of possible routes. The Davis report recommended a southern route. Davis also orchestrated the Gadsden Purchase in 1853 of what is now the southern portion of Arizona to provide a better route for a railroad to the West. Others, including Abraham Lincoln, were giving thought to a route that would run from Omaha to Sacramento. Once the South seceded from the Union in 1861, the northern route was chosen quickly by the Congress. The act of 1862 provided large federal subsidies, including huge grants of land. Much has been written about the transcontinental railroad as a major event in history and as a business proposition,[2] but for our purposes the important fact about the railroad is the boost it gave to San Francisco. The Bay Area had a spectacular bay to serve as a port and the only railroad connection to the East.

As the economy of northern California grew, San Francisco–Oakland became a center of shipping, mining, banking, railroading, and manufacturing. In 1880, the city of San Francisco had a population of 234,000, and the city of Oakland was home to 35,000 people. At this time Los Angeles and its surrounding county was little more than a small town of 34,000, but oil had been discovered. The Southern Pacific Railroad completed a line from San Francisco to Los Angeles in 1876, and the Santa Fe Railroad built the transcontinental railroad on the southern route to Los Angeles in the 1880s. The Port of San Pedro was developed during the latter years of the nineteenth century (and annexed by the city in 1907), so by 1900 the Los Angeles urban area had a population of 170,000 and was ready to boom.[3] The opening of the Panama Canal in 1914 also contributed to the growth of Los Angeles, after a pause during World War I.

The efforts to publicize Los Angeles as a great place to live definitely bore fruit (and vegetables and all sorts of other agricultural products as well). The population of the five-county urban area grew to 250,000 in 1900 and reached 2.6 million in 1930. That growth required housing, transportation, water, and jobs. Los Angeles developed as a city of largely single-family houses linked to the central business district and other destinations by a private system of street railways. Abu-Lughod (1999, p. 143) suggests that private mass transit was used to stimulate the demand for building lots and that the transit lines did not need to be profitable. Once the automobile had superseded the street railways as the more convenient means of transportation, the trolley lines disappeared. Early on it was clear that the lack of a dependable water supply would limit the growth of Los Angeles. The solution to the problem was the construction of the Los Angeles aqueduct, which opened in 1913. This facility, designed by famed city engineer William Mulholland, diverted water from the upstate Owens Valley and provided enough water for the city's growth for most of the first half of the twentieth century. The federal government constructed Hoover Dam on the Colorado River (and the supplementary Parker Dam) in the 1930s; these projects added greatly to the water supply for Los Angeles. Abu-Lughod (1999, p. 404) notes that the city fathers of Los Angeles had succeeded in using their influence to overcome the disadvantages of not having a natural harbor or an adequate water supply. As we have seen, the Santa Fe Railroad was convinced to use Los Angeles at its western terminus (rather than San Diego), the federal government paid to build the port, the federal Owens Valley Reclamation Service was persuaded to divert water to the city, and later Hoover Dam was built.

The infrastructure, the oil, and the rapid population growth in California provided the factors needed for economic growth. The manufacturing sector became a center for the production of oil equipment, automobiles and automotive equipment, furniture, glass, steel, aircraft, and a host of other products. The port of Los Angeles grew, thanks in part to the local oil industry. By the 1920s, the Los Angeles area was one of the world's major oil suppliers. And then, of course, there are the movies. D.W. Griffith moved to Los Angeles from New York in 1909, and by the 1930s the major movie studios in Hollywood (a neighborhood in Los Angeles) dominated the industry. Los Angeles continued to grow, even during the 1930s. Migration to the area continued. Migrants from the Dust Bowl of the southern Great Plains are remembered in story and song, but they were only a small portion of the thousands who came. As Abu-Lughod (1999, p. 245) recounts, by the end of the 1930s Los Angeles County area ranked first in the nation in agricultural wealth and income, first in aircraft (with employment of 120,000) and movies, second in auto assembling and tire production, third in furniture, fourth in women's apparel, and fifth overall in the value of industrial production. Then World War II turned Los Angeles into a huge industrial economy involving iron and steel, aircraft, ships, rubber products, nonferrous metals, machinery, and chemicals. All of this was facilitated by the harbor and the oil. The end of the war and the transition to the peacetime economy only meant continued growth for Los Angeles. Coping with that growth included a plan for the construction of a freeway network that was approved by the city council and county board of supervisors in 1941. Construction of the system started only after the end of the war.

The population of the state grew from 6.91 million in 1940 to 10.59 million in 1950. This growth of 53.3 percent is remarkable because it started with a large base of almost 7 million. As shown in Table 2.1, 7.06 million Californians (66.7 percent) lived in the two huge urban agglomerations of Los Angeles (4.65 million) and San Francisco–Oakland (2.24 million). Population growth in the two urban areas had matched the state's growth during the 1940s, with population increasing by 51.7 percent in the Los Angeles urban area and by 53.3 percent in San Francisco–Oakland. Recall that the population of the entire West was 19.56 million in 1950. Over one-half of that population (54.1 percent) lived in California, and over one-third (36.1 percent) lived in California's two huge urban areas. The migration of black population to California had increased substantially during the war so that in 1950, blacks constituted 4.9 percent of the Los Angeles area population and 6.6 percent of San Francisco–Oakland. Los Angeles had also attracted a significant number of migrants of Mexican descent, but their precise numbers are not known because the Census did not enumerate the "Hispanic" population at that time.

As shown in Table 2.2, the economy of the Los Angeles urban area provided 1.78 million jobs in 1950, of which 24.5 percent (436,000) were in manufacturing. While Los Angeles contained a huge manufacturing sector, its percentage of total employment was well below the national average of 29 percent. Less than half of the manufacturing employment (46.5 percent) was located in the city of Los Angeles. Median earnings of $2,997 for men and $1,224 for women were comparable to earnings in the major urban areas of the Northeast, in part because education levels were high—11.9 years for men and 12.0 years for women. This education level for men was the second-highest of any major urban area in the nation at that time, exceeded only by Washington, D.C. (see Table 1.2, p. 12).

Total employment in the San Francisco–Oakland area was 865,000, and only 19.9 percent of employment was in manufacturing. Transportation and wholesale trade contributed 110,000 jobs, which were 12.7 percent of the total. Median education levels and earnings were relatively high. Men's median education level was 11.7 years and women's 12.1 years, exceeded by the women of Washington, D.C., and Seattle (12.2 years). Median male earnings of $3,131 were among the highest in the nation. Only the northeastern manufacturing centers of Chicago, Detroit, Cleveland, and Milwaukee had higher median male earnings. Median female earnings of $1,529 were topped only by women's earnings in New York, Chicago, and Washington, D.C. The relatively high earnings in the two major California urban areas, coupled with the favorable weather, would prove to be powerful incentives for continued migration.

The other four urban areas of the West had grown rapidly in the 1940s, but were still rather small in 1950. These four urban areas include two other port cities, San Diego and Seattle, and two cities in the interior, Denver and Phoenix. As a result of World War II, the population of San Diego grew by 92.4 percent in the 1940s to 557,000. The growth of Seattle was not as spectacular —"only" 45.2 percent, to 734,000. Neither San Diego nor Seattle had attracted very many black migrants as of 1950. The Denver urban area, the economic capital of its region and state capital of Colorado, had a population of 564,000 in 1950. Growth in Denver in the 1940s was a substantial 38.3 percent, but this pales in comparison to the growth of California's urban areas. The black population of Denver was only 2.8 percent of the total. Phoenix began the 1940s with a population of only 186,000, which was smaller than the Peoria, Illinois, area, but it grew by 78.2 percent to reach 332,000 in 1950. Its black population was only 14,000 at that time. Arizona had been a state for only twenty-nine years in 1940, and the weather in the Valley of the Sun for much of the year can be described by two words—very hot.

The Seattle economy included a manufacturing sector that supplied only

20.4 percent of total employment, but transportation and wholesale trade employed 13.1 percent of the work force. Male median earnings of $3,103 were almost as high as in San Francisco–Oakland, and female median earnings of $1,269 were on a par with female earnings in Los Angeles. The education levels in Seattle of 11.8 years for men and 12.2 years for women were among the highest in the nation.

Ever since World War II, the San Diego economy has been dependent to a considerable degree on the U.S. military. Total government employment in 1950 was 17,300 (13.0 percent of the total). While the San Diego economy had a low proportion of manufacturing jobs of 15.7 percent (20,900 manufacturing jobs), 10,700 of those jobs were in transportation equipment (e.g., ships and aircraft). Median education levels in San Diego matched the levels in the other West Coast urban areas—11.8 years for men and 12.1 years for women. However, a relatively small manufacturing sector meant that earnings were not particularly high, at $2,610 for men and $1,031 for women. These earnings were well below the median earnings in neighboring Los Angeles—12.9 percent for men and 15.8 percent for women.

The Denver economy also included relatively few manufacturing jobs—16.6 percent of total employment. The finance, insurance, and real estate (FIRE) and business services, wholesale trade, and government sectors were all about the same size in Denver. Each provided 5.7 to 6.9 percent of total employment. Education levels were high—11.8 years for men and 12.1 years for women. But median earnings were a relatively unimpressive $2,741 for men and $1,151 for women. Once again, a small manufacturing sector was associated with relatively low median earnings.

Lastly, the Phoenix economy had very few manufacturing jobs and very low earnings. Only Miami had a smaller proportion of manufacturing employment than the 9.3 percent in Phoenix. Wholesale trade and government each employed 5.8 percent of the Phoenix work force. Median earnings of $2,271 for men and $923 for women resembled median earnings in the urban areas of the Deep South. The education level of 10.1 years for men was quite low compared to the other urban areas of the West, and the education level for women of 11.1 years was not very high either. In 1950 Phoenix was a minor urban area that had yet to make its mark.

The housing situation was roughly similar in five out of the six western urban areas. Vacancy rates in Los Angeles, San Francisco–Oakland, Seattle, Denver, and San Diego were between 5 and 7 percent. Vacancy rates in this range indicated a fairly tight market, but these markets were not as tight as many in the Northeast. These five urban areas had relatively few substandard housing units. The percentage substandard varied from a low of 9.0 percent in Los Angeles to a high of 15.6 percent in Denver. Indeed, the 9.0 for Los

Angeles and 9.5 for San Francisco–Oakland were the lowest in the nation. And, as one would have expected given the population growth, all five urban areas had experienced significant amounts of housing construction in the 1940s. In Denver, 27.2 percent of the units had been built since 1940, as had 44.5 percent of the units in San Diego. However, note that the percentage of units built in the 1940s was well below the percentage population increases in that same decade for all five urban areas. In contrast to these five urban areas, the housing situation in Phoenix was characterized by a high vacancy rate of 10.7 percent and, at 30.0 percent, a relatively high proportion of substandard units. A majority of the units in Phoenix had been built since 1940 (52.6 percent). None of the urban areas of the West was a major participant in the public housing program.

Conclusion

The term Sunbelt is a later invention. In 1950 the urban areas of the South and the West were very different. The major urban areas of the Deep South—Atlanta, Birmingham, and New Orleans—were characterized by high percentages of black population, low wages, low education levels, poor housing conditions, and, with the exception of iron and steel in Birmingham, little manufacturing. Dallas–Fort Worth and Houston, the major urban areas in Texas, were supported by the oil economy and had higher earnings, better housing conditions, and fewer black people than the urban areas of the Deep South. And in 1950, Miami was small (fewer than one-half million people) and only beginning its growth to become a major urban area. Blacks made up 21.8 percent of the population of the South in 1950, and 63.3 percent of blacks in the United States lived in that region.

The urban areas of the West were dominated by Los Angeles and San Francisco–Oakland. San Francisco had been given a head start by the Gold Rush and the transcontinental railroad, but Los Angeles had surpassed its northern neighbor by 1920, thanks in part to the water supply and port infrastructure provided with the cooperation of the federal government. World War II, the war in the Pacific in particular, had stimulated these two urban economies so that in 1950 the population of the Los Angeles area had reached 4.65 million and San Francisco–Oakland was home to 2.24 million. Together, 36 percent of the population of the West was located in just these two urban areas. They offered relatively good earnings and housing conditions and, of course, California weather. The other four urban areas of the West included the two other port cities of Seattle and San Diego, and the two interior cities of Denver and Phoenix. The populations of these urban areas were still fairly small in 1950—ranging from 332,000 in Phoenix to 734,000 in Seattle.

Phoenix differed from the other three in that median earnings were very low and housing conditions were poor. The urban areas of the West had small percentages of black population. All six were 6.6 percent or lower. In 1950, the black population of the West was only 571,000, which was 2.9 percent of the population of the West and 3.8 percent of the nation's black population.

The survey of the urban scene in 1950 concludes with the next chapter, which concentrates on the black population of the nation's major urban areas.

Notes

1. The others were New York, Philadelphia, Chicago, Buffalo, Cincinnati, St. Louis, Baltimore, and Boston.

2. See Ambrose (2000) for a popular and stirring account of the building of the transcontinental railroad.

3. Abu-Lughod (1999, p. 138) describes the first boom in Los Angeles that took place in the 1880s. Campaigns were mounted to bring settlers from the Midwest, and the local Chamber of Commerce convinced the railroads to lower the one-way fare from Chicago to Los Angeles to one dollar. The Chamber turned Los Angeles into the most publicized place in the United States.

3

An American Dilemma in 1950

On August 12, 1937, Frederick Keppel, president of the Carnegie Corporation, sent a letter to Professor Gunnar Myrdal of the University of Stockholm to invite him to become the director of a "comprehensive study of the Negro in the United States, to be undertaken in a wholly objective and dispassionate way as a social phenomenon" (Myrdal 1944, p. lix). The trustees of the Carnegie Corporation wished to support such a study, to be directed by a single individual who would come from abroad with a fresh mind, not influenced by traditional attitudes. The funding for the project was $300,000, which was a large sum for the time. Their search ended with Professor Myrdal, an economist who already had a strong reputation as a broader social scientist and public official. Agreement was reached, and Myrdal arrived in the United States on September 10, 1938, and began work on plans for the study. Much consultation was required, but Myrdal drew up a detailed work plan in the summer of 1939, and research on the various parts of the study commenced. Myrdal returned to Sweden in April 1940 after the German invasion of Denmark and Norway and did not return to the United States until March 6, 1941. The research staff continued the work during his absence, so Myrdal had an enormous set of reports upon which to draw as he began to draft *An American Dilemma* upon his return. The book was completed in October 1942, and consists of 45 chapters, 10 appendices, and 1,483 pages. The project produced thirty-five background research papers, and four other books were published by project researchers. On October 9, 1974, the Royal Swedish Academy of Sciences announced that the Nobel Prize in economics was to be awarded to Professor Gunnar Myrdal and Professor Friedrich von Hayek. The citation included the following statements:

> Mainly by directing most of his research on economic problems in the broadest sense, particularly the negro problem in the USA and the poverty

of developing countries, Myrdal has sought to relate economic analysis to social, demographic and institutional conditions.

When making its decision, the Academy of Sciences has attached great importance to the monumental work, *An American Dilemma: The Negro Problem and Modern Democracy* (1944). It is primarily in this massive work of scholarship that Myrdal has documented his ability to combine economic analysis with a broad sociological perspective.

The purposes of this chapter are to review some of this great work, and then to update material in *An American Dilemma* so as to depict the economic situation of urban black Americans in 1950. The basic conclusion is that there were powerful economic and social incentives for black Americans to migrate from the South to the major urban areas of the Northeast, and that they had responded to those incentives in the 1940s. Approximately 1.4 million black Americans, 9.3 percent of the nation's black population in 1950, migrated out of the South in the 1940s, and most of them moved to the cities of the Northeast.

The American Dilemma

The title of this book includes the word "crisis." The urban crisis that is the subject of this book and many others is something that happened to people and to places during a particular period of time. How is the urban crisis defined? Thomas Sugrue (1996, p. 3), in his prize-winning book *The Origins of the Urban Crisis*, provides a stark description of the places and people of the urban crisis with which most would agree:

> The story I tell is one of a city transformed. In the 1940s, Detroit was America's "arsenal of democracy," one of the nation's fastest growing boomtowns and home to the highest-paid blue-collar workers in the United States. Today, the city is plagued by joblessness, concentrated poverty, physical decay, and racial isolation. . . . Factories that once provided tens of thousands of jobs now stand as hollow shells, windows broken, mute testimony to a lost industrial past. . . . The faces that appear in the rundown houses, homeless shelters, and social agencies in these urban wastelands are predictably familiar. Almost all are people of color.

It is thus essential to focus on the black population. How did joblessness, concentrated poverty, racial isolation, and all of the other elements of the urban crisis come to be visited disproportionately on the urban black population? Sugrue argues that the roots of the urban crisis are in the 1940s and 1950s, so a good place to start to answer the question is with Myrdal.

Early in his book, Myrdal writes:

> The "American Dilemma," referred to in the title of this book, is the ever-raging conflict between, on the one hand, the valuations preserved on the general plane which we shall call the "American Creed," . . . and, on the other hand, the valuations on specific planes of individual and group living. (p. lxxix)

Those specific planes include many aspects, including group prejudice against other groups. The Declaration of Independence, a product of the Enlightenment of the eighteenth century, had stated "that all men are created equal, that they are endowed by their Creator with certain unalienable Rights, that among these are Life, Liberty, and the Pursuit of Happiness." Myrdal found in 1940 that Americans took this seriously, and recognized the disparity that still existed between the American Creed and the status accorded black Americans. Myrdal saw his task as finding out why.

Of course, the answer begins with slavery. Slavery itself was an ancient institution in no need of rationalization. It was early brought to America. But the Enlightenment and the Declaration of Independence presented Americans with the fundamental problem of how to "rationalize" slavery in the new nation. Many of the founders, including Washington and Jefferson, believed that slavery would fade away. They were content to leave the issue unresolved in the Constitution. Even the section that led to the outlawing of the slave trade does not mention slavery. Article I, Section 9 states: "The Migration or Importation of such Persons as any of the States now existing shall think proper to admit, shall not be prohibited by Congress prior to the Year one thousand eight hundred and eight."

But the matter of slavery did not turn out as some founders had hoped. The economics of southern agriculture changed with the invention of the cotton gin, and the Cotton South expanded rapidly from the original states all the way to the newer states of the South—all the way to Texas. Myrdal (pp. 87–88) found that the pro-slavery attitudes in the South grew stronger, but that "In the precarious ideological situation—where the South wanted to defend a political and civic institution of inequality which showed increasingly great prospects for new land exploitation and commercial profit, but where they also wanted to retain the democratic creed of the nation—*the race doctrine of biological inequality between whites and Negroes offered the most convenient solution*" (emphasis in original).

Myrdal found that the doctrine of equality embodied in the American Creed contributed to its opposite—the belief in natural inequality. The idea of natural inequality was bolstered both by "science" and everyday observation. By 1940, much scientific inquiry had undermined the doctrine of biological inequality of the races (and emphasized the importance of nurture over nature), but that doctrine was still alive in the minds of many because it definitely served a purpose. The foreigner Myrdal had some very tough things to say about the racial beliefs of whites in the 1940s, which he saw as the fundamental determinants of the quality of life for blacks. Further, he hypothesized that white prejudice and discrimination arising from white racial beliefs kept social and economic outcomes for blacks low, which in turn only fostered continuation of the racial beliefs. This is Myrdal's mechanism of the vicious circle.

Yet Myrdal saw reason for hope. A vicious circle might be made to work in reverse. If somehow white prejudice could be reduced, then social and economic outcomes for blacks could be raised, white racial beliefs would change, and so on. He saw many possible factors that might set off a cumulative improvement for blacks; for example, better employment opportunities would lead to greater incomes, better nutrition and health, and higher levels of education for children, which would tend to change white attitudes and lead to further improvements. Once again, the racial beliefs of whites were the critical factors in Myrdal's assessment—the answer to the "why" question.

The bulk of *An American Dilemma* is an examination of various aspects of the lives of black Americans up to 1940. The first topic is basic demographics: population growth and migration. A basic fact is the lack of migration of blacks from the South for over fifty years after the end of the Civil War. The Great Migration to the North during and after World War I is described, and explained partly by the shortage of labor caused by the war and the restriction on immigration from abroad after 1924. Six northern cities (New York, Chicago, Philadelphia, Detroit, Cleveland, and Pittsburgh) were shown to be major recipients of these migrants from the South. Blacks grew from less than 3 percent of the population of these cities in 1910 to 8 percent in 1940. In 1940, 48 percent of all blacks living in the North and the West were living in these six cities (Myrdal and the Census counted Maryland, Missouri, and Washington, D.C., as part of the South). He noted the real economic opportunity that existed in the northern cities, but he also noted the exaggerated claims of some labor agents and newspapers and the general "myth" of northern prosperity.

Myrdal then turned to economics, obviously one of his strengths. His summary of the situation is brief and to the point: "The economic situation of the Negroes in America is pathological. Except for a small minority enjoying upper or middle class status, the masses of American Negroes, in the rural South and in the segregated slum quarters in southern and northern cities, are destitute" (p. 205).

Furthermore, in accordance with the vicious circle, whether blacks were living in the grip of the share-cropping system of the South or in poverty in northern cities, Myrdal wrote, "Poverty itself breeds the conditions which perpetuate poverty" (p. 208). Our interest centers on urban areas, so a few of Myrdal's observations regarding economic conditions for urban blacks will be noted.[1] In the South, the employment of blacks outside of agriculture was confined to unskilled labor in certain industries such as lumber and planing mills, construction, railroads, longshore work, and domestic service in homes and hotels. Employment outside agriculture increased rapidly, and the employment of black males outside agriculture increased as well. But the percentage of black male workers in the South engaged in nonagricultural employment fell from 31.3 percent in 1890 to 21.1 percent in 1930. As we saw in Chapter 2, blacks were largely excluded from the growing southern textile industry. Some blacks were employed in the iron and steel industry, especially in and around Birmingham, but at low wages. The U.S. Bureau of Labor Statistics reported that in 1938 the average wage for black men in the iron and steel industry in the South was 54 cents per hour, compared to 75 cents per hour for whites. Male unemployment rates in the cities of the Deep South were higher for blacks than for whites. In New Orleans, the unemployment rates were 15.3 percent for black males and 10.2 percent for white males. In Atlanta and Birmingham, the black male unemployment rates were double those of whites; 13.9 percent and 6.7 percent in Atlanta, and 15.9 percent and 7.0 percent in Birmingham.

In the urban North in 1910, blacks were mainly relegated to work as domestics, laundresses, cooks, waiters, janitors, laborers, and so on. However, during World War I and during the 1920s, blacks gained footholds in the manufacturing sector in the North, primarily in iron and steel, machinery, and automobile factories. In 1938, the average wage for blacks in the iron and steel industry in the North was 74 cents per hour, compared to 86 cents per hour for whites. (Compare with the wages in the South cited above.) Some blacks gained employment in the apparel and slaughter and meat-packing industries. The author's father recalled working next to a black man on the disassembly line in Chicago's Union Stockyards in the 1930s. The work was difficult and dangerous, involving as it did rough men who wielded large knives. The Census of 1940 showed that unemployment rates were still quite high in the urban North, and much higher for blacks than for whites. Unemployment rates for males in March 1940 are shown in Table 3.1. The black male unemployment rate in Philadelphia was a very high 33.1 percent (versus 15.4 percent for white males). The average black male unemployment rate for the eight cities listed in Table 3.1 was 18.3 percent, compared to 10.9 percent for white males.

Myrdal only briefly discussed residential segregation. He believed that resi-

Table 3.1

Unemployment Rates in 1940 (in percent)

	Black men	White men
New York	20.1	15.2
Philadelphia	33.1	15.4
Cleveland	16.7	12.4
Detroit	16.1	9.7
Chicago	17.2	11.1
St. Louis	19.6	10.5
Baltimore	13.2	7.3
Washington, D.C.	10.6	5.4

Source: Myrdal (1944, p. 621).

dential segregation in southern cities was not especially high because whites derived benefit from having black domestic workers living nearby. There was "ceremonial" distance rather than physical distance between the races. As we shall see below, subsequent research has shown that racial segregation in southern cities was very high in 1940 and before. Myrdal noted that blacks in northern cities were confined to well-defined "black belts." He included more detailed discussions of Harlem in New York and the South Side Black Belt in Chicago, and discussed the use of racial covenants in the North (which were approved by the Federal Housing Administration in its mortgage insurance program). Myrdal saw residential segregation in the North as only one of many manifestations of white racial attitudes. He did not foresee that racial segregation in housing would become a central issue in later years.

Much of the remainder of *An American Dilemma* is an indictment of the political, legal, and social institutions of the South. The North came in for some criticism too, but Myrdal (p. 604) concluded that blacks in the North could "struggle for fuller social equality with some hope" because they had the vote, had some expectation of justice from the legal system, and could attend real schools (indeed, were forced to attend school). His lengthy examination of the South led him to conclude that the entire corpus of the mythical, political, legal, and social systems of the South essentially had but one purpose—white supremacy. Black Americans were the members of the lower caste of society, especially in the South, because there was no mobility out of caste. For example, Myrdal attributed the complete dominance of the Democratic Party in the South to the need to disfranchise the black population. Any political division might have led white factions to seek black political support. Furthermore, Myrdal concluded that this southern brand of "conservatism" was "a unique phenomenon in Western civilization in being married to an established pattern of *illegality*" (p. 440, emphasis in original). Conservatives in other places are the guardians of the law as they act to preserve the status quo. It was not so in the South, as the civil rights movement was to demonstrate in the 1950s and 1960s.

The final major section of *An American Dilemma* examined black society —including its leadership, its protest organizations, its churches and schools, and its press. Myrdal noted the tradition of accommodating leadership. The most important national organization at that time was the National Association for the Advancement of Colored People (NAACP), which had (and has) the long-run goal of full equality for blacks as American citizens. The NAACP was founded by white and black Americans in response to a race riot of whites against blacks in 1908 in Springfield, Illinois, the home of Abraham Lincoln. In 1940, the agenda of the NAACP for the foreseeable future included passage of anti-lynching laws and laws to eliminate debt slavery among sharecroppers and to establish enfranchisement of blacks in the South, equality in legal procedures, and equitable distribution of public education funds. The NAACP also advocated the longer-run goals of equal employment opportunity; equal pay for equal work; and the abolition of segregation, discrimination (including in the right to collective bargaining), and humiliation based on race. The black church, a center of social life and potentially a powerful institution, was seen by Myrdal as an ineffective vehicle for improving the general position of blacks, and the black clergy were seen as timid and disinterested in leading a "movement." However, it was a member of the black clergy, Martin Luther King, Jr., who would become the leader of the civil rights movement in the 1950s and 1960s. Myrdal praised the black press as "a fighting press" that provided a bitter and relentless critique of white America. The black press was serving to inform blacks of their situation and how it compared poorly against American ideals, and Myrdal (and many others) thought that this press would be enormously important in the future.

Myrdal summarized some basic facts of black society in America as follows:

- According to a study by E. Franklin Frazier (1939), blacks had a rate of illegitimate births that was eight times the rate for native whites and sixteen times the rate of foreign-born whites.
- Blacks had a higher percentage of "broken" families (30 percent) compared to native whites (20 percent), where broken families include married with spouse not present, widowed, divorced, and single family heads.
- Black church membership was high, services were emotional, and most black churches were small and poor.

- School attendance by black children had increased dramatically to 64.4 percent of people aged five to twenty in 1940 (compared to 71.5 percent for whites), but the educational attainment of adults aged twenty-five and over was low. Black adults had a median of 5.5 years of education in 1940, compared to 8.8 years for native whites. Fifteen percent of rural-farm blacks had no formal education at all, and only 1.2 percent of black adults had graduated from college (5.4 percent for whites). And the "separate but equal" schools of the South were separate, but not equal. Black schools provided fewer days of instruction and had low standards for teachers.
- Crime data of the day were incomplete and probably reflected unequal administration of justice, but blacks committed more crimes of violence than whites. According to the FBI *Uniform Crime Report* for 1940, arrests for criminal homicide were 19.8 per 100,000 population for blacks and 3.2 per 100,000 for whites. Arrest rates for robbery (31.7 versus 7.6), assault (116.4 versus 15.7), and most other crimes were substantially greater for blacks than for whites. But Myrdal (p. 979) asserted that arrest rates for middle- and upper-class blacks were no higher than for their white counterparts.
- Some black Americans had made significant achievements in various fields of entertainment and the arts, but few had made a mark in business or politics.

Myrdal ended his monumental treatise with the observation that the findings of social science will be put to work changing society for the better. He stated, "We are entering an era where fact-finding and scientific theories of causal relations will be seen as instrumental in planning controlled social change" (p. 1,023). The trend in history was toward greater realization of the American Creed, and the work of social science had already destroyed in the minds of educated people the idea of the biological inferiority of blacks (but not in the minds of people with little education). Myrdal saw the role of the federal government, including the Supreme Court, as being of increasing importance in bringing about social change. He used the words "social engineering."[2] Furthermore, social engineering had the potential to set off a "virtuous" circle in which white Americans would change their attitudes toward blacks as blacks made economic and social advances, which in turn would permit blacks to make additional advances, ad infinitum.

A critical question that will be examined in this book is whether Myrdal was correct in this final prediction in *An American Dilemma*. There is no question that *An American Dilemma* was highly influential. The NAACP Legal Defense and Education Fund used it as one basis for their argument in the case of *Brown v. Board of Education* in 1954. In this case, the Supreme

Court ruled that segregated schools violated the equal protection under the law mandated in the 14th Amendment. However, there are many conservatives who see the influence of *An American Dilemma* in a negative light. For example, the popular (and conservative) historian Paul Johnson (1997) thinks that the *Brown v. Board of Education* decision was the first of a series in which courts used legal decisions to attempt to improve society based on sociological findings. In his view, courts should make decisions that are applications of the Constitution, law, and precedent. Johnson labels this legal trend "the sinister legacy of Myrdal."[3]

Black Americans in Urban Areas of the Northeast: 1950

Our starting point is only a little over seven years after Myrdal completed *An American Dilemma*, but substantial changes had already taken place. The Census Bureau estimated that 1.7 million blacks migrated from the South in the decade of the 1940s. This is 11.3 percent of the entire black population of 15.0 million in 1950. Of these migrants, an estimated 450,000 went to New York, New Jersey, and Pennsylvania; 594,000 went to the east north central region (Ohio, Indiana, Illinois, Michigan, and Wisconsin), and 285,000 went to California. The black population of the South had increased only from 9.38 million to 9.52 million in the 1940s. What was the state of the black populations in the nation's major urban areas in 1950?

Basic population data for the seventeen major urban areas of the Northeast are shown in Table 3.2. The first two columns repeat the data on the total population of the urban area and the total black population of the urban area from Chapter 1. The third column shows the percentage of the black population that resided in the central city. For example, out of a total population of the New York urban area of 13.32 million, 1.013 million were black, and 73.2 percent of the black population lived in New York City. The fourth column contains what is called the segregation index for the black population in the central city (and another city, if listed). Columns 3 and 4 generally show that the vast majority of the black population lived in the central city (with a few exceptions, noted below), and that blacks who lived in the central city were highly segregated from the rest of the city's population. In short, blacks were largely confined to black neighborhoods in the central city.

The segregation index is the percentage of the black (or white/nonblack) population that would have to move in order to have perfect integration (explained below) in the central city at the residential block level; the figure is 87.3 for New York City. It is important that you understand the idea of a segregation index, so let us look at a couple of numerical examples. First, suppose that a city consists of four blocks, with 100 people living on each

Table 3.2

Black Population in Northeastern Urban Areas: 1950

Urban area	Population (1,000s)	Black population (1,000s)	Total black population in central city (percent)	Segregation index for city*
New York	13,318	1,020	73.2	87.3
				(76.9 Newark)
Chicago	5,495	587	83.8	92.1
Philadelphia	3,671	480	78.3	89.0
Detroit	3,016	358	83.8	88.8
Boston	2,370	52	76.9	86.5
				(75.6 Cambridge)
Pittsburgh	2,213	136	60.3	84.0
St. Louis	1,681	215	71.6	92.9
				(94.2 E. St. Louis)
Cleveland	1,466	152	97.4	91.5
Washington, D.C.	1,464	334	84.1	80.1
Baltimore	1,337	265	83.8	91.3
Minneapolis–St. Paul	1,117	13	100	86.0
				(90.0 St. Paul)
Buffalo	1,089	124	29.8	89.5
Cincinnati	904	95	92.6	91.2
Milwaukee	871	22	100	91.6
Kansas City	814	87	64.4	91.3
				(92.0 K.C., KS)
Indianapolis	552	65	98.5	91.4
Columbus	503	52	90.4	88.9

* *Source:* Taeuber and Taeuber (1965, p. 39).

block. One block is 100 percent black and the other three blocks are 100 percent white, so blacks make up 25 percent of the population of the city. One way to generate complete integration is to have all of the black people move to white blocks: 33 move to each of the three white blocks so each of those blocks has a population that is 25 percent black (33/133). The segregation index in this scenario began as 100 and is now 0, meaning that once 100 percent of the black population moved, integration was achieved and 0 percent need to move. Alternatively, suppose that all of the white people move to the black block, which now has a total population of 400 with 100 blacks and 300 whites. The segregation index began at 100 because 100 percent of the white population needed to move to achieve integration; after the move, the index is 0. Neither of these scenarios is realistic because they involve the abandonment of part of the city. More realistically, suppose that 25 blacks move into each of the three white blocks and replace 25 whites on each one.

The 75 replaced whites (25 from each white block) move into the formerly all-black block. Now each block is home to 100 people, 25 of whom are black. In all, 75 percent of the blacks moved and 25 percent (75 out of 300) of the whites moved. In this simple case, the initial segregation index is 100 (75 + 25) regardless of the specific pattern of moves needed to achieve complete integration. And full integration, with a segregation index of 0, reflects the proportions of the races citywide.

The segregation index for New York City of 87.3 indicates that this very high percentage of the black population would have had to move to achieve perfect integration at the block level with blacks constituting 9.48 percent of the population on each block. A quick glance at Table 3.2 shows that twelve of the other large central cities had segregation indexes that were higher than New York City's. The lowest index in the table is 80.1 for Washington, D.C., and the highest is 92.9 for the city of St. Louis (with an index of 94.2 for East St. Louis, across the Mississippi River in Illinois). The third column of Table 3.2 shows that, with a few exceptions, the vast majority of the black population resided in the central cities. The main exception is Buffalo, where only 29.8 percent of the black population lived in the city of Buffalo. However, the remaining 70.1 percent of the black population was concentrated in certain suburbs to the north and east of the central city. The next exception is Pittsburgh, where 60.3 percent of the black population lived in the central city. The remainder of the black population was concentrated in Steel Valley along the Monongahela River. The cities of Kansas City, Missouri, St. Louis, New York, and Boston had relatively low concentrations of the black population of the urban area (64.4, 71.6, 73.8, and 76.9 percent, respectively), but in each case there was a smaller city across a river that contained the bulk of the remaining black population (Kansas City, Kansas, East St. Louis, Illinois, Newark, New Jersey, and Cambridge, Massachusetts). Otherwise, the concentration of the black population inside the central city was very high—at 83.8 percent or greater. The pattern of the concentration of blacks in highly segregated neighborhoods of central cities was well established in 1950.

The segregation of a population can be one of four types:

- segregation by social and economic status, caused by tastes and social linkages;
- segregation related to ethnic group, which may in part stem from the timing of arrival of immigrants to the urban area;
- segregation caused by active discrimination against certain racial groups;
- segregation caused by prejudice against certain racial groups.

The first two on this list bring about voluntary segregation of groups, but the last two involuntarily segregate the victims of discrimination and prejudice. All of these factors were at work in the case of blacks in the urban North, but the evidence is strong that active discrimination was important in creating the high level of racial segregation. There is a long history of studies documenting the creation of the black "ghettoes" in the northern cities.[4] The tools used included racially restrictive covenants in deeds enforced by white neighborhood improvement associations, discriminatory real estate practices, and violence. As the demand for housing for the black population grew with migration to the northern cities, the practice known as block busting came into use. The process of expanding the supply of housing for the black population involved steering blacks to particular blocks adjacent to the existing black residential area and, at the same time, making good offers to white property owners on those blocks (and feeding their fears as well). This method was used by real estate brokers of both colors, and essentially was a compromise solution to the American dilemma of how to accommodate a growing black population while playing to white prejudice. The situation in northern cities with growing black populations was particularly tense in 1950 and before because the suburban housing boom was still in the future. Whites "defended" their neighborhoods with vigor, but later would use the suburbs as an escape mechanism.

One particularly contentious issue was the construction of public housing. The decision to allow blacks to move into the Sojourner Truth public housing development in northeast Detroit in 1942 was met with violence. As Sugrue (1996, pp. 73–75) indicates, after this riot the Detroit Housing Commission established a policy of racial segregation in public housing. No one was killed in this riot, but a major race riot in the summer of 1943 claimed the lives of thirty-four people, twenty-five of them blacks. Civil disturbances also took place in Chicago when black families moved into public housing located in white neighborhoods. The issue of public housing and where to build it would become even more contentious in the wake of the Housing Act of 1949, the law that promised a huge expansion of the public housing program.

We now turn from the housing situation to the labor market. Table 3.3 contains information about the status of black workers in the northeastern urban areas. The first three columns pertain to males, and columns four to six display the data for females. We see in the first column that the rate of labor force participation of black males (aged fourteen and up) varied from a high of 80.4 percent in the Detroit urban area to a low of 70.6 percent in the Columbus urban area. Labor force participation is the percentage of men who are working or who are looking for work (i.e., officially unemployed), and the national rate of labor force participation for men in 1950 was 86.4

percent. Black men in northeastern urban areas fell well short of this national average. The unemployment rate for black men varied from a very low 5.0 percent in the Washington, D.C., urban area to 15.1 percent in the Buffalo urban area. However, the unemployment rate for Washington, D.C., stands out; the next-lowest was 8.6 percent in Milwaukee, and at a time when the national unemployment rate for men was 5.1 percent, most of the urban areas had unemployment rates for black men in excess of 10 percent.

The median earnings for black men were highest in the Detroit urban area at $2,717, which was 82.9 percent of the median earnings for all employed men in the headquarters of the America auto industry. The median earnings for black men came closest to the overall male median in Detroit, mainly as a result of the auto industry and its union, the United Auto Workers. The lowest median earnings for black men were in the Baltimore urban area with $1,864, followed closely by the Cincinnati ($1,879) and St. Louis ($1,906) urban areas. In each case, the median earnings of black men were barely two-thirds of the median earnings for all men in those urban areas; these are the lowest relative earnings figures in the table. In short, black men in the urban areas of the Northeast faced relatively high unemployment rates and had relatively low earnings. But there was also substantial variation across these urban areas in unemployment and earnings. Black men fared best in Washington, D.C., with its low unemployment rate, and in the major manufacturing centers of Chicago, Detroit, Cleveland, and Milwaukee with their relatively high median earnings. Black men also did relatively well in Minneapolis–St. Paul, but very few black men lived and worked there in 1950. The New York metropolitan area did not offer black men an especially promising picture. Their unemployment rate was 11.5 percent, and the relatively modest median earnings of $2,100 were only 69.7 percent of the median for all employed men in that urban area. Also, black men did not do particularly well in heavily industrialized Pittsburgh; the unemployment rate was 13.2 percent, and median earnings were $2,114, which was 75.8 percent of the overall male median for Pittsburgh.

The position of black women in the labor markets of northeastern urban areas mirrored the position of black men and of women in general. Labor force participation was highest in the New York metropolitan area at 48.2 percent and lowest in Pittsburgh at 24.9 percent. The labor force participation rate for all women in the United States was 33.9 percent in 1950; black women in the major northeastern urban areas exceeded the national average everywhere except the heavily industrialized urban areas of Pittsburgh, Detroit, and Buffalo. The relatively high participation rates for black women stood in contrast to the relatively low participation rates for black men. Unemployment rates for black women in the northeastern urban areas exceeded the national unemployment rate for women of 5.7 percent in every

Table 3.3

Black Workers in Northeastern Urban Areas: 1950

Urban area	Male labor force (percent participation)	Male unemployment rate (percent)	Male median earnings (percent of median)	Female labor force (percent participation)	Female unemployment rate (percent)	Female median earnings (percent of median)
New York	279,500 (76.1)	11.5	$2,100 (69.7)	212,400 (48.2)	8.0	$1,302 (76.2)
Chicago	171,900 (78.0)	10.9	2,361 (73.6)	94,200 (39.4)	12.4	1,234 (76.6)
Philadelphia	120,600 (71.7)	14.9	2,051 (72.2)	74,800 (39.7)	9.1	1,058 (71.5)
Detroit	106,800 (80.4)	11.4	2,717 (82.9)	39,000 (28.8)	12.6	1,025 (69.1)
Boston	15,200 (72.7)	10.5	2,011 (72.6)	8,800 (40.9)	6.8	1,199 (84.8)
Pittsburgh	36,500 (73.4)	13.2	2,114 (75.9)	12,700 (24.9)	11.0	827 (71.7)
St. Louis	54,600 (73.2)	10.8	1,906 (66.8)	30,400 (35.5)	10.2	859 (63.4)
Cleveland	44,600 (79.2)	11.4	2,289 (72.3)	23,000 (37.8)	10.0	1,016 (72.6)
Washington, D.C.	93,500 (77.0)	5.0	2,137 (71.1)	67,100 (49.7)	6.7	1,343 (67.5)
Baltimore	71,700 (75.9)	9.8	1,864 (68.8)	41,900 (42.4)	8.8	844 (70.1)
Minneapolis– St. Paul	4,500 (73.8)	8.9	2,188 (72.5)	2,200 (40.0)	4.5	1,052 (78.4)
Buffalo	13,900 (79.0)	15.1	2,370 (78.9)	5,600 (31.5)	21.4	942 (73.8)
Cincinnati	25,200 (74.3)	14.3	1,879 (66.8)	14,500 (37.7)	10.3	853 (68.6)
Milwaukee	7,000 (80.0)	8.6	2,460 (76.9)	3,100 (37.3)	9.7	1,072 (78.3)
Kansas City	23,900 (74.4)	7.9	1,911 (66.2)	14,100 (39.4)	7.8	857 (62.3)
Indianapolis	18,300 (78.9)	9.3	2,084 (68.6)	10,600 (40.5)	8.5	919 (64.0)
Columbus	14,200 (70.6)	11.3	2,073 (73.2)	7,900 (39.9)	11.4	924 (65.3)

Source: Census of Population and Housing.

case except one—Minneapolis–St. Paul (which had a very small black population). Black women faced very high unemployment rates in the industrial centers of Detroit (12.6 percent) and Buffalo (21.4 percent). Median earnings for black women ranged from $844 per year in Baltimore to $1,199 in Boston and $1,343 in Washington, D.C. As was the case for black men, black women earned a percentage of the overall median female earnings that ranged from 62.3 percent in Kansas City to 84.8 percent in Boston.

This brief portrait of black Americans in the major urban areas of the Northeast has revealed that:

- Substantial numbers of blacks had migrated to many of these urban areas, and they lived primarily in segregated areas in the major central cities.
- Opportunities in the labor market were far better than in the urban areas of the South (as we shall see), but blacks in these urban areas faced high rates of unemployment (at a time when national unemployment was a relatively low 5.3 percent) and earnings that fell below median earnings.
- Black men had relatively low, and black women relatively high, labor force participation rates. A reasonable inference is that in the society of 1950, outcomes in the labor market for black men led black women to seek employment.

Black Americans in the Urban Areas of the South and West: 1950

We first examine the six urban areas in the South. The basic population data in Table 3.4 show that five of the six had sizable black populations in 1950 (Miami being the exception) that were primarily concentrated in the central city and highly segregated at the block level. Indeed, these data for the southern urban areas do not differ substantially from the corresponding figures for the northeastern urban areas. The percentage of the black population that lived in the central city varied from a low of 62.5 percent in Birmingham to 90.5 percent in New Orleans. And the segregation indexes were 84.9 (for New Orleans) and higher. The segregation level of 97.8 for the small black population of Miami was the highest of any of the twenty-nine cities shown in Tables 3.2 and 3.4. Myrdal's impression that segregation was lower in southern cities was incorrect; the black population was not interspersed among the white population at the block level. The segregation indexes for these southern cities for 1940 were all over 80. However, the segregation indexes for these cities were slightly lower in 1940 than in 1950, with the exception of Miami. Also, it is important to remember that the segregation indexes reported here are at the block level. It is possible that black residential blocks were more

Table 3.4

Black Population in Southern and Western Urban Areas: 1950

Urban area	Population (1,000s)	Black population (1,000s)	Total black population in central city (percent)	Segregation index for city* (percent)
Dallas–	976	123	76.4	88.4
Fort Worth				90.4
Houston	808	149	83.9	91.5
New Orleans	685	201	90.5	84.9
Atlanta	672	166	72.9	91.5
Birmingham	559	208	62.5	88.7
Miami	495	65	61.5	97.8
Los Angeles	4,664	226	75.7	84.6
San Francisco–	2,241	147	61.2	79.8
Oakland				81.2
Seattle	734	16	100	83.3
Denver	564	16	93.8	88.9
San Diego	557	17	88.2	83.6
Phoenix	332	14	35.7	n.a.

* *Source:* Taeuber and Taeuber (1965, pp. 40–41).

scattered in southern cities than in northeastern cities. The two largest black populations in the Northeast, in New York and Chicago, were largely confined to two well-established areas with clear boundaries—Harlem and the South Side Black Belt.

Sharp differences between the South and the Northeast emerge when we examine the labor market data in Table 3.5. The ability of black men to earn money in the southern urban areas was much lower. The labor force participation rates of black men were slightly higher in the southern urban areas—ranging from 73.3 percent in New Orleans to 84.1 percent in Miami (remember the national figure for men was 86.4)—and unemployment rates of black men were lower in the South, at 4.5 percent in Atlanta up to 9.5 percent in New Orleans. But median earnings for black men were very low. Median earnings were $1,457 in the Atlanta urban area (the lowest) and $1,803 in Houston (the highest). These median earnings figures are barely above 60 percent of the median for all men in these urban areas. The median earnings for black men in Dallas–Fort Worth of $1,503 were only 56.5 percent of the median earnings for all employed men in that urban area. In short, black men generally could readily find work in southern urban areas, but the pay was very low.

The situation faced by black women in the southern urban areas can likewise be summarized easily. Labor force participation rates were high—over 50 percent in Dallas–Fort Worth and Miami—and unemployment rates were

Table 3.5

Black Workers in Southern and Western Urban Areas: 1950

Urban area	Male labor force (percent participation)	Male unemployment rate (percent)	Male median earnings (percent of median)	Female labor force (percent participation)	Female unemployment rate (percent)	Female median earnings (percent of median)
Dallas–Fort Worth	34,700 (80.0)	5.2	$1,503 (56.5)	25,400 (52.2)	5.1	$661 (60.5)
Houston	43,300 (81.7)	5.5	$1,803 (62.1)	25,600 (43.9)	4.7	$747 (67.0)
New Orleans	47,500 (73.3)	9.5	$1,459 (66.1)	27,900 (35.6)	7.2	$682 (75.0)
Atlanta	42,100 (77.0)	4.5	$1,457 (63.1)	29,100 (44.2)	9.3	$674 (60.1)
Birmingham	50,900 (76.5)	9.0	$1,676 (73.1)	25,500 (32.4)	7.5	$467 (62.9)
Miami	19,600 (84.1)	4.6	$1,654 (65.9)	14,000 (54.7)	5.7	$866 (74.5)
Los Angeles	83,300 (77.5)	12.2	$2,169 (72.4)	48,800 (44.2)	10.9	$1,041 (85.0)
San Francisco–Oakland	61,400 (75.7)	16.1	$2,307 (73.7)	29,200 (41.2)	17.5	$1,023 (66.9)
Seattle	9,400 (72.9)	18.1	$2,183 (70.4)	3,700 (38.1)	13.5	$1,098 (86.5)
Denver	5,400 (75.0)	7.4	$1,882 (68.7)	3,100 (42.0)	5.5	$860 (74.7)
San Diego	6,000 (76.9)	8.3	$2,057 (78.8)	2,800 (36.8)	14.3	$877 (85.1)
Phoenix	5,200 (70.3)	19.2	$1,432 (63.1)	2,300 (32.4)	13.0	$707 (76.6)

Source: Census of Population and Housing.

lower than in the Northeast. Recall that the female labor force participation rate for the nation was 33.9 percent in 1950, but median earnings were very low. The median earnings for black women in Birmingham were $467 per year, which was 62.9 percent of the median for all employed women in this urban area. The highest median earnings for black women were in Miami at $866, but Miami had a small black population at that time. As in the Northeast, survival for urban black families often meant that women went to work—usually domestic work at very low wages.

The urban areas of the West fall into two categories. As Table 3.4 shows, the Los Angeles and San Francisco–Oakland urban areas had sizable black populations (226,000 and 147,000, respectively) and somewhat lower levels of segregation compared to the other major urban areas. In the case of Los Angeles, 75.7 percent of the black population lived in the central city, and these central city residents had a segregation index of 84.6. In San Francisco–Oakland, 61.2 percent of blacks lived in the two central cities, and their segregation indexes were 79.8 and 81.2. As we shall see, the two major urban areas of the West have a history of somewhat lower levels of segregation than do the urban areas of the Northeast and the South. The other four urban areas of the West had very small black populations in 1950 of only 14,000 to 17,000. These populations were highly concentrated in the central city (except for Phoenix) and were highly segregated at the block level.

The labor market outcomes for black Americans in the western urban areas generally resembled those of the northeastern urban areas. As shown in Table 3.5, black men in the West had low rates of labor force participation and faced high unemployment rates. Median earnings ranged from a low of $1,432 in Phoenix to a high of $1,882 in Denver. The important urban areas are Los Angeles and San Francisco–Oakland. Black men in Los Angeles had a labor force participation rate of 77.5 percent (compared to the national rate for all men of 86.4 percent), an unemployment rate of 12.2 percent, and median earnings of $2,169 (72.4 percent of the median for all employed men in the urban area). The labor force participation rate was lower (75.7 percent) and the unemployment rate higher (16.1 percent) in San Francisco–Oakland, but median earnings there were slightly higher at $2,307 (73.7 percent of the median for all employed men there). Black women in the western urban areas had high rates of labor force participation, high rates of unemployment, and low earnings. Median earnings for black women in the Los Angeles were $1,041, which was 85.0 percent of the median for all employed women in that urban area. Median earnings for black women in San Francisco–Oakland were $1,023—virtually the same as in Los Angeles—but this figure was only 66.9 percent of the median earnings of all employed women in northern California's major urban area.

Conclusion

The Carnegie Corporation had called attention to the plight of black Americans through the monumental study that was organized by Swedish economist Gunnar Myrdal. Myrdal's book, *An American Dilemma*, came out in 1944 and was highly influential among the American intelligentsia. Myrdal found that the old doctrine of racial inferiority was still alive in the minds of many white Americans, and that the institutions of the South were specifically designed to keep blacks "in their place." Myrdal was more hopeful about the situation of black Americans in the cities of the North. There, black people could vote, the system of justice was much fairer to blacks, and decent schools (for that time) were being provided. Work was available in the manufacturing plants. Black Americans were moving from the South to the northern metropolises to take advantage of both social and economic opportunity. Myrdal felt that the vicious circle in which black Americans were trapped might be reversed if further opportunities could be opened. The position of blacks depended upon the attitudes held by whites, and those attitudes could be changed, he believed, if blacks could improve their social and economic standing. Myrdal advocated "social engineering" to help bring about the changes that were needed. He did not say it directly, but a reasonable inference is that Myrdal believed that direct intervention by the federal government in the South would be needed.

The status of black Americans in 1950 was largely the same as the one Myrdal described for the early 1940s. About 1.7 million blacks had migrated from the South in the 1940s (11.3 percent of the total black population in 1950), and most had gone to the northern cities. Migration to the two major urban areas of the West, Los Angeles and San Francisco–Oakland, had also begun. Upon their arrival in the northern cities, blacks became largely concentrated in central cities and in highly segregated housing patterns. Opportunities in the labor market presented something of a mixed picture in that unemployment rates were higher in the Northeast, but median earnings were much greater than in the South. For example, black men in metropolitan Chicago had an unemployment rate of 10.9 percent and median earnings of $2,361, while black men in Atlanta faced an unemployment rate of only 4.5 percent and earned a median of $1,457. One approach is to compute the "expected" earnings as the median earnings times one minus the unemployment rate. For Chicago, this computation is 0.891 x $2361 = $2,104, while the computation for Atlanta is 0.955 x $1457 = $1,391. The "expected" earnings for black men in Chicago were 51.3 percent higher than for black men in Atlanta. Black women in Chicago faced an unemployment rate of 12.4 percent and had median earnings of $1,234, thus "expected" earnings of $1,081. Black women in Atlanta had a lower unemployment rate of 9.3 percent and lower earnings of $674, hence "expected" earnings of $611. Expected earnings for black women were 76.9 percent higher in Chicago than in Atlanta. These differences represent large economic incentives for migration. Further, the "social" incentives for migration to the North might have been even greater. The social status of blacks in the South had not yet changed much from the time when Myrdal wrote. The status of blacks in the northern cities left much to be desired, but presented a huge contrast to the South. Black Americans in the northern cities had the franchise, access to the legal system, and reasonably decent public schools. This last factor was especially important for the next generation of black Americans.

Notes

1. Our focus here is on conditions in the urban areas, but some of the other data in *An American Dilemma* (1944, p. 372) need to be mentioned. In a study of food consumption by nonrelief families in 1935–36 undertaken by the U.S. Department of Labor, it was found that 66 percent of southern black farm owners, sharecroppers, and tenants did not consume fresh fruit during a survey period of one week. Thirty-four percent of these families did not consume fluid milk and a like number did not consume eggs—for the entire week! The diets of white sharecroppers were better, but not by much.

2. Myrdal is regarded as the father of the Swedish social welfare state.

3. In *A History of the American People*, Johnson (1997, pp. 952–953) writes, "Who was Gunnar Myrdal? He was, essentially a disciple of Nietzsche and his theory of the Superman: Myrdal's belief that 'Democratic politics are stupid' and 'the masses are impervious to rational argument' led him to the social engineering of the Swedish Social Democratic Party, in which the enlightened elite took decisions on behalf of the people for their own good. Myrdal's book had a profound impact on the American intelligentsia." I have read nearly all of *An American Dilemma*, and I think that Johnson is given to overstatement.

4. See Massey and Denton (1993) for a survey of those studies. One particularly detailed study of Chicago by Drake and Cayton (1945) included maps showing the incidents of violence against blacks who attempted to move into white neighborhoods.

Part II

Urban Growth and Prosperity: 1950–1970

4

The Industrial Northeast and the Great Migration

The American economy had already entered the postwar boom period in 1950. The urban areas of the Northeast participated in that boom, but before we examine those seventeen, it is useful to review briefly this remarkable period in America. James Patterson (1996), in his volume in the Oxford History of the United States on the period, calls it the time of "Grand Expectations." The American economy stood largely unchallenged in the world. The world economy was built around the dollar as the reserve currency. Postwar prosperity was fueled by rapid growth in productivity. Output per worker increased by 3.3 percent per year from 1947 to 1965. Using the Rule of 72, this meant that output per worker doubled in twenty-two years. Median family incomes in real terms nearly doubled between 1949 and 1969, increasing by 99.4 percent. The population of the nation grew by 18.5 percent from 1950 to 1960, and then added another 13.4 percent in the decade of the 1970s to reach a total of 203.3 million. Gross domestic product (GDP) increased by 43.4 percent in the 1950s, so that decade produced an increase in GDP per capita of 20.9 percent. Partly because of the Vietnam War expenditures, economic growth was more rapid in the 1960s than in the 1950s; GDP increased by 50.4 percent in the 1960s, so GDP per capita increased by 32.6 percent. Over this twenty-year period, population increased by 34.4 percent, GDP increased by 115.6 percent, and GDP per capita grew by 60.4 percent. Nonagricultural employment grew from 45.2 million in 1950 to 54.2 million in 1960 and 70.9 million in 1970. The employment growth of 19.9 percent in the 1950s closely matched the population growth, but employment growth in the 1960s of 30.1 percent far exceeded the population growth of 13.4 percent. Three factors account for most of this discrepancy: the increased labor force participation of women, the decline in agricultural employment, and the entry into the work force of the first group of baby boomers.

The economy grew, but its composition was also changing away from the production and distribution of goods toward the service sector, broadly defined. Employment in goods-producing industries (manufacturing, construction, and mining) declined from 40.9 percent of total nonagricultural employment in 1950 to 37.7 percent in 1960 and 36.1 percent in 1970. (The percentage was to decline even more rapidly in the 1970s and 1980s to 28.4 percent in 1980 and 22.8 percent in 1990.) The share of employment in manufacturing fell from 33.7 percent in 1950 to 31.0 percent in 1960 and 27.3 percent in 1970.

America's period of economic boom lasted from the end of World War II to 1973 and ended with the onset of the period of what economists called "stagflation"—the combination of stagnant growth and inflation. Real gross domestic product (GDP) dropped in 1974 and 1975. The economy recovered from 1976 to 1979, but GDP dropped again in 1980, recovered somewhat in 1981, and fell again in 1982. Recovery resumed in 1983, but real GDP increased only by 23.3 percent in the decade of 1973 to 1983—an annual growth rate of 2.1 percent. The recessions of 1973–75 and the early 1980s are generally attributed to the two "oil shocks" of 1973 and 1979 and to the actions taken by the Federal Reserve to rein in inflation in the early 1980s. It is no accident that this period was also one of crisis for America's urban areas.

Economic growth and increasing prosperity had many causes and consequences. Here are a few:

- The baby boom began in 1946 and lasted until 1964. During these years 76.4 million babies were born. The birthrate had been 18 to 19 per 1,000 population in the 1930s, and increased to 26.6 in 1947 (the peak), remained at 24 or higher until 1959, and was above 20 until 1964. The birthrate then fell below 20, but by then the "baby boom generation" had been born. The baby boom was caused partly by the increasing prosperity, and then turned into a source of demand that sustained prosperity.
- Americans achieved much higher levels of education. In 1940, 49 percent of students graduated from high school; in 1970 this proportion stood at 76 percent. The GI Bill provided stipends for veterans to attend college or technical colleges, and the modern system of American higher education was the result. The boom in education was both cause and consequence of increasing economic prosperity.
- Americans spent their increasing incomes on new houses and automobiles (and many other goods as well). New houses and automobiles mean rapid suburban growth, a direct consequence of economic growth and prosperity. Home purchase was partly motivated by the increase in children, and it was facilitated by the FHA mortgage insurance program and the VA program that permitted veterans to purchase a home with little or no down payment.

- The introduction of a vast array of consumer products was also fueled by the growth in incomes. Those new consumer products included television and household appliances such as automatic washing machines, electric clothes dryers, automatic dishwashers, vacuum cleaners, electric ranges, refrigerators, and freezers. Other new products included the Polaroid camera, frozen foods, clothing made from new fibers, vinyl floors, transistor radios, stereo systems and long-playing records, and a wide array of plastic products. Indeed, the invention of the transistor in 1947 was the first step in the amazing computer revolution of later decades.

This author, who as a seven-year-old in 1950 had never seen a television program, in 1960 was driving a car to high school (from a suburban home) and was an avid TV viewer. Dating the end of an era in American urban history is somewhat arbitrary. The era in question is here called the period of urban growth. In this case, the dating options range from 1964, the year of the first urban riot of the period, to 1973, the year of the first oil shock. Two factors suggest that 1970 is a reasonable choice. First, the selection of an earlier date would miss the period of rapid economic growth in the mid to late 1960s. For example, 1963 to 1967 was the only period during which manufacturing employment in the city of Chicago increased. The increase was substantial—from 509,000 to 546,000, an increase of 7.4 percent in four years. However, by 1972 manufacturing employment in this major city had dropped to 430,000. Second, 1970 is a census year. The best data on urban areas are available only from census years.

The postwar economic boom also involved rapid growth in the West. As noted in the Introduction, population growth varied by region. Total population of the United States grew from 151 million in 1950 to 202 million in 1970. Growth in the West of 72.5 percent far exceeded the national growth of 34.1 percent. Population growth in the South was 31.6 percent, while the Northeast added 26.8 percent to its population. While the population of the Northeast grew at a less rapid rate than in the rest of the nation, its growth from 87.4 million to 110.8 million represented 45.5 percent of the nation's population increase. And as we have already seen, the black population of the Northeast more than doubled—from 4.96 million to 10.23 million. During these same twenty years, the black population of the South grew by only 12.0 percent, from 9.52 million to 10.65 million. The black population of the South continued to respond to the economic and social opportunities in the Northeast in this last era of the Great Migration.

Growth in the Northeastern Urban Areas

The task of this chapter is to examine how the metropolitan areas of the Northeast fared during this period of growth from 1950 to 1970. All of the metropolitan areas experienced significant growth, but their experiences varied widely from low growth in Pittsburgh to the boom in nearby Columbus.

The basic record of economic growth in the northeastern urban areas is shown in Table 4.1. The urban areas of the Northeast recorded remarkable gains in population, employment, and real income from 1950 to 1970. Average population growth for the seventeen areas was 46 percent, which far exceeded the population growth in the nation as a whole or the northeastern region. Population growth varied from a high of 93 percent in Washington, D.C. (as always, a special case), and 80 percent in Columbus to a low of just 19 percent in the Boston urban area. These figures refer to the geographic area defined by the Bureau of the Census as the metropolitan area in 1970. The four largest urban areas recorded strong population growth figures—32 percent for New York, 28 percent for Chicago, 33 percent for Philadelphia, and 49 percent for Detroit (the last above average for the seventeen urban areas). Employment growth for the same geographic areas averaged 43 percent and varied from the highs of 98 percent in Washington, D.C., and 81 percent in Columbus to the low of 19 percent in Pittsburgh. Employment growth in the four top urban areas fell short of the average for the seventeen, but displayed strong increases none the less. Employment in metropolitan New York increased by 29 percent, Chicago recorded a gain of 24 percent, Philadelphia grew by 36 percent, and employment in Detroit gained 40 percent. Median family income in real terms increased by an average of 89 percent in these seventeen urban areas. New York and Baltimore had the largest income growth of 104 percent, and Buffalo had the smallest increase at 65 percent.

Rapid population growth at the metropolitan level was accompanied by population decline in most of the central cities of the Northeast. Only the central cities of Milwaukee, Kansas City, Indianapolis, and Columbus added to their populations, and as shown in Table 4.1, these are the only central cities in the group that annexed significant amounts of land. The central city of Milwaukee added 12 percent to its population and 90 percent to its land area. The central cities of Kansas City, Indianapolis, and Columbus added huge amounts of land area and recorded population increases of 11 percent, 74 percent, and 44 percent, respectively. New York City added no land or population. The other twelve central cities declined in population and added little or no land area. The largest population decline in this group was the 27 percent drop in St. Louis, which was accompanied by a 34 percent increase in the urban area as a whole. The central cities of Boston, Pittsburgh, and Buffalo also lost at least 20 percent of their populations even as their urban areas grew by 19 percent, 21 percent, and 24 percent, respectively. The move to those new houses in the suburbs was on—facilitated by the increase in income to purchase automobiles and by the construction of highways on which to drive them.

Table 4.1

Urban Areas of the Northeast: 1950–1970 (percent change)

	Urban area population	Urban area employment	Median family income	Manufacturing employment (1947–1972)	Central city population	Central city area
New York	32	29	104	-8.6	0	0
Chicago	28	24	92	6.0	-7	7
Philadelphia	33	36	102	-6.3	-6	0
Detroit	49	40	70	-2.6	-18	0
Boston	19	27	64	-5.1	-20	0
Pittsburgh	21	19	87	-22.5	-23	2
St. Louis	34	27	100	0.8	-27	0
Cleveland	42	23	87	-2.0	-18	1
Washington, D.C.	93	98	89	140.8	-6	0
Baltimore	36	40	104	1.8	-5	0
Minneapolis–St. Paul	81	81	97	67.2	-11	5
Buffalo	24	21	65	-17.5	-20	4
Cincinnati	36	30	99	9.2	-10	
Milwaukee	51	43	87	3.4	12	
Kansas City	54	52	99	50.6	11	90
Indianapolis	63	54	91	20.3	74	292
Columbus	80	81	78	66.6	44	587
Mean	46	43	89	17.8	-2	242

Source: Census of Population and Housing and Statistical Abstract of the United States.

The rapid employment growth in the northeastern urban areas was accompanied by a dramatic shift in the industrial composition of employment. Table 4.1 shows that the average growth in manufacturing employment in the seventeen urban areas was 18 percent. However, this average is skewed by the huge 141 percent increase in Washington, D.C., from a very small base. If the nation's capital is excluded from the average, the figure falls to an increase of just 10 percent. Manufacturing employment declined in seven of the seventeen urban areas, including New York, Philadelphia, Detroit, Boston, Pittsburgh, Cleveland, and Buffalo. Indeed, the declines of 22 percent in Pittsburgh and 18 percent in Buffalo were harbingers of things to come.

In summary, the urban areas of the Northeast provide a stunning record of economic growth in the 1950–70 period. Population, employment, and median real family incomes grew rapidly, and this growth was accompanied by movement to the suburbs that, in some cases, meant population decline in the central city. These urban areas also experienced the shift away from manufacturing employment. Rapid productivity growth, coupled with increases in demand for nonmanufactured services (health care, restaurant meals, entertainment, vacations, and so on) meant that the demands of consumers for manufactured products could be satisfied with a declining fraction of the work force. A much more pronounced effect of this kind had already taken place in agriculture, of course.

Statistical Patterns of Urban Growth

This section explores some patterns in the data on urban growth shown in Table 4.1. Some of the hypotheses examined are based on an important earlier study by R.D. Norton (1979), which examined the largest thirty urban areas over the 1950–75 period. Norton's study is highly relevant to this section, so let us begin by reviewing his findings. The title of Norton's book is *City Life-Cycles and American Urban Policy*. His idea is that urban areas have life cycles, and his critical distinction for an American urban area is whether it grew to maturity before the age of the automobile, which he dated as 1910. Norton divided the thirty largest urban areas as of 1970 into three groups—the twelve that were the largest in 1910 (the industrial group), the twelve that were the smallest in 1910 (the young group), and a group of six urban areas that was in-between these two groups in size in 1910. Sixteen of the seventeen urban northeastern urban areas in this study were included in Norton's study. Norton excluded only Minneapolis–St. Paul. The "industrial" group includes eleven of the seventeen northeastern urban areas included in this study, plus San Francisco. Indianapolis and Columbus are included in the "young" group, and Washington, D.C., Milwaukee, and Kansas City are members of the "in-between" group. The "in-between" group also includes Los Angeles, New Orleans, and Seattle. The "young" group includes six of the urban areas of the South and West included in this study (Atlanta, Denver, Dallas, Houston, San Diego, and Phoenix) plus Memphis, Nashville, San Antonio, and Jacksonville, Florida. In short, the Norton's "industrial" group corresponds reasonably closely to the northeastern urban areas in this study.

The "industrial" group differed substantially from the "young" group in 1950. The average for manufacturing employment in the "industrial" group was 35 percent compared to 19 percent for the "young" group. The "industrial" group had population growth at the metropolitan level of 37 percent from 1950 to 1970, while the "young" group grew by 123 percent. The central cities of the "industrial" group added only 2 percent to their land area and declined in population by an average of 14 percent, while the central cities of the "young" group added an average of 676 percent of land area and increased in population by 115 percent. Population density in the "industrial" urban areas averaged 4,500 people per square mile in 1950 compared to 2,700 per square mile for the "young" urban areas, and the percentage of the housing stock built before 1939 was 49 percent for the former group and 22 percent for the latter group.

Norton (1979, p. 34) used data on the thirty metropolitan areas to create an equation for the change in central city population from 1950 to 1970. That equation is:

$$CCPOPGRO = -61.9 + 1.1 \, UAPOPGRO + 0.06 \, AREA$$

CCPOPGRO is the percentage change in the central city population, UAPOPGRO is the percentage change in the population of the urban area, and AREA is the percentage change in the land area of the central city. These results are highly statistically significant. They imply the following:

- If an urban area had no population growth, then its central city population (with no expansion of land area) would have declined by 61.9 percent. The typical "industrial" central city was located in an urban area with population growth of 37 percent and added no land area, so the equation says that the population of such a central city would have declined by 21 percent (actual decline was 14 percent).
- The population of the central city increased by 1.1 percent for each percentage increase in the population of the urban area (although this effect is not statistically significantly different from 1.0).
- Expansion of the land area of the central city by 1 percent increased the central city population by 0.06 percent.

Norton (1979) also studied employment in central cities in four categories —manufacturing, wholesale trade, retail trade, and selected services as defined by the Census of Business. These four categories contain only about half of total employment. He estimated an equation for the change in employment in these four categories in the central city over the period 1947 to 1972, with the following results:

$$CCEMPGRO = -46.6 + 1.0 \ UAEMPGRO + 0.03 \ AREA$$

Here, CCEMPGRO is the percentage change in employment in the central city in the four employment categories, UAEMPGRO is the percentage change for employment in these categories at the metropolitan level, and AREA is the percentage change in the land area of the central city. These results are also highly statistically significant, and have implications very similar to those of the central city population equation. A central city that is located in an urban area with no employment growth and with no ability to annex territory would have declined in employment (in the four categories) by 46.6 percent. Employment at the metropolitan level translated into employment growth in the central city with a coefficient of 1.0, and annexation of territory added to the employment base of the central city.

Norton's results tell us that growth at the metropolitan level is the critical factor in the fate of the central city. A metropolitan area that grew relatively slowly had a central city that lost population and employment. For a central city that was unable to annex territory, the "break-even" metropolitan growth of population for 1950 to 1970 was 56 percent (61.9 divided by 1.1). The break-even metropolitan growth in employment in the four categories was 46 percent. Here is where the idea of the life cycle of the urban area comes into play. The "industrial" group of urban areas had an average of 35 percent of employment in manufacturing 1950 and had subsequent growth of 37 percent in population and only 17 percent in employment in the four categories. The "young" group had only 19 percent of employment in manufacturing in 1950 and had population growth of 123 percent and employment growth of 160 percent. Norton argued that there was a strong connection between the manufacturing base in 1950 and subsequent metropolitan growth. An urban area with a strong reliance on the old manufacturing base was a victim of the forces of change—Joseph Schumpeter's "creative destruction."

What statistical patterns emerge if attention is restricted to the seventeen major urban areas of the Northeast? First, let us examine growth at the met-ropolitan level. Population and employment growth appear to be negatively related to the size of the manufacturing base in 1950. For this comparison I exclude Washington, D.C. (with its manufacturing base of just 7 percent in 1950). The eight urban areas with the largest manufacturing bases in 1950, shown in Table 4.1, had average manufacturing employment that was 40 percent of total employment and population growth from 1950 to 1970 of 35 percent, while the other eight had 29 percent of employment in manufacturing in 1950 and population growth of 50 percent. Total employment growth for these two groups was 29 percent and 49 percent, respectively. However, it is also apparent that smaller urban areas may tend to grow more rapidly in percentage terms simply because they begin with a smaller base. Both of these ideas can be tested together.

A multiple regression was computed using the data for the sixteen urban areas (excluding Washington, D.C.), with the following results:

$$\text{EMPGRO} = 159.64 - 1.37 \text{ MFG} - 9.84 \text{ LNPOP}$$
$$(4.14) \quad (2.32) \quad (1.99)$$

Here EMPGRO is percentage employment growth in the urban area for 1950 to 1970, MFG is the percentage of employment in manufacturing in 1950, and LNPOP is the natural logarithm of the population (in thousands) of the metropolitan area in 1950. The R-square for the estimated equation is 0.394 (indicating that the equation accounts for 39 percent of the variation in percentage employment growth), and the t statistics are in parentheses. The coefficients of both variables are statistically significant at the conventional 95 percent level. (A t statistic of about 2.0 or greater indicates that the estimated coefficient in question is highly unlikely to be zero, in fact 95 percent or more unlikely). The coefficient on the manufacturing base variable says that an urban area with a larger initial concentration in manufacturing of 1 percent had lower subsequent total employment growth of 1.37 percent over twenty years. The coefficient of the natural log of population controls for initial size and indicates that larger metropolitan areas did indeed tend to grow more slowly in percentage terms. For example, the Chicago metropolitan area had manufacturing employment of 37.5 percent in 1950 and population of 5,493 (8.611 in natural logs). These values mean that employment growth in metropolitan Chicago would have been predicted to have been 23.5 percent (compared to the actual of 24 percent). This simple model explains 39 percent of the variation in employment growth for the 16 urban areas—quite a respectable finding.

The same model was estimated for population growth in the sixteen metropolitan areas, but in this case the size of the initial manufacturing base is not statistically significant once the size of the urban area is included. The estimated equation is:

$$POPGRO = 157.50 - 0.79 \text{ MFG} - 11.70 \text{ LNPOP}$$
$$(3.80) \quad (1.25) \qquad (2.20)$$

Here POPGRO is the growth of the population of the urban area. The R-square for this estimated equation is 0.282, and the coefficient of LNPOP is highly statistically significant (but the coefficient of MFG is not). Populations of smaller metropolitan areas grew more rapidly in percentage terms, and any relationship to the initial manufacturing base is quite weak. Indeed, dropping LNPOP from the estimation results in a coefficient of MFG of −1.08 that is still not statistically significant.

Population growth in the central city can be explained statistically quite well using Norton's (1979) approach. The estimated equation is:

$$CCPOPGRO = -23.35 + 0.41 \text{ UAPOPGRO} + 5.21 \text{ LNAREA}$$
$$(2.49) \quad (2.17) \qquad\qquad (4.05)$$

Here LNAREA is the natural log of the increase in land area of the central city (with zero coded as 0.1). The R-square for this estimated equation is 0.600, and the coefficients of both variables are highly statistically significant. The constant term of −23.35 says that a central city with no ability to annex territory and in an urban area with no population growth would have declined by 23.35 percent. The coefficient on population growth at the metropolitan level says that a 1 percent increase in this growth was associated with greater population growth (or less population decline) in the central city of 0.41 percent, a result that is much smaller than Norton's (1979) finding of 1.1 percent. However, it turns out that population growth in the central city was more closely associated with employment growth in the urban area. The estimated equation for the sixteen urban areas is:

$$CCPOPGRO = -26.06 + 0.58 \text{ EMPGRO} + 4.99 \text{ LNAREA}$$
$$(2.72) \quad (2.33) \qquad\qquad (3.69)$$

The R-square for this estimated equation is 0.631, which is slightly greater than the R-square of 0.600 for the model that includes urban area population growth instead of employment growth. The coefficient of employment growth is highly statistically significant, and it indicates that greater employment growth of 1 percent was associated with population growth in the central city that was 0.58 percent higher. When we put all of these results together, we see that urban areas that were more heavily concentrated in manufacturing and were larger in 1950 had lower employment and population growth at the metropolitan level and lower population growth in the central city. All of these results pertain to the sixteen major urban areas of the Northeast (excluding the special case of Washington, D.C.). But these findings in no way negate the observation that these urban areas produced a remarkable record of growth from 1950 to 1970. Lastly, attempts to find correlations between growth in median real family income were unsuccessful. In particular, growth in real family income was not related to the size of the manufacturing base in 1950. This result perhaps is not surprising because the increase in labor productivity tended to increase wages in manufacturing, while slower demand growth tended to depress manufacturing wages.

Summary

This chapter has documented the remarkable record of growth and prosperity achieved by the major urban areas of the Northeast in the twenty years after 1950. Population, employment, and median family incomes grew rapidly as the nation pursued, in James Patterson's (1996) words, "Grand Expectations." Life for the typical American in one of these major metropolitan areas was quite different in 1970 compared to 1950. Real family incomes doubled and the baby boom generation was born. Indeed, the last of the baby boomers had entered first grade in 1970. Growth of these urban areas was accompanied by population decline in the older, larger central cities as people were attracted to the suburbs in record numbers. We shall turn to the issues and problems related to suburbanization and central city decline in later chapters. The purpose of this chapter has been to document the strong growth that was dominant during these twenty years. The next chapter is a similar examination of the urban areas of the Sunbelt.

5

The New Sunbelt Takes Off

The sharp distinction between the major urban areas of the South and West began to break down during 1950 to 1970. Recall that population growth in the South was 31.6 percent during this time, compared to 72.5 percent in the West. However, the three urban areas with the greatest growth during this period are Phoenix, San Diego, and Miami. Furthermore, population growth in percentage terms in Dallas–Fort Worth, Houston, and Atlanta exceeded the growth in the other urban areas of the West (Los Angeles, San Francisco, Seattle, and Denver). New Orleans and Birmingham lagged behind, but still recorded growth that was comparable to that achieved by the urban areas of the Northeast. And growth in median family incomes in real terms was rapid across the board in these twelve major urban areas. The format of examining first the urban areas of the South shall be followed.

Major Urban Areas of the South: 1950–1970

The basic data on the growth of the urban areas of the Sunbelt are shown in Table 5.1. The two major urban areas in Texas had similar amounts of growth during the twenty years. In Dallas–Fort Worth and Houston, urban area populations increased by 149 and 136 percent, and employment boomed at 148 and 137 percent, respectively. The population of Dallas–Fort Worth reached 2.43 million, and Houston was 1.90 million. The percentage of employment in Dallas–Fort Worth engaged in manufacturing actually increased from 20.9 percent in 1950 to 24.4 percent in 1970 (but declined in Houston from 22.3 percent to 18.9 percent). Both central cities annexed major amounts of territory, and the central city population increased by 107 percent in Houston and by 73 percent in Dallas and Fort Worth. Median family incomes in real terms increased by 97 percent in Dallas–Fort Worth and by a somewhat smaller 90 percent in Houston.

Table 5.1

Major Urban Areas of the Sunbelt: 1950–1970 (percent change)

	Urban area population	Urban area employment	Median family income	Manufacturing employment (1947–1972)	Central city population	Central city area
Dallas–Fort Worth	149	148	97	204	73	129
Houston	136	137	90	142	107	171
New Orleans	46	37	104	17	4	0
Atlanta	131	140	123	113	50	256
Birmingham	32	34	100	24	–8	22
Miami	226	223	95	1,009	35	0
Los Angeles	102	106	95	121	43	3
San Francisco–Oakland	60	74	96	12	–7	0
Seattle	97	100	97	71	14	18
Denver	110	126	100	170	24	42
San Diego	144	196	91	211	108	219
Phoenix	192	224	119	253	444	1,350
Mean	119	129	99	196	74	184

Sources: Census of Population and Housing and Statistical Abstract of the United States.

The Texas urban areas contrast sharply with New Orleans and Birmingham. Population growth in the New Orleans metropolitan area was 46 percent (to an even 1.00 million), while Birmingham recorded only 32 percent population growth and remained well below 1 million at 738,000. These are comparable to population growth in the northeastern urban areas during the same years. Employment growth was 37 percent and 34 percent, respectively. Birmingham began the period with the largest percentage of employment in manufacturing in the twelve Sunbelt urban areas (26.0 percent), but this percentage fell to 17.1 percent in 1970. The city of New Orleans was unable to annex territory, and the central city population increased by only 4 percent. The city of Birmingham added 22 percent to its land area, but still the population of the central city fell by 8 percent. Nevertheless, real median family incomes increased by 104 percent in the New Orleans metropolitan area and by 100 percent in metropolitan Birmingham. As we saw with the northeastern urban areas, more rapid population and employment growth did not necessarily mean more rapid income growth.

During these years, the Atlanta metropolitan area began its drive to become the economic capital of the Southeast. Population growth was 131 percent (to reach 1.60 million), and employment growth was an even more rapid 140 percent. The expansion of manufacturing was even greater, so that the percentage of employment in manufacturing increased from 19.5 percent in 1950 to 22.0 percent in 1970. What is more, real median family income increased by 123 percent, the largest increase of any of the twenty-nine urban areas in this study. The central city expanded its area by 256 percent, and its population increased by 50 percent. Then there is Miami. The metropolitan area population increased by an amazing 226 percent in twenty years. The population was only 559,000 in 1950, and ended the decade of the 1960s at 1.89 million. Population growth was fueled by retirees and immigrants from Latin America (including refugees from Cuba, of course). Employment increased by 223 percent, and real median family income increased by 95 percent. The central city did not add to its land area, but its population increased by 35 percent.

Each of these southern urban areas represents something of a special case. Dallas–Fort Worth and Houston both benefited from the booming Texas oil, cattle, and agricultural economy, but Houston also is a major port of location of the oil-refining industry. New Orleans is also a major port and part of the oil economy, but as an older city, it performed poorly compared to Houston. Birmingham is an older city in the heart of the Deep South that includes a significant iron and steel industry. The performance of New Orleans and Birmingham is reminiscent of some of the urban areas in the Northeast. Atlanta became the urban growth pole for the Southeast during this time. Miami's growth was the result of the increasing trend of retirees to move to the South as well as the revolution in Cuba that drove away many of its middle-class people (as well as others).

Urban Areas of the West

As always, the discussion of urban areas of the West begins with Los Angeles and San Francisco–Oakland. The two California behemoths were magnets for Americans from all parts of the nation. Los Angeles was an urban area of 4.93 million people in 1950 (the third-largest in the nation), and it more than doubled in twenty years to 9.97 million, an increase of an amazing 102 percent. No urban area in the United States had ever added over 5 million people in twenty years, and it is highly likely that this will never happen again in America. Metropolitan Los Angeles quickly surpassed the Chicago urban area in the early 1950s to become the nation's number two metropolis. Employment grew at an even faster rate, with an increase of 106 percent. The chief source of population growth was migration from other locations in the country. The vast majority (71.6 percent) of residents of metropolitan Los Angeles in 1970 were non-Hispanic whites, and 92.5 percent of this group was native born. Hispanics constituted 14.0 percent of the population, blacks were 7.8 percent, and Asians were only 2.6 percent of the total. The ethnic makeup of the metropolitan area would change dramatically in the 1970s and 1980s, but in 1970 the metropolitan area was a non-Hispanic white person's world. Growth in median family income in real terms was a robust 95 percent over the twenty years. While the city of Los Angeles was unable to add any significant amount of land area (3 percent), the population of the central city increased by 43 percent, the largest increase for any of the land-locked central cities in this study.

Growth of this enormous magnitude involved great expansion of the boundaries of urban development. Most of the growth was accommodated within Los Angeles County, which increased from a population of 4.15 million in 1950 to 7.04 million in 1970. However, Orange County to the South increased from a mere 216,000 in 1950 to 1.42 million in 1970. Orange County includes Disneyland (opened in 1955) and, perhaps more importantly, the Irvine Ranch development. The other three counties of Ventura, San Bernardino, and Riverside increased from a combined population of 556,000 in 1950 to 1.52 million in 1970. Growth was facilitated by the construction of a vast network of freeways, which also opened up large areas for industrial development as the metropolitan area was transformed into a production center for the nation and the world from its position on the Pacific Rim. Total employment more than doubled, but the percentage of employment engaged in manufacturing did not change, remaining at 24.5 percent. Employment was stimulated by defense spending on aircraft, ships, and many other products. Manufacturing employment in the metropolitan area increased by 121 percent from 1947 to 1972.

Growth in metropolitan San Francisco–Oakland was at a slower pace than in Los Angeles. Population grew by 60 percent over the twenty years to 3.11 million in 1970, and employment growth was 74 percent. Manufacturing declined from 19.9 percent to 15.4 percent of total employment, although it did increase by 12 percent from 1947 to 1972. Growth of median family income in real terms of 96 percent matched Los Angeles almost exactly. Neither of the central cities was able to add territory, and their combined population declined by 7 percent. Expansion of the San Francisco–Oakland urban area also involved the construction of a freeway network, as well as the San Francisco Bay Bridge, which connects the two cities. As in Los Angeles, employment growth was partly fueled by defense spending (including spending for the Vietnam War) and by the growth in international trade with Japan and other Asian nations.

The other two major urban areas on the Pacific Coast also grew by leaps and bounds. The population of metropolitan Seattle increased by 97 percent, and employment there grew by 100 percent. The percentage of workers engaged in manufacturing increased from 20.4 percent in 1950 to 23.1 percent in 1970, thanks to Boeing and other manufacturers. The San Diego urban area grew more rapidly than any other metropolis on the Pacific Coast. Population increased by 144 percent in twenty years, and employment grew by an astounding 196 percent. Median family income in real terms increased by 97 percent in Seattle and by 91 percent in San Diego. The city of Seattle added 18 percent to its land area and 14 percent to its population. In contrast, the city of San Diego more than tripled in size (an increase in land area of 219 percent) and added 108 percent to its population.

The two urban areas of the interior West, Denver and Phoenix, present a contrast. Growth in Denver was rapid, but did not approach the growth rate of Phoenix, the urban area with the largest percentage growth in the West. Population in the Denver urban area increased by 110 percent (and employment increased 126 percent). The population of the urban area was well over 1 million in 1970 at 1.24 million. Real median family income exactly doubled. The central city added 42 percent to its area, and population grew by 24 percent. Metropolitan Phoenix almost tripled in population (up 192 percent), and employment jumped 224 percent in a mere twenty years. Phoenix joined the industrial economy as its percentage of employment in manufacturing increased from 9.3 percent in 1950 to 18.4 percent in 1970. Real median family income increased by 119 percent, which was well above the average for the Sunbelt urban areas of 99 percent.

What accounts for the enormous growth in the urban areas of the West? The population of the region increased from 19.56 million in 1950 to 33.73 million in 1970, an overall increase of 14.17 million (72.5 percent). The population growth in the six urban areas was 9 million, which is 63.5 percent of the total population growth in the entire region. The Los Angeles metropolitan area grew by 5.04 million, which accounts for 35.6 percent of the population growth in the West. The state of California grew from a population of 10.59 million (54.1 percent of the population of the West) to 19.95 million (59.1 percent of the West's total). California accounts for 66.1 percent of the population growth of the West from 1950 to 1970. Population growth in California and in the urban areas of Seattle, Denver, and Phoenix of 11.36 million accounts for 80.2 percent of population growth in the West. In short, the growth of the West took place in California and in a few urban areas not located in California.

What were the causes of this growth, with its particular pattern? The definitive study has yet to be done, but some reasonable hypotheses include:

- California took off as a result of the military expenditures associated with World War II. Industrial growth, especially in the Los Angeles metropolitan area, was fed by economies of agglomeration that really had not existed before. The urban infrastructure of Los Angeles discussed in Chapter 2 played an important role. Infrastructure investment continued with the construction of freeway systems.
- The "dust bowl" era of the 1930s pushed migrants from the Great Plains to California to work in agriculture and other industries. This was also part of the take-off.
- California weather attracted people from the other regions of the nation, especially retirees.
- The increasing volume of international trade with Asian nations stimulated growth in the port cities of Los Angeles, San Francisco–Oakland, and San Diego (as well as Seattle).

The interior urban areas of Denver and Phoenix are different cases. Denver is the economic capital of a vast region of the Great Plains and Rocky Mountains. It serves as a distribution center and provides business and professional services for its region, so economic growth in this market area stimulated the Denver economy. Phoenix was a relatively small urban area of just 332,000 people in 1950—only 56 percent the size of Denver's 590,000 population. As we shall see, its growth to 968,000 in 1970 was just the beginning of the creation of a major urban area. In 1950, Phoenix was only thirty-nine years removed from the admission of Arizona as a state. Surely the widespread use of air conditioning was critical for Phoenix. The Valley of the Sun is very hot (but it's a dry heat, they will tell you). Retirees and others found that the Phoenix area is a good place to spend at least part of the year. One of the first to "winter" in the Phoenix area was the famous architect Frank Lloyd Wright, who founded Taliesin West in the early 1930s. By 1970 Phoenix was more than an old frontier city with retirees from the North. It included some industry as well. Manufacturing employment increased from 11,000 in 1950 to 73,000 in 1970.

Statistical Analysis of Urban Growth in the Sunbelt

This section follows the comparable section of Chapter 4 in testing hypotheses pertaining to urban growth in the twelve metropolitan areas of the Sunbelt from 1950 to 1970. It turns out that both population growth and employment growth at the metropolitan level were strongly negatively related to the percentage of employment in manufacturing in 1950. The estimated equation for population growth is:

$$POPGRO = 246.69 - 7.04 \text{ MFG}$$
$$(5.57) \quad (3.01)$$

The R-square is 0.434, and the t-statistic in parentheses indicates that the coefficient on percentage of employment in manufacturing is highly statistically significant. The equation says that metropolitan population growth was reduced by 7.04 percent if the percentage of employment in manufacturing was 1 percent greater in 1950. The result for metropolitan employment growth is virtually identical:

$$EMPGRO = 272.33 - 7.90 \text{ MFG}$$
$$(5.54) \quad (3.05)$$

The R-square for this estimated equation is 0.429, and the coefficient of MFG says that employment growth was 7.9 percent less if manufacturing employment in 1950 was 1 percent greater. These results emerge because Phoenix is included in the data. Phoenix had a very low percentage of employment in manufacturing in 1950 of only 9.3 percent and had very high population and employment growth (192 percent and 224 percent). Phoenix is one reason the equation explains 43 percent of the variation in the dependent variables. Additional tests showed that neither population nor employment growth was related to the initial size of the urban area (contrary to the results for the Northeast).

The increase in median family income in real terms was negatively related to the size of the urban area in 1950. The estimated equation is:

$$\text{MFIGRO} = 123.95 - 3.66\,\text{LNPOP}$$
$$(11.51)\ (2.23)$$

Here MFIGRO is the percentage change in real median family income for 1949 to 1969, and LNPOP is the natural logarithm of the population (in 1,000s) in 1950. The R-square for the estimated equation is 0.266. The result is picking up on the fact that the greatest increases in real median family income occurred in Atlanta and Phoenix, two of the smaller urban areas in 1950, and that income growth in Los Angeles and San Francisco–Oakland (by far the two largest urban areas) was below the average of 99 percent for the twelve urban areas.

The last result is an equation for population change in the central city. In this case Phoenix is omitted from the data because it is an exceptional case with central city population growth of 444 percent that was coupled with an increase in land area of 1,350 percent. The result obtained for the eleven remaining central cities of the Sunbelt is similar to the finding for the central cities of the Northeast in that central city population change was related to employment growth in the urban area and the increase in central city land area. The estimated equation is:

$$\text{CCPOPGRO} = -13.89 + 0.29\,\text{EMPGRO} + 0.24\,\text{AREA}$$
$$(0.80)\ (2.00)\qquad\qquad (2.15)$$

Here AREA is the percentage increase in the central city land area. The R-square for the estimated equation is .653, and the coefficients of both variables are statistically significant at the conventional 95 percent level. The equation says that a 1 percent increase in employment growth in the urban area was associated with a larger central population growth of 0.29 percent. (Recall that the coefficient on employment growth for the northeastern central cities is 0.53.) Also, the equation says that a 1 percent greater increase in land area was associated with central city population growth that was 0.24 percent larger.

These results provide a reasonably straightforward picture of growth in the urban areas of the Sunbelt and their central cities. Urban population and employment growth were negatively associated with the initial concentration of employment in manufacturing. Growth of median family income in real terms was larger in the smaller urban areas. Central city population growth was related to employment growth in the urban area and to expansion of central city land area.

This chapter and the previous one examined the growth of the twenty-nine urban areas in this study at an aggregate level. Other than some discussion of population change in the central city, these chapters have not looked inside the urban areas to examine their changes in spatial patterns. This is the task of the next two chapters. Chapter 6 is a study of suburbanization, including description, causes, and some consequences. Chapter 7 is a further dissection of the urban areas with a view toward finding signs of trouble that presaged the urban crisis of the later decades.

6

Suburbanization: 1950–1970

It can be argued that suburbanization is the most important economic and social trend of the second half of the twentieth century in America. While the major urban areas contained sizable suburban populations in 1950, suburban growth after 1950 was unprecedented. As Jackson (1985, p. 283) noted, the suburban population in the nation's metropolitan areas increased from 36 million in 1950 to 74 million in 1970, and that growth of suburban populations accounts for 74 percent of total population growth of 51.4 million over these two decades. In 1970, more people lived in suburbs than in central cities. Population growth from 1950 to 1970 in the suburbs of the twenty-nine metropolitan areas included in this study was 28.7 million, which accounts for 55.8 percent of the nation's population growth. As the data in Tables 6.1 and 6.2 show, population growth in the suburbs of the five largest metropolitan areas (New York, Los Angeles, Chicago, Philadelphia, and Detroit) was 13.4 million, and just the suburbs of New York and Los Angeles together added up to 8.45 million people. Much has been written about suburbanization—pro and (mostly) con. The purposes of this chapter are first to describe the extent and nature of suburbanization of our twenty-nine metropolitan areas, and then to explore the causes and consequences of this great economic and social transformation.

Suburban Population Growth in the Northeast

As we saw in Chapter 4, the average population growth for the seventeen metropolitan areas of the Northeast was 46 percent from 1950 to 1970, and their central cities declined by an average of 2 percent. The data in Table 6.1 imply that the average population growth in the suburbs of these seventeen urban areas was 107 percent—more than double in twenty years. Suburban population growth varied from 35 percent in metropolitan Boston to 281 percent for

Table 6.1

Suburbs of the Northeastern Urban Areas: 1950–1970

	Suburban population 1950 (1,000s)	Suburban population 1970 (1,000s)	Suburban housing units 1970 (1,000s)	Suburban vacancy rate 1970 (percent)	Suburban ownership rate 1970 (percent)	Central city ownership 1970 (percent)
New York	5,426	9685	3,011	3.7	64.2	23.6
Chicago	1,872	3,646	1,011	3.2	74.2	34.9
Philadelphia	1,598	2,929	881	2.8	72.8	59.7
Detroit	1,164	2,980	881	3.2	80.0	60.0
Boston	1,910	2,585	802	2.8	62.6	27.2
Pittsburgh	1,541	2,164	690	3.3	73.0	50.1
St. Louis	976	1,834	578	5.1	74.7	40.5
Cleveland	789	1,668	520	2.8	72.9	46.1
Washington, D.C.	858	2,447	768	4.4	55.2	28.2
Baltimore	586	1,183	354	3.8	70.0	44.4
Minneapolis–St. Paul	381	1,454	364	3.6	77.3	52.4
Buffalo	508	886	267	2.6	74.4	44.0
Cincinnati	555	987	299	3.7	74.1	38.5
Milwaukee	293	687	200	2.5	75.0	47.3
Kansas City	441	876	286	4.6	71.3	58.1
Indianapolis	339	501	163	5.0	74.2	61.3
Columbus	250	586	183	4.7	71.7	51.0
Means				3.6	71.6	45.1

Source: Census of Population and Housing.

Minneapolis–St. Paul. Also, recall that four of the central cities (Milwaukee, Kansas City, Indianapolis, and Columbus) added large amounts of land area that otherwise would have been suburbs. The suburbs of New York grew by 4.26 million, suburban Chicago added 1.77 million, Philadelphia's suburbs grew by 1.33 million, and the population of suburban Detroit increased by 1.82 million.

The percentage increase in the suburban population was associated with two variables: the population growth rate of the metropolitan area and the amount of land area added to the central city. The estimated equation for the 17 metropolitan areas of the Northeast is:

$$\text{SUBPOPGRO} = -2.48 + 2.54 \text{ POPGRO} - 0.20 \text{ AREA}$$
$$(4.94)\ (7.27) \qquad\qquad (4.15)$$

Here SUBPOPGRO is the percentage increase in the suburban population from 1950 to 1970, POPGRO is the percentage increase in the population of the metropolitan area over the same period, and AREA is the percentage increase in the land area of the central city. The R-square for the estimated equation is 0.769, and the t statistics in parentheses indicate that the coefficients of both variables are highly statistically significant. The coefficient of metropolitan population growth of 2.54 says that higher metropolitan growth of 1 percent was associated with suburban population growth that was 2.54 percent greater. The coefficient of the increase in central city land area says that a central city that increased its land area by 10 percent reduced the increase in the suburban population by 2 percent because that population was annexed to the central city.

Table 6.1 also shows some basic data on the suburban housing markets in these metropolitan areas as of 1970. The table shows that vacancy rates in the suburbs were quite low—an average of 3.6 percent. These vacancy rates varied only slightly from urban area to urban area. The largest vacancy rate was 5.1 percent in suburban St. Louis, and the lowest was 2.6 percent in the suburbs of Buffalo. What is also striking about these suburban housing markets are the high rates of home ownership. The average for the seventeen suburban areas was 71.6 percent, compared to an average of 45.1 percent for the central cities. Clearly, households that moved to the suburbs tended to purchase homes in the process. The ownership rates were lowest in suburban Washington, D.C. (55.2 percent), Boston (62.6 percent), and New York (64.2 percent), but the ownership rates in their central cities were quite low at 28.2 percent, 27.2 percent, and 23.6 percent, respectively. Ownership rates in each of the other fourteen suburban areas exceeded 70 percent, topped by suburban Detroit with 80.0 percent.

Suburban Population Growth in the Sunbelt

The suburbs in the urban areas of the Sunbelt grew very rapidly, even though most of them gave up land to the central city. The data in Table 6.2 imply that the average population growth in these twelve suburban areas was 218 percent from 1950 to 1970. Suburban Los Angeles grew by 4.2 million, from 2.96 million in 1950 to 7.16 million in 1970, an increase of 141 percent. The suburbs of San Francisco–Oakland increased from 784,000 to 2.03 million (up 128 percent). And the suburbs of Miami grew from 330,000 to 1.55 million, increasing 371 percent. Two other suburban areas, Dallas–Fort Worth and Denver, also more than quadrupled.

Population growth in the suburbs of the Sunbelt was closely associated with the growth of the population of the metropolitan area, moderated by the ability of the central city to annex territory. The estimated equation for the twelve suburban areas is:

$$\text{SUBPOPGRO} = -0.12 + 1.22 \, \text{POPGRO} -0.20 \, \text{AREA}$$
$$(0.14) \; (3.16) \qquad\qquad (3.51)$$

The R-square for this estimated equation is 0.722, and the t statistics in parentheses indicate that the coefficients of both variables are highly statistically significant. The coefficient of metropolitan population growth of 1.22 means that a larger increase in this variable was associated with a 1.22 percent greater increase in the suburban population. In other words, the suburban population increase in percentage terms closely followed the percentage increase in the metropolitan population. The coefficient of the percentage increase in the land area of the central city is negative, indicating that a 10 percent increase in central city land area was associated with a smaller increase in the suburban population by 2 percent. As with the northeastern suburban areas, this effect simply means that the central city annexed some population that otherwise would have been located in the suburbs.

Table 6.2 also provides a snapshot of the suburban housing markets in the twelve urban areas as of 1970. The average vacancy rate in these markets was 4.9 percent, which was greater than the average vacancy of 3.6 percent in the suburban Northeast. Two suburban areas had relatively high vacancy rates: suburban Houston's was 9.2 percent and the Seattle suburbs recorded 8.7 percent. It would appear that construction ran ahead of demand in these two suburban areas. The rate of home ownership averaged 68.6 percent for the twelve suburban areas, which is almost 20 percentage points greater than the average central city ownership rate of 49.2 percent. As in the Northeast, people who moved their households to the suburbs tended to become home owners.

Table 6.2

Suburbs of the Sunbelt Urban Areas: 1950–1970

	Suburban population 1950 (1,000s)	Suburban population 1970 (1,000s)	Suburban housing units 1970 (1,000s)	Suburban vacancy rate 1970 (percent)	Suburban ownership rate 1970 (percent)	Central city ownership 1970 (percent)
Dallas–Fort Worth	263	1,195	390	7.4	70.7	55.5
Houston	212	670	215	9.2	73.7	52.6
New Orleans	115	407	163	7.1	71.0	38.4
Atlanta	360	1099	397	4.9	67.6	41.1
Birmingham	233	437	138	4.7	76.0	54.0
Miami	330	1,553	571	6.9	59.7	43.0
Los Angeles	2,964	7,156	2,452	6.1	54.7	48.5
San Francisco–Oakland	784	2,032	672	3.2	70.9	38.2
Seattle	266	918	301	8.7	72.8	54.2
Denver	174	724	174	3.5	73.6	50.7
San Diego	223	661	209	6.2	63.2	50.7
Phoenix	225	386	141	5.0	69.1	63.8
Means				4.9	68.6	49.2

Source: Census of Population and Housing.

Two suburban areas (Los Angeles and Miami) recorded home ownership rates that were well below average and below 60 percent. The ownership rate in suburban Los Angeles of 54.7 percent was only 6.2 percentage points greater than the ownership rate in the central city, so on this measure the central city and suburban housing markets in Los Angeles are fairly similar—unlike the other twenty-eight metropolitan areas in this study.

Causes of Suburbanization

The two previous sections make it obvious that the basic cause of suburban population growth was the population growth of the metropolitan area, coupled with the fact that no central city was able to annex all of the newly developed residential areas. The most extreme case of annexation was Phoenix, which expanded its land area from 17.1 to 248 square miles—an increase of 1,350 percent! And yet the population located outside the city of Phoenix increased from 225,000 to 386,000 (up 71.6 percent). The population of the city of Phoenix did increase from 107,000 to 582,000, so the central city captured 74.7 percent of the growth, but not all of it. Also, the city of Indianapolis expanded to be identical in size to its central county, an increase in land area of 587 percent. As a result, the population of the central city increased from 427,000 to 745,000. The suburbs outside of Marion County had population growth from 339,000 in 1950 to 501,000 in 1970, so the central city captured 66.2 percent of the total population growth. Houston was the other central city that captured more than 50 percent of the population growth in the metropolitan area (637,000 out of 1.10 million, or 58.2 percent). The city of Houston was able to do this by using the Texas law that gives the central city the option to annex territory before any other municipality. Otherwise, rapid population growth at the metropolitan level outstripped the ability of central cities to annex territory.

The basic reason that population growth means suburbanization is that urban areas build out more than they build up. The existing housing stock cannot easily be torn down and replaced with denser developments. In economic terms, the elasticity of the housing supply is far greater at the edge of the developed area than inside it. A percentage increase in the price of housing calls forth a larger percentage increase in supply at the fringe than in the interior of the urban area. This effect is particularly in play when demand increases rapidly, as it did in the 1950s and 1960s.

Beyond this fundamental reason, several other forces were at work behind the suburbanization of the period. Kenneth Jackson, in his popular history of suburbanization, provided a convenient catalog of these factors. Jackson (1985) argued that economic factors were more important than social factors.

The economic factors behind suburbanization include:

- The increase in income and wealth during these years created demand for bigger and better houses. An important part of the "American Dream" is a home of one's own with a yard and all the rest, but fulfillment of the dream requires money, which (as we saw in Chapters 4 and 5) Americans gained in the 1950s and 1960s. American also used their increased income to purchase automobiles, which were a necessary part of suburbanization.
- American urban areas had inexpensive land at the urban fringe. Land in America is plentiful, and many of the urban areas are surrounded by flat land that is easy to build upon.
- Transportation costs within urban areas declined substantially, especially with the construction of the freeway systems. The stories of the Eisenhower Interstate Highway System and the huge increase in automobile ownership are told below.
- Another factor is the low cost of construction, which includes the balloon-frame house. America was blessed with a plentiful supply of lumber as well.
- Government played a facilitating role. Government provided the FHA (Federal Housing Authority) and VA (Veterans Administration) mortgage insurance programs, which meant that lenders could offer long-term loans at low rates of interest and low down payments. Home owners can deduct mortgage interest payments and local property taxes on their federal income tax forms. These tax deductions became ever more important as federal income tax rates increased during and after World War II. Renters are not eligible for these tax deductions. And, during these decades, local governments did not hamper the efforts of private developers to build housing by imposing tight controls on the use of land.
- Lastly, Jackson (1985) pointed out that the basic free-market orientation of the American economic system produces land speculators, subdivision developers, building contractors, realtors, and lending institutions. These are the people on the supply side of suburbanization.

Some social factors can also be cited as causes of suburbanization. Jackson (1985) believes that Americans seek a balance between urban, communal life and pastoral, country life. Suburban living provides a good combination —access to employment, shopping, and other aspects of urban life along with the detached house in a safe, quiet, and peaceful place. Americans are not unique in seeking this balance, but they do have the ability to exercise their choices. Prior to the 1950s many American expressed a longing for a life in the suburbs but were unable to achieve this ambition. This author's father grew up in the inner city of Chicago in the 1920s and 1930s and, once he had achieved some measure of economic success, moved repeatedly to the fringe of the urban area in which he was living. Furthermore, there are negative aspects of life in the central city that many seek to avoid. These include crowded conditions, crime, noise, and air pollution. Another social factor is race. White Americans sought to avoid living among black Americans, and studies of housing prices and rents indicate that they are willing to pay for this preference. In most cases, white Americans used avoidance behavior rather than overt acts of discrimination. Theories and empirical studies of racial segregation are discussed in the next chapter.

Urban economists such as Hoover and Vernon (1959)—and all urban economists ever since this book was published—frame the choice of residential location within an urban area as a trade-off between "spacious living and easy access." When the New York Metropolitan Study was conducted in the late 1950s, access to employment still usually involved being located near the downtown area. Spacious living, on the other hand, was (and is) the single-family house with a yard in the suburbs. Land near downtown is too expensive for this kind of spacious living. This is another way of making the point that many Americans seek a balance between city and country living. The theoretical breakthrough in the field of urban economics came when William Alonso (1964) and Richard Muth (1969) formulated an economic model of this trade-off. The basic idea is that households choose to locate at the distance from downtown at which the additional cost of locating one mile further away is just balanced by the saving in housing costs—the marginal cost of distance equals the marginal benefit of distance. The marginal cost of distance is the additional cost of commuting to the job in or near downtown. For the automobile driver the cost consists of additional expenditures on gas and oil, wear and tear on the auto, and, most importantly, the additional time needed to commute one more mile 240 times per year. The benefit of greater distance is the reduction in the price of housing. The price of a house of a given level of quality declines with distance to downtown because the price of land declines with distance. Why does the price of land decline with distance from downtown? This happens because commuting costs rise with distance from downtown. If one lives at a greater distance from downtown, one is willing to bid a lesser amount for the land because that land carries a higher commuting cost. That land is of lower "quality" in that sense.

The Alonso-Muth theory can be expressed as a simple equation:

Marginal cost of distance = Marginal benefit of distance
or,
Travel cost per mile = Change in price of housing per mile

Muth (1969) broke the price of housing into two components: the "price" for a standardized quantity of housing times the amount of housing—the quantity. The idea is that a larger, fancier house embodies a larger amount of housing. For example, suppose a five-room, two-bedroom house with one bathroom and a lot that is 30 feet by 100 feet is one unit of standardized quantity. A seven-room, three-bedroom house with two bathrooms on a lot of 50 by 150 might then be two units of standardized quantity. You can imagine what 1.5 units of standardized quantity would be. The Alonso-Muth equation then becomes:

Travel cost per mile = Quantity of housing x change in "price" per mile

This equation has interesting implications. Suppose that travel cost per mile is reduced by the construction of a freeway, for example. It now takes less time to get downtown. You may say, "Of course, people will tend to move farther away from downtown." The equation says the same thing. The equation has become an inequality:

Travel cost per mile < Quantity of housing x change in "price" per mile

The household can now be better off by moving one mile farther away from downtown because it saves more in its housing costs than the cost of additional travel. The household keeps moving until the equality of marginal cost and marginal benefit of additional distance is established once again. The reduction in travel cost per mile induces households to adjust the right-hand side of the equation by selecting a distance from downtown with a smaller change in the "price" of a standardized house as distance increases. It is an empirical fact that this "price" of housing declines by smaller and smaller amounts as distance from downtown increases. The new equilibrium location for the household therefore is at a greater distance from downtown. As large numbers of households make this adjustment, the spatial pattern of the housing "price" adjusts, too.

Employment Location Patterns

A fundamental economic factor that has not yet been mentioned is the changing location pattern of employment in urban areas. As discussed in Chapter 1, American urban areas began as centers of trade and industry, with most of that activity located in and around the central business district. Residential areas (with population-serving employment) were located outside the central area of business and industry. Urban economists refer to this configuration as the "monocentric" city. However, it was not long before some industries sought out locations that were removed from the dense and congested downtown areas. Early examples are the Union Stockyards and the McCormick Reaper Works in Chicago, discussed in Chapter 1. The rail and highway systems in the urban areas of the 1950s and 1960s provided ample sites for industry. Firms found that expansion of their operations could most easily be accomplished with a move away from the center of the city. Furthermore, newer production methods called for single-story factories, and distribution systems called for single-story warehouses with adequate exterior space for vehicles and easy access to highways. Inexpensive land in the suburbs facilitated the suburbanization of industry. Workers followed.

The massive growth of population (and thus consumer demand) in the suburbs brought with it massive growth in suburban retailing and other activities that directly serve consumers. Suburban shopping centers had existed for many years, but the development of the auto-oriented shopping center took off in the 1950s. The idea was to provide free parking and immediate access to a wide variety of stores. Suburban shopping centers began as relatively small developments, but these early facilities were superseded by the huge shopping malls that could provide even more shopping options. At the same time, downtown retailers found themselves under increasing pressure, and consumers used their automobiles to go shopping in the suburbs. Downtown retailing declined in the 1950s and eventually virtually disappeared in some places, such as downtown Detroit. This shift in the location of retailing jobs and related employment provided further impetus for suburbanization of the population.

Meyer, Kain, and Wohl (1965) were among the first to study the changing location pattern of employment in American's urban areas. Their book on the "urban transportation problem" was and is highly influential, and will be discussed at greater length in the next chapter. Their study began with a detailed look at employment location trends in thirty-nine major metropolitan areas. Their list of metropolitan areas includes twenty-seven of the twenty-nine included in this study. They did not include New York and Birmingham, and their list includes San Antonio, Tampa, Dayton, Louisville, Memphis, Oklahoma City, Akron, Jersey City, Newark, Portland (Oregon), and Rochester (Dallas and Fort Worth were included separately). They examined, for 1948 to 1958, the changes in population and changes in employment in four categories—manufacturing, wholesale trade, retail trade, and selected services—the industries covered by the Census of Business that is conducted every five years. They were careful to adjust the data for annexations by the central city. Their basic finding is that population in the central cities increased by 0.2 percent per year, and that suburban population growth was 9.8 percent per year over these ten years. Central city employment in two categories declined. Central city manufacturing employment fell by 0.6 percent per year, and central city retail jobs declined by 0.4 percent per year. However, wholesale trade and selected services added jobs in the central city. Central city wholesale trade employment increased by 0.7 percent per year, while service sector employment increased by a relatively robust 2.7 percent per year. But the most important trend they discovered was the employment growth in the suburbs. Suburban manufacturing jobs grew by 15.0 percent *per year*, and suburban employment growth in the other three sectors was even more rapid. Wholesale trade jobs increased by 29.4 percent per year, followed by selected services with employment growth of 24.4 percent per year and retail trade at 16.0 percent growth per year. They pointed out that the jobs in retail trade and selected services primarily serve the nearby population, but it is striking that suburban employment in these categories grew at rates that far exceeded the suburban population growth rate. Furthermore, the location choices of manufacturers and wholesale trade firms are largely "exogenous" with respect to household location choices. These trends in employment location were seen as strong incentives for further suburbanization of the population.

McDonald (1984) provided a detailed look at employment location trends in the Chicago metropolitan area. Unlike Meyer, Kain, Wohl (1965), this study examined all categories of employment in as much detail as the data sources permitted. Data availability varies across employment sectors. A summary of McDonald's findings is as follows.

- Manufacturing employment in the city of Chicago was 668,000 and 185,000 in the suburbs in 1947. Manufacturing in the central city fell continuously, reaching 509,000 in 1963. Suburban manufacturing jobs increased to 339,000 in that year. Total manufacturing employment was identical in these two years (853,000 and 848,000), but over 150,000 jobs had "migrated" to the suburbs. Actually, the change in location pattern was the result of deaths of firms in the central city, births of firms in the suburbs, employment declines of firms in the city, and growth of firms in the suburbs. Only a relatively small amount of the net change can be explained by the direct relocation of firms from the central city to the suburbs. Central city manufacturing employment increased to 546,000 in 1967 during the boom period of the 1960s, and suburban manufacturing jobs increased to 420,000. The increase in employment of 118,000 was shared between city and suburbs at 31 percent and 69 percent. But then disaster struck in the city. Manufacturing employment in the city of Chicago fell to 430,000 in 1972, a drop of 21 percent in just five years. At the same time, total manufacturing employment in the metropolitan area declined from 966,000 to 892,000. The decline in the central city of 116,000 exceeded the total decline of 74,000, so suburban manufacturing employment increased by 42,000. What happened between 1967 and 1972? This time period includes the fateful year of 1968, the year in which riots occurred in the city in the wake of the assassination of Martin Luther King, Jr., and at the time of the Democratic National Convention that was held in Chicago.

- Wholesale trade employment in the central city was fairly stable (138,000 in 1948 and 131,000 in 1967), but then fell to 101,000 in 1972. Wholesale trade in the suburbs increased steadily from a mere 17,000 in 1948 to 98,000 in 1972.
- Central city employment in retail trade fell from 249,000 in 1948 to 210,000 in 1963, bounced back to 218,000 in 1967, and then declined to 193,000 in 1972. Retail trade jobs in the central business district fell by 50 percent—from 65,000 in 1948 to 32,000 in 1972. Suburban retailing boomed—from 105,000 jobs in 1948 to 260,000 in 1972, the first year in which suburban retail jobs exceeded the jobs in the central city.
- Comprehensive data on employment in other sectors are available at the county level (in a data source called County Business Patterns). McDonald (1984) reported that employment in Cook County (the central county) in services and finance, insurance, and real estate (FIRE) increased dramatically. Service sector employment increased from 194,000 in 1956 to 496,000 in 1977, and FIRE employment in Cook County grew from 127,000 in 1956 to 202,000 in 1977. Both of these sectors were highly centralized in Cook County in 1956, but became more decentralized over time. Suburban employment in services increased from 14,000 in 1956 to 104,000 in 1977. Employment in FIRE was only 5,000 in the suburbs in 1956, but grew to 28,000 in 1977. However, another data source suggests that very little of the employment growth in services and FIRE took place in the central city. The data source is the enumeration of journeys to work in the decennial census. This source shows that service employment in the central city increased from 287,000 in 1960 to 311,000 in 1970, and that employment in FIRE increased from 101,000 to 109,000 over this same period.
- The remaining sectors include construction; transportation, communication, and utilities (TCU); and government. Not surprisingly, construction employment declined in the central city and increased in the suburbs. The decline in the city was from 65,000 in 1960 to 48,000 in 1970. Employment in TCU in the city fell from 156,000 to 118,000 over these same years. Growth occurred in the rest of Cook County and in the other suburban areas. Lastly, local government employment in Cook County

increased from 137,000 in 1962 to 195,000 in 1977, but one suspects that most (if not all) of this growth was in suburban Cook County because these jobs mainly serve the resident population. Federal civilian employment was stable in Cook County (59,000 in 1962 and 58,000 in 1977) and in the rest of the metropolitan area as well (11,000 in both years).

The total picture is one of large employment declines in the central city, especially after 1968. The two sectors of growth for the city, services and FIRE, did not come close to offsetting the massive employment declines in manufacturing and the more modest declines in wholesale trade, retail trade, TCU, and construction.

What were the location patterns of population and employment in a major metropolitan area of the 1950s? What was the net outcome of the forces that have been described in this and the previous chapters? The New York Metropolitan Study of the late 1950s was designed to answer this question in great detail. This study provides a high-definition snapshot of the nation's largest urban area as of 1956. There is much to learn from the ten published volumes of what still stands as the largest study ever of an American urban area. The central volume in the study for our present purposes is the volume by Edgar Hoover and Raymond Vernon (1959), titled *Anatomy of a Metropolis: The Changing Distribution of People and Jobs Within the New York Metropolitan Region.* That region was defined as consisting of twelve counties in the state of New York, nine in New Jersey, and one in Connecticut. The Hoover and Vernon (1959) study is used at various places in this book, with the one county in Connecticut excluded. Hoover and Vernon divided the metropolitan area into three large areas—the core area, the inner ring of suburban counties, and the outer ring of counties. The core was defined as four of the five boroughs of New York City (Manhattan, Brooklyn, the Bronx, and Queens—excluding Staten Island) and Hudson County, New Jersey (the city of Newark and nearby areas). The inner ring consists of three counties in the state of New York (Staten Island, Westchester, and Nassau) and four counties in New Jersey (Union, Essex, Passaic, and Bergen). The outer ring includes five counties in the state of New York, four counties in New Jersey, and the one in Connecticut (which is excluded here).

Table 6.3 displays the location of population and employment (by industry category) for these broad zones, with Manhattan broken out from the core area. This table shows that the total population of 15.34 million was concentrated in the core area outside of Manhattan (6.42 million people) and in the inner ring (4.57 million people). The employment of 6.55 million was heavily concentrated in the core area, with 2.72 million on Manhattan Island and 1.58 million in the rest of the core area. However, in 1956 the inner ring of

Table 6.3

Population and Employment Location Patterns: New York Metropolitan Area in 1956 (1,000s)

	Manhattan	Rest of core*	Inner ring	Outer ring	Total
Population	1,811	6,225	4,573	2,566	15,335
Employment	2,718	1,584	1,572	677	6,551
Manufacturing	532	540	518	188	1,778
Wholesaling	269	89	70	16	444
Finance	220	35	51	9	315
Other office	610	92	133	44	879
Retail trade & services	412	351	320	116	1,199
Construction	60	62	78	29	229
Health care & other	616	413	401	175	1,605

*Rest of core consists of Brooklyn, Queens, the Bronx, and Hudson County, New Jersey (Newark).
Source: Adapted from Hoover and Vernon (1959, p. 248).

suburban counties contained almost as many jobs as did the core area outside Manhattan—a total of 1.57 million. The growth of suburban jobs was much in evidence in 1956.

Table 6.3 also shows that the location pattern varied considerably by industry. Manufacturing jobs were evenly distributed among Manhattan, the rest of the core, and the inner ring. Each zone contained about 520,000 to 540,000 jobs. In contrast, employment in wholesale trade, finance, and other office jobs was very heavily concentrated in Manhattan. Manhattan was home to 60.6 percent of wholesale trade employment and 69.8 percent of jobs in the financial sector, and 69.4 percent of employment in other office categories. As one would expect, employment in retailing and consumer services more closely followed the location of the population. However, Manhattan had 11.8 percent of the population and still contained 34.4 percent of employment in this sector. The largest number of construction jobs was located in the inner ring. The "other" category, which was primarily health care, had a pattern that was similar to retail trade and consumer services. Manhattan was home to 38.3 percent of these jobs. These location patterns essentially confirm some of the observations about employment in metropolitan Chicago that were made above. A great deal of manufacturing employment (40.5 percent) had taken up locations in the suburbs. Retail trade and consumer services had followed the population and provided large numbers of jobs in the core areas outside of Manhattan and in the inner ring of suburban counties.

Table 6.4

Journey-to-Work Matrix: New York Metropolitan Area in 1956 (1,000s)

Zone of residence	Manhattan workplace	Rest of core workplace	Inner ring workplace	Outer ring workplace	Total
Manhattan	440	86	36	5	567
Rest of core	1,432	1,175	142	4	2,753
Inner ring	527	224	1,143	62	1,956
Outer ring	51	29	88	408	576
					5,852
Total	2,450	1,514	1,409	479	

Source: Adapted from Hoover and Vernon (1959, pp. 282–283).

The location of population and employment produced a very interesting journey-to-work pattern, which is shown in Table 6.4. The New York Metropolitan Study conducted a special journey-to-work survey for 1956, and this table contains a short version of the commuting matrix. Table 6.4 has the workplace locations arrayed across the top of the table, and the residence locations listed down the left-hand side. The same four broad areas are used— Manhattan, the rest of the core area, the inner ring of suburban counties, and the outer ring. The table is read as follows. There were 440,000 workers who lived in Manhattan and worked there as well. The rest of the core (Brooklyn and so on) sent 1.43 million workers to Manhattan each day, and 86,000 commuters traveled from Manhattan to the rest of the core. Table 6.4 reveals some fascinating facts. First, the largest number of workers lived and worked in the same zone. The figures for those who lived and worked in the same zone are on what is called the "main diagonal" of the travel matrix. The sum of these figures is 3.17 million, which is 54.1 percent of the estimated total trips to work in the table of 5.85 million. This fact is particularly striking for the inner and outer rings. Of the 1.96 million workers who lived in the inner ring, 58.4 percent worked there as well. And of the 576,000 workers who lived in the outer ring, 70.8 percent (408,000) chose not to commute to the three inner zones. The largest number of inward commuters was the 1.43 million workers who lived in the rest of the core area who traveled to Manhattan. The next-largest group of inward commuters was the 527,000 residents of the inner ring who also traveled to Manhattan for work. But only 51,000 made the lengthy commute from the outer ring to Manhattan. In sum, 2.35 million workers made the inward commute. On the other side of the coin, Table 6.4 shows that only 335,000 workers commuted from an inner zone to an outer zone. Only 5.7 percent of the work trips involved "reverse commuting." For example, only 5,000 workers traveled from Manhattan to the outer ring.

Tables 6.3 and 6.4 depict metropolitan New York in 1956 as still a place with a centralized employment pattern and commuting flows to match. However, Table 6.4 also shows that more than half of the workers lived and held jobs in the same broad zone. This finding implies that the growth of employment in suburban areas would attract population, and declines in employment in the inner city would cause population to fall as well. Lastly, Table 6.4 shows that "reverse commuting" was rare. This would change.

One can argue that New York commuting patterns were far from typical of commuting in other urban areas because New York has, by far, the most extensive system of public transportation in the nation. One indicator of this was the choice of transportation mode for people who entered the Manhattan central business district on a typical day. Hoover and Vernon (1959, p. 209) reported that 3.32 million people entered the central business district on a typical business day in 1956, and that 1.97 million came by rapid transit (59.3 percent), 246,000 by bus, and 233,000 by commuter railroad. The choice of mode was auto (including taxi) for 736,000 travelers (22.2 percent). Other modes (truck, trolley, ferry) accounted for the other 131,000. In all, 73.9 percent came by public transportation (transit, commuter rail, or bus). Consequently, it is worthwhile to examine the pattern in another metropolitan area. A good candidate is Detroit, which conducted its own survey of commuting in 1953. These data were reported by Meyer, Kain, and Wohl (1965) in sufficient detail that an estimate of the journey-to-work matrix could be computed. Detroit was an auto-oriented metropolitan area even in 1953 (no surprise there). The choice of travel mode for the trip to work was 64.7 percent auto driver, 14.1 percent auto passenger, 20.8 transit rider (i.e., bus), and 0.4 percent other modes.

The journey-to-work matrix for the Detroit metropolitan area in 1953 is shown in Table 6.5. The total volume of daily trips was estimated to be 1.07 million. The metropolitan area was broken down into six rings. Ring 1 is the downtown area narrowly defined. Only about 4,000 workers lived in this zone in 1953. The other rings contain both residences and places of work. The table shows that large numbers of workers live in the same ring as their places of work. The total for these groups is 342,000, or 32.0 percent of total employment depicted in the table. This percentage is smaller than the figure presented above for New York, but only four rings were used for New York journey-to-work matrix. The wider the ring, the less likely it will be that the commuter traveled across a ring boundary. Inward commuting was the dominant pattern for the trip to work in Detroit in 1953. Almost half of the commuters (496,000, or 46.4 percent) had a trip to work to a ring inside the ring of residence. Rings 1, 2, and 3 were all popular choices for inward commuting trips; Ring 1 (downtown narrowly defined) attracted

Table 6.5

Journey-to-Work Matrix: Detroit Metropolitan Area in 1953 (1,000s)

Residence ring	Ring 1 workplace	Ring 2 workplace	Ring 3 workplace	Ring 4 workplace	Ring 5 workplace	Ring 6 workplace
Ring 1	4.0	0	0	0	0	0
Ring 2	20.0	53.4	61.9	32.0	8.5	4.4
Ring 3	36.4	72.8	138.3	63.5	17.9	6.6
Ring 4	24.7	35.1	63.5	63.2	18.6	6.3
Ring 5	20.2	21.7	44.2	40.7	46.2	12.1
Ring 6	7.6	14.1	24.9	30.2	30.3	37.1

Source: Adapted from data presented in Meyer, Kain, and Wohl (1965).
Note: Average distance to the center for each ring is as follows:

Ring 1	0.5 miles	Ring 4	8 miles
Ring 2	2.5 miles	Ring 5	11.5 miles
Ring 3	5 miles	Ring 6	18 miles

109,000 commuters, Ring 2 (average distance of 2.5 miles from the center) was the destination for 144,000 inbound commuters, and Ring 3 (average distance 5 miles) attracted 133,000, as well as 62,000 who traveled out from Ring 2. A larger percentage of commuters in Detroit than in New York traveled outward. A total of 232,000 workers (21.7 percent) had jobs located in a ring that was farther from the center than their place of residence. The comparable figure for New York was only 5.7 percent. As was mentioned, the New York journey-to-work matrix has only four rings instead of six, but the difference in the proportion of reserve commuters is still notable. The larger figure for Detroit probably reflects the much greater reliance on the private auto for the trip to work. The private auto is the mode that can be used conveniently for the reverse commute, as opposed to public transit, which is mainly focused on the trip to downtown. Nevertheless, the data for Detroit also show the tendency of workers to live and work in the same ring. And the data also show that far more workers commuted inward than outward in 1953. Another journey-to-work matrix (also with six rings) for metropolitan Chicago as of 1956 and presented in McDonald and McMillen (2007, p. 350) shows a pattern very similar to that for Detroit. Workers who lived in the same ring as the workplace made up 32.9 percent of the total. Inward commuters were 48.1 percent, and reverse commuters were the remaining 18.9 percent of the total.

Highways and Automobiles

Suburbanization of population and employment was facilitated by the construction of freeway systems in the1950s and 1960s. That "age of the automobile (and truck)" had begun in the 1920s, and the system of streets and
highways of that day was built to accommodate the Model T, Model A, and
other popular cars of the time. But after World War II it became clear that the
existing highways were inadequate for the growing volume of auto and truck
travel. Kenneth Jackson (1985, pp. 248–251) picks up the story from there. The
New York World's Fair of 1939 included an exhibit built by General Motors
called "Futurama." The city of the future in that exhibit was to be served by
a system of elevated freeways with cars moving at speeds of over 100 miles
per hour. The exhibit had 50,000 miniature cars zooming into and around a
model city. General Motors and other organizations such as the Automobile
Manufacturers Association, state highway administrators, and the American
Trucking Association in 1943 joined together as the American Road Build-
ers Association to lobby for a national system of modern highways. By the
mid-1950s many others had joined the movement for the creation of a new
system of superhighways.

As it happened, the Cold War also provided motivation to build a national
highway system. One strategy for surviving a nuclear attack was to decentral-
ize the population. At a more practical level, such a highway system would
permit military forces to be moved around the nation quickly. Hitler had such
a system (the autobahn) built in Germany in the 1930s.

These pressures led President Dwight D. Eisenhower in 1954 to appoint
a committee to study the issue. The committee was chaired by former army
general Lucius Clay, a member of the board of directors of General Motors.
It was not surprising that the committee recommended a massive highway
system, and Congress passed the Interstate Highway Act in 1956. The act
called for a system of 41,000 miles (which eventually became 42,500 miles),
and provided that the federal government would pay 90 percent of the cost
of construction. President Eisenhower signed the bill, giving four reasons
for his approval:

- Current highways were unsafe.
- The existing system produced traffic jams that wasted time and
  money.
- Businesses suffered from high transportation costs, largely because of
  wasted time.
- Modern highways could be used for quick evacuation of cities in case
  of nuclear attack.

Table 6.6

Automobile Registrations in the United States (1,000s)

	1950	1970	Percent change
Total	40,185	88,393	120
Northeast	23,629	46,735	98
New York state	3,240	5,968	84
South	9,786	25,226	158
Texas	2,311	5,104	111
West	6,770	16,432	143
California	3,937	9,821	149

Source: Statistical Abstract of the United States (1951 and 1971).

As Jackson (1985, p. 249) noted, very little was said about the impact of such a system on urban areas. Perhaps few people understood how a system of modern highways would have a profound effect on the location patterns in an urban area. Some urban areas, such as New York, Chicago, and Los Angeles, already had elaborate plans for new highway systems, so in these instances the Interstate Highway Act simply funded the construction of systems that were already on the drawing boards. Funding of the 90 percent was provided by the creation of the Highway Trust Fund. The money in this fund comes from the federal gasoline tax, and cannot be diverted to other uses. Within a decade, most of the Eisenhower Interstate Highway System had been completed. The construction of modern highways through existing cities with dense development was disruptive, and the experience of those years surely is partly behind the more recent movement against the construction of more highways. Many homes and businesses had to be relocated to create the multi-lane highways with their expansive (and safe) interchanges. Such relocation itself was a factor in moving population and employment to the suburbs.

The new highway system came at a critical time because Americans were using their increasing income to buy more automobiles by the millions. A quick look at automobile registrations for the forty-eight states and Washington, D.C., is provided in Table 6.6. Total registrations went from 40.2 million in 1950 to 88.4 million in 1970, an increase of 120 percent. (Recall that the increase in population over these two decades was 34.1 percent.) Autos in the Northeast increased by 98 percent (with a population increase of 26.8 percent). The South had the largest increase in cars—158 percent—even though its population growth was just 31.6 percent. And the West, with its population growth of 72.5 percent, had 143 percent more cars in 1970 than in 1950. Table 6.6 also shows auto registrations for the top state in each region.

In 1970, California led the nation in number of cars by a wide margin. Its 9.82 million cars topped the state of New York by 3.85 million.

Summary

This chapter has described the rapid pace of suburbanization in America's major urban areas during the 1950–70 period, and identified the major causes of what may well be the most significant social and economic force of that time. The basic point is that rapid growth in population and employment was accommodated primarily by building out, rather than by building up. Indeed, the additional forces leading to suburbanization were so strong that some central cities declined even as their metropolitan areas grew rapidly. Those forces were primarily economic in nature: rapid growth in household income, which could be used to buy houses and automobiles, reduction in commuting costs from the construction of freeways, cheap suburban land and low costs for building materials, and federal policies that encouraged suburban development of single-family homes. And most important of all, perhaps, was the motivation of households to seek a balance in the trade-off between "spacious living and easy access." People seek both the city and the country in some optimal mix.

What could have been wrong with all of this? Millions and millions of Americans succeeded in attaining some version of the "American Dream" during these years. What was going wrong is the topic of the next chapter.

7

Signs of Trouble Ahead

The economic growth and increasing prosperity enjoyed by most Americans in the 1950s and 1960s have been documented in the previous three chapters. The nation's urban areas grew rapidly, and the suburbs accommodated that growth. But in retrospect we know that all was not well in many of America's metropolitan areas. In particular, the urban black population did not participate fully in the prosperity of the time. Black people moved to the major urban areas in large numbers but found housing segregation and limitations on job opportunities. This chapter examines the status of the urban black population in the 1950s and 1960s and discusses causes of the tensions that produced the urban crisis. Housing segregation and employment are the primary topics, but access to consumer goods and public services such as schools is also discussed. The chapter concludes with an examination of the public housing and urban renewal programs, the introduction of which was presented in Chapter 3.

Housing Segregation in the Northeast

The pattern of residential segregation of the black population was well established in 1950, as shown in Chapter 3. Some of the data from that chapter are repeated in Tables 7.1 and 7.2. Table 7.1 shows that a total of 3.17 million black people lived in the seventeen northeastern central cities included in this study in 1950, which amounts to 21.1 percent of the nation's black population in that year. Actually, the black population in the northeastern central cities was heavily concentrated in eight cities—New York, Chicago, Philadelphia, Detroit, St. Louis, Cleveland, Washington, D.C., and Baltimore. These central cities housed 2.72 million black people in 1950. The Great Migration brought black people to these cities in large numbers, and by 1960 their population in the seventeen central cities was 4.82 million, which amounted to 25.6 percent of the nation's black population. Those top eight central cities were home to

4.12 million black people at that time. The increase in the black population in the seventeen central cities was almost as great in the 1960s as it had been in the 1950s. By 1970, the black population in the seventeen cities had more than doubled to 6.42 million, representing 28.4 percent of the total black population of the nation. The percentage of the nation's black population located in just these seventeen central cities had increased by 7.3 percentage points in twenty years—during a time when the nation's black population had grown by exactly 50 percent. Those top eight central cities were home to 4.97 million black people in 1970. New York City had a black population of 1.59 million in 1970, and the city of Chicago was home to 1.10 million.

Given that the black population in the seventeen central cities had more than doubled, and given that the total population of these cities had changed very little from 1950 to 1970, the percentage of the central city population that was black also more than doubled, from an average of 13.9 percent in 1950 to 28.7 percent in 1970. The increase in this percentage varied. The percentage of blacks in the city of Chicago increased from 13.6 to 32.8, and the percentage of blacks in the city of Detroit jumped from 16.2 to 43.7 in twenty years. Washington, D.C., had become a majority black city by 1960 (53.9 percent) and was 71.0 percent black in 1970. The cities of Baltimore, Detroit, and St. Louis were all above 40 percent black in 1970. On the other end of the spectrum, the cities of Minneapolis and St. Paul were only 4.0 percent black in 1970.

Table 7.1 shows that all of the seventeen central cities had large increases in their black populations in the 1950s and 1960s. (Minneapolis–St. Paul saw its black population increase by 131 percent.) However, even with these large increases, the pattern of racial segregation was maintained across the board. Table 7.2 displays the segregation indexes for the seventeen central cities for 1950 (repeated from Chapter 3), 1960, and 1970. These are indexes of segregation at the block level. The comparable index for Minneapolis for 1970 was not computed. The mean of the segregation indexes for the other sixteen central cities was 89.2 in 1950, 87.2 in 1960, and 84.2 in 1970. The pattern of segregation of the black population had not changed much. The decline in the segregation index from 89.2 to 84.2 means that the number of black people who would "move" hypothetically to have an even distribution at the block level in the central city had been reduced by 5.0 percent.

Table 7.2 also shows the percentage of the black population of the metropolitan area that lived in the central city in 1970. With a few exceptions, this percentage was well over 80 percent. The exceptions are metropolitan areas with a large inner suburb that contained a large black population: Newark, New Jersey, for New York City; Camden, New Jersey, for Philadelphia; the Steel Valley towns for Pittsburgh; East St. Louis, Illinois, for St. Louis; and Kansas City, Kansas, for

Table 7.1

Black Population in Urban Areas of the Northeast: 1950–1970

	Central city black population 1950 (1,000s)	Central city black population 1960 (1,000s)	Central city black population 1970 (1,000s)	Central city percent black 1950	Central city percent black 1960	Central city percent black 1970
New York	748	1,088	1,590	9.5	14.0	20.1
Chicago	492	813	1,103	13.6	22.9	32.8
Philadelphia	376	535	654	18.1	26.5	33.6
Detroit	300	482	660	16.2	28.9	43.7
Boston	40	68	105	5.0	9.8	16.4
Pittsburgh	82	102	105	12.1	16.9	20.2
St. Louis	154	216	254	18.0	28.8	40.8
Cleveland	148	251	288	16.2	28.7	38.3
Washington, D.C.	281	412	538	35.0	53.9	71.0
Baltimore	222	326	420	23.4	34.7	46.4
Minneapolis–St. Paul	13	21	30	1.6	2.6	4.0
Buffalo	37	73	94	6.4	13.7	20.3
Cincinnati	88	109	125	17.5	21.7	27.6
Milwaukee	22	65	105	3.5	8.8	14.6
Kansas City	56	84	112	12.3	17.6	22.1
Indianapolis	64	99	134	15.0	20.8	18.0
Columbus	47	78	100	12.5	16.6	18.5
Total	3,170	4,822	6,417			
Mean				13.9	21.6	28.7

Source: Census of Population and Housing.

Table 7.2

Segregation of the Black Population in Urban Areas of the Northeast: 1950–1970

	Segregation index for central city 1950	Segregation index for central city 1960	Segregation index for central city 1970	Percent of black population in central city 1970
New York	87.3	79.3	73.0	65.3
	(76.9 Newark)	(71.6 Newark)	(74.9 Newark)	
Chicago	92.1	92.6	88.8	89.6
Philadelphia	89.0	87.1	85.2	77.5
Detroit	88.8	84.5	80.9	87.2
Boston	86.5	83.9	79.9	82.7
Pittsburgh	84.0	84.6	83.9	61.8
St. Louis	92.9	90.5	89.0	67.0
	(94.2 E. St. L.)	(92.0 E. St. L.)		
Cleveland	91.5	91.3	89.0	86.5
Washington, D.C.	80.1	79.7	77.7	76.4
Baltimore	91.3	89.6	88.3	85.7
Minneapolis– St. Paul	86.0	79.3	n.a.	93.8
	(90.0 St. P.)	(87.3 St. P.)		
Buffalo	89.5	86.5	84.2	86.2
Cincinnati	91.2	88.1	83.7	82.2
Milwaukee	91.6	88.1	83.7	98.1
Kansas City	91.3	90.8	88.0	70.4
	(92.0 KC, KS)	(91.5 KC, KS)		
Indianapolis	91.4	91.6	88.3	97.8
Columbus	88.9	85.3	84.1	94.3
Mean	89.0	86.6	84.2	82.5

Sources: Taeuber and Taeuber (1965); Massey and Denton (1993).

Kansas City, Missouri. The remaining exception is Washington, D.C., with 76.4 percent of the black population of its metropolitan area. However, the population of the central city was 71.0 percent black in 1970, so it is not surprising that some of the "tipping" mechanism had spilled over into the nearby suburbs.

The small decline in segregation indexes probably does not mean very much because the indexes shown in Table 7.2 measure that amount of movement needed to have integration just within the central city. All of the central cities had increases in the percentage of the population that was black, so the "target" percentage for full integration had moved up. Table 7.1 shows that the percentage of the central city population that was black had been an average of 13.9 percent in 1950; it had increased to 21.6 percent in 1960 and 28.7 percent in 1970.

In summary, the two decades of the 1950s and 1960s were a time of rapid increase in the black populations of the central cities of the Northeast. During this time, the pattern of racial segregation was maintained. A more detailed look at the pattern of rapid black population growth and maintenance of segregation in Chicago is provided below.

Housing Segregation in the Sunbelt

Chapter 3 also demonstrated that segregation was very high in the West and, contrary to Myrdal's conjecture, also very high in the urban areas of the South. Data on the black population in the Sunbelt urban areas are found in Tables 7.3 and 7.4. Table 7.3 shows that the black population in the twelve central cities increased from 1.00 million in 1950 to 1.62 million in 1960 and 2.22 million in 1970. In 1970, 9.8 percent of the nation's black population lived in the twelve central cities of the Sunbelt included in this study. Together the twenty-nine central cities included in this study were home to 38.2 percent of the nation's black population in 1970.

Of the six central cities in the South, only Miami did not have a large black population. The six central cities of the South had an average black population of 26.4 percent in 1950; this average increased to 29.7 percent in 1960 and 35.0 percent in 1970. Table 7.4 shows that segregation in these six central cities was very high in 1950 and remained so. The average of the segregation indexes for Dallas, Houston, New Orleans, Atlanta, Birmingham, and Miami was 90.5 in 1950, actually increased to 93.2 in 1960, and was 89.7 in 1970. Remarkably, all six indexes increased between 1950 and 1960, and then all declined slightly in 1970. Segregation by this measure was consistently slightly higher in the South than in the Northeast.

In the West only Los Angeles and San Francisco–Oakland had large numbers of black residents. The black population of the city of Los Angeles increased from 171,000 in 1950 to 504,000 in 1970, and the combined central cities of San Francisco and Oakland increased from 90,000 to 221,000 black population. The larger increase occurred in the city of Oakland, which had 47,000 black residents in 1950 and 125,000 in 1970. Table 7.3 shows that the black population remained less than 10 percent of the populations of the cities of Seattle, Denver, San Diego, and Phoenix. The segregation indexes for the cities of the West shown in Table 7.4 indicate a high level of segregation in 1950. Segregation indexes are not available for Phoenix. The average for the six cities (including Oakland as a separate city) in 1950 was 83.6. This average declined somewhat to 78.4 in 1960. Indexes are not available for Seattle, Denver, San Diego, and Phoenix for 1970 on the same basis because Massey and Denton (1993) did not compute them (most likely because of their small

Table 7.3

Black Population in Urban Areas of the Sunbelt: 1950–1970

	Central city black population: 1950 (1,000s)	Central city black population: 1960 (1,000s)	Central city black population: 1970 (1,000s)	Central city percent black 1950	Central city percent black 1960	Central city percent black 1970
Dallas–Fort Worth	94	185	288	13.2	17.9	23.3
Houston	125	215	317	21.0	22.9	25.7
New Orleans	182	234	267	31.9	37.3	45.0
Atlanta	121	186	255	36.6	38.2	51.3
Birmingham	130	135	126	39.9	39.6	41.9
Miami	40	65	76	16.1	22.3	22.7
Los Angeles	171	335	504	8.7	13.5	17.9
San Francisco–Oakland	90	158	221	7.8	14.3	20.5
Seattle	16	27	38	3.4	4.8	7.2
Denver	15	30	47	3.6	6.8	9.1
San Diego	15	34	53	4.5	5.9	7.6
Phoenix	5	21	28	4.7	4.8	4.8
Total	1,004	1,625	2,220			
Mean				16.0	19.0	23.1

Source: Census of Population and Housing.

Table 7.4

Segregation of the Black Population in Urban Areas of the Sunbelt: 1950–1970

	Segregation index for central city 1950	Segregation index for central city 1960	Segregation index for central city 1970	Percent black population in central city 1970
Dallas– Fort Worth	88.4	94.6	92.7	87.3
Houston	91.5	93.7	90.0	83.0
New Orleans	84.9	86.3	83.1	82.4
Atlanta	91.5	93.6	91.5	82.0
Birmingham	88.7	92.8	91.5	58.1
Miami	97.8	97.9	89.4	28.5
Los Angeles	84.6	81.8	78.4	60.7
San Francisco	79.8	69.3	55.5*	67.0
(Oakland)	(81.2)	(73.1)		
Seattle	83.3	79.7	n.a.	90.5
Denver	88.9	85.5	n.a.	94.0
San Diego	83.6	81.3	n.a.	85.5
Phoenix	n.a.	n.a.	n.a.	84.8

*Segregation index for city of San Francisco only.
Sources: Taeuber and Taeuber (1965); Massey and Denton (1993).

black populations). The segregation index for the city of Los Angeles declined from 84.6 in 1950 to 81.8 in 1960 and 78.4 in 1970, which is similar to the size of the declines recorded in the central cities of the Northeast. However, the index for the city of San Francisco fell from 79.8 in 1950 to 69.3 in 1960 and 55.5 in 1970. No other city in this study has such a record of reduction in the segregation index.

The available data show that segregation levels in the six central cities of the South and in Los Angeles was quite similar to those observed in the central cities of the Northeast. Four of the cities of the West (Seattle, Denver, San Diego, and Phoenix) had small black populations in 1970.

Black Population Growth and Segregation in Chicago

The black population of the city of Chicago increased from 492,000 in 1950 to 813,000 in 1960 and 1.103 million in 1970, an increase of 611,000 in twenty years. This increase in just one city represents 8.1 percent of the total increase in the black population of the nation, and yet the segregation index started at 91.1, increased to 92.6, and fell slightly to 88.8. Segregation can remain only so high in the face of massive population increase if neighborhoods change from all-white to all-black on a large scale. Chicago's black neighborhoods as of 1950 could not possibly have accommodated such a large population increase.

The pattern of racial transition can be tracked using the data on the Chicago community areas. The seventy-seven areas had been designated in 1930, and the first published report of these data was edited by Ernest Burgess and Charles Newcomb and published by the University of Chicago Press in 1933. The community areas with significant numbers of black residents in 1970 are listed in Table 7.5. The first community area listed is the Near North Side, located just north of downtown Chicago. The next six community areas listed are on the West Side of the city, and the remaining twenty-four are located on the city's South Side. The table shows the population of each of these community areas in 1950, 1960, and 1970, along with the percentage of black residents in each of these years. The table also shows the number of housing units in the community area in each year, and has a brief note that characterizes that community area. Only six of the thirty-one community areas were predominantly black in 1950. Fourteen of these community areas underwent racial transition from predominantly white to predominantly black (69 percent or more) during the 1950–70 period. Ten of the remaining eleven were in the process of transition from white to black occupancy in 1970, and only one was to remain racially mixed—the Near North Side. However, the Near North Side was actually highly segregated because it consisted of public housing projects that were virtually all black and nearby areas where high-income whites lived. The remaining forty-six community areas in Chicago contained few black residents in 1970.

The city of Chicago was (and is) highly racially segregated. In addition, the black population of the city occupied housing that was of significantly lower quality than the average for the city. The data for 1960 are striking in this regard. The city of Chicago contained 1,214,958 housing units in that year. Of this total, 11.4 percent lacked some aspect of standard plumbing, which is regarded as a flush toilet, a bathtub or shower, and both cold and hot water. Substandard units are either deteriorating or dilapidated, and 15.3 percent of the units in Chicago were so rated by the census takers. Also, 11.2 percent of the units were regarded as crowded, which means that the unit houses more than 1.0 persons per room. The black population of the city occupied 233,494 housing units in 1960, of which 19.4 percent lacked some aspect of standard plumbing. Substandard units were 30.7 percent of the total occupied by blacks, and 27.4 percent of the 233,494 units were crowded. In fact, of the 981,464 units that were *not* occupied by blacks in 1960, 9.8 percent lacked plumbing, 11.6 percent were in substandard condition, and 7.3 percent were crowded. Note that blacks, who constituted 22.9 percent of the population of

Table 7.5

Neighborhood Racial Transition in Chicago: 1950–1970

Community area	Population	Percent black	Housing units	Notes
8 Near North Side				
1950	89,196	20	27,248	Mixed area; public
1960	75,509	31	38,243	housing and high
1970	70,269	37	38,958	income
23 Humboldt Park				
1950	76,199	0	22,633	
1960	71,609	1	23,919	Beginning
1970	71,726	19	23,360	transition
25 Austin				
1950	132,180	0	41,451	
1960	125,133	0	44,554	In transition to
1970	127,981	33	44,841	black area
26 West Garfield Park				
1950	48,443	0	14,553	
1960	45,611	16	14,590	Transition to black
1970	48,464	97	13,171	area completed
27 East Garfield Park				
1950	70,091	17	21,509	
1960	66,871	62	20,353	Transition area and
1970	52,185	98	16,065	riot area in 1968
28 Near West Side				
1950	160,362	41	41,164	
1960	126,610	53	37,057	Demolition for
1970	78,703	72	23,706	U of I in 1960s
29 North Lawndale				
1950	100,489	13	28,009	Transition
1960	124,937	91	30,212	complete; riots
1970	94,772	96	25,342	in 1968
33 Near South Side				
1950	11,317	69	2,875	
1960	10,350	77	3,803	Old black area in
1970	8,767	85	3,223	decline
35 Douglas				
1950	78,745	97	21,474	
1960	52,325	92	15,816	Old black area in
1970	41,276	86	15,738	decline

(continued)

Table 7.5 *(continued)*

Community area	Population	Percent black	Housing units	Notes
36 Oakland				
1950	24,464	77	7,869	
1960	24,378	98	7,834	Old black area in
1970	18,291	99	5,686	decline
37 Fuller Park				
1950	17,174	50	4,147	
1960	12,181	96	2,954	Demolition for
1970	7,372	97	2,287	Ryan Expressway
38 Grand Blvd.				
1950	114,557	99	31,598	
1960	80,036	99	26,486	Old black area in
1970	80,150	99	25,948	decline
39 Kenwood				
1950	35,705	10	12,771	
1960	41,533	84	15,428	Transition and then
1970	26,908	79	11,597	decline
40 Washington Park				
1950	56,856	99	16,477	
1960	43,690	99	15,878	Stable old black
1970	46,024	99	15,890	area
42 Woodlawn				
1950	80,699	39	27,624	
1960	81,279	89	29,616	Transition, then
1970	53,814	96	22,255	decline
43 South Shore				
1950	79,336	0	27,930	
1960	73,086	10	30,001	In transition to all-
1970	80,660	69	33,359	black area
44 Chatham				
1950	40,845	1	13,162	
1960	41,962	64	14,378	Transition to black
1970	47,287	98	16,900	area completed
45 Avalon Park				
1950	11,358	0	3,335	
1960	12,710	0	3,913	Transition to black
1970	14,412	83	4,206	area completed
46 South Chicago				
1950	55,715	5	14,931	
1960	49,913	5	15,622	In transition to
1970	45,655	22	15,759	black area
47 Burnside				
1950	3,551	0	869	To become 89 per-
1960	3,463	0	1,057	cent black in 1980
1970	3,181	3	1,036	

(continued)

Table 7.5 *(continued)*

Community area	Population	Percent black	Housing units	Notes
48 Calumet Heights				
1950	9,349	0	2,651	
1960	19,352	0	5,677	In transition to
1970	20,123	45	6,108	black area
49 Roseland				
1950	56,705	18	16,066	
1960	58,750	23	18,328	In transition to
1970	62,512	55	19,557	black area
50 Pullman				
1950	8899	0	2,430	
1960	8412	0	2,795	In transition to
1970	10,893	51	3,685	black area
53 West Pullman				
1950	29,265	0	8,285	
1960	35,397	0	10,613	In transition to
1970	40,318	17	12,496	black area
54 Riverdale				
1950	9790	84	2,017	
1960	11,448	90	2,295	Public housing
1970	15,018	95	3,471	area
67 West Englewood				
1950	62,842	6	17,732	
1960	58,516	12	18,224	In transition to
1970	61,910	48	18,511	black area
68 Englewood				
1950	94,134	10	28,059	
1960	97,595	69	27,157	Transition, then
1970	89,713	96	25,234	decline
69 Greater Grand Crossing				
1950	61,753	6	18,786	
1960	63,169	86	18,749	Transition, then
1970	54,414	98	18,476	decline
71 Auburn-Gresham				
1950	60,978	0	17,758	
1960	59,484	0	19,448	In transition to
1970	68,854	69	20,663	black area
73 Washington Heights				
1950	24,488	0	6,947	
1960	29,793	13	9,068	In transition to
1970	36,540	75	10,098	black area
75 Morgan Park				
1950	22,618	40	6,053	
1960	29,912	35	7,858	In transition to ma-
1970	31,016	48	9,050	jority black area

Sources: Local Community Fact Book: Chicago Metropolitan Area (1963 and 1995).

the city, occupied 19.2 percent of the housing units. No wonder many of those units were regarded as crowded. In short, the system of supplying housing to the growing black population by racial transition of neighborhoods left the black population living in crowded conditions in units many of which lacked plumbing and were in substandard condition. The white population relinquished neighborhoods grudgingly. In the meantime, the intensive use of the existing housing stock in black neighborhoods resulted in units that were split into smaller units (sometimes without complete plumbing facilities) and deteriorating conditions.

The story of racial transition on the West Side of the city in the community areas of North Lawndale, East Garfield Park, West Garfield Park, and Austin has been told in great detail by Amanda Seligman (2005). Table 7.5 shows that the first three had rapid and complete racial transitions during 1950 to 1970, and that Austin was in the process of racial transition in 1970. Seligman (2005) shows that the racial transition has a more complex history than many realize. She refers to the study of Detroit by Sugrue (1996) to the effect that some white neighborhoods were "defended," while others went "undefended." The white residents of the West Side conducted a multifaceted defense. Some real estate agents clearly were "block busters" and "panic peddlers," but others saw themselves as advocates of open housing and providers of legitimate services to people in need of better homes. Some community organizations were organized simply to keep black people out of white neighborhoods, while others attempted to prevent "white flight," promote integration, and move the city to enforce its own building code and provide other public resources for the area. Some organizations condoned violent protests against certain real estate agents, while others extolled the virtues of the West Side and pointed out that the nearby suburbs were expensive and required that the family own two cars. Others tried to slow down the entry of black households by promoting open housing in other locations. Much controversy surrounded the public schools. Movement of black families into an area often increased public school enrollment and created crowded conditions in schools. The movement of elementary school boundaries set off loud and detailed protests. Interracial violence occurred in the public high schools, especially Austin High School. Seligman (2005) points out that violence perpetrated by whites on the West Side against new black residents and real estate agents was not publicized very much. However, some rioting by blacks against the police and local businesses took place in 1965 and 1966, and this got much attention in the local press—including the neighborhood newspapers. The major riots on the West Side after the murder of Martin Luther King, Jr., in 1968 were national news, of course. Several blocks on the two major business streets in the area were burned, and the businesses never returned. In the end, Seligman (2005) concludes that West Garfield Park and Austin failed to become integrated neighborhoods for many reasons.

Housing Prices and Home Ownership

The previous section showed that the black population of Chicago occupied a housing stock of lower quality than did other Chicagoans in 1960. Was this caused simply by their relatively low incomes, or did the pattern of segregation and neighborhood succession produce additional adverse outcomes for black households in the housing market? Research that has been conducted since the 1940s has demonstrated that:

- Rents and housing prices were higher in black neighborhoods than in white neighborhoods when the black population was increasing rapidly, as it was in the 1950s and 1960s. Demand growth, coupled with slower response on the supply side, drove up rents and prices for units in the black residential areas that were comparable to lower-priced ones in white areas. Later in the 1970s and 1980s, after whites had moved away to the suburbs in large numbers, rents and prices for comparable units (in neighborhoods of comparable quality) were no longer higher in the black neighborhoods. Indeed, rents and prices in many inner-city black neighborhoods collapsed because of the severe social problems in those areas. Housing abandonment occurred in many areas as rents and prices fell so low that it became uneconomical to continue to use the housing units.
- Heads of black households faced discrimination in the quest to become home owners. Black households had (and have) lower rates of home ownership than do comparable white households. The relative lack of home ownership is damaging to the black community because ownership is a primary means used by most households to build wealth, and because home owners generally take pride in their property and create better neighborhoods.

This section examines some of the huge volume of research that has been conducted on these points.

A study by Haugen and Heins (1969) took a nicely direct approach to the question of black versus white rents. They examined the ratio of median rent paid by black households to the median rent paid by white households in sixty-nine major metropolitan areas in 1960. All twenty-nine of the metropolitan areas included in this study were included in their data. They hypothesized that this ratio of median rent would be higher if:

- the speed at which the white population moved away from the central city had been *lower*, measured as the rate of increase in the suburban white population from 1950 to 1960;
- the rate of black population growth in the urban area had been *greater* during 1950 to 1960;
- the black population was more heavily centralized (higher proportion in the central city).

Haugen and Heins (1969) also included three "control" variables—the ratio of the percentage of dilapidated units occupied by blacks versus whites, the ratio of the median number of rooms in the units occupied by blacks and whites, and the ratio of black to white median incomes for renters. Haugen and Heins (1969) estimated a multiple regression model, and found that two of their three primary hypotheses were confirmed for 1960. In particular, the rate of black population growth had a strong positive effect on the ratio of black to white rents, as did the extent to which the black population was concentrated in the central city. The rate of white population growth in the suburbs did not have a statistically significant effect on the rent ratio. However, note that their results did not say whether blacks or whites paid higher rents for equivalent units.

The question of who actually paid more for the housing unit of equivalent quality can only be answered by using data on individual properties so that one can introduce extensive "controls" for the features of the unit and the neighborhood in which it is located. Perhaps the best study of rents in the 1960s was conducted by King and Mieszkowski (1973). First, recall the discussion in Chapter 3 of racial prejudice and discrimination. Racial prejudice is an aversion to an individual member of a racial group regardless of the attributes of that person. Racial discrimination means taking action against a person from a particular racial group because of membership in that group, such as charging a higher rent or paying a lower wage rate. Racial prejudice is passive; racial discrimination is active. In the urban housing market racial prejudice means that one moves away—avoids the other group—when that group starts to move into the neighborhood (or next door). Racial discrimination can mean a simple refusal to rent or sell housing, and it can also mean taking action to try to make sure that one's neighbors discriminate as well.

King and Mieszkowski (1973) pointed out that it is important to separate the demand and supply factors. If prejudice on the part of whites is the only racial factor operating, the aversion of whites for blacks will lead to supply adjustment, which will cause rents and prices to be lower for blacks than for the whites who avoid them. The rent or price differential is a measure of the preference that whites have for avoiding blacks. However, if whites actively discriminate against blacks and refuse to rent or sell to them when black demand grows, then blacks will pay higher rents and prices because supply has been limited. This latter effect was found by Haugen and Heins (1969), for example. King and Mieszkowski (1973) studied rents paid by blacks and whites in New Haven, Connecticut, during 1968–69. They examined rents paid by white and black households in two types of areas, the interior of the black residential area and the racial boundary areas, compared to the rents paid by whites in the interior white areas. A large number of variables was used to control for variations in the quality of the housing units and the neighborhoods in which they were located. The results showed that white rents in the boundary areas were 7 percent lower than rents in the white interior. Rents paid by blacks in the boundary areas were equal to white interior rents, so there was a 7 percent difference between white and black rents in the boundary area. This is their estimate of the effect of racial prejudice, the aversion of whites for blacks. Also, they found that all rents (paid by whites and blacks) in the black interior were 9 percent higher than rents in the white interior. This result suggests limitations on the expansion of the black residential areas during a period of demand growth. By the way, the whites who lived in the black interior evidently did not harbor racial prejudice.

Another study by Berry (1976) examined the housing market in Chicago during 1968–72. He found that prices paid for comparable houses were lower in the white areas near the black and Hispanic areas than in the white areas that were removed from the racial borders. However, he also found that prices were lowest of all in the traditional black and Hispanic neighborhoods. Prices in the zones of recent black and Hispanic expansion were about equal to the prices paid in the white border areas. Berry (1976) attributed these results to two factors:

- By the late 1960s and early 1970s, the rate of increase of the black population had dropped significantly.
- Housing construction in the suburbs had drawn whites away from the central city in large numbers, so that racial succession took place more rapidly than before.

Most of the many other early studies of housing rents and prices and race are reviewed by Kain and Quigley (1975).

The earliest detailed studies of race and home ownership were conducted by Kain and Quigley (1972) and McDonald (1974). These studies confirmed that, holding constant income and other household characteristics, blacks had lower rates of home ownership than did whites in St. Louis and Detroit of the 1960s. This racial difference in home ownership rates was estimated to have been roughly 9 to 10 percentage points. The raw difference in home ownership was much greater, but income differences and household composition differences accounted for most of this "raw" difference. Yet there was still that 10 percent that could not be accounted for. Both Kain and Quigley (1972) and McDonald (1974) attributed part of this difference in home ownership rates to restrictions on the nature of the supply of houses available to blacks in St. Louis and Detroit. Kain and Quigley (1972) found, observing cities, that the extent to which the black home ownership rate fell short of the rate expected based on income and household composition was negatively correlated with the percentage of units in the central city designated as single-family housing. McDonald introduced a variable that measured the type of structure occupied by the household and found that, in the days before condominium conversions, home ownership was strongly positively related to living in a single-family house. This factor reduced the racial difference in home ownership by about one-half. Both Kain and Quigley (1972) and McDonald (1974) concluded that full racial equality in home ownership would require both that residential lending be offered in a nondiscriminatory manner, and that additional areas of single-family houses be made available to black households.

The Poor Pay More

The housing market was not the only market for consumer goods in which urban blacks (and others) were disadvantaged. David Caplovitz (1963) stated the problem succinctly in his book *The Poor Pay More*. The poor paid more in many ways. Poor neighborhoods were not provided with supermarkets, which take advantage of economies of scale to deliver groceries at relatively low prices. Instead, poor neighborhoods were served by "mom-and-pop" food stores with no economies of scale and higher prices. The chain drugstores with their economies of scale also tended to avoid the inner city, so the poor had to obtain medicines and sundries at smaller stores. Furniture and appliance stores would often sell to the poor on credit, at high interest rates. Banks and savings and loan associations avoided the inner city altogether, leaving the poor to deal with "currency exchanges." The poor worker would have to pay a fee to cash his or her paycheck, instead of depositing it in a bank checking account. It was no coincidence that much of the anger and resentment expressed in the urban riots of the 1960s was directed at retail establishments.

Employment Discrimination

Black workers in the United States experience discrimination in employment. That discrimination takes many forms. Discrimination can take place at every stage of the process of getting educated, seeking job training, searching for work, getting placed in a position, being paid for the work that one does, and getting promoted (or demoted or fired). Chapter 3 provided an update to 1950 of Myrdal's (1944) *An American Dilemma*. Did the situation change very much over the next twenty years? The situation changed because of the migration of black people from the South to the Northeast and to Los Angeles and San Francisco–Oakland, where opportunities for education and employment were better. The Great Migration definitely had a purpose. The other great migration of the time was the movement from rural to urban areas of the South. However, once black people arrived in the great cities of the Northeast, California, and the South, they found that they faced difficulties:

- Racial segregation in housing confined most black children to schools that were de facto segregated. Educational outcomes were not equal.
- Those seeking job training found discrimination in the training offered by some unions and employers.
- The job search process was often not an open process for black workers. Jobs were often filled by word of mouth or by hiring from union halls. There were, however, significant exceptions to this discrimination in the auto industry and others.
- Placement in a position might be influenced by race as well. For example, employers might not wish to place blacks in positions in which they would be dealing with the public, especially the white public.
- Black workers got paid less for equal work. This rather narrow issue was studied intensively, and there was a consistent finding that black workers in many industries were paid less than white workers of equal qualification and/or responsibilities. Masters (1975) and F. Wilson (1979) documented this racial wage differential in detail for 1959 and 1969.
- Black workers faced discrimination in promotion. And, since they often were the last to be hired, they were the first to be fired.

Most of these points had been documented for 1939 and 1949 by Nobel Prize–winning economist Gary Becker (1971) in his first book, *The Economics of Discrimination*.

Employment of Blacks in the Northeast

This section looks at the net outcome of all of the forces discussed above as of 1970. Basic data on the labor market outcomes for black workers in the metropolitan areas of the Northeast are shown in Table 7.6. This table shows that the average labor force participation rate for black males (aged sixteen and over) in the seventeen urban areas was 71.8 percent. The national average for all men (aged sixteen and over) was 79.7 percent, and the national average for black men was 76.5 percent at that time. This means that 28.2 percent of black males in the seventeen urban areas chose not to work or look for work. The average unemployment rate for black males in the seventeen urban areas was 7.0 percent, compared to the national male unemployment rate of 4.4 percent in this year of low unemployment. The unemployment rate for all black men in the nation was 7.3 percent. The net outcome was that, on average, 66.7 percent of black males in the seventeen urban areas were employed in 1970, compared to 76.2 percent for all men and 70.9 for all black men in the nation. This recitation of facts shows that looking only at the unemployment rate does not give the complete picture. Black men in these urban areas have relatively low rates of labor force participation. People choose not to participate in the labor force for many reasons such as school attendance, advancing age, disability, and so on. But other people do not participate because they perceive that the chances of finding work are not good. It is telling that the labor force participation rates of black men in the northeastern urban areas were below the averages for all men and all black men as well.

The labor force participation rate of black men varied from a low of just 63.8 percent in Pittsburgh and 68 to 69 percent in St. Louis, Buffalo, and Cincinnati, to 74 percent or more in Detroit, Cleveland, Washington, D.C., and Milwaukee. None of these urban areas had a labor force participation rate that exceeded the rate for all men in the nation or all black men in the nation. Statistical analysis reported below shows that the rate of labor force participation for black men was related to the unemployment rate and earnings.

The average for the seventeen urban areas of median earnings for black men who worked full time was $6,360. The comparable average for all men was $8,482, so black men who were employed earned, on average, 75.0 percent of the earnings of all men in these urban areas. In short, black men had lower labor force participation, high unemployment if they did participate, and lower earnings if they found work.

Table 7.6 shows that the relative of median earnings of black men, compared to all men in the same urban areas, varied from a high of 79.6 percent in Columbus to a low of 70.4 percent in Minneapolis–St. Paul. Perhaps what is notable about these figures is that their variation from urban area to urban area in the Northeast is not very large.

Given that black men in the seventeen urban areas had relatively low rates of labor force participation, it is perhaps not surprising that black women had relatively high participation rates. Table 7.6 shows that the average of the labor force participation rates for black women in the seventeen urban areas was 49.7 percent, which was substantially greater than the national average

Table 7.6

Black Employment and Relative Earnings: Northeastern Urban Areas for 1970

	Male labor force participation (percent)	Male unemployment rate (percent)	Relative earnings for black males*	Female labor force participation (percent)	Female unemployment rate (percent)	Relative earnings for black females*
New York	72.5	5.4	0.746	48.1	5.2	0.953
Chicago	73.1	6.5	0.785	45.9	7.7	0.995
Philadelphia	71.8	6.4	0.723	49.0	6.4	0.969
Detroit	74.0	9.0	0.792	45.7	10.8	0.929
Boston	71.8	6.6	0.720	47.7	5.2	0.947
Pittsburgh	63.8	7.8	0.787	38.1	8.1	0.863
St. Louis	67.8	9.8	0.708	47.8	9.2	0.871
Cleveland	74.0	7.3	0.791	49.6	6.5	0.921
Washington, D.C.	76.5	3.9	0.709	58.8	4.2	0.905
Baltimore	71.4	5.4	0.730	51.2	6.5	0.873
Minneapolis–St. Paul	72.8	6.5	0.704	53.6	4.8	0.980
Buffalo	68.9	9.2	0.795	44.7	11.2	0.959
Cincinnati	69.1	6.7	0.756	49.3	8.0	0.859
Milwaukee	76.3	8.1	0.745	52.8	8.3	0.940
Kansas City	73.9	6.5	0.712	54.0	6.8	0.818
Indianapolis	72.2	8.1	0.746	55.7	8.1	0.913
Columbus	70.4	5.6	0.796	53.6	5.2	0.909
Mean	71.8	7.0	0.750	49.7	7.2	0.918

*Ratio of median earnings of black workers to median earnings for all workers of the same sex in the metropolitan area.
Source: Census of Population and Housing.

for all women of 43.3 percent. The participation rate for all black women in the nation was 49.5 percent—close to the average for the seventeen urban areas. Black women had an average unemployment rate of 7.2 percent in the seventeen urban areas, which exceeded the unemployment rate for all women in the nation of 5.9 percent, but was less than the national black female unemployment rate of 9.3 percent. In the end, the average employment rate for black women in these urban areas was 46.1 percent, compared to 40.8 percent for all women in the nation. As in 1950, black women in the northeastern urban areas worked more than did all women in the nation, and black men in these same urban areas worked less than did all of the nation's men.

How do the earnings of black women compare to all women? Table 7.6 shows that black women in the seventeen urban areas earned, on average, almost as much as did all women in these urban areas. Black women in these urban areas had average earnings of $3,706, which was in fact 91.8 percent of the comparable average for all women in the same urban areas. Since their earnings were close to earnings for all women, one might say, "Well, no wonder so many black women were working." Black women in Washington, D.C., had median earnings of $4,643, and women in New York and Chicago earned $4,348 and $4,488, on average. Otherwise, the median earnings for black women in the other urban areas fell below $4,000—some well below $4,000. Black women in the Pittsburgh urban area had median earnings of only $3,149, so their rate of participation in the labor force was a low 38.1 percent.

In summary, black men in the seventeen urban areas faced severe disadvantages in the labor markets, but black women attempted to compensate. Black women in these urban areas had higher rates of labor force participation than did all women, and their median earnings were close to the median earnings of all women (in contrast to black men in these same urban areas).

Black Employment in the Sunbelt

The South and the West continued to be very different regions for black workers in 1970. While rates of labor force participation were similar in these two regions, unemployment rates for both black men and black women were much lower in the South, while earnings were considerably greater for both black men and black women in the West. Indeed, as in 1950, earnings for full-time black workers in the southern urban areas were still very low.

The data in Table 7.7 show that the mean labor force participation rate for men in the six urban areas of the South was 72.2 percent in 1970, which is quite close to the average participation rate in the urban areas of the Northeast. However, the average unemployment rate for black men in these six urban

Table 7.7

Black Employment and Relative Earnings: Sunbelt Urban Areas in 1970

	Male labor force participation (percent)	Male unemployment rate (percent)	Relative earnings of black males*	Female labor force participation	Female unemployment rate	Relative earnings of black females*
Dallas–Fort Worth	75.8	4.8	0.635	57.7	5.9	0.705
Houston	74.4	3.9	0.652	52.3	6.4	0.664
New Orleans	67.7	7.7	0.635	41.8	9.2	0.681
Atlanta	74.9	3.8	0.624	55.7	5.9	0.711
Birmingham	64.2	5.1	0.697	39.8	10.0	0.592
Miami	76.3	4.3	0.664	58.4	5.0	0.729
Los Angeles	72.1	10.1	0.782	49.6	9.4	0.906
San Francisco–Oakland	71.0	11.0	0.771	56.5	10.3	0.874
Seattle	73.8	12.5	0.787	55.4	13.9	0.956
Denver	75.0	5.9	0.731	55.6	5.6	0.948
San Diego	72.0	9.5	0.761	45.9	8.9	0.849
Phoenix	67.1	7.3	0.660	45.2	6.4	0.745
Mean	72.0	7.2	0.700	51.1	8.1	0.780

*Ratio of median earnings for black workers to median earnings for all workers of the same sex in the metropolitan area.
Source: Census of Population and Housing.

areas was only 4.9 percent, which exceeded the national unemployment rate for all men by only 0.5 percent. Metropolitan New Orleans recorded a low black participation rate of 67.7 percent and a relatively high unemployment rate of 7.7 percent. The lowest black male participation rate was the 64.2 percent in Birmingham. Together, the labor force participation rate and the unemployment rate yield an average employment rate for black males in the six urban areas of the South of 68.0 percent, compared to 76.2 percent for all men in the United States and 70.9 for all black men in the nation.

Black men in the southern urban areas had low earnings. The average of the median earnings for full-time black male workers in the six urban areas of the South was only $4,864, which was just 65.1 percent of the corresponding average for all male workers in those metropolitan areas. The corresponding average for the northeastern urban areas was 75.0 percent.

Once again, given that black men in the southern urban areas had somewhat low labor force participation and very low earnings, it is not surprising that black women had a high rate of labor force participation. The average of the participation rates for the six southern urban areas was 50.1 percent (slightly above the average for the northeastern urban areas), and it varied from a low of 39.8 percent in the industrial Birmingham metropolitan area to 58.4 percent in the Miami urban area. The average of the black female unemployment rates was 7.1 percent, which was close to the figure for the northeastern urban areas. However, the earnings of black women in the southern urban areas were very low. The average of the full-time median earnings for black women in the six urban areas was just $2,439, which falls far below the figure for the Northeast of $3,706. The average of the median earnings of black women compared to all women in the six urban areas was only 68.0 percent, compared to 91.8 percent in the Northeast.

The labor market outcomes for black workers in the western urban areas resemble those for blacks in the Northeast. Black men had the same average labor force participation rate in the six urban areas of the West (71.8 percent) as did black men in the northeastern metropolitan areas. At 9.4 percent, the average for the unemployment rates was somewhat greater in the West, but the average for median earnings of $6,344 was virtually equal to the $6,360 recorded in the Northeast. Black women in the western urban areas had an average labor force participation rates of 51.4 percent, which is comparable to the averages found for the other two regions. Their average unemployment rate of 9.1 percent was two points higher than in the other regions, but this was compensated by average median earnings for the six urban areas of $3,675 (close to the figure for the Northeast of $3,706). Actually, median earnings for full-time black women were relatively high in the Los Angeles, San Francisco–Oakland, and Seattle urban areas and, in contrast, quite low in metropolitan Phoenix. In short, with the exception of the labor market faced by black women in the Phoenix urban area, male and female black workers in the western metropolitan areas faced conditions that were similar to those that their counterparts faced in the northeastern urban areas.

Let us now take a look specifically at Los Angeles. Black men in metropolitan Los Angeles had a labor force participation rate of 72.1 percent and a high unemployment rate of 10.1 percent in 1970. Median earnings of black men were $6,647, which was 78.2 percent of median earnings for all men in that metropolitan labor market. In short, the participation rate was close to average for major urban areas, the unemployment rate was well above average, and median earnings were also above average for urban black men. Black women also had a typical labor force participation rate, 49.6 percent, and faced a high unemployment rate of 9.4 percent. Median earnings for black women of $4,041 were a relatively high 90.6 percent of the median earnings for all women in this labor market. In other words, Los Angeles was neither the best nor the worst labor market for black men and black women in 1970.

Statistical Analysis of Labor Force Participation

The decision to participate in the labor force has been found to respond to economic opportunity, and black workers are no exception. Better job prospects such as higher wages and a lower unemployment rate will induce more people to enter the labor force to seek and find employment. Statistical analysis has been performed to test these ideas for the black workers in the twenty-nine major urban areas included in this study. The estimated equation for black male workers is:

$$MLFP = 65.78 + 1.91 \ MEARN - 0.77 \ MUNEMP$$
$$(13.88) \ \ (2.03) \quad\quad\quad (2.31)$$

Here MLFP is the labor force participation rate for black males aged sixteen and over in the metropolitan area, MEARN is median earnings (in thousands of dollars) for black males in the urban area, and MUNEMP is the unemployment rate for black males in the urban area. The R-square for the estimated equation is only 0.126, but the t values shown in parentheses indicate that the coefficients of the two variables are statistically significant. The coefficient of median earnings says that an increase in median earnings of black males of $1,000 was associated with an increase of labor force participation of 1.9 percent, which does not seem to be a very large effect given that black men earned an average of just $6,360 in the northeastern urban areas. The coefficient on the unemployment rate indicates that an increase in the unemployment rate of one percentage point was associated with a reduction in labor force participation of 0.77 percent.

The results for black women indicate that the estimated response to variations in median earnings was not statistically significant. The estimated equation for black females in the twenty-nine urban areas is:

$$FLFP = 49.59 + 2.11 \ FEARN - 0.86 \ FUNEMP$$
$$(8.39) \ (1.46) \qquad (2.02)$$

Here FLFP stands for the labor force participation of black females in the urban area, and the other two variables are the female versions of median earnings and the unemployment rate. The R-square for this estimated equation is 0.125, and only the coefficient of the unemployment rate is statistically significant. This coefficient is comparable to the coefficient in the male labor force participation equation. An increase in the unemployment rate of black females of one percentage point was associated with a reduction in their labor force participation of 0.86 percent.

This brief statistical analysis has shown that black workers responded to employment opportunities—measured as median earnings and the unemployment rate—by adjusting their rates of labor force participation. But these responses were not estimated to be very large.

Public Housing and Urban Renewal

The initiation of the federal public housing and urban renewal policies was discussed in Chapter 1. The Housing Act of 1949 was landmark legislation that set a target of 810,000 additional public housing units to be built in the next six years, and established what became known as the urban renewal program. Recall that the federal public housing program called for "equivalent demolition" of slum housing. The urban renewal program authorized local governments to apply for federal funds to pay two-thirds of the cost of slum clearance projects in which the local government's power of eminent domain would be used to clear land and sell it to developers. All public housing and urban renewal projects were to be initiated by local officials.

The National Advisory Commission on Urban Problems was established by President Lyndon B. Johnson in 1967, and it conducted a detailed evaluation of these programs in 1968. The commission found that the total stock of public housing in the nation had increased from 170,000 in 1949 to 440,000 in 1960 and 667,000 in 1968. The public housing program had fallen far short of the goal of almost 1 million public housing units by 1955. Initiation of public housing projects rested with the local authorities, and opposition by local populations to public housing doubtless slowed construction. The commission also discovered that some of the urban renewal projects involved demolition of the slum housing without any specific plans for subsequent development (National Advisory Commission on Urban Problems 1968).

A summary of this evaluation for the cities of the Northeast is shown in Table 7.8, and the corresponding data for the Sunbelt urban areas are displayed in Table 7.9. New York City clearly was the leader in implementing the public housing program. It provided 64,633 public housing units in 1968, an increase of 50,462 units since 1949. Table 7.7 shows that equivalent demolitions were only 22,717 (in spite of federal policy), and that urban renewal demolitions were 33,697 slum housing units. The commission computed the net change that resulted from the public housing and urban renewal programs as plus 8,219 units. Public housing in New York City was a successful program. One index of this success is the vacancy rate, which stood at only 0.2 percent (129 units out of 64,633) in 1967. The public housing authority had a waiting list that was 762 times the number of vacant units. One reason for this enormous waiting list was the relatively high income limit in use. The income limit for a public housing resident in 1967 was 1.71 times the federal poverty income level of $3,365 for a family of four. New York City received praise from the commission for its public housing program, which included a good effort to provide units in most areas of the city.

The city of Chicago was also a big participant in the public housing program, but its story is in contrast to that of New York City. Chicago had added 24,477 units from 1949 to 1967 to reach a total of 32,960 units. Equivalent demolitions were only 5,358 units, but the urban renewal program had removed another 26,058 units, so the net increase in units from the two programs was only 1,564. The demand for units was very strong at that time. The vacancy rate was a minuscule 0.5 percent in 1967, and the waiting list was 126 times the number of vacant units. However, the local officials in Chicago had placed the public housing units largely in the segregated black neighborhoods of the south and west sides of the city. Arnold Hirsch (1983) referred to the process of selecting sites for public housing as the "making of the second ghetto." Shortly after the National Advisory Commission on Urban Problems issued its report, the Chicago Housing Authority was sued on behalf of some public housing tenants on the grounds that site selection had been conducted in a racially discriminatory manner. A federal court in 1969 decided the famous *Gatreaux* case in favor of the plaintiffs and ordered that additional public housing in Chicago be built in other areas of the city—that is, white neighborhoods. This court decision essentially brought the construction of public housing in Chicago to an end.

Table 7.8 shows that the cities of Philadelphia, Boston, Pittsburgh, Washing-

Table 7.8

Public Housing and Urban Renewal Demolitions: Northeastern Central Cities

	Public housing units: 1949	Public housing units: 1967	Equivalent demolitions as of 1963	Urban renewal demolitions 1949–1967	Net change	Vacant rate in public housing	Wait list/ vacant units	Income limit/ poverty level
New York	14,171	64,633	22,717	33,697	8,219	0.2	762	1.71
(Newark)	(2,711)	(10,891)	(3,517)	(5,486)	(1,888)	(2.2)	(22)	(1.36)
Chicago	8,483	32,960	5,358	33697	1,564	0.5	126	1.34
Philadelphia	3,248	15,719	6,280	15,836	−6,417	1.4	30	1.13
Detroit	4,879	8,180	847	11,216	−3,883	0.9	21	1.28
Boston	5,102	10,973	8,480	8,906	−6,413	5.3	12	1.13
Pittsburgh	4,463	12,270	3,330	7,191	−1,287	5.8	11	1.31
St. Louis	1,315	7,245	2,022	9,156	−3,933	13.0	1.04	1.31
Cleveland	5,179	7,458	3,977	5,095	−1,614	2.1	13	1.31
Washington, D.C.	3,147	10,056	1,941	7,127	988	1.3	24	1.16
Baltimore	5,021	10,335	8,810	8,661	−7,136	2.0	12	1.08
Minneapolis–St. Paul	464	5,643	661	9,471	−4,489	0.5	190	1.27
Buffalo	2,571	4,370	1,800	2,715	−145	2.9	5	1.49
Cincinnati	3,818	6,222	3,084	9,012	−5,874	2.3	4	1.19
Milwaukee	615	3,066	423	3,703	−1,060	4.6	2	1.13
Kansas City	0	2,383	1,171	3,173	−1,961	14.0	0.16	1.07
Indianapolis	748	748	0	0	748	0	n.a.	1.34
Columbus	1,352	2,881	1,193	3,309	−1621	0.8	56	1.31

Source: National Advisory Commission on Urban Problems (1968).

Table 7.9

Public Housing and Urban Renewal Demolitions: Sunbelt Urban Areas

	Public housing units: 1949	Public housing units: 1967	Equivalent demolitions as of 1963	Urban renewal demolitions 1949–1967	Net change	Vacant rate in public housing	Wait list/ vacant units	Income limit/ poverty level
Dallas	1,750	6,372	946	0	5,426	12.0	1.3	0.98
(Fort Worth)	(502)	(1,074)	(2,082)	(0)	(–1,008)	(16.5)	(0.6)	(0.8)
Houston	2,251	2,599	2,210	0	389	4.3	9.6	0.9
New Orleans	5,381	12,270	4,071	342	7,857	0.7	76	0.89
Atlanta	5,188	8,982	5,466	6,264	–2,748	0.9	26	0.95
Birmingham	2,768	5,523	3,156	2,102	265	0.7	15	1.07
Miami	1,318	4,458	1,736	959	1,763	1.4	74	1.16
Los Angeles	3,468	9,287	1,689	4,641	2,957	3.6	4.5	1.28
San Francisco	1,741	5,883	3,234	5,554	–2,905	1.1	54	1.25
(Oakland)	(922)	(2,016)	(920)	(1,674)	(–578)	(0.5)	(120)	(1.07)
Seattle	1,068	3,520	511	190	2,819	1.3	36	1.25
Denver	770	3,596	3,030	852	–286	1.0	25	1.07
San Diego	n.a.	n.a.	n.a.	n.a.	n.a.	n.a.	n.a.	n.a.
Phoenix	604	1,604	737	0	871	2.6	5	1.04

Source: National Commission on Urban Problems (1968).

ton, D.C., and Baltimore all had stocks of public housing in excess of 10,000 units in 1967, but with the exception of the nation's capital, these cities had removed more units through equivalent demolition and urban renewal than had been constructed. The other cities of the Northeast had fewer than 10,000 units. A notable case is St. Louis, with a stock of 7,245 public housing units, of which 13.0 percent stood vacant in 1967. The waiting list was equal only to the number of vacant units. Furthermore, equivalent demolition and urban renewal had removed 3,933 more units than had been constructed. Shortly after the commission conducted its study, St. Louis demolished its largest public housing project, the Pruitt-Igoe development. New York City and Chicago together had constructed 74,939 public housing units between 1949 and 1967, but the other fifteen major central cities of the Northeast had added just 65,627 units. And fourteen of the fifteen cities had removed more housing units through equivalent demolition and urban renewal than public housing units had been built.

What can account for this outcome? Why did cities not participate more fully in the public housing program, and why did slum units demolished exceed public housing units built? One reasonable answer is that the boom in housing construction in the suburbs and the decline in population of the central city meant that the filtering mechanism was supplying housing for low-income households. The need for public housing that had been perceived in 1949 was no longer acute. The private market was working—and producing a highly segregated housing market. Local officials may have felt that the private market was producing a satisfactory outcome, and that it was best not to take action that would be opposed by their white constituents.

Table 7.9 shows that the principal participant in the public housing program in the Sunbelt was New Orleans. The stock of public housing in New Orleans was 12,270 units in 1967, an increase of 6,889 from 1949. The equivalent demolition and urban renewal program had eliminated 4,413 slum units, so the net addition of these two programs was 7,857 units. The program had a very low vacancy rate of 0.7 percent (86 vacant units) and a waiting list that was 76 times the number of vacant units. The income limit was a relatively low 0.89 times the poverty level for a family of four of $3,365. The fact that public housing was in such great demand surely reflected the poverty in New Orleans. The huge city of Los Angeles had only 9,287 public housing units in 1967, and all of the other cities of the Sunbelt had fewer than 9,000 units. The public housing programs in the Sunbelt cities had low vacancy rates with the exception of Dallas and Fort Worth, which had rates of vacancy of 12.0 percent and 16.5 percent, respectively. The waiting list in Dallas was only 1.3 times the number of vacant units, and in Fort Worth the number of vacant units actually exceeded the waiting list. Public housing in Dallas–Fort Worth evidently was poorly managed.

Empirical research by Murray (1983, 1999) has investigated the question of whether the construction of public housing tended to "crowd out" construction of private housing units. Murray used national data on the public and private housing stocks, and found no evidence that additions to the stock of public housing subsequently reduced the stock of private housing. One might think that construction of public housing units would have reduced the demand for private housing by low-income households, and therefore tended to reduce the private housing stock. Murray's explanation for his finding is that public housing, with its low rent, provides an opportunity for females with children and the elderly to establish separate households. Most public housing units are occupied by female-headed families or the elderly. In effect, the demand for housing units by low-income people seems to have been somewhat elastic in that the provision of more public housing leads to the creation of more separate low-income households. Murray did not investigate the effect of the "equivalent demolition" provision on the stock of private housing, nor did he comment on the concentration of poverty that was produced by some of the large public housing projects in major cities.

Summary

This rather long chapter shows that black residents of the major urban areas of the nation in 1970 were segregated in residential areas with a housing stock of relatively low quality, paid relatively high rents and housing prices for units of a given quality level, faced higher prices and lower availability for consumer goods, sent their children to de facto segregated schools, and experienced discrimination in all aspects of employment. The strongly rising economic tide of the 1950s and 1960s discussed in Chapters 4, 5, and 6 had not lifted all of the boats—or at least had not lifted all of them to the same degree. Prejudice and discrimination on the part of the white population operated to hold back the black population. Whether the black population also was responsible for its own poverty and social problems because of a "culture of poverty" is discussed at length in Chapter 12. Anyone who had been aware of all of these conditions in 1964 should not have been surprised that eventually there would be some form of protest in response. What no one could have known at that time is that the urban crisis that emerged in the 1960s was to involve deep descent in the inner cities into high crime and other social pathologies that were exacerbated by conditions in the national economy in the 1970s. The next chapter discusses the first of the urban riots of the 1960s in New York City and Los Angeles, and examines the psychological basis of the "dark ghetto" as postulated by Kenneth B. Clark (1965).

8

August 1965

Chapter 7 examined the segregation and employment difficulties faced by black Americans in the major central cities during the time of rapid urban growth in the 1950s and 1960s. As it happened, the situation provided a combustible mixture that could turn into "civil disorder" after a seemingly minor provocative event. Urban riots were nothing new, but the rioting that began in New York City in July 1964 was of a different kind. Previously, most urban riots were largely perpetrated by whites against blacks who had "invaded" residential areas, recreational facilities, or other places that whites had thought were reserved for them. Rioters protested decisions to locate public housing in white neighborhoods, for example. The urban riots of the 1960s were largely perpetrated by blacks. They involved arson and other forms of unlawful behavior in black neighborhoods directed at institutions that were thought to be oppressive. Retails stores were frequent targets, in part because consumer goods could be obtained by looting as well.

New York City, 1964

Many students of the era, including Abu-Lughod (1999), believe that the first urban riot of the 1960s type took place in New York City in July 1964. As Abu-Lughod points out, New York City had a history of building a large amount of subsidized housing that was offered on a nondiscriminatory basis. There was a tradition of appointing blacks to higher positions and to civil service jobs, and the mayor's office had set up institutions intended to defuse racial tensions. But New York City was home to 1.09 million black people in 1960 (and had added one-half million more by 1970), and many of them were segregated in the huge areas of Harlem in Manhattan and Bedford-Stuyvesant in Brooklyn. The 1964 rioting was triggered by an altercation on July 15 in Manhattan between black teenagers and a build-ing janitor. It eventually led to the fatal shooting of a fifteen-year-old black boy by an off-duty white policeman. This shooting escalated into a battle between seventy-five policemen and hundreds of black youth, who had seen the dead boy. Many of the black youth saw the police as "oppressors" intent on maintaining the system of segregation. This incident produced rioting in both Harlem and Bedford-Stuyvesant that lasted for six nights. Abu-Lughod (1999, p. 209) states that as many as 4,000 people participated in vandal-ism, looting, or attacks on police. The rioting produced lots of broken glass, looted stores, streets littered with rubbish and broken glass, and a great deal of blood. After the riots had run their course, one rioter was dead, 118 were injured (although many more were treated in local hospitals), and 465 had been arrested. Abu-Lughod's judgment is that the rioting in New York was "an early warning that despite the progress made in the civil rights move-ment and the apparent health of the American economy, troubles lay ahead" (1999, p. 211).

A keen observer of the New York urban scene in general and the riots of 1964 in particular was Kenneth B. Clark. Professor Clark began his career as a research associate with Gunnar Myrdal's project for the Carnegie Corpo-ration in the early 1940s, and in 1964 was a professor of psychology at the City University of New York. He is a founder of Harlem Youth Opportuni-ties Unlimited (HARYOU), an organization financed in 1962 by the federal government and the mayor of New York City to study the conditions faced by youths in Harlem in preparation for setting up youth development programs. He spent the next two years studying youth in Harlem and the wider issues of blacks in heavily segregated urban neighborhoods in New York, areas he chose to call dark ghettoes. In July 1964 he was at work on his best-known book, *Dark Ghetto: Dilemmas of Social Power* (1965). In his foreword to this book, Gunnar Myrdal writes, "He is desperately anxious that the ugly facts of life in the Negro ghetto become really known to the ruling white majority. Among these facts of life, one most difficult to convey is how it feels to be enclosed by segregation" (Clark 1965, p. x).

In Myrdal's words, Clark's book is "an attempt to understand the com-bined problems of the confined Negro and the problems of the slum" (1965, p. xxii). Clark found that many people in the black urban slums believe that they are destined to remain there and suffer low social and economic status. The book is a detailed psychological examination of the pathologies that exist as consequences of the lack of both opportunity and power to change one's status. A selective list of the chapters and their topics can summarize the thrust of Clark's analysis:

- Social Dynamics of the Ghetto
  Economic and Social Decay
  Housing Decay
  Dynamics of Underemployment
  The Cycle of Family Instability
- The Psychology of the Ghetto
  Fantasy Projections
  Sex and Status
  The Negro Matriarchy and the Distorted Masculine Image
- The Pathology of the Ghetto
  Emotional Illness
  Homicide and Suicide
  Delinquency
  Drug Addiction
- Ghetto Schools: Separate and Unequal
  The Debate on the Causes of Inferiority
  Educational Atrophy: The Self-Fulfilling Prophecy
  Defeatism in Ghetto Schools

In assembling many of his facts and figures, Clark drew on his background as one of the researchers who worked on the 1954 *Brown v. Board of Education* case for the National Association for the Advancement of Colored People. He showed that students in the elementary schools in Central Harlem were two years behind their counterparts in the rest of the city in reading comprehension, word knowledge, and arithmetic. The IQ scores for sixth-grade students in Central Harlem were 86.3, compared to 99.8 for the rest of the city (1965, pp. 122–123).

Clark's strategy for change was to mobilize power to counteract the forces that resist change. He argued that blacks must convince the white majority that the situation he described hurts the entire nation, including the white majority itself. In his view, ethical appeals would not work unless tied to more concrete economic concerns. He was not an advocate of public demonstrations, which he thought would have decreasing impact. He believed blacks must use intellectual power coupled with appeals to morality. It is interesting that he was critical of the strategy pursued by Martin Luther King, Jr., because he felt that King's approach of nonviolent, passive resistance had been far more effective in the South than it would be in the North. The complex patterns of discrimination in housing, employment, and education in the northern cities could not be dramatized by King's approach, which included, in Clark's view, the admonition to "love the oppressor." King's methods called upon the Christian tradition, but Clark stated that:

A deeper analysis, however, might reveal an unrealistic, if not pathological, basis in King's doctrine as well. It is questionable whether masses of an oppressed group can in fact "love" their oppressor. The natural reactions to injustice, oppression, and humiliation are bitterness and resentment. The form which such bitterness takes need not be overtly violent, but the corrosion of the human spirit which is involved seems inevitable. It would appear, then, that any demand that a victim love his oppressor—in contrast with a mere tactical application of nonviolent, dignified resistance as a moral rebuke with concomitant power to arouse the conscience and effectiveness of others—imposes an additional and probably intolerable psychological burden. (1965, p. 218)

And in the end, white society must take up the cause as well. Clark saw the taunting of police by New York rioters in 1965 as an invitation to the police to act as the oppressors they were thought to be. While many of the looters were just looters, some of the rioters felt that they had nothing to lose and, as Clark asserted, "[The rioter's] acts were a desperate assertion of his desire to be treated as a man. He was affirmative up to the point of inviting death; he insisted upon being visible and understood. If this is the only way to relate to society at large, he would rather die than be ignored" (1965, p. 16).

Watts

The next chapter in the story brings us to August 1965. The Watts riot was sparked on August 11 by an alleged act of police brutality that involved the arrest of a young black motorist who was drunk and driving dangerously. Violence took place on a massive scale, with the rioting lasting five days. Thirty-four people were killed, at least 1,000 were wounded, and property damage was estimated at $200 million. White-owned stores in the Watts area were targets. It was estimated that about 35,000 blacks took part in the rioting, and that 16,000 police and National Guardsmen were needed to quell it. The violence took place in an area of 46.5 square miles. Rioters looted stores, set fires, attacked whites who happened to be passing by, stopped cars and set them afire, had gun battles with police, and threw rocks and aimed gunfire at firemen. The rioting in New York City during the previous summer pales in comparison.

We turn now to the report of the Governor's Commission on the Los Angeles Riots (1965), often known as the McCone Commission. This report was subsequently subject to considerable criticism, but its analysis illuminates several points. The McCone Commission noted that many believed that the urban problems in the cities of the Northeast were far less acute in Los Angeles. A study by the Urban League, cited by the commission, ranked Los Angeles first among sixty-eight major cities in a study of ten basic aspects of life for blacks—housing, employment, income, schools, and so on. The commission stated that the black areas of Los Angeles were not slums, noting that Watts consisted mainly of single-family houses that were owner occupied. The riot area contained parks and playgrounds. Blacks in Los Angeles were not discriminated against in voting or public accommodations, the commission asserted. The McCone Commission explained the riot as follows:

- The black population in Los Angeles County had increased rapidly from 75,000 in 1940 to 650,000 in 1965. Most of this increase was through migration from the South. These migrants had high hopes for social and economic advancement, but their hopes were not fulfilled. Further, the McCone Commission asserted that many of the recent migrants were "totally unprepared to meet the conditions of modern urban life. At the core of the cities where they cluster, law and order have only tenuous hold; the conditions of life itself are often marginal; idleness leads to despair and finally, mass violence supplies a momentary relief from the malaise" (1965, p. 3).
- A series of aggravating events took place in the year prior to the riot. The federal poverty programs of the Johnson administration were delayed in arriving, and did not live up to expectations. Civil disorder in other cities, such as New York, had gone unpunished, and this was widely reported. Advocates of civil disorder and violence to right wrongs were being publicized. And the voters of California by a two-thirds majority had passed Proposition 14, which repealed the state's Fair Housing Act.

The McCone Commission called the Watts riot "an explosion—a formless, quite senseless, all but hopeless violent protest—engaged in by a few but bringing great distress to all" (1965, p. 4).

The commission placed great stress on what they called the spiral of failure in the schools. The disadvantaged child arrives at school unprepared because of a deficient home background, falls farther and farther behind as the years pass, leaves school, and becomes part of the ranks of the unemployable. Schools that are dominated by children of this sort are abandoned by the parents of children who have more advantaged backgrounds, which only makes the problems worse. In short, the McCone Commission introduced its own version of the vicious circle.

After stating that the rioters had no moral or legal justification for their actions, the McCone Commission made a set of sweeping policy recommendations for improving the lives of the black and Hispanic population of the state. This effort would require heavy financial costs and large adjustments on the part of the rest of society, but the commission believed that the failure to undertake their program would have even higher costs. In that sense they were in tune with Kenneth Clark. Their basic policy prescriptions were three:

- To reduce the lack of job opportunity, immediately institute a comprehensive cooperative program of training and employment that would involve the black community, government at all levels, employers, and organized labor. The robust local economy provided a good environment that should be of benefit to all.
- Invest in a new and costly approach to the education of black children that would include early childhood education, small classes, and remedial instruction.
- Instruct law enforcement agencies to emphasize crime prevention, and to improve their means of handling community relationships and complaints from citizens.

Critics of the McCone Commission, such as Abu-Lughod (1999), found that the commission's emphasis on the failure of federal poverty programs to live up to their publicity and on exhortations to violence as causes of the riot was naïve. Furthermore, some subsequent survey research showed that many blacks in Los Angeles had hoped that the riots would call attention to real grievances. The study by Tomlinson and Sears (1967) found, in a survey of residents of the riot zone, that 56 percent of respondents believed that the riot had a purpose. Of those who thought there was a purpose in the rioting, 41 percent thought it would call attention to the problems faced by blacks, 33 percent believed it relieved pent-up frustrations, and 26 percent thought it would communicate to the powers that be and thereby improve conditions. In short, many blacks felt that the riot was not necessarily "quite senseless." And, perhaps most telling of all, the McCone Commission never recommended integration.

On August 12, the day after the Watts riot began, a much smaller riot began on the west side of Chicago. The precipitating incident took place outside a fire station that was being picketed by a civil rights group for its failure to hire blacks. Peaceful picketing had gone on for four weeks, but on that day a fire truck went out of control and killed a black woman. The picketers broke windows in the fire station and in nearby stores. A protest rally the following day drew a crowd that was in a mood to cause further damage. Some fires were set and some windows were broken. Police arrested about 100 protestors. A committee was formed to advocate a set of solutions to Mayor Richard Daley.

Also on August 12 this author attended Professor Kenneth Clark's class at the Harvard Summer School. Clark greeted the news of the start of the Watts riot with mixed emotions. Obviously riots are not good. But, as he had expressed in *Dark Ghetto*, rioting could in part be an expression of desperation that could not be ignored. Professor Clark could at least take some consolation in his belief that he had communicated with his class effectively. He called us an integrated audience, which is high praise from him. This author vividly remembers Professor Clark on that day.

Part III

The Years of Urban Crisis

9

The Great Society and the Urban Riots

Nineteen sixty-four and 1965 are watershed years in American urban history. Martin Luther King, Jr., and the civil rights movement achieved major victories with passage of the Civil Rights Act of 1964 and the Voting Rights Act of 1965 and decided to move the campaign to the inner city of Chicago. President Lyndon Johnson declared war on poverty and followed up with the most massive set of social programs since the New Deal. And some citizens of the Watts area of Los Angeles expressed their views on the urban condition by rioting; many more citizens followed up with more than 700 urban civil disturbances in the next six years. We are still living in the aftermath of Dr. King, the Great Society, and the urban riots. It is worthwhile to review these events of the turbulent 1960s.

The Great Society

On January 8, 1964, President Johnson's stirring State of the Union address began with these words:

> Let this session of Congress be known as the session which did more for civil rights than the last hundred sessions combined; as the session which enacted the most far-reaching tax cut of our time; as the session which declared all-out war on human poverty and unemployment in these United States; as the session which finally recognized the health needs of all our older citizens; as the session which reformed our tangled transportation and transit policies; as the session which achieved the most effective, efficient

foreign aid program ever; and as the session which helped to build more homes, more schools, more libraries, and more hospitals than any single session of Congress in the history of our Republic.[1]

Presidents rarely say such things. A few moments later he declared, "This administration today, here and now, declares unconditional war on poverty in America. I urge this Congress and all Americans to join with me in that effort."

Congress completed action on the Civil Rights Act of 1964. The bill had been sent to Congress by President John F. Kennedy on June 19, 1963. The House of Representatives promptly passed the bill on February 10, 1964, and it passed the Senate and was signed into law by President Johnson on July 2, 1964. The Civil Rights Act was a major victory for the Civil Rights movement. Its major features are as follows:

- Title I barred unequal application of voter registration requirements (but did not abolish literacy tests);
- Title II outlawed discrimination in public accommodations such as hotels, restaurants, and theaters engaged in interstate commerce (but exempted private clubs);
- Title III authorized the U.S. Attorney General to file suits to force school desegregation;
- Title VI prohibited discrimination on the basis of race, color, or national origin in programs that receive federal funds; and
- Title VII outlawed discrimination in any employment on the basis of race, national origin, gender, or religion, and prohibited retaliation against employees who oppose such unlawful discrimination. Title VII created the Equal Employment Opportunity Commission to investigate, mediate, and file lawsuits on behalf of employees. Title VII is perhaps the most far-reaching part of the Civil Rights Act in that it eventually changed attitudes and how the labor market operates.

The President followed up on March 16, 1964 with his "Proposal for a Nationwide War on the Sources of Poverty." The Economic Opportunity Act of 1964 was passed by Congress later in the year. The act created the Office of Economic Opportunity (OEO), which was headed by Sargent Shriver. The OEO initiated these programs:

- Community Action programs in the inner city,
- Job Corps to train young men for skilled employment,
- Neighborhood Youth Corps to put semi-skilled urban youth to work,
- Upward Bound to help able students,

- work-study program in which the government and colleges share the cost of hiring student workers, and
- Volunteers in Service to America (VISTA), the domestic Peace Corps.

OEO was not funded lavishly, but the president was far from finished with his agenda. A major revision of the food stamp program was also approved in 1964. The Food Stamp Act of 1964 was passed on August 31, 1964, and changed the program from one that used agricultural surpluses into a broad, means-tested "voucher" program to enable the poor to buy more and better food.

Even as the Civil Rights Act and the Economic Opportunity Act were moving toward final passage in Congress, President Johnson addressed the graduating class of the University of Michigan in May 1964 with the words, "We have the opportunity to move not only toward the rich society and the powerful society, but upward to the Great Society." In the summer of 1964 he set up 135 task forces to study a huge array of social problems. After the election in November he moved ahead with an enormous set of proposals. The State of the Union message of January 4, 1965, outlined proposals for medical care for the elderly, medical research, doubling the war on poverty, enforcement of the Civil Rights Act and elimination of barriers to the right to vote, changes in the immigration law, programs for education at all levels, programs to control crime, and programs for the cities to be administered by a new Department of Housing and Urban Development.

The Democratic Party had overwhelming control of both houses of Congress as a result of the 1964 election and quickly passed the president's proposals. The major legislation in 1965 included:

- Elementary and Secondary Education School Act of 1965, passed April 9, allocated $1 billion to schools with high concentrations of low-income students; created preschool programs (such as Head Start), bilingual education, and a variety of school counseling programs, and funded school libraries;
- Manpower Act of 1965, passed April 26, providing more job training funds;
- Older Americans Act of 1965, passed July 14;
- Social Security Amendments of 1965, passed July 30, creating Medicare (health insurance for the elderly) and Medicaid (medical care for those on welfare and other indigent people);
- Voting Rights Act of 1965, passed August 6, putting an end to literacy tests and authorizing the Department of Justice to send voting registrars to localities that had a history of denying people the right to vote— effectively enfranchising the black population of the South;

- Housing and Urban Development Act of 1965, passed August 10;
- Public Works and Economic Development Act of 1965, passed August 26;
- Department of Housing and Urban Development Act, passed September 9, creating the Department of Housing and Urban Development (HUD);
- Law Enforcement Assistance Act of 1965, passed September 22;
- National Foundation of the Arts and the Humanities Act of 1965, passed September 29;
- Amendment to the Immigration and Nationality Act, passed October 3, abolishing the restrictive 1924 Immigration Quotas Act and providing for liberalized entry based on family relationships and occupational qualifications;
- Heart Disease, Cancer, and Stroke Amendments of 1965, passed October 6;
- Economic Opportunity Amendments of 1965, passed October 9, adding to the OEO budget;
- Higher Education Act of 1965, passed November 8.

In addition, amendments to the Water Pollution Control Act and the Clean Air Act authorized the federal government to set standards for water quality and automobile emissions.

More programs were passed during the following years of the Johnson administration. The Department of Transportation was created in 1966. The Demonstration Cities and Metropolitan Development Act of 1966 created the Model Cities program. The program was administered by HUD and provided funds for more comprehensive efforts to improve cities. The goals of the program included rehabilitation, social service delivery, and citizen participation. Cities selected neighborhoods for this more comprehensive planning and treatment effort. The program generated controversy over control of the federal funds and was ended in 1974.

President Johnson's momentum in domestic policy slowed greatly after the escalation of the Vietnam War and the mid-term elections of 1966, but he did succeed with the Fair Housing Act of 1968 (Title VIII of the Civil Rights Act), which prohibits discrimination in the sale, financing, or rental of housing because of race, color, religion, sex, handicap, familial status, or national origin. Also, the Housing Act of 1968 was a major revision of federal housing policy. Analysts at HUD estimated that 26 million housing units would be needed between 1969 and 1978, and set a goal of 6 million subsidized units. The Housing Act of 1968 adopted this goal. The most important new programs were those that provided assistance through subsidized interest rates to families with modest incomes. Buyers could qualify for a mortgage interest rate as low as 1 percent, and developers of rental housing for low-income tenants had a similar opportunity. The homeownership subsidy program was operated through the Federal Housing Administration (FHA). The rules of the programs were such that the families targeted by these programs had incomes between the level that qualifies one for public housing and an upper limit—a range of roughly $4,000 to $6,500 per year. These programs were in place until 1974, when they were replaced by the Housing and Community Development Act of 1974. The 1968 Act increased subsidies to poor families in public housing by lowering the rents that they were required to pay, and provided additional funds for the construction of more public housing. Several features of the Act aimed to transform the urban renewal program into a program to help people who live in blighted or slum areas in accordance with the original intent of the program. Housing on urban renewal sites had been primarily for middle- and upper-income households, so the Act required housing for low- and moderate-income households in urban renewal projects for predominantly residential use. The Act attempted to attack the practice of "red-lining" of inner city areas by mortgage lenders by permitting the FHA to insure mortgages and the financing of repair and rehabilitation for houses located in older, declining urban areas. The higher conventional standards for FHA mortgage insurance need not apply. Lastly, the 1968 Act created the Government National Mortgage Association (GNMA, or "Ginny Mae"). GNMA was set up as an arm of HUD to issue securities backed by mortgages created under the various federal assistance programs. The Federal National Mortgage Association (FNMA) was changed to be a government-sponsored private corporation that would issue securities backed by private mortgages and not be subject to disadvantageous federal accounting procedures. GNMA was later changed to be a government-sponsored private corporation as well.

During the 1960s, the number of recipients of the nation's basic welfare program, Aid to Dependent Children (ADC), was greatly expanded. The total number of ADC recipients in the nation was 3.08 million in 1963, and this number nearly tripled to 10.81 million in 1973 even as the economy grew during these years and the poverty rate reached its all-time low of 11.1 percent of the population. Average benefit levels per family increased from $115 to $195 per month over this same period (a real increase of 20 percent). The dramatic increase in welfare recipients was the result of a series of policy changes that began in 1961, when federal law was changed to permit states to make ADC payments to families with an unemployed father. Ultimately, twenty-six states adopted this change. In 1966, the U.S. Department of Health, Education, and Welfare issued rules forbidding at-home eligibility checks, and legal services lawyers began to file cases challenging eligibility restrictions. In 1968 and 1969, the U.S. Supreme Court struck down the man-in-the-house

Table 9.1

ADC Recipients and Benefits

	Recipients (1,000s) 1960	Recipients (1,000s) 1973	Average benefit ($ per month) 1960	Average benefit ($ per month) 1973
California	283	1,330	168	211
New York	275	1,190	178	290
Illinois	154	773	168	262
Michigan	96	600	132	250
Pennsylvania	205	606	122	237
New Jersey	57	420	106	252
Ohio	111	497	122	175
Total	1,181	5,416		
Average			142	240

eligibility restriction and the one-year state residency requirement. And in 1967 Congress adopted the "thirty-and-a-third" rule. This rule encouraged welfare recipients to work by exempting the first $30 of earnings per month and reducing the ADC benefit by two-thirds of additional earnings (instead of dollar for dollar, as under the old rules). This last change in the program meant that many more families fell below the income level at which they qualified for some ADC benefit.

Much of the increase in ADC recipients occurred in the large, urban states. Numbers of recipients and average benefit levels for selected states are shown in Table 9.1. Together these seven states account for 55 percent of the increase in the number of ADC recipients.

Congress passed 226 out of 252 of President Johnson's legislative proposals by the end of his term. The effectiveness (or lack thereof, or even harm) of the Great Society programs has been a source of unending debate ever since. Many of these issues will be discussed in later chapters. But there can be no question that these programs are fundamental to the nation's landscape. Imagine a world without the Civil Rights Act, the Voting Rights Act, Medicare, Medicaid, the Equal Employment Opportunity Commission, federal aid to education, the Department of Housing and Urban Development, the Department of Transportation, and so on.

The Urban Riots

The United States has a long history of civil disturbances related to race. Prior to the 1940s most of those incidents involved whites attacking black people and property. Some urban rioting similar to the riots of the 1960s took place in 1943, but these were far fewer in number. The period of 1964 to 1971 was a period of widespread urban rioting that is unique in American history. The nation has experienced a small number of large-scale urban riots since 1971, such as Miami in 1980 and Los Angeles in 1992, but there has been no repeat of the riots of the 1960s.

My wife Glena and I were witnesses to the civil disturbance that took place in New Haven, Connecticut, during August 19–23, 1967. On these five nights, rocks and bottles were thrown at cars, windows were broken, stores were looted, and fires were started (one fire destroying a large, multifamily building). We saw the looting of a drugstore across the street from our apartment. Our landlord owned a small grocery store in the building adjacent to our apartment, and he sat up every night with a shotgun in his lap. His store was not looted. It is difficult to assess the amount of danger we were in, but the memory of those nights is lasting.

The sociologist Seymour Spilerman (1970) devised a definition of a race riot that has been in use since the early 1970s. An incident counts as a race riot if it was a spontaneous event with at least thirty participants, some of whom were African American, and if the incident resulted in property damage, looting, or other "aggressive behavior." Excluded are incidents that took place in school settings or were related to organized protests. An updated version of Spilerman's data is now the standard enumeration of the urban riots of 1964 to 1971. During these eight years there were 752 riots in which 228 people were killed, 12,741 injured, and 69,099 arrested. There were 15,835 incidents of arson. The peak year for rioting was 1968, with 289 riots in which 66 people died, 5,302 were injured, and 31,680 were arrested. Incidents of arson numbered 5,302. The vast majority of the riots were relatively minor incidents; no deaths occurred in 684 out of the 752 riots, for example. The worst riots in terms of lives lost were Detroit in July 1967 (43 deaths), Los Angeles in August 1965 (34 deaths), and Newark in July 1967 (24 deaths)—44 percent of the deaths occurred in these three major riots. Table 9.2 is a year-by-year enumeration of the riots of 1964–71.

What caused these riots, and what were their consequences? Consider first the causes. The National Advisory Commission on Civil Disorders (Kerner Commission), which was appointed in 1967 by President Johnson to examine the riots of 1967, issued its report in March 1968, which famously stated: "This is our basic conclusion. Our Nation is moving toward two societies, one black, one white—separate and unequal" (National Advisory Commission on Civil Disorders 1968).

The Kerner Commission blamed the riots on racial discrimination in employment, education, welfare, and housing. The commission's detailed study of the riots in 1967 contained the following conclusions:

Table 9.2

The Urban Riots

	1964	1965	1966	1967	1968	1969	1970	1971	Total
Number of riots	11	11	53	158	289	124	68	38	752
Days of riots	34	20	109	408	739	284	126	82	1,802
Killed	2	35	11	83	66	13	13	5	228
Injured	996	1,132	525	2,801	5,302	861	710	414	12,741
Arrested	2,917	4,219	5,107	17,011	31,680	4,730	2,027	1,408	69,099

- The riots involved mostly young black men who were acting against white society, authority, and property. Many of these participants were high school dropouts who were unemployed or worked in menial jobs.
- Initial damage estimates were exaggerated.
- The overwhelming majority of persons killed or injured were black civilians.
- A series of incidents, capped by a final incident, led to disorder. Often these incidents were police actions in a black neighborhood.
- Rioting usually began with rock and bottle throwing, and escalated to looting and (sometimes) worse.
- The riots were not planned or directed by any organization or group, but militant organizations and individuals sought to encourage violence and added to the atmosphere of violence.
- The Kerner Commission found deeply felt grievances among the residents of the riot areas in Detroit and Newark (the two largest riots of 1967). The grievances that were felt most intensely were regarding police practices, unemployment and underemployment, and inadequate housing. The residents also expressed dissatisfaction with education, the administration of justice, federal programs, welfare programs, consumer and credit practices, and recreation facilities. They felt that the political system and grievance mechanisms were ineffective, and that whites had disrespectful attitudes toward blacks.

These findings led the commission to search for the basic causes of the urban riots. The commission concluded that white racism is essentially responsible for the explosive mixture that has been accumulating in our cities since the end of World War II. Among the ingredients of this mixture are:

- pervasive discrimination and segregation in employment, education, and housing, which have resulted in the continuing exclusion of large numbers of blacks from the benefits of economic progress;
- black in-migration and white exodus, which have produced the massive and growing concentrations of impoverished blacks in our major cities, creating a growing crisis of deteriorating facilities and services and unmet human needs; and
- the black ghettos, where segregation and poverty converge on the young to destroy opportunity and enforce failure. Crime, drug addiction, dependency on welfare, and bitterness and resentment against society in general, and white society in particular, are the result.

These factors were the explosive mixture, but not the immediate causes of the riots at that particular time. What other specific ingredients set off the riots?

The commission concluded that there were unfulfilled expectations after the success of the civil rights movement in the South (leading to the Civil Rights Act of 1964, the Voting Rights Act of 1965, and other legislative and judicial victories). Furthermore, a climate of encouraging violence had been created by the actions of some southern whites against the civil rights movement and by some protesters. There was a "new mood" among some young blacks that included increased self-esteem and racial pride coupled with a feeling of powerlessness—all expressed by the words "Black Power." Finally, the police departments of the day were dominated by white officers, and they came to symbolize white racism and discrimination. The commission's report is a detailed examination of all of these factors.

The commission advocated a broad social program to open up employment and educational opportunity, to expand welfare, and to break down patterns of segregation in housing. Racial discrimination existed in every urban area to some extent, but while riots were numerous, only a few were major incidents. Was it possible to pinpoint specific causes of the riots after the fact?

Researchers such as Spilerman (1970) and others took up the challenge of identifying the proximate causes of the riots. The only variables that consistently were related to severe riots are the size of the African American population and region—rioting was less likely in the South than in the Northeast, Midwest, and West. One study found that riots were less likely and less severe if the rate of homeownership among African Americans was higher. Otherwise, as William Collins and Robert Margo (2004), the authors of the most recent studies of the riots, put it, "conditional on black population size and region, severe riots were essentially idiosyncratic events." In most cases there was some specific event that triggered the riot. For example, the spark for the Watts riot of 1965 was an incident involving an African American motorist and white police officers. The Detroit riot of 1967 started with a police raid on an after-hours bar. And, as all will recall, the murder of Dr. Martin Luther King, Jr., in April 1968 set off riots around the nation. Collins and Margo (2004, 2005) found that rioting in the wake of the King assassination was less likely in places where it rained on the critical nights.

The research thus tells us that, for an urban area not located in the South with a large African American population, a major riot was essentially a random event. However, much more can be said about the consequences of a major riot. Collins and Margo (2004, 2005) have investigated the effects on the labor market and the housing market. Negative effects are found in both markets in the sense that African Americans who lived in the central cities with severe riots had lower increases in household income and housing prices than did their counterparts in cities that did not experience a severe riot. Both of these outcomes may reflect a greater propensity of more prosperous African Americans to move out of those central cities where major riots occurred. Collins and Margo found that these effects could be seen in 1970, and persisted at least to 1980. Indeed, the negative effect on the value of houses owned by African Americans in the riot cities, relative to other cities, increased in the 1970s.

A detailed examination of the census tracts where rioting took place in Cleveland, Detroit, Los Angeles, Newark, and Washington, D.C., shows that the population in those tracts fell by 33 percent from 1960 to 1980, while the population in the other census tracts in those cities changed only a small amount (they actually declined by 2 percent). The starkest example is Cleveland; the population of the riot tracts was 71,575 in 1960, 45,487 in 1970, and 25,330 in 1980—a decline of 65 percent over twenty years. The rest of Cleveland lost 32 percent of its population during the same time. Cleveland, Detroit, Newark, and Washington, D.C., were declining central cities during those twenty years. In contrast, the population of the city of Los Angeles increased by a robust 20 percent from 1960 to 1980; with a 23 percent increase in the nonriot tracts and a 1 percent decrease in the riot tracts. It is reasonably clear that a major riot had severe and long-lasting effects on the places where it occurred and on the people who remained. Those who could do so abandoned the riot-torn areas of the city.

Martin Luther King, Jr., in Chicago

On January 26, 1966, Martin Luther King, Jr., his wife Coretta, and their four children moved into an apartment in a black slum on the West Side of Chicago. King and his organization, the Southern Christian Leadership Conference (SCLC), had selected the inner city of Chicago for the next phase of the civil rights movement. With passage of the Civil Rights Act of 1964 and the Voting Rights Act of 1965, SCLC saw the Chicago effort as the first attempt to attack economic discrimination rather than lack of voting rights or public access. The campaign included a huge rally at Soldier Field and a march to City Hall, at which King presented his demands for open housing and jobs in all-white industries.

The purpose of King's Chicago campaign was to show that race was a national problem, and in this it succeeded in spectacular fashion. He led an integrated march into the all-white Marquette Park neighborhood on the South Side, and was hit by a rock thrown from a crowd of thousands of angry whites. "I have never seen such hate in my life," King said. But the marches to Marquette Park and Cicero, a suburb adjacent to the West Side of Chicago, produced no substantial results. Mayor Daley dispatched police to defend the marchers, met with King, and spoke in conciliatory tones. Dr. King and

Mayor Daley met at a "summit" in August 1966 and crafted an agreement that pledged effort on open housing and research to track progress. Obviously the campaign did not end segregation, but Dr. King's biographer, Taylor Branch (2006), concludes that it did start a process of change. And without Chicago, Dr. King would have been regarded more as a regional figure than a national hero.

The murder of the apostle of nonviolence in 1968 set off what was probably the largest concentration of urban rioting in the nation's history.

Conclusion

What are we to make of this amazing time? I think that we can conclude that the urban crisis had begun. President Johnson and the Congress recognized that the society faced serious domestic problems centered in cities. They responded in 1965 with the greatest flurry of social policy legislation since the New Deal. At the same time—four days after the passage of the Voting Rights Act of 1965 and in the middle of this flurry of federal government action—the urban riots began in earnest in Watts. The peak years for civil disturbances were 1967 and 1968, two and three years after the Great Society programs had been enacted. The Kerner Commission blamed many factors for the riots, but among those factors cited were unfulfilled expectations after the civil rights and Great Society victories. Is this a credible conclusion? Did people really expect major changes that quickly? The urban crisis had begun, and it was to get much worse in many respects before it began to get better.

Note

1. The quotes from President Johnson are taken from *Public Papers of the Presidents of the United States: Lyndon B. Johnson, 1963–64*. Washington, DC: U.S. Government Printing Office, 1965.

10
Urban Employment Trends in the Northeast

This chapter is a depiction of the urban crisis in the major urban areas of the Northeast. The crisis was most severe in the 1970s, and continued in the decade of the 1980s in most of these urban areas. Data on population, employment, income, poverty, and housing are used to highlight the severe problems experienced by all of the major northeastern urban areas. The contrasts between the 1970–90 period and the previous twenty years are startling. The population of the seventeen northeastern metropolitan areas in this study grew by an average of 40 percent from 1950 to 1970, but population growth during 1970–90 averaged only 5.6 percent. Five metropolitan areas experienced population declines from 1970 to 1990—New York, Detroit, Pittsburgh, Cleveland, and Buffalo. Population did not change in metropolitan Boston, and the Philadelphia, St. Louis, and Milwaukee metropolitan areas grew by 2.0 percent or less. The real increase in median family incomes in these metropolitan areas was 89 percent on average for 1949 to 1969, but was only 7.6 percent from 1969 to 1989. Median family real income actually declined (by 1.5 percent) in metropolitan Detroit. The central cities suffered severe problems, which are discussed in detail in Chapter 13. As we saw in Chapter 4, central cities in the Northeast lost population during 1950–70. Four central cities annexed territory and gained population—Milwaukee, Kansas City, Indianapolis, and Columbus. The thirteen central cities that were unable to annex territory lost an average of 13.2 percent of their population during this period, but those same central cities lost an average of 21.9 percent of their population from 1970 to 1990. In addition, Milwaukee, Kansas City, and Indianapolis did not annex territory and also lost population over the 1970–90 period. Only Columbus added territory and gained population. The poverty rate in the seventeen central

Table 10.1

Population and Employment in Metropolitan New York: 1970–1990

	1970	1980	1990
Population (1000s)			
New York City	7,895	7,072	7,323
Suburbs	9,685	9,880	10,181
Total	17,580	16,952	17,504
Black population (percent)			
New York City	20.1	24.0	25.6
Suburbs	9.0	9.8	10.5
Total	14.0	15.7	16.8
Employment of residents (1000s)			
New York City	3,205	2,925	3,264
Suburbs	3,859	4,485	5,161
Total	7,064	7,410	8,425
Poverty rate (percent)			
New York City	14.8	20.0	19.3
Suburbs	6.7	8.	6.5
Total	10.3	13.0	11.9

Source: HUD State of the Cities Data.

cities increased from 14.7 percent in 1970 to 20.6 percent in 1990, and many neighborhoods became areas in which poverty was highly concentrated.

As usual, we begin with New York.

New York

The urban problems faced by New York City are evident in the basic data on population, employment of residents, and poverty shown in Table 10.1. The population of the city fell by 823,000 people in the 1970s, a decline of 10.4 percent. The rest of the metropolitan area gained only 195,000 people, so the population of the entire metropolitan area dropped from 17.58 million to 16.95 million over these ten years. Population grew at both the metropolitan and central city levels in the 1980s, but the 1990 Census found New York City with a population of 7.23 million, which is 572,000 fewer than its population in 1970. The population of the metropolitan area in 1990 had not yet regained its 1970 level. The number of employed residents of New York City declined by 8.7 percent in the 1970s even though total employment in the metropolitan area increased by 4.9 percent. The ratio of employment to population increased in the metropolitan area from 40.2 percent to 43.7 percent, but this ratio for New York City increased only from 40.6 percent to 41.4 percent. The poverty rate in New York City jumped from 14.8 percent to 20.0 percent, so the number of people in poverty in the city increased from 1.17 million to 1.41 million. The poverty rate in the city had exceeded the national poverty rate of 12.6 percent by 2.2 percent in 1970. The national poverty rate was 13.0 percent in 1980, so the difference between New York City and the nation had increased to 7.0 percent. Perhaps even more telling is the finding by Jargowsky (1997) that the number of people who were living in high-poverty areas (poverty rate greater than 40 percent) increased from 300,527 to 1,002,015. The 1970s were a very bad decade for New York City.

Decline in New York City was not spread evenly. For example, the South Bronx became known as the worst slum in America after a visit by President Jimmy Carter in 1977. As described by von Hoffman (2003), the decline of the South Bronx after 1970 is startling. An area consisting of the neighborhoods called Hunt's Point, Crotona Park East, Morrisania, Melrose, and Longwood had a population of 247,000 in 1970 housed in 55,400 housing units. In 1980 the population was only 91,800, and the number of standing housing units had dropped to 36,100. Crotona Park East was home to 61,400 souls in 1970, but only 13,400 were there in 1980. The devastation of the housing stock in this neighborhood almost defies description: the number of units fell from 18,800 in 1970 to 6,200 in 1980. The South Bronx stabilized and started to revive in the 1980s. Population increased to 100,600, but the number of housing units declined to 33,400. The story of the revival of the South Bronx will be told in Chapter 15.

The racial composition of New York City was changing somewhat as well. The black population percentage increased from 20.1 percent to 24.0 percent in the 1970s, and then increased slightly again in the 1980s to 25.6 percent. Overall, the percentage of blacks in the population increased modestly from 14.0 percent to 16.2 percent from 1970 to 1990. The percentage of the population of New York City that was of Puerto Rican heritage increased from 10.3 percent to 12.2 percent in the 1970s and remained constant in the 1980s. As we shall see, these changes are modest compared to the experience of some of the other major central cities in the Northeast.

A notable event in the history of New York is the near-bankruptcy of the city. The headline in the New York *Daily News* on October 29 proclaimed, "FORD TO CITY: DROP DEAD." The Ford in question is, of course, the president of the United States, and "drop dead" refers to the lack of interest by the federal government in bailing out the municipal government. Simply stated, the New York City fiscal crisis stemmed from expenditures in excess of income that had become so large that banks refused to continue to lend money to the city. The budget gap was being filled by short-term borrowing (which is technically illegal), delays in payments, overestimates of projected income, and questionable accounting methods. As Abu-Lughod (1999) re-counts, the New York fiscal crisis has been examined in depth by numerous investigators. Their basic conclusion is that New York City was providing more services for its residents than other cities, and that it relied heavily on its own tax revenues. For example, while the expenditures on welfare in most states were shared equally between the state and the federal government, New York City was obliged to pay half of the state's share. New York City also provided transit, health care, and education services that went well beyond those provided in other cities such as Chicago and Los Angeles. The recession of 1973–75 precipitated by the first oil price shock meant that tax revenues fell and expenditures on welfare and other services increased. The resolution of the New York fiscal crisis involved scaling back services (including programs at the City University of New York), increased taxes, and increased revenues from the state of New York and, ultimately, from the federal government—but only after the creation of the Municipal Assistance Corporation by bankers. This private corporation required retrenchment by the city in exchange for support of a bond issue. Also, the state of New York now supervises the fiscal operations of the city more carefully.

The New York metropolitan area began its comeback from the 1970s after the recession of 1982. As Table 10.1 shows, employment in the metropolitan area increased by 13.7 percent in the 1980s as population increased by only 3.3 percent. New York City gained 3.5 percent in population, and the number of residents who were employed increased by 11.6 percent. However, the poverty rate in the city did not respond, changing only slightly to 19.3 percent. The number of poor people in New York City in 1990 was 1.41 million—identical to the number in 1980.

The metropolitan area was undergoing an economic transformation in the 1970s and 1980s that is illustrated in Table 10.2. Total employment increased from 7.06 million to 8.43 million during these twenty years, but employment in manufacturing fell from 1.61 million to 1.18 million, a decline of 26.4 percent. Manufacturing employment was 22.7 percent of total employment in 1970, but provided only 14.0 percent of the jobs in 1990. The sources of employment growth were in professional services and, to a lesser extent, in finance, insurance, and real estate (FIRE) and in business services. The larg-est component of professional services is health services, followed by legal services, educational services (private), and social services. Employment in professional services almost doubled over the 1970–90 period from 1.20 million to 2.21 million. This growth was fueled by the increased demand for health care created in large part by the Medicare and Medicaid programs passed during the Johnson administration. Finance, insurance, and real estate, as well as business services (accounting, computer services, and so on), also

Table 10.2

Employment by Industry in Metropolitan New York (1,000s)

	1970	1980	1990
Total	7,064	7,410	8,425
Manufacturing	1,607	1,522	1,183
FIRE*	546	680	889
Business services	302	437	489
Professional services	1,196	1,629	2,212
Other	3,413	3,142	3,652

* Finance, insurance, and real estate.
Source: HUD State of the Cities Data.

contributed to employment growth in metropolitan New York. The FIRE sector added 343,000 jobs over twenty years, including 209,000 jobs in the 1980s. Business services employment grew by 61.9 percent from 1970 to 1990. The economic transformation of metropolitan New York (and the other urban areas of the Northeast) involved a sharp reduction in employment in manufacturing, rapid increase in the demand for health care and other professional services, and a large shift to financial and business services. The growth in financial and business services in New York is thought to be partly a result of its status as a "global city."

A brief depiction of housing in metropolitan New York is shown in Table 10.3. The number of housing units in the city remained roughly constant over the twenty-year period. The vacancy rate in the city increased from a very low 2.7 percent in 1970 to over 5 percent in 1980 and 1990, so the number of occupied units actually declined by 1.7 percent in the 1970s (and then increased by 1.1 percent in the 1980s). However, the vacancy rate in New York City is quite low compared to other major central cities of the Northeast. The number of housing units in the metropolitan area increased by 8.1 percent in the 1970s even though the population declined. Household sizes continued to decline. Housing units increased another 5.4 percent in the 1980s. The vacancy rate increased from 3.2 percent in 1970 to 5.2 percent in 1990. As one would expect, the rate of home ownership in New York City is low—less than 30 percent during this period. Home ownership did increase in the 1980s from 23.4 percent to 28.7 percent.

How did the population and employment in New York during the 1970s and 1980s compare to forecasts? Such a comparison is useful because it illustrates whether the crisis of the 1970s was anticipated by the forecasters. One set of forecasts is in print. The New York Metropolitan Study discussed in Chapter 4 included a comprehensive set of forecasts of population and employment

Table 10.3

Housing Units in Metropolitan New York (1,000s)

	1970	1980	1990
Housing units			
New York City	2,917	2,941	2,979
Suburbs	3,011	3,466	3,773
Vacancy rate (percent)			
New York City	2.7	5.2	5.4
Suburbs	4.0	4.2	5.1
Ownership rate (percent)			
New York City	23.6	23.4	28.7
Suburbs	64.1	64.5	67.5

Source: HUD State of the Cities Data.

for 1965, 1975, and 1985. Those forecasts were published in Vernon (1960) in the final volume of the series titled *Metropolis 1985*. The population of the metropolitan area (excluding Connecticut) was projected to increase by 18.9 percent from 1955 to 1965, 14.5 percent over the 1965–75 decade, and then another 12.9 percent by 1985 for a total increase of 53.7 percent. The projected population for 1985 was 22.3 million for the metropolitan area. Given the actual population figures of 16.95 million for 1980 and 17.50 million for 1990, the actual population for 1985 was about 17.25 million—a forecast error of 29 percent. As Vernon (1960, p. 290) recounts, the New York forecasters were working from a set of national population forecasts provided by the Bureau of the Census that turned out to be too high. The national population forecasts were 217 million for 1970 (7.4 percent too high) and 262 million for 1980 (16 percent too high). The population of the nation was projected to increase by 73.3 percent from 1955 to 1985. The New York forecasters expected that their metropolitan area would grow more slowly than the nation, but they still overestimated the local growth.

The forecasters with the New York Metropolitan Study did project a decline in the population of New York City from 7.90 million in 1965 to 7.76 million in 1975 and 7.69 million in 1985. While they missed the magnitude of the decline, they did anticipate that the central city even of a metropolitan area that was growing briskly would lose population to the suburbs.

Employment was projected to increase in the metropolitan area by 12 to 15 percent per decade for 1956 to 1985, reaching 9.0 million in 1985. This was an overestimate of about 12 percent (not bad), as actual employment was approximately 8.0 million in 1985. Employment located in New York City (by place of work) was projected to increase by 13 percent over the twenty-nine years from 1956 to 1985. This projection was coupled with the expectation that some older areas of the city outside the central business district would lose jobs as employers sought newer facilities. In summary, the forecasts provided by the New York Metropolitan Study in the late 1950s overstated the growth of the metropolitan area—especially the population growth—but they did foresee some population decline in the city and employment decline in the city's older industrial districts. The fact that growth at the metropolitan level was overstated is not surprising, given the recent history. And the hint of problems for the central city was prescient. As we shall see, the forecasts that were made for Chicago at the same time were not as accurate, or as prescient.

Chicago

Unlike the New York metropolitan area, metropolitan Chicago did not experience population loss. Otherwise, the patterns are similar. As shown in Table 10.4, population growth in the metropolitan area was slow in the 1970s and 1980s; total growth for the twenty years was 5.7 percent, which matches the population growth of 5.1 percent for the entire Northeast. The population of the central city declined by 358,000 in the 1970s (10.6 percent loss) and 221,000 in the 1980s (7.4 percent). The population of the city decline of 579,000 was 17.2 percent of the population of 3.36 million in 1970. Slow overall population growth, coupled with a strong trend of movement to the suburbs, translated into a large loss for the central city—larger in percentage terms than the population loss in New York City. As in New York, the decline in the central city was not spread evenly.

The population of the city of Chicago became increasingly black in the 1970s, going from 32.8 percent in 1970 to 39.5 percent in 1980. The black population in the city increased from 1.103 million to 1.188 million during this decade, an increase of 85,000. The black population of the suburbs increased by 102,000—from 128,000 to 230,000. The decade of the 1980s is a different story for the black population of metropolitan Chicago. The total black population declined slightly from 1.418 million to 1.410 million, and the black population in the central city fell from 1.188 million to 1.076 million as the black population in the suburbs increased by 104,000. This represents a different version of a familiar pattern: slow or no growth at the metropolitan level, coupled with movement to the suburbs, means decline in the central city. But this time it is the black population of metropolitan Chicago.

The employment data in Table 10.4 show that total employment in the metropolitan area grew by a relatively robust 23.7 percent from 1970 to 1990 as the baby boomers grew up and joined the work force and as women increasingly sought employment. However, the number of employed residents of the

Table 10.4

Population and Employment in Metropolitan Chicago: 1970–1990

	1970	1980	1990
Population (1,000s)			
Chicago	3,363	3,005	2,784
Suburbs	3,646	4,241	4,626
Total	7,009	7,246	7,410
Black population (percent)			
Chicago	32.8	39.5	38.6
Suburbs	3.8	5.4	7.2
Total	17.7	19.6	19.0
Employment of residents (1,000s)			
Chicago	1,390	1,237	1,209
Suburbs	1,549	2,091	2,426
Total	2,939	3,328	3,635
Poverty rate (percent)			
Chicago	14.4	20.3	21.6
Suburbs	4.2	4.9	5.1
Total	9.1	11.3	11.3

Source: HUD State of the Cities Data.

central city declined. The employment decline of Chicagoans in the 1970s was 13.0 percent, which exceeds the decline in population over the same period of 10.6 percent. During the 1980s, the number of employed Chicago residents fell by only 2.3 percent as the population fell by 7.4 percent. The poverty rate of city residents jumped from 14.4 percent in 1970 to 20.3 percent in 1980, and ended the decade of the 1980s at 21.6 percent. Poverty became increasingly concentrated in certain areas of the central city. Jargowsky (1997) shows that the number of people living in high-poverty areas increased from 156,270 in 1970 to 396,200 in 1990. The city was losing population in large numbers (including some of its black population in the 1980s), and those who remained increasingly were impoverished. In relative terms, the suburbs prospered as the central city became smaller and poorer.

Metropolitan Chicago also was undergoing a major transformation of its economy during these years. Total employment increased by 23.7 percent from 1970 to 1990 (from 2.94 million to 3.64 million), but employment in its large manufacturing sector declined from 856,000 to 700,000. Manufacturing was 29.1 percent of total employment in 1970, and this proportion had dropped to 19.3 percent in 1990. The sectors of employment growth were professional services, business services, and FIRE. Employment in professional services increased from 422,000 in 1970 to 818,000 in 1990, a level that exceeds employment in manufacturing. The decline in employment among residents of the central city is a result of the drop in manufacturing employment for this group. The number of central city residents who were employed in manufacturing fell from 404,000 in 1970 to 225,000 in 1990.

The housing market in the metropolitan area reflects the decline of the central city and the growth of the suburbs. Total housing units increased by 20.5 percent over the twenty years (from 2.22 to 2.67 million units), and the overall vacancy rate increased modestly from 4.6 percent to 6.1 percent. But the number of units in the central city fell from 1.21 to 1.13 million over this same period, a drop of 76,000 units (6.3 percent). Furthermore, the vacancy rate in the central city increased from 5.8 percent to 9.3 percent from 1970 to 1990, which implies that the decline in occupied units was 111,000 (9.8 percent). Some neighborhoods, especially those in the black residential areas of the south and west sides of the city, experienced huge losses of population and housing units. For example, von Hoffman (2003) shows that the population of the black Near–South Side fell from 177,100 in 1970 to 99,800 in 1990. The number of housing units in this same area fell from 62,100 to 49,000, and the vacancy rate increased from 7.9 percent to 18.6 percent. In many instances housing units were simply abandoned by their owners when rents could no longer cover operating expenses. The situation in the suburbs was quite different. The total number of housing units in the suburbs increased from 1.01 to 1.54 million (52.4 percent) and, in spite of this huge growth, the vacancy rate remained low at 2.8 percent in 1970 and 3.8 percent in 1990.

A good approach to understanding these basic facts about the housing market is called the filtering model. The idea is that new units are built in the suburbs in response to consumer demand. If the number of new units built exceeds the growth in demand, then some older units will become vacant and ultimately will be removed from the housing stock because it is no longer profitable to operate them. Those vacant units tend to be concentrated in certain areas of the inner city that are no longer attractive places to live. Such places enter a vicious circle of decline as vacancy and abandonment beget more vacancy and abandonment.

What accounts for the decline of the city of Chicago during these years? The basic explanations are pretty straightforward. First, population growth of the metropolitan area slowed to its lowest rate in history of 2.26 percent in the 1980s (compared to 2.67 percent in the 1930s and 3.38 percent in the 1970s). Slow population growth for the metropolitan area over the 1970–90 period was especially damaging to the central city for (at least) three reasons:

- The system of expressways was completed in the decade of the 1960s, with the last leg of the system opening in 1970. This system reduced

commuting times significantly and enabled people to move to new houses in the suburbs. The expressway system was relatively uncongested in the 1970s and 1980s (in contrast to the current situation).
- Employment opportunities in the central city outside of the downtown area declined as manufacturing declined and employment growth took place in the suburbs.
- The riots of 1968 were fresh in the minds of Chicagoans of all races.

All of this amounts to a double-barreled assault on the central city—slow overall growth with strong incentives to move to the suburbs.

Did the official forecasters for the metropolitan area foresee any of this? The short answer is "no." The official forecasts began with the work of the Chicago Area Transportation Study (CATS) in the late 1950s. The task of this agency is to forecast the demand for transportation facilities and formulate the transportation plan for the metropolitan area. Their first tasks therefore were to project population and employment for a target year, which was 1980. Those projections were much too high, and the possibility that the central city might decline was not discussed. These projections are discussed in detail in McDonald (1988). CATS assumed that the population of the metropolitan area would grow at the same rate as the nation's population. This assumption led to a population projection of 9.5 million (for a five-county metropolitan area) in 1980, compared to an actual population of 7.48 million—an overestimate of 27 percent. CATS projected that the population of the city of Chicago would level off at 3.7 million (compared to 3.0 million in 1980). The projection for total employment for 1980 exceeded the actual employment level for this same five-county area by 34 percent. The projection for manufacturing employment of 1.4 million was too high by 61 percent. One should not make too much of these overestimates. Transportation planners must make plans that can accommodate growth, and the failure to have a plan when growth comes as a surprise is very inefficient. What is important is that, because growth was expected to continue unabated, the transportation planners did not have a plan in place for what actually happened—slow metropolitan growth and central city decline.

Philadelphia and Detroit

Philadelphia and Detroit were similar in total size but provide some contrast in the paths that they followed during the urban crisis period. Philadelphia suffered through the 1970s, but showed signs of revival in the 1980s—especially in employment growth. The decline of the central city slowed significantly. The record of employment in the Detroit urban area is not as bad as one might

Table 10.5

Metropolitan Areas of the Northeast: 1970–1990 (in percent)

	Population growth	Employment growth	Median family income growth	Manufacturing employment 1970
New York	−3.3	19.3	14.5	22.7
Chicago	5.7	23.7	6.3	29.1
Philadelphia	0.8	21.3	16.3	28.2
Detroit	−1.1	14.4	−1.5	35.7
Boston	0.0	28.1	5.0	22.8
Pittsburgh	−10.8	4.3	1.8	30.5
St. Louis	1.5	26.4	8.5	26.7
Cleveland	−9.0	4.3	−3.2	34.4
Washington, D.C.	31.9	72.4	26.9	6.6
Baltimore	14.0	43.4	19.4	22.8
Minneapolis–St. Paul	25.2	63.1	12.0	24.1
Buffalo	−11.9	6.5	−5.8	32.3
Cincinnati	6.0	33.3	7.4	31.1
Milwaukee	2.0	22.3	2.9	33.6
Kansas City	14.5	38.2	7.9	20.8
Indianapolis	10.6	38.6	4.0	29.9
Columbus	18.6	50.4	7.4	23.8
Mean	5.6	30.0	7.3	26.8

Source: HUD State of the Cities Data.

have guessed, but the overall decline in metropolitan population, coupled with a huge exit of the white population from the central city to the suburbs, left the city of Detroit largely black and increasingly poor. The basic data on these urban areas and their central cities are found in Tables 10.5 and 10.6.

The Philadelphia story for the 1970s and the 1980s is a combination of the New York and Chicago stories. Table 10.5 shows that the population of the metropolitan area declined from 4.88 million in 1970 to 4.78 million in 1980 (as in New York), and then rebounded to 4.92 million in 1990 to finish with an increase of 0.9 percent over the twenty years. The population of the city of Philadelphia dropped in the 1970s from 1.95 million to 1.69 million (a decline of 13.4 percent in this one decade). The subsequent decline in population to 1.59 million in 1990 was "only" 6.0 percent. Here is the familiar story: in this case, no growth at the metropolitan level and a very large decline in the central city of 363,000 people (18.6 percent) over twenty years. The central city was able to expand its land area slightly from 128.5 to 135.1 square miles, but the effects of this expansion are negligible.

Table 10.6

Central Cities of the Northeast: 1970–1990 (in percent)

	Population change	Poverty in 1970	Poverty in 1990	Black population 1970	Black population 1990
New York	−7.2	14.8	19.3	20.1	25.6
Chicago	−17.2	14.4	21.6	32.8	38.6
Philadelphia	−18.6	15.1	20.3	33.6	39.5
Detroit	−32.0	14.7	32.6	43.7	75.5
Boston	−10.5	15.5	18.7	16.4	24.0
Pittsburgh	−28.8	15.0	21.4	20.2	25.7
St. Louis	−36.2	19.9	24.6	40.8	47.4
Cleveland	−32.6	17.1	28.7	38.3	46.2
Washington, D.C.	−19.8	16.3	16.9	71.7	65.2
Baltimore	−18.8	18.0	21.9	46.4	59.0
Minneapolis– St. Paul	−14.0	10.6	17.7	4.0	10.5
Buffalo	−29.2	14.8	25.6	20.3	30.5
Cincinnati	−19.6	17.1	24.3	27.6	37.9
Milwaukee	−12.4	11.2	22.2	14.6	30.3
Kansas City	−8.3	12.5	15.3	22.1	29.4
Indianapolis	−1.9	9.5	12.5	18.0	22.4
Columbus	17.2*	13.2	17.2	18.5	22.4
Mean	−17.1	14.7	21.2	28.8	37.1

* Land area of central city increased by 41.8 percent.
Source: HUD State of the Cities Data.

The black population of the metropolitan area increased by 10.0 percent over the period from 844,000 to 928,000, and all of that growth took place in the suburbs. The black population in the central city actually declined slightly from 654,000 in 1970 to 627,000 in 1990, so the suburban black population increased from 190,000 to 301,000. The movement of the black population to the suburbs was similar to the trend in metropolitan Chicago.

Employment in the metropolitan area increased by 21.3 percent to 2.36 million from 1970 to 1990, but employment of central city residents dropped by 14.6 percent. However, most of that growth in employment took place in the 1980s. Employment in 1980 was only 4.8 percent higher than in 1970. The familiar economic transformation took place in Philadelphia. Manufacturing employment declined from 28.2 percent to 16.7 percent of total employment, figures that are quite similar to those for Chicago. The number of central city residents employed in manufacturing fell from 192,000 to 88,000. Metropolitan employment in professional services doubled, from 302,000 to 618,000; the latter figure far exceeds manufacturing employment of 393,000 for 1990.

Employment in business services also doubled from 60,000 to 120,000. A major study of the Philadelphia economy by William Stull and Janice Madden (1990) was titled *Post-Industrial Philadelphia: Structural Changes in the Metropolitan Economy*. One result of these changes in population and employment was that the poverty rate for central city residents increased from 15.1 percent in 1970 to 20.6 percent in 1980, and then held steady at 20.3 percent in 1990. This outcome for central city poverty is virtually identical to those for New York and Chicago. Jargowsky (1997) computed that the number of people living in high-poverty areas increased during the 1970s from 112,000 to 267,000, and then declined slightly to 242,000 in 1990.

The housing market reflects the shift of population to the suburbs. The number of housing units increased from 1.55 million in 1970 to 1.93 million in 1990 (24.1 percent increase) while, somewhat unexpectedly, the number of units in the central city did not change (673,000 in 1970 and 674,000 in 1990). The vacancy rate in the metropolitan area increased from a low 3.6 percent to 6.6 percent, and this included a jump in the central city vacancy rate from 4.6 percent to 9.5 percent in 1980 and 10.5 percent in 1990. The number of vacant units in the city of Philadelphia was 71,000 in 1990, compared to 31,000 in 1970.

In a nutshell, the decade of the 1970s was a very bad one for the Philadelphia metropolitan area and especially for its central city. The metropolitan population declined, total employment increased by only a small amount, and the central city suffered large declines in population and employment while poverty and vacant housing units increased. But the 1980s tell a somewhat different story. The metropolitan population grew by a modest 2.9 percent, and the population decline in the central city slowed down. Total employment increased by a healthy 15.7 percent, fueled largely by professional services, and housing vacancies remained stable. Philadelphia could, perhaps, look forward to better days.

Metropolitan Detroit in 1970 differed from other metropolitan areas in two important respects. Employment was (and is) heavily concentrated in manufacturing in general and automobiles in particular, and as noted in the previous chapter, Detroit suffered the worst urban riot of the 1960s in terms of lives lost. The 1970s were disastrous for the city of Detroit, and the 1980s were no better. Recounting the facts is a sad duty.

The metropolitan population declined from 4.49 million in 1970 to 4.39 million in 1980 and 4.27 million in 1990. Detroit, Cleveland, and Pittsburgh are the only major metropolitan areas that experienced population declines in both decades. The population of the city of Detroit dropped by 32.0 percent in twenty years—from 1.51 million to 1.03 million. At the same time, the black population in the central city increased from 660,000 to 776,000 over the twenty years, so the black population percentage in the city of Detroit increased from 43.7 percent to 75.5 percent. The population of the suburbs increased from 2.98 million to 3.24 million, and the black population percentage in the suburbs increased only slightly from 3.3 percent to 5.0 percent. Metropolitan Detroit became the most racially divided major urban area between the central city and the suburbs.

Employment increased in both decades—by 6.6 percent in the 1970s and 7.3 percent in the 1980s—to reach 1.92 million in 1990. Manufacturing employment fell from 598,000 in 1970 to 474,000 in 1990, a decline of 20.7 percent that is not out of line with the experience of the other major metropolitan areas of the Northeast. Recall that the decline in manufacturing employment in metropolitan New York was 26.4 percent over the two decades. Manufacturing was still 35.7 percent of total employment in the Detroit metropolitan area in 1970, and this percentage fell to 24.7 in 1990. However, the total number of residents of the city of Detroit who were employed fell from 562,000 in 1970 to 336,000 in 1990, a startling decline of 40.2 percent. Manufacturing employment of central city residents dropped from 186,000 in 1970 to 69,000 in 1990. Poverty among central city residents increased from 14.7 percent to 21.9 percent from 1970 to 1980, a result that is similar to New York, Chicago, and Philadelphia. But then the central city poverty rate in Detroit shot up to 32.4 percent in 1990 instead of remaining stable, as it did for these other central cities.

As in the other metropolitan areas, employment growth was led by professional services (66.8 percent increase over twenty years). Business services and finance, insurance, and real estate also registered strong gains in employment. Together these three sectors added 278,000 jobs from 1970 to 1990, but these jobs were largely taken by suburbanites.

The housing market added units even as the population declined. Total units in the metropolitan area increased by 18.1 percent (from 1.41 million to 1.67 million) between 1970 and 1990, and the vacancy rate actually changed very little—from 4.2 percent to 5.1 percent. However, the number of units in the city of Detroit fell from 529,000 to 410,000, a decline of 22.5 percent. The vacancy rate in the central city increased from 5.9 percent to 8.7 percent, so the number of occupied units fell by 24.1 percent (from 498,000 to 378,000). This decline in occupied units is commensurate with the population decline of 32.0 percent, and brings to mind the image of abandoned houses burning on Devils' Night, October 30. The Centers for Disease Control (1997) reported that Halloween pranks turned destructive in the late 1970s and that, during the three-day period at the end of October 1984, 810 fires were reported in the city of Detroit (over 600 above the average for a three-day period). The Devils' Night phenomenon has since been brought under control (more or less) by a citywide anti-arson campaign.

How can one summarize the experience of Detroit in the period of the urban crisis? Total employment actually did pretty well, and the decline in manufacturing jobs was not any worse than in other major northeastern urban areas. But metropolitan Detroit ceased to be a destination for migration, and total population fell throughout the 1970s and 1980s. Aided by an excellent system of expressways, the white population of the city of Detroit moved to the suburbs in large numbers, falling from 851,000 in 1970 to 252,000 in 1990. All of the major retailers left downtown Detroit as retailing shifted to the suburbs. The central city became largely black and increasingly poor, with a poverty rate of 32.4 percent in 1990. The suburbs grew and remained almost exclusively white. It is apparent that the central city became one of the worst examples of the vicious circle in which bad trends feed and reinforce each other. The Devils' Night phenomenon (and other crime) does not help a city retain its middle class.

Boston and Pittsburgh

As has been noted previously, Boston and Pittsburgh were roughly equal in size and had relatively small central cities and black populations in 1950. Their paths diverged in the 1950s and 1960s, and continued to diverge during the urban crisis period. The Boston metropolitan area had a larger population than did metropolitan Pittsburgh in 1970, and that difference increased as Pittsburgh lost metropolitan population and Boston did not. Total employment was stagnant in the manufacturing urban area of Pittsburgh as manufacturing declined, and Boston gained substantial numbers of jobs in the "new economy."

The population of metropolitan Boston declined from 3.23 million in 1970 to 3.15 million in 1980, and then recovered to 3.23 million in 1990. Population of the city of Boston fell from 641,000 to 563,000 in the 1970s (12.2 percent), but increased slightly to 574,000 in 1990. The black population increased somewhat—from 127,000 (3.9 percent) to 198,000 (6.1 percent) for the metropolitan area but remained relatively low. The black percentage for the central city increased from 16.4 percent to 24.0 percent. The economy of the metropolitan area generated an employment increase of 28.1 percent from 1970 to 1990 to reach 1.71 million, and the number of employed residents of the city of Boston also increased 8.2 percent to 290,000. The ratio of employment to population increased in twenty years from 41.3 percent to 52.8 percent (with approximately the same number of people). Manufacturing has always been a relatively small part of the metropolitan economy compared to several other urban areas in the Northeast; manufacturing was 22.8 percent of total employment in 1970, and this number fell to 15.1 percent in 1990. The decline in manufacturing jobs from 304,000 to 257,000 was a comparatively modest 15.5 percent. At the same time, employment in professional services grew by 81.9 percent (from 281,000 to 511,000), and business services and finance, insurance, and real estate added 116,000 jobs.

While a majority of the "beantowners" were working, one discouraging note is the poverty rate in the central city, which increased from 15.5 percent in 1970 to 20.2 percent in 1980. However, the central city poverty rate declined modestly to 18.7 percent in 1990. Median family income (in 1999 dollars) advanced modestly in the 1970s (from $40,000 to $42,000 in the metropolitan area and $26,900 to $28,700 in the central city), but median incomes moved up briskly in the 1980s—to $54,000 at the metropolitan level and $39,200 in the central city. For the most part, the people of metropolitan Boston were working and prosperous in 1990. The housing market reflected that prosperity; total units increased by 24.6 percent, and the number of units in the central city increased by 7.8 percent. The overall vacancy rate increased from a low 3.6 percent to 5.2 percent, and the increase in the vacancy rate in the central city from 6.4 percent to 8.6 percent meant that the number of occupied units in the central city increased by only 5.1 percent.

The Pittsburgh story resembles the Detroit story in some respects. The population was 2.68 million in 1970 and decline in the metropolitan area was 4.2 percent in the 1970s. Population actually declined by a larger amount of 6.8 percent in the 1980s. The population of the city of Pittsburgh stood at 520,000 in 1970 (down from 677,000 in 1950), and it fell to 424,000 in 1980 and 370,000 in 1990. Remarkably, the central city does not account for the population decline. The population of the suburbs fell from 2.16 million in 1970 to 2.03 million in 1990. The Pittsburgh and Buffalo metropolitan areas have the distinction of having the only entire suburban areas to lose population. The major cause (and consequence as well) of population loss was the stagnant employment picture. Total employment did increase from 963,000 to 1,004,000 over the twenty years, but this increase of only 4.3 percent fell far short of the number of jobs needed by the baby boomers and females who were entering the work force. Employment in manufacturing (largely the steel industry) fell by 46.9 percent—from 294,000 to 156,000. Employment in professional services increased by 120,000, from 161,000 to 281,000, and business services and FIRE together registered a gain from 69,000 to 120,000, but these gains were not enough to turn the Pittsburgh economy around.

The number of central city residents who were employed fell from 193,000 in 1970 to 155,000 in 1990, and the central city poverty rate increased from 15.0 percent in 1970 to 16.5 percent in 1980 (less than other central cities of the Northeast) to 21.4 percent in 1990 (in line with other northeastern central cities). The number of housing units in the central city declined by 10.5 percent and the number of occupied units fell by 13.5 percent, even as the total number of units in the metropolitan area increased by 14.8 percent.

The black population of the metropolitan area remained relatively small for a northeastern urban area (6.3 percent in 1970 and 7.5 percent in 1990). The black population of the central city fell from 105,000 to 95,000 over the twenty years, but the proportion of the population of the city of Pittsburgh that was black increased from 20.2 percent to 25.7 percent. The size of the suburban black population increased from 65,000 in 1970 to 84,000 in 1990. In short, both whites and blacks were moving to the suburbs, even as the total population of the suburbs was declining.

St. Louis, Cleveland, Washington, D.C., and Baltimore

The next group of urban areas had populations of 2.1 to 3.2 million in 1970, and represents a wide diversity of experiences in the era of the urban crisis. Metropolitan Cleveland and its central city, with the heavy concentration in manufacturing, suffered badly. The St. Louis urban area also had a bad time of it, but its record is not as dismal as that of Cleveland. In contrast, the Baltimore metropolitan area did well compared to most of the northeastern urban areas, and Washington, D.C., grew rapidly and experienced sizable growth in median family incomes.

St. Louis is another metropolitan area with little population growth and a rather small central city that declined by a large percentage. The metropolitan area population went from 2.46 million in 1970 to 2.41 million in 1980 to 2.49 million in 1990—very little change. The city of St. Louis started the period at 622,000 people (down from 857,000 in 1950), and it dropped to 453,000 in 1980—a decline of 27.2 percent in a single decade. The city fell further to 397,000 in 1990 for an overall decline of 36.2 percent in twenty years. The suburbs gained 14.2 percent in population from 1.83 million to 2.10 million. Housing units in the suburbs increased from 578,000 to 825,000 and units in the central city fell from 238,000 to 195,000. The vacancy rate in the city increased from 9.6 percent in 1970 to 15.3 percent in 1990, so the number of occupied units fell from 215,000 to 165,000 (a drop of 23.2 percent). As the filtering model of the housing market implies, suburban housing construction coupled with slow demand growth means that housing units in the central city will become vacant and, ultimately, be demolished.

The black population in the metropolitan area increased modestly from 379,000 to 422,000 over the twenty years and declined in the central city from 254,000 to 188,000. The black population in the suburbs thus increased from 125,000 to 234,000. St. Louis is another example of the net movement of both white and black populations to the suburbs as the overall population of the metropolitan does not change.

Metropolitan St. Louis did experience employment growth of 26.4 percent, with about equal growth in both decades. Manufacturing employment held up relatively well. The decline from 251,000 to 225,000 was only 10.4 percent in twenty years. Manufacturing provided 26.7 percent of total employment in 1970, and its share fell to 19.0 percent in 1990. As is the case for all of the other urban areas, professional services, business services, and FIRE provided most of the employment growth. In this case, the three sectors increased from 219,000 to 419,000 employees over the 1970–90 period. The employment of residents of the city of St. Louis fell from 232,000 in 1970 to 162,000 in 1990, a decline of 30.2 percent (compared to a central city population decline of 36.2 percent). The poverty rate for the metropolitan area was 10.8 percent in both 1970 and 1990, but the poverty rate in the central city was a relatively high 19.9 percent in 1970. The central city poverty rate increased to 21.6 percent in 1980 and 24.6 percent in 1990, but this increase was smaller than in most of the major northeastern central cities. Median family income in the metropolitan area (1999 dollars) increased slowly from $47,000 in 1969 to $49,800 in 1979 to $51,000 in 1989. Median family income for central city residents fell steadily from $37,100 to $35,000 to $32,600 for these same years.

The case of St. Louis can be characterized by an absence of population growth, rapid decline of the central city as the suburbs grew, decent employment growth, but only slow growth in median family incomes in real terms (and income decline in the central city). There was little to suggest that the St. Louis metropolitan area was prepared to make a resurgence in the 1990s. Indeed, St. Louis was known primarily for the Gateway Arch and the demolition of a major failed public housing project, Pruitt-Igoe, in 1972. This project was built in 1956 and consisted of 33 eleven-story buildings with 2,870 units; it was declared unsalvageable in 1972.

Cleveland's experience was in many ways worse than that of St. Louis. Metropolitan population declined in both decades—from 2.42 million in 1970 to 2.28 million in 1980 and 2.20 million in 1990 for a total decline of 9.0 percent. The city of Cleveland suffered a large loss of population, primarily in the 1970s. In 1970 the city had a population of 751,000, and the decline was 177,000 (23.6 percent) over the next ten years. The population continued to decline during the 1980s from 574,000 to 506,000, for a total loss of 32.6 percent. It is a familiar story. The housing units in the suburbs increased from 520,000 to 672,000 (a 29.2 percent increase) while the number of occupied units in the central city fell from 248,000 to 199,000 and the total number of central city units was reduced from 264,000 to 224,000.

The black population of the metropolitan area increased from 333,000 to

377,000 (13.2 percent), and the number of black people who resided in the central city fell from 288,000 to 234,000. The suburban black population increased from 45,000 to 143,000, so here is yet another case of both white and black net migration from central city to the suburbs. The migration of whites was much larger, so the percentage of the central city population that was black increased from 38.3 percent in 1970 to 46.2 percent in 1990.

The employment record in Cleveland is particularly dismal. Total employment was 963,000 in 1970 and increased by only 4.3 percent over twenty years, even as the baby boomers and females entered the work force. Manufacturing employment did not do well; employment fell by 100,000—from 331,000 to 231,000. Cleveland's heavy concentration in manufacturing of 34.4 percent in 1970 clearly hurt its job market in the subsequent two decades. Growth of employment in professional services from 145,000 to 245,000 exactly offset the loss of manufacturing jobs, and business services and FIRE added 40,000 jobs (from 71,000 to 111,000)—the exact increase in employment from 1970 to 1990. The number of central city residents who were employed fell by 36.2 percent, from 287,000 to 183,000, matching the population decline in percentage terms. The poor employment picture meant that the poverty rate in the metropolitan area increased from 8.8 percent in 1970 to 12.0 percent in 1990. Central city poverty started at a high level of 17.1 percent in 1970 and increased to 22.1 percent in 1980 and 28.7 percent in 1990. Median family incomes fell by 3.2 percent at the metropolitan level ($50,600 in 1969 and $49,000 in 1989), and dropped by 26.9 percent in the central city (from $41,300 to $30,200). Clearly the story of Cleveland is one of the worst.

As always, Washington, D.C., is a special case of a special place. The metropolitan area experienced strong growth during the twenty years; metropolitan population increased from 3.20 million in 1970 to 4.22 million in 1990 (31.9 percent) and total employment increased by 72.4 percent (from 1.39 million to 2.40 million). However, even this strong growth performance could not prevent central city decline. The population of the city of Washington, D.C., fell from 757,000 in 1970 to 607,000 in 1990. One might have guessed that the employment growth occurred in government jobs. While government did employ more people (300,000 in 1970 under President Richard Nixon, 362,000 in 1980 under President Jimmy Carter, and 362,000 in 1990 under President George Bush), that growth was far exceeded by jobs in professional services. This sector expanded from 256,000 jobs in 1970 to 633,000 in 1990. In addition, business services and FIRE increased from 120,000 to 334,000. Was the employment growth fueled by the effort of influence government and its expenditures (lobbyists, professional associations, lawyers, and so on)?

The population growth was accommodated by a huge increase in suburban housing. The number of units in the suburbs increased from 768,000 to 1.39

million over twenty years. The number of units in the central city remained stable at 278,000 in 1970 and 277,000 in 1990, but the central city vacancy rate did increase from 5.4 percent to 9.7 percent, and the number of occupied units declined from 263,000 to 250,000 (4.9 percent). Thus there is some evidence of the adverse effect of the filtering mechanism at work on the central city.

The strong job market meant that the poverty rate in the metropolitan area actually declined from a relatively low 8.7 percent in 1970 to a very low 6.6 percent in 1990. The central city poverty rate was stable at 16.3 percent in 1970 and 16.9 percent in 1990 (but it had popped up to 18.6 percent in 1980). The record for real median family income is impressive—showing an increase in the metropolitan area from $55,800 in 1970 to $70,800 in 1990. Median family incomes in the central city also increased from $43,500 in 1970 to $48,700 in 1990.

The changes in the racial makeup of Washington, D.C., are interesting. In 1970, the black population of the metropolitan area was 704,000, of whom 538,000 lived in the central city. The central city was 71.1 percent black. By 1990, the total black population had grown to 1.06 million, an increase of 50.6 percent, but the black population of the central city had declined to 396,000. The central city was 65.2 percent black in 1990, a lower percentage than in 1970 by 4.9 percent. The black population of the suburbs increased from 166,000 to 664,000. The black population of the nation's capital was joining the ranks of suburbanites as in no other urban area of the Northeast.

The Baltimore metropolitan area actually performed relatively well during the urban crisis period. Population increased by 14.0 percent from 2.09 million to 2.38 million, and total employment grew by a strong 43.4 percent. The population of the central city did fall from 906,000 in 1970 to 736,000 in 1990 (18.8 percent decline), but the number of employed central city residents declined by only 11.2 percent from 356,000 to 316,000.

Manufacturing employment was a relatively small 22.8 percent of total employment in the metropolitan area in 1970, and its share dropped to 12.1 percent in 1990. Strong employment growth was recorded in professional services (up 116.8 percent from 137,000 to 297,000 in twenty years) and in business services and FIRE (up 146.8 percent from 62,000 to 153,000). Baltimore was joining the "new economy" in a pretty big way. The strong job market meant that poverty in the metropolitan area actually declined—from 11.1 percent in 1970 to a very low 10.1 percent in 1990. Central city poverty was a relatively high 18.0 percent in 1970, but it increased only modestly to 21.9 percent in 1990. Median family income grew in real terms in the metropolitan area from $47,500 in 1970 to $56,700 in 1990—an increase of 19.4 percent over twenty years. Median family income in the central city did decline from $40,000 to $37,900. But even the housing market in the central city did not suffer as much as in other major cities of the Northeast. The number of units in the suburbs increased by 277,000 (an increase of 78.2 percent from 354,000 in 1970), but the number of units in the central city remained stable (305,000 in 1970 and 303,000 in 1990). The number of vacant units in the central city did increase from 16,000 to 27,000, so there is evidence of the filtering mechanism at work.

The black population of the Baltimore metropolitan area increased by 24.9 percent—from 490,000 in 1970 to 612,000 in 1990. All but 14,000 of this growth took place in the suburbs, as the black population of the central city increased marginally from 420,000 to 434,000. The percentage of the central city population that was black increased from 46.4 percent in 1970 to 59.0 percent in 1990. The corresponding figures for the metropolitan area are 23.5 percent in 1970 and 25.7 percent in 1990.

Five More Urban Areas

Next comes the diverse group of five smaller urban areas that includes Minneapolis–St. Paul, Buffalo, Cincinnati, Milwaukee, and Kansas City.

Minneapolis–St. Paul survived the 1970s and 1980s relatively well. Total population increased from 2.03 million in 1970 to 2.20 million in 1980 and 2.54 million in 1990, an increase of 25.2 percent in twenty years. The population of the twin central cities fell from 744,000 to 641,000 (14.0 percent decline) during the 1970s, but declined no further in the 1980s and finished the decade at 640,000. The housing market in the Twin Cities did not suffer the same malady as most of the other large northeastern metropolitan areas. Housing construction in the suburbs was robust, suburban units increased from 362,000 to 718,000 (98.3 percent) from 1970 to 1990, but the number of units in the two central cities actually increased from 275,000 to 289,000. The vacancy rate in the central cities did increase from 3.6 percent to 6.2 percent, so the number of occupied units increased by a modest 6,000 units.

The racial makeup of Minneapolis–St. Paul started to change during 1970–90. The number of black residents of the metropolitan area increased from 32,000 (1.6 percent) to 88,000 (3.5 percent), and the percentage of black residents in the central cities increased from 4.0 to 10.5 percent.

Minneapolis–St. Paul is notable for its employment growth. The metropolitan area employment total increased from 839,000 to 1.37 million over the twenty years, an increase of 63.1 percent. Remarkably, manufacturing employment increased—from 202,000 to 268,000, which is a hefty 32.7 percent increase. Employment in the three sectors of the "new economy," professional services, business services, and FIRE, increased by 117.3 percent (from 237,000 to 515,000). This employment growth meant that the number of residents of the central cities who were employed did not change, but stood at 327,000 in both 1970 and 1990. However, the transition to the new economy did not go smoothly for the poor; the poverty rate in the central cities was 10.6 percent in 1970s and increased somewhat to 12.4 percent in 1980. The 1980s brought an even larger increase in central city poverty, to 17.7 percent. With the exception of this discouraging note, the Twin Cities avoided the worst of the urban crisis.

The story of Buffalo brings us back to the urban crisis with a vengeance. The population of the metropolitan area fell from 1.35 million in 1970 to 1.19 million in 1990, and the central city dropped from 463,000 to 328,000 (29.2 percent decline). The population of the suburbs declined from 886,000 to 861,000, matching the Pittsburgh suburbs in that respect. Housing units in the suburbs increased from 267,000 to 338,000 over twenty years, and the number of units in the central city declined from 166,000 to 152,000. The central city vacancy rate doubled from 4.9 percent to 10.2 percent. Employment growth over twenty years was a weak 6.5 percent from 511,000 to 544,000. Manufacturing declined from 165,000 to 102,000 jobs. Employed residents of the central city declined from 172,000 to 131,000, and the central city poverty rate increased from 14.8 percent in 1970 to 20.7 percent in 1980 to 25.6 percent in 1990. Median family income in the metropolitan area declined in real terms from $40,000 in 1970 to $37,700 in 1990, as median family income in the central city fell from $29,800 to $24,800. The black population of the metropolitan area increased by 10.0 percent—from 109,000 to 120,000. The black population remained heavily concentrated in the central city (94,000 in 1970 and 100,000 in 1990), so the percentage of the central city population that was black increased from 20.3 percent in 1970 to 30.5 percent in 1990. Buffalo experienced the urban crisis, albeit on a smaller scale than Detroit, Cleveland, et al.

The Cincinnati experience was between that of Minneapolis–St. Paul and Buffalo. The metropolitan population increased over the twenty years from 1.44 million to 1.53 million (6.0 percent increase), and total employment increased by 33.3 percent (from 543,000 to 724,000). Manufacturing employment declined from 169,000 to 144,000, but growth in professional services, business services, and FIRE more than made up for this loss by adding 122,000 jobs (from 125,000 to 247,000). The central city lost people, declining from 453,000 to 364,000, and the number of central city residents who were employed declined from 175,000 to 159,000. The central city poverty rate was a relatively high 17.1 percent in 1970, and it increased to 24.3 percent in 1990 as some of the middle class exited to the suburbs. Jargowsky's (1997) computation is that the number of residents of high-poverty areas increased from 55,000 in 1970 to 74,000 in 1990.

The housing market in the central city held up relatively well. The suburbs added 141,000 units from 1970 to 1990 (299,000 up to 440,000 units), and the central city stock remained stable—falling only from 172,000 to 169,000. Furthermore, the central city vacancy rate increased from 7.3 percent to 8.6 percent, so the number of occupied units did fall by 5,000—from 159,000 to 154,000. The black population of the metropolitan area increased by 25.0 percent (from 152,000 to 190,000), so blacks made up a modestly increasing percentage of the metropolitan population (10.6 percent in 1970 and 12.5 percent in 1990). The percentage of the black population residing in the central city declined from 82.2 percent in 1970 to 72.6 percent in 1990, but the number of black central city residents increased from 125,000 to 138,000, resulting in an increase in the percentage of black central city residents from 27.6 percent to 37.9 percent.

Milwaukee's experience was close to that of Cincinnati. The metropolitan population growth was only 2.0 percent over the twenty years (from 1.40 million to 1.43 million), and the central city population declined from 717,000 to 628,000. The percentage of the central city population that was black increased from 14.6 percent (105,000) to 30.3 percent (190,000), and very few of the black population lived in the suburbs (1.9 percent in 1970 and 3.1 percent in 1990). Employment grew from 574,000 to 702,000 (22.3 percent increase) in the metropolitan area. Manufacturing employment declined from 193,000 to 169,000 (although it showed an increase to 209,000 in 1980), so the percentage of jobs in manufacturing declined from a relatively high 33.6 percent to (a still relatively high) 24.1 percent. Even the old industrial town of Milwaukee added a large number of jobs in the "new economy," from 134,000 to 255,000 in the professional services, business services, and FIRE sectors. Unfortunately, central city poverty increased sharply, from 11.2 percent in 1970 to 22.2 percent in 1990, and median family incomes (1999 dollars) in the central city declined from $46,300 to $38,000. Median family income in the metropolitan area was pretty stagnant, increasing only from $50,900 to $52,400 over the twenty years.

Housing construction in the suburbs from 1970 to 1990 matched the growth in demand. Suburban units increased from 200,000 to 305,000, and units in the central city actually increased from 246,000 to 254,000. The central city vacancy rate increased slightly from 3.6 percent to 5.3 percent, so the number of occupied units in the central city also increased from 237,000 to 241,000. In summary, the Milwaukee urban area had a relatively weak job market that produced stagnant family incomes and central city poverty and, perhaps as a result, the suburbs did not experience a construction boom sufficient to devastate the central city housing market.

The experience of Kansas City resembles that of Minneapolis–St. Paul, which is a relatively good record. Metropolitan population grew by 14.5 percent over the twenty years (from 1.38 million to 1.58 million), and the central city declined from 507,000 to 435,000 (8.3 percent). Employment growth was a strong 38.2 percent (from 573,000 to 792,000), and manufacturing employment held steady at 119,000 in 1970 and 118,000 in 1990, after increasing to 135,000 in 1980. Employment in professional services, business services, and FIRE more than doubled from 135,000 to 288,000, and the number of central city residents who were employed remained steady at 215,000 in 1970 and 212,000 in 1990. The strong job market meant that central city poverty increased by a relatively small amount, from 12.5 percent in 1970 to 15.3 percent in 1990. Median family incomes (1999 dollars) increased at the metropolitan level from $46,900 to $50,600 over the 1970–90 period and fell only slightly in the central city from $45,000 to $44,300.

Suburban housing construction was strong, but there was some increase in the housing stock in the central city as well. Units in the suburbs increased by 266,000—from 196,000 to 462,000 over twenty years. The central city housing stock increased from 192,000 units to 201,000, and the number of occupied units in the central city increased slightly from 176,000 to 178,000.

The racial makeup of the metropolitan area changed somewhat as the black population grew from 159,000 to 199,000 (11.5 percent in 1970 and 12.6 percent in 1990). The black population of the central city increased from 112,000 in 1970 to 128,000 in 1990, which means that the central city went from 22.1 percent to 29.4 percent black. More than half of the black population increase (24,000 out of 40,000) took place in the suburbs.

Indianapolis and Columbus

Lastly, we come to the two metropolitan areas that had joined the ranks of the majors during the twenty years prior to 1970. Was their record during urban crisis years very different from that of other northeastern urban areas? How do they compare to urban areas such as Minneapolis–St. Paul and Kansas City?

The Indianapolis metropolitan area had a population of 1.25 million in 1970, and growth of 10.6 percent brought the total to 1.38 million in 1990. The Columbus urban area grew from 1.13 million to 1.34 million (19.4 percent) over the same twenty years. This growth rate was comparable to the growth in Minneapolis–St. Paul of 25.2 percent, less than the 31.9 percent growth for Washington, D.C., and somewhat greater than the 14 percent growth recorded by the Baltimore and Kansas City urban areas. So among the major urban areas of the Northeast, Columbus ranked third in population growth during the urban crisis years. On this one criterion Columbus did relatively well but was by no means far above the crowd.

The population of the city of Indianapolis (which included the entire central county) decreased slightly from 745,000 in 1970 to 731,000 in 1990. Employment growth in the metropolitan area was a strong 38.6 percent—from 502,000 to 696,000—and the number of central city residents who were employed increased from 303,000 to 369,000 (21.8 percent). Manufacturing employment declined from 150,000 to 130,000 (and from 29.9 percent to 18.7 percent of total employment). Employment in professional services, business services, and FIRE increased from 113,000 to 242,000 (up 114.2 percent). The strong job market kept the central city poverty rate relatively low—at 9.5 percent in 1970 and 12.5 percent in 1990. However, median family incomes did not increase rapidly in the urban area. The median in 1970 in real terms was $48,100 and $50,000 in 1990, an increase of 4.0 percent in twenty years. And median family income in the central city fell from $48,300 in 1970 to $46,900 in 1990 (down 2.9 percent).

The housing stock grew in both the suburbs and the central city. Suburban units increased from 163,000 in 1970 to 250,000 in 1990, and units in the central city grew from 252,000 to 319,000 over this same period. The central city vacancy rate stood at 6.3 percent in 1970 and 8.5 percent in 1990. The black population of metropolitan Indianapolis increased from 137,000 in 1970 to 181,000 in 1990, a growth of 32.1 percent that exceeds overall population growth of 24.3 percent. The black population remained largely confined to the central city—134,000 in 1970 and 164,000 in 1990. The central city was 18.0 percent black in 1970 and 22.4 percent black in 1990.

A quick summary of the Indianapolis experience during the urban crisis years is that population growth was above average for a northeastern urban area, the job market did well in terms of jobs created (but not in terms of median family incomes), and the central city did not suffer much decline or increase in poverty. Indeed, the central city added 67,000 housing units. In these respects, the city of Indianapolis did rather better than Minneapolis–St. Paul, Baltimore, and Kansas City.

As noted above, the population of the Columbus urban area increased from 1.13 million to 1.34 million over the twenty years. In addition, the central city population grew from 540,000 to 633,000 (up 17.2 percent). The city of Columbus was unusual among northeastern central cities in its ability to annex territory. The land area of the city expanded from 134.6 square miles to 190.9 square miles (a 41.8 percent increase). The central city added housing units as well—from 182,000 to 277,000—as the housing stock of the urban area increased from 365,000 to 546,000. The central city vacancy rate did increase from 5.1 percent to 7.3 percent, but the number of occupied units in the city of Columbus increased from 173,000 to 257,000. The black population of the urban area increased from 106,000 to 162,000 (up 52.8 percent), and remained largely concentrated in the central city (100,000 in 1970 and 142,000 in 1990). The central city was 18.5 percent black in 1970 and 22.4 percent black in 1990.

The Columbus job market expanded from 450,000 to 677,000 jobs (up 50.4 percent), and the number of central city residents who were employed rose from 221,000 to 326,000. Manufacturing employment declined by 10,000 (from 107,000 to 97,000), but the new economy sectors of professional services, business services, and FIRE expanded from 119,000 to 264,000. As elsewhere, not everyone easily made the economic transition. Central city poverty increased from 13.2 percent in 1970 to 17.2 percent in 1990. Median family incomes grew at the metropolitan level by 7.4 percent (from $46,000 to $49,400) and were steady in the central city at $44,200 in both 1969 and 1989.

In short, Columbus had sizable population growth at the metropolitan level and in the central city, coupled with strong employment growth. The only negative outcome was the increase in poverty in the central city from 13.2 percent to 17.2 percent. The ability of the central city to expand its land area clearly was to its advantage, an advantage that other northeastern central cities did not possess.

Urban Crisis in the Northeast: Manufacturing Matters

The discussion of each of the seventeen major urban areas of the Northeast during the twenty years from 1970 to 1990 has shown that their experience varied widely, and it leads to summary statements that can be subjected to a statistical test. First, urban areas that began the period with a heavier concentration in manufacturing seem to have had greater difficulties. Data to test this idea have been assembled in Tables 10.5 and 10.6. The results are a striking confirmation of the basic idea.

Consider employment growth. The percentage employment change in the metropolitan area from 1970 to 1990 is made simply a linear function of the percentage of total employment in manufacturing in 1970, with the regression result that

$$\text{EMPGROW} = 87.41 - 2.14 \, \text{MANUF}, \, R^2 \, (\text{adj.}) = .558$$
$$(6.79) \quad (4.60)$$

The t statistics are in parentheses. Employment growth was reduced by 2.2 percent if the percentage of employment in manufacturing was 1.0 percent higher in 1970, and the result is highly statistically significant. Because employment growth is determined partly by population growth (and vice versa), perhaps a better measure of employment growth is the growth in employment minus the growth in population. In this case the regression result is that

$$\text{EMPGROW} - \text{POPGROW} = 48.10 - 0.91 \text{ MANUF. } R^2 \text{ (adj.)} = .597$$
$$(9.47) \quad (4.97)$$

Here we see that employment growth in excess of population growth was reduced by 0.91 percent as the percentage of employment in manufacturing was 1 percent greater in 1970.

Next, consider the percentage in median family income in the metropolitan area (1999 dollars) from 1970 to 1990 as a linear function of manufacturing in 1970. The result is that

$$\text{INCOMEGROW} = 34.04 - 0.99 \text{ MANUF. } R^2 \text{ (adj.)} = .654$$
$$(6.98) \quad (5.59)$$

This shows that the growth of median family income in real terms over a twenty-year period was reduced by 0.99 percent for a concentration that was one percentage point greater in 1970, and this result is also highly statistically significant. Finally, consider the increase in the poverty rate in the central city. It, too, is related to the initial concentration in manufacturing employment according to

$$\text{CHCCPOV} = -3.45 + 0.35 \text{ MANUF, } R^2 \text{ (adj.)} = .586$$
$$(1.74) \quad (4.86)$$

Each percentage of total employment in manufacturing was associated with an increase in central city poverty rate of 0.35 percent, and, once again, the result is highly statistically significant. One might argue that the inclusion of Washington, D.C., in the data involves including an urban area that was very different from the others (and with a very low concentration in manufacturing and a high growth rate). All of the statistical tests were performed after Washington, D.C., was dropped from the data, and the results changed very little. The R-squares declined, but the coefficients of the manufacturing variable did not change appreciably and remained highly statistically significant.

Another set of tests examined the levels of central city poverty in 1970 and 1990. These tests show that the central city poverty level was related to the black population percentage in the central city in 1970, but it was not related to the concentration in manufacturing employment at the time. The estimated coefficient is 0.11 (and is highly statistically significant), which indicates that a central city with a black population that was 1.0 percent higher had a poverty rate in 1970 that was 0.11 percent greater. However, the central city poverty rate in 1990 is related to the poverty rate in 1970 and to the concentration in manufacturing employment in 1970, and not related to the black population percentage in the central city in 1990. The coefficient of the central city poverty rate in 1970 is 1.05, and the coefficient on the manufacturing variable is 0.35; both are highly statistically significant.

Finally, it is obvious that population and employment growth are highly correlated. That is indeed the case: the correlation is .902, and the estimated equation is

$$POPGROW = -12.81 + 0.64 \; EMPGROW$$
$$(6.90) \quad (12.21)$$

In this case no causation can be inferred because causation runs both ways.

The main discussion in this chapter has shown that the seventeen major urban areas of the Northeast had rather different experiences during the years of the urban crisis. We have also begun to see that the urban crisis had many dimensions, and discussion of this will continue in the following chapters. Nevertheless, the simple statistical tests reported in this section highlight the important roles that the concentration in manufacturing employment played. Urban areas such as Detroit, Pittsburgh, Cleveland, Buffalo, Cincinnati, and Milwaukee that began the urban crisis period with heavy concentrations in manufacturing suffered the most. These six urban areas had a concentration in manufacturing that exceeded 30 percent and a mean of 32.9 percent compared to the average for the seventeen urban areas of 26.8 percent. These six urban areas had an average population decline of 4.1 percent over twenty years, compared to the average for the seventeen urban areas of 6.4 percent population growth.

Whose Urban Crisis Was Worst?

Is it possible to say which urban area (and its central city) had the worst urban crisis? One approach to this question is simply to create an index of economic crisis that is a combination of the variables examined in this chapter. The exercise reported here uses metropolitan population growth, metropolitan employment growth, change in median family real income, central city population loss, and the increase in the central city poverty rate. The seventeen urban areas are ranked on each of these five variables, and the ranks are added together, with the results shown in Table 10.7. The seventeen urban areas seem to form three groups: those that had the worst economic outcomes, those that

Table 10.7

Urban Crisis Rankings: Northeastern Metropolitan Areas (changes from 1970 to 1990)*

	Metro population change	Metro employment change	Median income change ($ 1999)	Central city population change	Central city poverty change	Total index	Index rank
New York	14	13	4	3	7	41	8
Chicago	8	10	12	8	12	48	11
Philadelphia	11	12	3	9	9	44	9
Detroit	13	14	15	15	12	59	14
Boston	12	8	11	5	4	40	7
Pittsburgh	16	16	14	13	10	69	15
St. Louis	10	9	6	17	8	50	12
Cleveland	15	16	16	10	17	74	16
Washington, D.C.	1	1	1	12	1	16	1
Baltimore	5	4	2	7	11	29	6
Minneapolis–St. Paul	2	2	5	7	11	27	4
Buffalo	17	15	17	14	15	78	17
Cincinnati	7	7	8	11	12	45	10
Milwaukee	9	11	13	6	16	55	13
Kansas City	4	6	7	4	2	23	3
Indianapolis	6	5	12	2	3	28	5
Columbus	3	3	8	1	6	21	2

* The rank is from 1 (the best) to 17 (the worst) of the 17 metropolitan areas. The total index is the sum of the five ranks.
Source: HUD State of the Cities Data.

had the best, and those that fell somewhere in the middle. The five urban areas with the worst scores on this index are (in order, from the worst) Buffalo, Cleveland, Pittsburgh, Detroit, and Milwaukee—manufacturing cities all. The first four are probably no surprise, and it is striking that the four are located within a relatively small area of the industrial "heartland." The next group is (from the bottom) St. Louis, Chicago, Cincinnati, Philadelphia, New York, and Boston. This diverse group includes the three largest urban areas in the Northeast. The members of the top group are (from the bottom) Baltimore, Indianapolis, Minneapolis–St. Paul, Kansas City, Columbus, and Washington, D.C. However, as we shall see in Chapter 13, the placement of Washington, D.C., at the top of the group must be tempered by the shockingly high murder rate in the central city. The top group consists of urban areas that are located away from the core industrial area of the Northeast (Washington, D.C., Baltimore, Kansas City, and Minneapolis–St. Paul), or are the two "newer" major metropolitan areas of the Northeast (Indianapolis and Columbus).

11

Urban Growth in the Sunbelt: 1970–1990

We now turn to the urban areas of the Sunbelt during the years of urban crisis. Since the 1965 Watts riot in Los Angeles signaled the beginning of the nation's urban crisis, we can ask whether there really was anything resembling an urban crisis in the Sunbelt that was similar to the experience of the northeastern urban areas. The basic answer to that question is "yes," but the underlying reasons differ from city to city. Several of the central cities in the Sunbelt experienced the urban crisis. Those include all of the six central cities of the South—Dallas–Fort Worth, Houston, New Orleans, Atlanta, Birmingham, and Miami. The average of the poverty rates for these six central cities was 19.4 percent in 1970 and increased by 6.2 percentage points to 25.6 percent poverty in 1990. The city of Miami recorded the highest poverty rate in the group with 31.2 percent in 1990. Three of the central cities—Atlanta, New Orleans, and Birmingham—lost population in sizable amounts (20.7, 16.2, and 11.6 percent, respectively). The central cities of the West include Los Angeles, San Francisco–Oakland, Seattle, Denver, San Diego, and Phoenix. The urban crisis is much less in evidence in these western cities. This group of central cities had a low average poverty rate of 12.4 in 1970, and this average had increased to 15.4 percent in 1990. Three of the western central cities (Seattle, San Francisco–Oakland, and San Diego) experienced small increases in poverty that averaged 2.0 percent, but Los Angeles, Denver, and Phoenix had increases in poverty of 5.9, 3.6, and 2.4 percent, respectively. Only the central city of Los Angeles in the West had an increase in poverty that was similar to the increases experienced in the South. Also, recall that the seventeen central cities of the Northeast saw poverty increase from 14.7 percent to 20.6 percent from 1970 to 1990, the same 5.9 percentage point increase as in the city of Los Angeles. The only western central city to lose population was Denver, which declined 9.2 percent from 1970 to 1990.

The Urban Areas of the South

Some background on the oil and gas industry is needed to understand the history of some of the urban areas of the South during this period. The oil patch experienced prosperity in the 1970s as the price of crude oil jumped fourfold and then more than doubled again. The oil and natural gas business has many aspects, all of which exist in Texas. A few facts are needed as background. First, we need the basic facts about oil prices. The nominal price of Saudi Arabian crude oil increased from $2.10 per barrel in 1973 to $9.60 in 1974, and it continued to drift up to $13.34 in 1979. The second jump in the price occurred in 1980, when the price was raised to $26.00 per barrel. Subsequent increases brought the price to $34.00 in 1982. The price started to fall in 1984 to $29.00, and then the Saudis dropped the price to $16.15 in 1987. Additional reductions brought the price down to $13.15 in 1989. Prices paid by refineries in the United States followed this price path. The refinery price started at $4.15 per barrel in 1973, jumped to $9.07 in 1974, increased further to $17.72 in 1979, jumped to $28.07 in 1980 and $35.24 in 1981, declined to $26.75 in 1985, and then dropped to $14.55 in 1986. The refinery price remained below $18 per barrel up through 1989, popped up to $22.22 in 1990, and then settled down below $19 for the next five years.

Clearly this price history provided a strong incentive to produce crude oil and to find more. However, crude oil production in Texas peaked in 1972 at 1.26 billion barrels, and it has declined continuously since then.

By 1980, crude oil production had declined to 0.93 billion barrels, and in 1990 production was down to 0.66 billion barrels, just over half of its peak. Nevertheless, the oil prices brought forth a dramatic increase in drilling and exploration. The rig count increased by 70 percent between 1973 and 1975. The second major price spike in 1980 produced a further increase in drilling and exploration in Texas—up 71 percent from 1979 to 1981. The drop in the oil price in 1986 caused drilling and exploration to fall—by more than half in 1986 alone. The rig count in 1991 was only one-fourth of its level in 1981. The Handbook of Texas Online states that the Texas oil and gas industry had what probably was its last boom in the 1970s and early 1980s. The petroleum industry was more than one-quarter of the state's economy in 1981, but it fell to less than half that level by 1991. One-third of employment in the oil and gas industry was lost between 1982 and 1994.

Texas

Dallas–Fort Worth

Dallas–Fort Worth maintained its status as the largest metropolitan area in the South as of 1990. Population increased from 2.43 million in 1970 to 3.05 million in 1980 and 4.04 million in 1990—a growth of 66.0 percent in twenty years. Total employment doubled over these same years, from 1.03 million in 1970 to 1.53 million in 1980 and 2.08 million in 1990. Even manufacturing employment increased briskly, from 251,000 in 1970 to 371,000 in 1990. Employment in professional services almost tripled from 141,000 to 400,000 over the twenty years. The poverty rate in the "metroplex" was stable at 11.2 percent in 1970, 10.0 in 1980, and 11.9 percent in 1990. However, the rapid growth in employment did not prevent the central cities from experiencing an increase in poverty. The poverty rate in the combined central cities of Dallas and Forth Worth started at 13.4 percent in 1970, increased marginally to 14.1 percent in 1980, but then jumped to 17.8 percent in 1990. Median family incomes in the metropolitan area increased in real terms nicely in the 1970s—from $46,100 to $50,000 (an increase of 8.5 percent from 1969 to 1979). Median incomes did increase during the 1980s, albeit at a slower pace, to $51,600 (up 3.2 percent). As discussed below, the oil patch problems had a much larger impact on Houston and New Orleans.

The black population of the metropolitan area increased from 330,000 in 1970 to 560,000 in 1990, an increase of 69.7 percent that matches the growth in total population of 66.0 percent. The number of housing units in the urban area increased by 103.2 percent over this same period. The vacancy rate of 10.8 percent in 1990 exceeded the 7.2 percent recorded for 1970, suggesting some degree of overbuilding.

The land area of the two central cities increased from 471 square miles in 1970 to 624 square miles in 1990, a jump of 32.5 percent, so the examination of central city data over time loses some of its meaning. (One would prefer to study central city performance holding land area constant.) The population of the two central cities increased from 1.24 million in 1970 to 1.46 million in 1990 (up 17.6 percent). The black population of the central cities increased from 23.3 percent to 26.9 percent, which is not a particularly large increase. The average increase in the black population proportion in the northeastern central cities was 8.3 percent (from 28.8 to 37.1 percent). However, the increase in the black population proportion in the central cities of 3.6 percent is fairly close to the increase in the poverty rate in the central cities of 4.4 percent.

During the 1970s and 1980s, Dallas–Fort Worth was a major participant in the Sunbelt boom, and there is scant evidence of an urban crisis of the type that happened in the Northeast. The timing of the increase in the metropolitan housing vacancy rate and poverty rate in the two central cities that occurred in the 1980s is roughly coincident with the rough times in the oil patch as the price of crude oil fell from the heights it reached in the late 1970s. Otherwise, Dallas–Fort Worth seems to have shrugged off the oil patch problems and moved on.

Houston

How did Houston fare during this period? We shall see that the oil market ups and downs had a larger impact on Houston than on Dallas–Fort Worth. The population of the Houston metropolitan area increased from 1.90 million in 1970 to 2.75 million in 1980, a jump of 44.7 percent in just ten years. Population continued to increase in the 1980s, but at a slower pace of 20.6 percent to 3.32 million. Likewise, total employment jumped 79.5 percent—from 769,000 in 1970 to 1.38 million in 1980. Cowboys were becoming urban cowboys in the 1970s. The employment level of 1.62 million in 1990 was a further increase of 17.1 percent that was actually less than the rate of population growth during the decade. Manufacturing employment in the urban area increased from 145,000 in 1970 (18.9 percent of total employment) to 248,000 in 1980 (18.0 percent of the total), but then declined to 217,000 (down to 13.4 percent of the total) in 1990.

The economic difficulties that Houston experienced in the 1980s were caused by the drop in the price of oil and the decline in crude oil production. The Center for Public Policy of the University of Houston (2004) reported that the energy-dependent employment base in the metropolitan area declined from 317,000 in 1985 to 256,000 in 1990, a drop of 19.2 percent. The effects can be seen in the poverty and median income data. The poverty rate in the metropolitan area fell from 12.8 percent in 1970 to 10.3 percent in 1980, but increased to 15.1 percent in 1990. The poverty rate in the central city started at 13.9 percent in 1970, fell to 12.7 percent in 1980, and then increased to a northeastern-like 20.7 percent in 1990. Median family income (1999 dollars) increased from $45,900 to $55,800, a 21.6 percent jump from 1970 to 1980, but then fell to $49,600 in 1990 (down 11.1 percent). Up and down indeed. The housing market also reflects the up-and-down pattern. Total housing units increased from 642,000 to 1.11 million from 1970 to 1980. The vacancy rate increased from 8.4 percent to 11.6 percent, so there is evidence of some overbuilding during the boom years. Housing units increased to 1.36 million in 1990 (up another 22.3 percent), and the overall vacancy rate remained stable at 11.9 percent. However, during the 1980s the vacancy rate in the central city showed signs of trouble. The vacancy rate in the city of Houston increased from 8.0 percent to 11.1 percent from 1970 to 1980, in line with the urban area as a whole. However, the central city vacancy rate of 14.9 percent in 1990 was a sign of a depressed housing market.

The city of Houston also was able to annex territory during these years, so the land area increased from 434 square miles in 1970 to 540 square miles in (a 24.4 percent increase). The Texas law gives the central cities more authority to annex territory than is the case in most other states. The population of the central city increased from 1.23 million in 1970 to 1.63 million in 1990 (32.3 percent), and most of that increase took place in the 1980s, when 362,000 more people became Houstonians. The black population of the metropolitan area increased from 382,000 in 1970 to 604,000 in 1990, an increase of 58.1 percent that fell considerably short of the overall population increase of 74.6 percent. The percentage black population of the central city remained fairly stable at 25.7 in 1970 and 27.7 in 1990.

The Houston story during the 1970s and 1980s is therefore a combination of the Sunbelt boom coupled with the up-and-down oil market. The decline in real family income, increases in central city poverty, and the housing vacancy rate in the central city in 1990 are evidence of economic difficulties, but these difficulties arise from a source that is largely unlike those in the Northeast.

The Deep South

New Orleans

We now turn to the three urban areas of the Deep South—New Orleans, Atlanta, and Birmingham. The New Orleans economy is also strongly influenced by the oil market, and its record resembles that of Houston, only worse. The population of the urban area increased in the 1980s from 1.14 million to 1.30 million (14.0 percent), and then fell slightly to 1.28 million (down 1.5 percent). The city of New Orleans is not able to annex territory, and its population declined continuously from 593,000 in 1970 to 558,000 in 1980 and 497,000 in 1990 (down 16.2 percent in twenty years). The black population of the urban area increased from 324,000 (28.3 percent of the total) to 444,000 (34.6 percent of the total) from 1970 to 1990 (up 37.0 percent). The population of the central city was 45.0 percent black in 1970, and this proportion increased to 61.6 percent in 1990. Total employment in the metropolitan area increased nicely during the 1970s from 399,000 to 544,000 (36.3 percent), but then declined to 541,000 in 1990. The number of central city residents who were employed increased from 210,000 in 1970 to 221,000 in 1980, and then fell to 190,000 in 1990.

The oil and gas business is big in Louisiana as well as in Texas. And as in

Texas, crude oil production in Louisiana peaked in 1972 at 0.58 billion barrels, and it has declined virtually continuously since then. Production had dropped to 0.20 billion barrels in 1980, and declined more slowly in the 1980s to reach approximately 0.16 barrels in 1990. Crude oil production in offshore wells is also important to Louisiana. Production from this source increased in the 1970s and 1980s, but has declined in recent years. Louisiana is also a big player in the oil refining business. Its oil refineries increased their production capacity dramatically from 0.44 billion barrels per year in 1970 to 0.90 billion barrels in 1980. Capacity remained at this level throughout the 1980s. Production in the state's twenty-six refineries typically exceeds 90 percent of capacity. However, on balance the oil and gas industry reduced employment opportunities and income for the residents of the Pelican State during 1970–90, largely because the state is simply running out of its oil and gas reserves.

The data on poverty and median family incomes reflect the employment trends. The poverty rate in the metropolitan area fell from 20.1 percent in 1970 to 17.4 percent in 1980, but then increased to 21.3 percent in 1990. The poverty rate in the central city was 26.4 percent in both 1970 and 1980, and then increased to 31.6 percent in 1990—encompassing one-third of the residents of the city of New Orleans. This poverty rate was higher than in any of the central cities of the Northeast in that year, the city of Cleveland being the highest with a poverty rate of 28.7 percent. Median family incomes (1999 dollars) in the metropolitan area increased by 13.5 percent from 1969 to 1979 ($39,300 to $44,600), and then gave it all back by declining to $39,200 in 1990 (down 12.1 percent). Median family incomes in the central city increased slightly in the 1970s from $33,800 to $34,400, and then fell in the 1980s to $29,800.

The New Orleans housing market added 121,000 units in the 1970s (from 371,000 to 492,000), and then added only 43,000 units in the 1980s. The vacancy rate remained stable in the 1970s at 7.6 percent in 1970 and 8.0 percent in 1980, but stood at 12.2 percent in 1990. The number of housing units in the central city increased from 208,000 in 1970 to 226,000 in 1980 and held steady at 224,000 in 1990. However, the central city vacancy rate, which was 8.0 percent in 1970 and 8.7 percent in 1980, popped up to 16.0 percent in 1990. That amounts to an additional 16,000 vacant units in 1990 compared to 1980.

New Orleans is the oldest urban area in the South, and its economy is subject to the ups and downs in the oil market. Further, unlike most of its Sunbelt counterparts, the central city is unable to annex territory. All of this added up to an urban area with its own urban crisis in the 1980s that certainly resembles the pattern experienced by the northeastern urban areas in the 1970s (and a few in the 1980s).

Atlanta

Metropolitan Atlanta arguably is the new economic capital of the "Old South." Its performance in the 1970s and 1980s was remarkable—pure Sunbelt boom. However, the central city is small, unable to annex territory, and experienced some bad inner-city problems. The population of the metropolitan area increased from 1.76 million in 1970 to 2.23 million in 1980 and 2.96 million in 1990, an increase of 67.8 percent in twenty years. The black population increased by 138.9 percent—from 311,000 to 743,000 to reach 25.1 percent of total population. Atlanta attracted both white and black migrants in large numbers. Total employment more than doubled in twenty years from 741,000 to 1.57 million. Even manufacturing employment increased—from 163,000 in 1970 (22.0 percent of the total) to 219,000 in 1990 (13.9 percent of the total). Employment in the new economy sectors of professional services, business services, and finance, insurance, and real estate (FIRE) more than tripled from 172,000 to 542,000. Median family incomes (1999 dollars) increased steadily from $45,500 in 1970 to $47,800 in 1980 and $55,100 in 1990—an increase of 21.1 percent over twenty years. The metropolitan poverty rate fell from 12.8 percent in 1970 to 10.1 percent in 1990. The housing market expanded from 568,000 units to 1.22 million units during these years, although the vacancy rate did increase from 4.9 percent in 1970 to 9.7 percent in 1990. Metropolitan Atlanta was booming.

But the story is different for the city of Atlanta. The central city declined in population even as the metropolitan population was growing very rapidly. The central city population of 497,000 in 1970 dropped to 425,000 in 1980 and 394,000 in 1990—a decline of 20.7 percent. The number of employed residents of the central city fell from 211,000 to 176,000 (down 16.6 percent). The central city also became increasingly black: 51.3 percent in 1970 and 66.8 percent in 1990. Actually, the size of the black population in the central city was stable at 255,000 in 1970 and 263,000 in 1990. The black population of the suburbs increased from 56,000 to 480,000 in twenty years. While the poverty rate in the metropolitan area declined, the central city poverty rate jumped from 19.8 percent in 1970 to 27.5 percent in 1980 and remained at that level (27.3 percent in 1990). The central city housing market shows evidence of the negative consequences of the filtering mechanism. The number of units in the central city increased from 171,000 to 182,000 from 1970 to 1990, but the vacancy rate shot up from 5.0 percent to 14.8 percent. The increase in vacant units of 18,000 exceeded the number of new units by 7,000.

Decline in the central city occurred in certain inner-city neighborhoods. Hoffman (2003) studied four predominantly black high-poverty areas in Atlanta to the east and south of downtown, and found that population in these areas declined from 36,000 in 1970 to 19,000 in 1990. The number of housing units fell from 12,156 to 9500, and the vacancy rate increased from 10.3 percent to 19.8 percent, so the number of occupied units dropped from 10,900 to 7,617. The poverty rate in these areas was a very high 41.9 percent in 1970, and it climbed to 50.2 percent in 1990.

Atlanta presents a rather surprising picture. The metropolitan area boomed and attracted large numbers of both white and black migrants and generated rising real incomes. However, in the midst of all this prosperity the central city experienced an urban crisis of northeastern proportions.

Birmingham

The Birmingham urban area did not reach a population of one million in the twentieth century. The population of 738,000 in 1970 did grow in each decade—to 815,000 in 1980 and 840,000 in 1990, for a total increase of 13.8 percent. The black population of the metropolitan area increased only 11.1 percent (from 217,000 to 241,000). Employment grew rather well from 270,000 in 1970 to 381,000 in 1990 (up 41.1 percent). The larger employment gain occurred in the 1970s (70,000 out of a total increase of 111,000). Manufacturing employment fell from 65,000 to 54,000 over the twenty years, but jobs in professional services, business services, and FIRE more than doubled—from 63,000 to 144,000. This outcome may be a bit of a surprise. Birmingham was joining the new economy and the "new South."

The strong employment growth produced gains in median family incomes (1999 dollars) at the metropolitan level. Median family income of $37,700 in 1970 increased to $42,700 in 1980 and $43,000 in 1990. The metropolitan poverty rate fell from 19.2 percent in 1970 to 15.2 percent in 1980 (and held steady at 15.1 percent in 1990). Clearly the 1970s were the better decade for Birmingham, but the urban area did not have to give back any of the economic gains in the 1980s as did Houston and New Orleans.

The city of Birmingham was unable to annex territory. As we have seen, a metropolitan area that does not grow rapidly typically experiences decline in the central city, and Birmingham is no exception. The population of the central city fell from 301,000 in 1970 to 266,000 in 1990 (down 11.6 percent). The number of employed residents of the central city fell slightly, from 115,000 to 111,000, even as the metropolitan job market was growing rapidly. Median family incomes in the central city (1999 dollars) held steady in the 1970s ($35,100 in 1969 and $34,900 in 1979), but fell in the 1980s to $32,100 in 1989. The central city poverty rate started high, at 22.7 percent in 1970, remained stable at 22.0 percent in 1980, and then increased to 24.8 percent in 1990. The black population of the central city increased from 126,000 to

168,000, so the percentage of black population in the central city increased from 41.9 percent to 63.2.

Metropolitan Birmingham had some success, especially during the 1970s, with joining the new economy of the South. However, its central city became increasingly black and had a poverty rate that remained stubbornly high.

Miami

Miami is another Sunbelt boomtown, but its sources of growth differ from those of Atlanta. Miami is a destination for retirees and the gateway of the United States to Latin America. Refugees from Cuba add to the mix as well. Commerce in Miami comes in many forms. For example, as their brochures suggest, the Miami tourism bureau regards the 1980s television show *Miami Vice* as an important part of the city's history.

Metropolitan Miami had a population of 1.89 million in 1970, jumping to 2.64 million in 1980 and 3.19 million in 1990. This growth of 69.1 percent in twenty years slightly exceeds the growth of Atlanta of 67.8 percent and Dallas–Fort Worth of 66.0 percent (but is slightly less than the 74.6 percent increase in Houston). Total employment doubled from 751,000 to 1.51 million over the twenty years despite of the cancellation of *Miami Vice*. Manufacturing is not a large part of the Miami economy, but it did increase from 96,000 jobs in 1970 to 159,000 jobs in 1980 (and held at 159,000 in 1990). Manufacturing employment was only 10.6 percent of total employment in 1990. Professional services, business services, and FIRE increased from 189,000 jobs in 1970 to 544,000 jobs in 1990. Median family incomes (1999 dollars) at the metropolitan level increased from $42,400 in 1970 by 5.7 percent to $44,800 in 1990. This is a relatively modest increase over twenty years in the face of a huge increase in employment, and it probably reflects the migration from Latin America. The foreign-born population of the metropolitan area increased from 19.0 percent in 1970 to 33.6 percent in 1990. The Hispanic population of the metropolitan area was 621,000 in 1980 (23.5 percent of the total), and their numbers grew to 1.06 million in 1990 (33.1 percent of the total population). The metropolitan poverty rate stood at 12.9 percent in 1970, declined slightly to 12.7 percent in 1980, and then increased to 14.9 percent in 1990.

The city of Miami had a small increase in population of 7.2 percent from 1970 to 1990—from 335,000 to 359,000. In 1970, 43.2 percent of the city's population was foreign born, and this proportion increased to 59.7 percent in 1990. The Hispanic population was 55.9 percent of the central city population in 1980, increasing to 62.1 percent in 1990.[1] The central city is small, consisting of only 35 square miles, and is unable to annex territory. The poverty rate was a relatively high 20.4 percent in 1970, increasing to 24.5 percent in 1980 and 31.2 percent in 1990 to equal the poverty rate in the city of New Orleans. Median family incomes in the central city declined in real terms from $33,200 in 1970 to a very low $26,500 in 1990.

The housing market added 632,000 units from 1970 to 1990, an increase of 90.8 percent from 696,000 to 1.33 million. The vacancy rate increased from 6.5 percent to 8.1 percent. The city of Miami experienced the adverse consequences of the filtering mechanism. The central city contained 125,000 units in 1970 with a vacancy rate of only 4.5 percent. The number of units increased to 143,000 in 1990 and the vacancy rate increased to 12.8 percent, so the increase in the number of vacant units of 13,000 was 72.2 percent of the increase in the number of units in the central city.

Metropolitan Miami boomed in the 1970s and 1980s, but it was struggling to absorb the immigrants from Latin America. This is evident in the data for the city of Miami, which show increasing poverty and declining family median real incomes.

Los Angeles

Let us now head to the West. When we last visited the Los Angeles metropolitan area, it had doubled in population from 4.93 million in 1950 to 9.97 million in 1970. Never before in U.S. history had such a large metropolitan area grown so rapidly. The strains created by that growth surely played a role in creating the tensions that produced the Watts riot of 1965. The city of Los Angeles had increased in population by 42.9 percent from 1950 to 1970 (from 1.97 million to 2.82 million), and the black population of the central city had jumped from 171,000 to 504,000. The Great Migration had included a western component. The metropolitan area added another 4.56 million people from 1970 to 1990, reaching a population of 14.53 million. The population of the central city also increased, to 3.48 million in 1990. The central city expanded its land area by a mere 1.1 percent (from 464 to 469 square miles), so this population growth represents an increase within a given area. However, the black population of the central city declined by 8.5 percent to 461,000 even as the black population of the metropolitan area increased from 830,000 to 1.17 million. The black population of the suburbs increased from 326,000 in 1970 to 710,000 in 1990, so that 60.6 percent of the black population was living in the suburbs.

The ethnic picture of metropolitan Los Angeles after 1970 must include two additional groups—Hispanics and Asians. Table 11.1 shows the ethnic composition of the metropolitan area for 1970, 1980, and 1990. This table shows that most of the population growth after 1970 was among the Hispanic and Asian groups. The Hispanic population increased from 1.4 million to 4.7

Table 11.1

Ethnic Groups in Metropolitan Los Angeles (1,000s)

	1970	1980	1990
All Hispanics	1,400	2,862	4,698
Foreign born	28%	42%	50%
Born in Mexico	20%	33%	36%
Asians	256	596	1,327
Foreign born	42%	63%	69%
Blacks	781	1,044	1,146
Foreign born	0%	2%	3%
Non-Hispanic whites	7,136	7,021	7,194
Foreign born	7%	8%	8%
Other or unknown	399	—	166

Note: Black Hispanics are classified as Hispanic.
Source: Adapted from data in Abu-Lughod (1999, p. 373).

million in twenty years, and the number of foreign-born Hispanics increased from 398,000 to 2.36 million. The number of residents in the metropolitan area who were born in Mexico increased from 79,000 in 1970 to 861,000 in 1990. The ethnic Asian community increased in numbers from 256,000 in 1970 to 1.33 million in 1990, and the number of foreign-born Asians increased from 109,000 to 912,000 during these twenty years. These two groups account for 90.7 percent of the population growth, and the source of much of total growth—some 60.6 percent—was migration from outside the United States. This is in dramatic contrast to the previous twenty years, in which the growth was largely the result of internal migration within the United States. How did the metropolitan economy fare during these years?

Total employment in the metropolitan area increased from 3.96 million in 1970 to 6.98 million in 1990—growth of 76.2 percent compared to the population increase of 45.7 percent. Employment growth was across the board. Manufacturing increased from 966,000 (24.4 percent of total employment) to 1.36 million (19.4 percent of total employment). Employment in professional services, business services, and FIRE more than doubled from 1.03 million to 2.31 million. The number of employed residents of the central city increased from 1.16 million to 1.67 million (43.7 increase, compared to the central city population growth of 23.8 percent), but this growth could not prevent an increase in poverty. The poverty rate in the metropolitan area increased from 10.2 percent in 1970 to 13.1 percent in 1990. This increase was largely the result of the increase in poverty in the city of Los Angeles—from 13.0 percent in 1970 to 16.4 percent in 1980 to 18.9 percent in 1990. Median family incomes (1999 dollars) increased at the metropolitan level from $49,400 in 1970 to $55,400 in 1990, but declined in the central city from $47,500 to $46,200.

The housing market in the metropolitan area was booming, but did not outstrip the growth in demand. The number of housing units increased from 3.53 million in 1970 to 5.21 million in 1990 (up 47.6 percent, compared to population growth of 45.7 percent). As a result, the vacancy rate was stable at 5.5 percent in 1970 and 5.9 percent in 1990. The number of units in the central city increased from 1.08 million to 1.29 million over the same twenty years, an increase of 20.5 percent compared to the population growth of 23.8 percent. The central city vacancy rate barely moved; 4.2 percent vacant in 1970 and 5.3 percent vacant in 1990.

This very brief examination of the Los Angeles metropolitan area during the urban crisis period has shown that, in spite of the tremendous growth in population and employment, the central city experienced an increase in poverty and a decline in median family incomes that is similar to some of the central cities of the Northeast. However, in contrast to the northeastern central cities, these problems are surely related to the difficulties associated with the massive migration from abroad. It is well known that foreign immigrants with limited ability in the English language also initially have limited ability to earn income. It is also known that their earnings advance over time and eventually catch up with the native born, provided that the job market is favorable.

San Francisco–Oakland

The second urban area of the West, San Francisco–Oakland, had a population in 1970 of 3.11 million, which was less than one-third of that of the Los Angeles metropolitan area in the same year. Population growth was a relatively sedate 577,000 (18.6 percent) from 1970 to 1990—partly because sizable growth took place in the adjacent booming area of Silicon Valley. The San Jose metropolitan area grew from a population of 1.06 million in 1970 to 1.50 million in 1990. The population of the two central cities remained stable at 1.08 million in 1970 and 1.10 million in 1990. The black population of the metropolitan area increased from 330,000 to 415,000, but it increased only marginally in the central cities from 221,000 to 239,000. The black population made up 10.6 percent of the metropolitan population and 20.5 percent of the central city population in 1970, and these proportions increased slightly to 11.3 percent and 21.8 percent in 1990.

Employment growth in the San Francisco–Oakland metropolitan area was a robust 48.0 percent, from 1.30 million to 1.93 million. Manufacturing employment recorded a gain of 17.4 percent from 201,000 (15.4 percent of total employment) to 236,000 (down to 12.2 percent of total employment).

Employment in professional services, business services, and FIRE more than doubled from 389,000 to 783,000. Employment of central city residents increased from 474,000 to 555,000 with a constant population.

The strong job market was reflected in the data on poverty and median family incomes. The poverty rate for the metropolitan area started at a relatively low 9.8 percent in 1970 and ended the period with an even lower 9.2 percent in 1990. The central city poverty rate was reasonably stable at 15.0 percent in 1970 and 16.1 in 1990. Median family incomes in real terms in the metropolitan area shot ahead by 21.3 percent (from $53,400 to $64,800), and the central city median family income increased from $46,100 to $50,500 (up 9.5 percent).

As in metropolitan Los Angeles, the housing market avoided overbuilding. The housing units in the metropolitan area increased from 1.30 million in 1970 to 1.49 million in 1990 (an increase of 32.3 percent compared to the population increase of 18.5 percent), and the vacancy rate was quite low at 3.9 percent in 1970 and 4.9 percent in 1990. Housing units in the central city increased from 457,000 to 482,000, and the vacancy rate of 5.0 percent in 1970 increased only to 6.4 percent in 1990.

At last we have found a major urban area that appears to have avoided the major economic aspects of the urban crisis during 1970 to 1990. The strong job market translated into a central city with a poverty rate that increased only by 1.1 percent, a median family income that increased by 9.5 percent, and a housing vacancy rate that remained relatively low at 6.4 percent as more central city housing was built.

Other Major Urban Areas of the West

Our final group of Sunbelt metropolitan areas consists of Seattle, Denver, San Diego, and Phoenix. The Seattle metropolitan area avoided the major negative economic aspects of urban crisis. The only major negative outcome was a modest increase in the central city poverty rate from 10.0 percent in 1970 to 12.4 percent in 1990. Metropolitan population increased nicely from 1.45 million in 1970 to 2.03 million in 1990, while the central city remained stable at 531,000 in 1970 and 516,000 in 1990. Central city population had dipped to 494,000 in 1980 but had recovered most of the loss by 1990. The city of Seattle did not annex territory during this period, remaining at 84 square miles. The black population is not large in Seattle—42,000 in 1970 (38,000 in the central city) and 79,000 in 1990 (51,000 in the central city).

Metropolitan employment increased by 90.2 percent over the twenty years (from 571,000 to 1.09 million). Manufacturing employment increased by 61.4 percent from 132,000 to 213,000, and the three "new economy" sectors of professional services, business services, and FIRE more than doubled from

157,000 to 382,000. The number of central city residents who were employed rose from 229,000 to 286,000. This strong job market produced a low poverty rate and a nice gain in median family incomes at the metropolitan level. The poverty rate was a low 7.5 percent in 1970, and it remained low at 7.6 percent in 1990. The median family income (1999 dollars) increased by 10.5 percent from $52,400 to $57,900 over the twenty years in the metropolitan area. As noted above, the poverty rate in the central city did increase from 10.0 percent in 1970 to 12.4 percent in 1990, but central city median family incomes advanced from $49,600 to $53,600 (up 8.1 percent).

The Seattle housing market actually tightened over the period. Housing units in the metropolitan area increased from 523,000 in 1970 to 847,000 in 1990 (up 62.0 percent compared to population growth of 40.3 percent), but the vacancy rate declined from 8.0 percent to 4.4 percent. Furthermore, the central city added housing units (from 222,000 to 248,000), and the vacancy rate declined from 7.1 percent to 4.7 percent.

The case of Denver is not as favorable as that of Seattle. The Denver economy grew strongly in the 1970s, but its growth slowed in the 1980s and produced an increase in the central city poverty rate and a drop in median family incomes in the central city, even as the land area of the central city increased by 61 percent. Population increased strongly from 1.10 million in 1970 to 1.64 million in 1990 (up 48.5 percent), but the population of the central city fell from 515,000 to 468,000 (down 9.2 percent). This decline in the central city population occurred in spite of the fact that the city of Denver expanded its land area from 95 to 153 square miles between 1970 and 1990. Blacks did not make up a large part of the population, numbering 50,000 (47,000 in the central city) in 1970 and 92,000 (58,000 in the central city) in 1990. Total employment increased from 457,000 in 1970 to 738,000 in 1980 and 869,000 in 1990 (up 61.5 percent in the 1970s and up an additional 17.8 percent in the 1980s), and the number of central city residents who were employed also increased from 218,000 to 250,000 in the 1970s and declined to 236,000 in 1990. Manufacturing jobs increased from 72,000 to 108,000 from 1970 to 1980 (50 percent increase) and then remained at that level in 1990, and professional services, business services, and FIRE increased from 132,000 to 327,000 jobs, with more than half of that increase (54.9 percent) coming in the 1970s.

The strong job market produced a metropolitan poverty rate that was low in 1970 at 9.4 percent and changed only to 9.7 percent in 1990 (after declining to 8.2 percent in 1980). Median family incomes (1999 dollars) in the metropolitan area increased nicely from $48,200 in 1969 to $54,200 in 1979 (up 12.4 percent in a decade), and remained stable at $54,100 in 1990. Clearly the Denver economy was very strong in the 1970s, but tailed off somewhat in the 1980s. The effects of the slower economy of the 1980s are seen most clearly in the poverty and income data for the central city. The central city poverty rate was 13.5 percent in 1970, barely moved to 13.7 percent in 1980, and then increased to 17.1 percent in 1990. Central city median family incomes increased from $43,800 in 1969 to $44,800 in 1979, and then backed up to $43,000 in 1990.

The metropolitan housing market increased from 368,000 units in 1970 to 581,000 units in 1980, and the vacancy rate increased from 3.9 percent to 6.3 percent. The 1980s saw a further expansion of the housing market to 720,000 units, and the vacancy rate increased to 9.0 percent. A vacancy rate in housing at this level is an indicator of a market that is somewhat overbuilt.

San Diego is another case of a booming Sunbelt urban area. Population increased from 1.36 million in 1970 to 2.50 million in 1990, an increase of 83.9 percent in just twenty years. The central city included a great deal of undeveloped land in 1970 so that, even though no new land was annexed, the city of San Diego increased from 697,000 to 1.11 million. The ethnic composition of the population includes a major increase in the Hispanic population. Black residents of the urban area increased from 62,000 (53,000 in the central city) to 151,000 (100,000 in the central city). But the largely Hispanic foreign-born population increased from 96,000 (53,000 in the central city) to 429,000 (232,000 in the central city). Only 7.1 percent of the population of the urban area was foreign born in 1970, and this proportion increased to 17.2 percent in 1990. The Hispanic population in the metropolitan area was 275,000 in 1980, and this group increased to 499,000 in 1990. Slightly fewer than half of this group lived in the central city (131,000 in 1980 and 224,000 in 1990).

Employment boomed in San Diego, rising from 561,000 in 1970 to 1.26 million in 1990 (a remarkable increase of 123.9 percent in twenty years). Manufacturing employment more than doubled from 73,000 to 158,000, and employment in professional services, business services, and FIRE more than tripled from 123,000 to 427,000. The booming job market produced strong increases in median family incomes at both the metropolitan and central city levels. The median family income (1999 dollars) in the metropolitan area of $53,400 in 1990 was 16.6 percent greater than the $45,900 figure for 1970, and the central city median family income increased from $46,000 to $52,800 as well. However, the booming job market could not prevent the poverty rate in the metropolitan area from increasing slightly, from 10.0 percent in 1970 to 11.3 percent in 1990. The central city poverty rate increased from 11.0 percent to 13.4 percent, which suggests that the central city experienced some difficulties absorbing the immigrant population into the job market.

The housing market showed no signs of being overbuilt. Housing units more than doubled—from 450,000 to 935,000 over the twenty years—and the vacancy rate actually fell slightly from 6.0 percent to 5.1 percent. The central city housing market expanded from 241,000 units to 429,000 units, and the vacancy rate moved down from 5.8 percent to 5.3 percent.

Last, we look at Phoenix, the metropolitan area in this study that grew most rapidly. Phoenix became a popular destination for retirees from the North in addition to being a booming Sunbelt economy. The population of the urban area more than doubled from 1.04 million in 1970 to 2.24 million in 1990. Total employment almost tripled from 392,000 to 1.06 million (up 169.1 percent, to be exact). The land area of the central city increased from 248 to 420 square miles, so comparisons of the city of Phoenix in 1990 with its 1970 version are flawed. Nevertheless, the data for the central city show some signs of urban problems. The poverty rate at the metropolitan level fell from 12.3 percent in 1970 to 11.0 percent in 1980, and then increased to 12.9 percent in 1990. The central city poverty rate was actually lower than the metropolitan poverty rate in 1970 and 1980 (11.6 percent in 1970 and 11.1 percent in 1980), but increased to 14.2 percent in 1990. Median family incomes (1999 dollars) increased in the metropolitan area from $44,100 in 1969 to $46,400 in 1979 and $47,600 in 1989. The central city also registered an increase in median family incomes in the 1970s from $45,200 in 1969 to $46,700 in 1979, but then dipped to $45,900 in 1990.

The ethnic composition of Phoenix was changing during these years, but not nearly as much as in Los Angeles and San Diego. The foreign-born population of the metropolitan area was only 40,000 (3.9 percent of the total population) in 1970, and their numbers increased to 162,000 (7.2 percent) in 1990. The black population was a mere 33,000 in 1970, and this group increased to 75,000 in 1990, but the proportion of the population that was black changed only from 3.2 percent to 3.4 percent. The Hispanic population was 226,000 in 1980 (14.1 percent of the total in the urban area) and increased to 374,000 (16.7 percent of the urban area).

The housing market became overbuilt during the twenty-year period. Housing units in the metropolitan area were 336,000 in 1970, and mushroomed to 950,000 units in 1990. The vacancy rate was a low 4.7 percent in 1970, but stood at 11.7 percent in 1990, probably in anticipation of further growth (which did occur, as we shall see).

The Sunbelt Metropolitan Areas: A Statistical Summary for 1970–1990

This section pulls together basic data on the metropolitan areas of the Sunbelt for 1970 to 1990 and presents a statistical summary. The data for the twelve metropolitan areas are presented in Table 11.2, and data for their central cities are shown in Table 11.3.

Table 11.2

Metropolitan Areas of the Sunbelt: 1970–1990 (in percent)

	Population growth	Employment growth	Median family income change	Manufacturing employment 1970	Foreign born 1970	Foreign born 1990
Dallas–Fort Worth	66.0	1,010.9	11.9	24.4	1.6	7.9
Houston	74.6	110.7	8.1	18.9	2.6	13.3
New Orleans	12.3	35.6	−0.3	14.0	2.3	4.1
Atlanta	67.8	118.8	21.1	22.0	1.0	3.9
Birmingham	13.8	41.1	14.1	17.1	0.6	1.1
Miami	69.1	101.1	5.7	12.8	19.0	33.6
Los Angeles	45.7	76.2	12.1	24.4	2.6	13.3
San Francisco–Oakland	18.6	48.0	21.3	15.4	10.9	21.1
Seattle	40.0	90.2	10.5	23.1	5.9	8.4
Denver	48.5	90.2	12.2	15.8	3.2	5.0
San Diego	83.9	123.9	16.6	13.0	7.1	17.2
Phoenix	115.4	169.1	7.9	18.4	3.9	7.2
Mean	54.6	92.3	11.8	18.3	5.7	12.5

Source: HUD State of the Cities Data.

Table 11.3

Central Cities of the Sunbelt: 1970–1990 (in percent)

	Central city population change	Change in land area	Poverty rate 1970	Poverty rate 1990	Black population 1970	Black population 1990
Dallas–Fort Worth	17.6	32.5	13.4	17.8	23.3	26.9
Houston	32.3	24.4	13.9	20.7	25.7	27.7
New Orleans	−16.2	0	26.4	31.6	14.1	18.5
Atlanta	−20.7	0	19.8	27.3	51.3	66.8
Birmingham	−11.6	0	22.7	24.8	41.9	63.2
Miami	7.2	0	20.4	31.2	14.1	18.5
Los Angeles	19.2	1.1	13.0	18.9	17.9	13.2
San Francisco–Oakland	1.9	4.0	15.0	16.1	20.5	21.8
Seattle	−2.8	0	10.0	12.4	7.2	9.9
Denver	−9.2	61.0	13.5	17.1	9.1	12.4
San Diego	57.8	0	11.0	13.4	7.6	9.0
Phoenix	68.9	69.4	11.6	14.2	3.2	3.4
Mean	12.0	16.0	15.9	20.5	22.2	27.9

Source: HUD State of the Cities Data.

The average population growth for the twelve metropolitan areas was 54.6 percent, compared to 6.4 percent for the seventeen metropolitan areas of the Northeast. Employment growth averaged 92.3 percent over the twenty years, compared to 30.0 percent for the Northeast. The manufacturing base of the Sunbelt urban areas was 18.3 percent of total employment in 1970 (versus 26.8 percent in the northeastern urban areas), and median family incomes in real terms advanced 11.8 percent on average (compared to a somewhat lower 7.6 percent for the northeastern seventeen). Some of the Sunbelt metropolitan areas experienced large increases in migration from abroad. The largest increases in foreign-born populations occurred in Los Angeles, Miami, San Francisco–Oakland, Houston, and San Diego.

The twelve central cities of the Sunbelt gained 12.0 percent population over the twenty years on average, compared to an average loss of 17.1 percent in the northeastern central cities. The central city poverty rate increased from 15.9 percent to 20.5 percent on average, compared to an increase from 14.7 percent to 20.6 percent for the central cities of the Northeast. However, as noted in the introduction to this chapter, the central cities of the South experienced the larger increases in poverty of 6.2 percentage points, compared to 3.0 percentage points for the central cities of the West. The black population of the Sunbelt central cities increased from 22.2 percent to 27.9 percent, a smaller increase than the one for the northeastern central cities of 28.8 percent to 37.1 percent.

Basic regression analyses were computed in order to summarize the data in Tables 11.2 and 11.3. First of all, none of the variables in the tables "explains" the growth of the population of the metropolitan area. Population growth of the northeastern metropolitan areas was negatively related to the size of the manufacturing base in 1970, but this relationship did not hold for the Sunbelt metropolitan areas. Population growth and employment growth were highly correlated ($R^2 = .959$), but no causal inference can be made because the causation runs both ways. Employment growth was also not related to the size of the manufacturing base in 1970 (as it was for the Northeast), but employment growth was statistically significantly related to the poverty rate in the central city in 1970 (Ccpov70), according to:

$$EMPGROW = 104.25 - 3.12\ CCPOV70, \quad R^2\ (adj.) = .199$$
$$(3.88) \quad (2.19)$$

The central city poverty rate was higher in the southern central cities than in the western central cities by 7.1 percent in 1970, and this difference is statistically significant. The difference between the southern and western central city poverty rates was 10.2 percent in 1990, and this difference is also statistically significant. A final regression related the change in poverty in the central city in 1990 (CCPOV90) to the initial poverty rate in 1970 and the increase in the foreign-born population in the metropolitan area (CHFB), with the following results:

$$CCPOV90 = 1.75 + 1.27\ CCPOV70 + 0.29\ CHFB,\ R^2\ (adj.) = .878$$
$$(0.64)\quad(9.02)\qquad\qquad(2.15)$$

This equation says that the central city poverty was higher the greater was the initial poverty rate in 1970 (as also was found for the northeastern central cities), plus an additional amount that was related to the increase in the foreign-born population. An increase in the foreign-born population of 1 percent was associated with a higher central poverty rate with a coefficient of 0.29, and this coefficient is statistically significant. This effect is particularly evident in the cases of Los Angeles, Houston, and Miami.

Additional assessment of the Sunbelt central cities is presented in Chapter 13.

Note

1. The use of the term Hispanic follows the U.S. Bureau of the Census definition. The 2000 Census asked, "Is this person Spanish/Hispanic/Latino?" If the respondent indicated Puerto Rican, Mexican, Mexican American, Chicano, Cuban, or other Spanish/Hispanic/Latino, then the person is classified Hispanic. The method is one of self identification. It is unclear whether all persons of Latin American origin consider themselves to be Hispanic. The methods for defining and identifying race and ethnicity continue to be a major topic of research.

12

New Urban Scholarship

The crisis in urban America stimulated a great deal of scholarly research from the 1960s onward. The purpose of this chapter is to provide a brief overview of the main themes of this huge outpouring of research work in economics and sociology. Other fields such as urban geography, urban transportation, and psychology also were involved heavily, but the work in these fields is less germane to the themes in this book. The work of the social psychologist Kenneth Clark on the pathology of the black inner city has already been highlighted, as has the report of the National Advisory Commission on Civil Disorders, more commonly known as the Kerner Commission report.

Urban Economics and the Urban Crisis

Urban economics grew out of the earlier field of land economics, which concentrated on understanding the nature of the use of both rural and urban land. Many identify the founding of urban economics as a separate field in economics with the publication of the basic theory of urban land use, William Alonso's book *Location and Land Use* (1964). Research in the basic economics of urban areas, including the work of Alonso, was funded by an organization called Resources for the Future, which had obtained funding from the Ford Foundation for the purpose. As is their wont, economists tend to develop theoretical models before they wade into the social and economic problems of the day. Alonso's theory of the urban land market, based on the notion of bid rent for urban sites, was well timed to bring economists into the study of the urban crisis.

Under the sponsorship of Resources for the Future, the field of urban economics developed rapidly in the 1960s. Very quickly the field was organized around a short list of topics. The leading textbook in the field—*Urban*

Economics by Edwin S. Mills, a professor at Princeton University—was first published in 1972. The topics included in the text are as follows:

- urbanization and growth of urban areas
- theory of land rent and land use
- efficient use of resources and equity in income distribution (standard microeconomic theory)
- trends in suburbanization
- urban problems, including
  a. poverty
  b. housing, slums, and urban renewal
  c. urban transportation
  d. financing local government
  e. pollution and environmental quality

Note that the book begins with an exploration of the growth of urban areas, which is followed by economic theory—theory of land rent and land use and an explication of basic microeconomic theory of the efficient allocation of resources and the question of equity in the distribution of income. These theoretical topics are followed by a description of the trends in suburbanization along with the economic explanation for the trends. The theoretical explanations for suburbanization boil down to two simple reasons: the decline in the time cost of commuting by car, and the increase in real incomes leading to an increased demand for new houses that would need to be built in the suburbs. Next is a laundry list of urban problems that clearly was motivated by the urban crisis that began at the time Mills's book was being written. Other college reading materials followed the same basic outline. The popular book *Readings in Urban Economics* by Matthew Edel and Jerome Rothenberg (1972) includes these topics:

- location theory and metropolitan growth
- intraurban location and land use
- housing
- segregation and ghetto poverty
- congestion and pollution
- urban transportation
- urban public finance

In the 1970s, many urban economists learned the field from these two books. Note that urban crime was not included in the list of topics. However, the economics of crime emerged as a separate subfield, starting with the well-known article by Gary Becker (1968) titled "Crime and Punishment: An Economic Approach." Becker posited that criminals can at least in part be understood as economic men (yes, mostly men) who respond to incentives just as anyone else. In their case, the incentives include the probabilities of capture and conviction as well as the severity of punishment. This approach has proved to be fruitful. Debate on incentives and criminals was sidetracked for a while on whether capital punishment served as a deterrent to murder (an issue still unresolved), but the basic approach has been proven valid in many studies.

One result of this definition of the field of urban economics was that research tended to become compartmentalized. Major exceptions to this tendency toward compartmentalization are discussed below. Economic theory as applied to urban areas received a great deal of attention, but those models largely were studied essentially with disinterest in the urban crisis of the day. A great deal of research on urban housing was conducted. Much was learned about how to model an urban housing market. The field of housing economics became very technical, but most of the research was not connected well to the other aspects of the urban crisis. Indeed, as the two previous chapters have suggested, urban housing problems are probably more a result of the urban crisis than a cause. The fields of environmental economics, urban transportation, and urban public finance became sub-specialties in their own right. The field of urban public finance included the study of the fiscal problems of central cities, so this field was connected to the urban crisis and the vicious circle experienced by the central cities. However, most of the research effort in urban public finance delved (some might say was sidetracked) into deeper theoretical analyses of what is known as the "vote with the feet" theory of local public goods. This theory is interesting in its own right and is applicable to the suburbs of major metropolitan areas, but has little or no relevance for large central cities. The study of segregation and inner-city poverty was the topic most closely connected to the urban crisis, and some of the studies did a pretty fair job of trying to understand urban crisis dynamics.

Perhaps the most influential single study of that time was an article by John F. Kain (1968) titled "Housing Segregation, Negro Employment, and Metropolitan Decentralization." Kain introduced his study with the following:

> This paper investigates the relationship between metropolitan housing market segregation and the distribution and level of nonwhite employment. Numerous researchers have evaluated the effects of racial discrimination in the housing market. Others have investigated discrimination in employment and have attempted to determine the extent to which the higher unemployment rates among Negroes are attributable to causes other than

racial discrimination, such as lower levels of educational attainment. However, possible interactions between housing segregation and nonwhite employment and unemployment have been all but ignored. To the author's knowledge, the research reported here is the first to link discrimination in the housing market to the distribution and level of nonwhite employment in urban areas. Hypotheses evaluated in this paper are that racial segregation in the housing markets (1) affects the distribution of Negro employment and (2) reduces Negro job opportunities, and that (3) postwar suburbanization of employment has seriously aggravated the problem. (1968, p. 175)

These hypotheses were tested using data from the 1950s for Chicago and Detroit. Scholars subsequently debated hotly the power of the statistical tests performed by Kain, but there is no question that belief in these hypotheses was and is influential among scholars, public officials, and the public in general. The general point here is that Kain set out to provide a more complete picture of the urban crisis by linking two topics—housing market segregation and employment location patterns.

Another important study by David Bradford and Harry Kelejian (1973) proposed an "econometric model of flight to the suburbs." They studied eighty-seven large metropolitan areas in 1960, with these results:

- A middle-class family was more likely to live in the suburbs (rather than the central city) the higher the poverty rate in the central city 1950, the higher the median family income of the urban area, and the lower the net public fiscal surplus enjoyed by middle-class residents of the central city.
- A poor family was more likely to live in the suburbs if the suburbs contained more older housing (and the central city less older housing), and if the net public fiscal surplus in the central city was lower.

Net public fiscal surplus refers to the general expenditures by local government per capita minus an estimate of the taxes paid per capita by middle-class and poor families. Their general conclusion is succinct and even includes the term vicious circle:

> Our result concerning the effect of the percentage poor in the central city on the middle class clearly supports the view that central cities are caught in a vicious circle, whereby the more rapidly the middle-class families move to the suburbs, the greater is the incentive for the exodus of those remaining. The feedback relationship is both direct—the location of the middle class depends directly on the fraction of the population in the central city that is

poor—and indirect, through the fiscal system—the fewer the middle-class families in the city, the heavier tax burden on all remaining families, especially the remaining middle-class families.

The Bradford-Kelejian study thus succeeds in linking the location decisions of middle-class households to the location of poor households and to the fiscal problems of the central city, and they linked the fiscal problems of the central city to the location decisions of middle-class households. However, left unsaid was why middle-class families evidently had an aversion to living in a city with a greater percentage of poor families. As we shall see, the sociological literature provided many answers to this question.

The attempts to formulate a comprehensive modeling approach to urban problems got off on what some regarded as the wrong foot. MIT engineer Jay Forrester (1969) published the book *Urban Dynamics*, in which he attempted to link many aspects of the urban economy, including business location, employment and unemployment, labor spatial and occupational mobility, the housing market, housing policy, and migration to the urban area. One of the major conclusions of the study was that policies to improve the housing stock of an urban area would be self-defeating because of the additional migration that would be stimulated. However, a detailed critique of the book by Jerome Rothenberg (1974), which appeared as the first article in the first issue of the *Journal of Urban Economics* (edited by Edwin Mills), concluded that the Forrester model was based on weak methodological presumptions, misleading structure of explanatory relationships, and specific parameter values that are arbitrary or often at variance from existing empirical data. In particular, the specific effect of housing availability on the migration of underemployed households was at variance with the facts. Such households in fact have not been found to pay much attention to housing availability, but rather respond to employment opportunity, higher wages, lower unemployment rates, and the like.

Some urban economists set out in the 1970s and 1980s to provide the synthesis needed to understand the urban crisis more fully. The work of R.D. Norton was emphasized in the earlier chapters on the 1950–70 period. Three additional serious empirical attempts are discussed here.

The first is a major study by Bradbury, Downs, and Small (1982) that was undertaken at the Brookings Institution, a major independent research organization located in Washington, D.C. The study, which was supported by both the Ford Foundation and the federal government, was prompted by the increase in urban problems in the 1970s. At the time, it was assumed that the federal government had a major responsibility to help the central cities and the poor who lived in them, but there was little research to serve as a guide to policy.

The study was intended as a guide to policy, but also turned out to provide more understanding of the processes of change in urban areas. The study of 120 large urban areas for the years 1960 to 1975 began by replicating Norton's (1979) equation for central city population growth, with the result that

$$\text{CCPOPGRO} = -16.9 + 0.71 \ \text{UPOPGRO} + 1.01 \ \text{ANNEX,}$$

where CCPOPGRO is the percentage change in the population of the central city, UPOPGRO is the same for the urban area, and ANNEX is the percentage increase in the population due to annexations over the period. The R-square for the equation is 0.87. The equation shows that if the urban area had no population growth, the central city would have declined by 16.9 percent over the fifteen-year period. The next task was to investigate the sources of population growth in the urban area, and Bradbury, Downs, and Small (1982) found that employment growth was the chief source of population growth (with a coefficient of 0.74). What determined employment growth? The main factor was population growth (both natural increase and migration), with a coefficient of 0.88. Three factors had positive, but weak, effects on employment growth—per capita income level and increase and a favorable industry mix in 1960. Population density and local taxes had negative effects on employment growth. An additional finding was that per capita income growth was a function of employment growth, moderated by population growth. The next task was to examine the central city. In summary, they found that the urban area was less decentralized if the central city had greater employment growth, if the urban area had lower income and fewer black people, if the central city had newer housing, and if the central city school system also served some of the suburbs. Greater employment growth in the central city depended upon employment growth in the urban area and other variables such as income growth in the city and low unemployment in the city. In summary, they found that a central city does poorly in employment growth if it is located in a large urban area with slow population growth, high income, rapid income growth, high population density, high taxes in the central city, and a bad mix of industries. The study found that there are some factors that can be manipulated by public policy. The central city is not just a prisoner of the growth rate of the urban area.

Bradbury, Downs, and Small (1981) did a study entitled *Futures for a Declining City: Simulations for the Cleveland Area.* In this study they constructed a simulation model based on metropolitan Cleveland and ran a "base case" projection for the years 1980 to 1990. They then introduced several policies designed to stimulate population and employment in the central city. Those policies were:

- a job stimulus package for the central city,
- a housing rehabilitation program for the central city,
- a transit improvement program,
- a program for fiscal equalization between city and suburbs, and
- a suburban growth control system.

All of these policy packages had the desired effects to some degree. The job stimulus package increased employment, but had only a minor effect on population in the central city. The housing rehabilitation program had the opposite effects. Transit improvement increased jobs in the downtown area but had no effect on population in the central city. Both the fiscal equalization program and the suburban growth controls increased population and employment in the central city. Based on these simulations, the fiscal equalization and the suburban growth controls seemed to have the largest positive impacts on the central city.

The last economic study considered here is the book by Thomas Stanback (1991) titled *The New Suburbanization: Challenge to the Central City*. In this study, Stanback took a close look at the suburbs, something that Bradbury and other researchers had not done. He studied fourteen of the largest urban areas over 1969–87 and found that important changes had taken place since the 1970s. First, the downtown areas had been transformed and rebuilt by the growth of the service sector. Most downtown workers commute from the suburbs, but some had decided to live near downtown. Second, the new suburbanization had created large centers of employment that place the suburbs in direct competition with downtown. Third, the demand for workers had shifted in favor of workers with higher levels of education. These changes have made the old industrial areas of the central city even more disadvantaged than ever. The data compiled by Stanback (1991) were used by McDonald (1997) to estimate an equation for employment growth in the central county for 1969–87 (CCEMPGRO), with the result that:

$$CCEMPGRO = 1.27 + 0.43 \; SUBEMPGRO - 2.82 \; CCPOP\%$$

Here SUBEMPGRO is suburban employment growth and CCPOP% is the percentage of the population of the central county that is located in the central city. The *R*-square is 0.67, and the equation says that employment growth in the central county is 0.43 percent greater if employment growth in the suburbs is 1 percent higher. Suburban employment growth generates employment growth in the central county. Also, the equation says that central county employment growth was lower the more closely the central county was identified with the central city. A similar result was found for population growth in the central county:

$$CCPOPGRO = 0.08 + 0.45 \text{ SUBPOPGRO} - 1.45 \text{ CCPOP}\%$$

The R-square for this equation is 0.65. The basic message of Stanback's book is that central counties on balance benefited from suburban growth, which by 1990 was taking partly the form of suburban agglomerations of service sector employment in office campuses.

Urban Sociology and the Urban Crisis

Work in urban sociology on racial segregation, urban education, urban crime, and urban poverty is discussed here. The field of urban sociology had been founded at the University of Chicago in the 1920s, and many descriptive studies of social and ethnic groups in urban areas had been conducted. In addition, two simple theoretical frameworks had been devised to understand the social layout of the urban areas of the 1920s, 1930s, and 1940s. The first is the concentric rings model, in which the urban population arranges itself in concentric rings of increasing income and more expensive housing. In this model, new migrants to the city first live in the inner ring and then move to outer rings as they achieve some economic success. The second framework is called the sector model, in which particular areas extend from near the central business district outward. These pieces of the urban pie are thought to be similar in ethnic identification and economic status. For example, the black population is generally of lower income than white ethnic groups, and tends to expand outward along a small number of radii. These are apt descriptions of the social geography of urban areas that are still in use, although adapted to the more dispersed urban areas of today.

The study of segregation was highlighted by the landmark study of Karl and Alma Taeuber (1965) entitled *Negroes in Cities: Residential Segregation and Neighborhood Change*. This important study made extensive use of data from the U.S. Bureau of the Census to document the extent of segregation of the black population and other ethnic groups in American's cities for 1940, 1950, and 1960. One basic finding is that blacks were far more racially segregated than were other groups such as Hispanics, Asians, and various groups of European origin. Furthermore, economic factors explained very little of the extent of segregation of blacks. They also investigated the process of neighborhood racial change, in which residential areas tend to "tip" from white to black occupancy once some tipping point of black occupancy had been reached. Further, they observed that the suburbanization of the white population, beginning in the 1950s, was associated with an expansion of the residential areas occupied by blacks in many cities. This expansion resulted in an increased degree of segregation of middle-class blacks from black people of lower class. This study has been highly influential and its findings are still relevant in the twenty-first century.

The study of student achievement in schools received a major boost from the work of James Coleman and his associates (U.S. Department of Education 1967) in the famous study *Equality of Educational Opportunity*, which is usually called the "Coleman Report." This study was sponsored by the U.S. Office of Education in order to discover the factors that contribute to educational achievement in elementary and secondary education. The Coleman Report achieved its fame from the finding that the economic and educational backgrounds of the students' families were more highly correlated with student achievement than were the various schooling input measures. The nature of the student body mattered far more than school resources. Given that the urban black population had lower education levels and income and was highly segregated, these findings suggested that racial and economic segregation would lead to lower achievement among the more disadvantaged students, so that economic inequalities would persist. This study set off a steady stream of studies that continues to this day. More recent research has identified schooling inputs that do matter for student achievement, such as teacher education and experience. One research issue arose very soon after the Coleman Report was released. It turned out that many of the measures of schooling inputs and the socioeconomic status of the students in the school are correlated. Indeed, the correlations were sufficiently high that it was difficult to identify any truly independent contribution of schooling inputs, given that the socioeconomic background of the student body was included in the statistical analysis. This issue was highlighted in the volume edited by Frederick Mosteller and Daniel Moynihan (1972) that was devoted to early further studies along Coleman Report lines. This problem of correlation between background variables and policy variables produced a call for careful experimentation to determine more precisely the educational policies that make a difference for student achievement. This issue also suggests that a vicious circle mechanism may be at work in this arena. A school in the central city loses some middle-class students because they move to the suburbs for some reason unrelated to school quality (e.g., the parents want to buy a new house). The socioeconomic status of the students in the school declines, and this possibly leads to some withdrawal of resources from the school as well. Both of these declines lead to further withdrawal of middle-class students from the school, and so on. The correlations between the schooling inputs and the socioeconomic status of the students therefore are indirect evidence of the vicious circle. This idea is applied to larger matters pertaining to the urban crisis in the next chapter.

The increase in the study of crime was no doubt in response to the shocking

Table 12.1

Crime in the United States: 1960–1990 (per 100,000)

	Murder	Rape	Robbery	Assault	Burglary	Larceny-theft	Auto theft
1960	5.0	9.5	59.9	85.1	502.1	1,024	181.7
1965	5.1	12.0	71.2	109.8	653.2	1,314	254.6
1970	7.8	18.5	171.4	163.0	1,071	2,079	453.7
1975	9.6	26.3	220.8	231.1	1,532	2,805	473.7
1980	10.2	36.8	251.1	298.5	1,684	3,167	502.2
1985	7.9	37.1	208.5	302.9	1,287	2,901	462.0
1990	9.4	41.2	257.0	424.1	1,236	3,195	657.8

Source: U.S. Department of Justice, Federal Bureau of Investigation, *Crime in the United States,* various issues.

increase in crime that occurred beginning roughly in 1965. Table 12.1 shows the official crime rate figures for the nation for 1960 to 1990. Compared to other advanced nations such as Great Britain, Japan, and Germany, crime in the United States was and still is very high. The homicide rate in 1990 was 9.4 per 100,000 people, compared to 1.1 in Great Britain, 1.1 in France, and 1.2 in Germany. The FBI keeps track of crimes that are reported to the police in the seven categories shown in the table. Between 1960 and 1980, the amount of crime reported to the police tripled from 1,867 to 5,950 crimes per 100,000. Most researchers on crime think that this increase is exaggerated because of an increase in crime reporting, but no one thinks that crime did not increase greatly. The murder rate doubled between 1965 and 1980, from 5.1 to 10.2 per 100,000. Murder is a crime that is virtually always reported.

Criminologists sought to understand why crime increased and how it can be reduced. A book edited by the eminent social scientist James Q. Wilson (1983) endeavored to summarize what had been learned in the previous fifteen years. It is telling that the sponsor of the volume stated in the preface that "Two lessons emerged from the experiences of the decade: first, that crime was a far more intractable problem than we had earlier been led to believe; and second, that there was clear room for improvement in our deployment of resources to control crime" (1983).

The topics of some of the essays in the Wilson volume indicate the foci of research on crime:

- violent predators as sources of criminal activity
- criminogenic traits of offenders
- crime and the family

- crime in the schools
- crime and unemployment
- controlling criminogenic commodities: drugs, guns, and alcohol
- strategies for police
- prosecution and sentencing
- parole and other policies pertaining to ex-offenders
- prisons and controlling crime through imprisonment

The causes of crime were sought inside the minds of the offenders, in their immediate family environment, and in the larger social environment. Attempts to control crime focused on control of drugs, guns, and alcohol, policing strategies, and policies regarding prosecution, sentencing, and imprisonment. One result of the studies was the decision to enforce harsher sentences, which increased the prison population dramatically in the 1990s. These matters are discussed at greater length in later chapters.

The study of urban poverty has generated much controversy along the way, beginning with the famous Moynihan report on the black family (U.S. Department of Labor 1965). This report, with the formal title *The Negro Family: The Case for National Action*, was conducted by the late Senator Daniel Moynihan when he was working for the U.S. Department of Labor in the 1960s. Using census data, Moynihan pointed out the relationship between black poverty and family structure—namely, the decline in marriage and the increase in out-of-wedlock births and female-headed families. The reaction to the Moynihan report was quite negative among "liberals," who felt that he was "blaming the victim." The issue is the direction of causation. Does a lack of economic opportunity, especially for black men, lead to the decline in marriage and families with children headed by females, or is there a "culture of poverty" that has been internalized by black people of the lower class that leads to the disintegration of the family and poverty? If it is the latter, then poverty will not be reduced appreciably until that culture is changed, because people will be unresponsive to changes in the economic and social external environment (except perhaps in the very long run). If it is the former, then poor people will respond to the provision of real economic and social opportunity. During the 1970s, some conservatives seized upon the "culture of poverty" theory to argue that providing the usual anti-poverty programs will do very little good until poor people are ready to become responsible members of society. Various programs were cut, and the real value of welfare benefits was permitted to erode. It was clear that this is not what Moynihan had intended, but it happened.

Interest in the sociological study of poverty revived in the late 1970s and early 1980s largely for two reasons. First, the disastrous situation of the inner cities in the 1970s was obvious. Second, a new term was popularized—the underclass. (Note: Sociologists study social classes, so they used the term.) Popular use of the term dates from 1981, when Ken Auletta published a series of three articles in the *New Yorker*. These articles became his book *The Underclass* (1982). Auletta was not the first to use the term. Earlier writers had used it to refer to those who were poor for long periods of time. But the term took on a new meaning. The eminent sociologist William J. Wilson used this new meaning in his highly influential 1978 book, *The Declining Significance of Race*. In that book he proposed the idea that, while many blacks increasingly were achieving higher levels of education and joining the ranks of the middle class, "new barriers (other than pure racial discrimination) create hardships essentially for the black underclass" (1978, p. 2). The nature of these new barriers is discussed in detail below. Wilson (1978, p. 115) stated that the process of suburbanization created a vicious circle of relocation of the middle class to the suburbs, the point that had been demonstrated empirically by Bradford and Kelejian (1973).

In *The Truly Disadvantaged: The Inner City, the Underclass, and Public Policy* (1987), Wilson refined the definition of underclass as follows:

> Today's ghetto neighborhoods are populated almost exclusively by the most disadvantaged segments of the black urban community, that heterogeneous grouping of families and individuals who are outside the mainstream of the American occupational system. Included in this group are individuals who lack training and skills and either experience long-term unemployment or are not members of the labor force, individuals who are engaged in street crime and other forms of aberrant behavior, and families that experience long-term spells of poverty and/or welfare dependency. These are the populations to which I refer when I speak of the *underclass*. (1987, p. 8)

The underclass is thus defined as black people who live in high-poverty neighborhoods and who are not engaged in standard labor market behavior and instead commit crimes (or are involved in other sorts of aberrant behavior) or are dependent on welfare. In Wilson's view, the basic cause of the growth of the underclass is social isolation, not a culture of poverty. The geographic concentration of the underclass means that their access to employment, marriage partners, good schools, and conventional role models is sharply limited. Social isolation was increased by the movement of successful blacks away from the traditional black neighborhoods in the city. Social isolation does not mean that some cultural features are not important. Rather, the culture in the underclass neighborhoods responds to the lack of social connection to the mainstream society.

Wilson then launched into a description of what he calls the "the tangle of pathology in the inner city"—the increases in crime, drug addiction, out-of-wedlock births, female-headed families, and welfare dependency (1987, p. 21). He did not mince words. Since he was a faculty member at the University of Chicago at the time, many of his examples were drawn from the inner city of Chicago. He began with violent crime. The number of murders committed in the city of Chicago jumped from 195 in 1965 to 810 in 1970, a rate of 24.1 per 100,000. There were 736 murders in the city in 1980, and 81 (11 percent) took place in one black police district on the South Side that contained 3.4 percent of the population of the city. That makes the murder rate in this small area 83 per 100,000 in that year (compared to the national average of 10.2), which by no means was the worst year in Chicago. This particular police district, the Wentworth District, contained the infamous Robert Taylor Homes, a massive high-rise public housing project of twenty-eight sixteen-story buildings that housed perhaps 25,000 to 27,000 people (including several thousand who were not registered with the public housing authority). Wilson reported that all of the residents of the Taylor Homes were black and that 93 percent of the families with children were headed by females (1987, p. 25). Of those families with children, 83 percent received welfare (Aid to Families with Dependent Children). He also reported that 70 percent of murder victims in Chicago were black, and that 80 percent of murderers (for whom race could be determined) were black. The leading cause of death for black men aged nineteen through thirty-four was murder. It was safer for a young black man to be a member of the armed forces than to be a resident of the inner city of Chicago.

Wilson then examined facts on family dissolution and welfare dependency. He noted that Moynihan expressed concern in 1965 that 25 percent of all black families in the United States were headed by women (Wilson 1987). That proportion increased to 40 percent in 1979 and 43 percent in 1983. The percentage of families with children headed by females in 1970 was 33.0 percent, increased to 48.7 percent in 1980, and hit 56.2 percent in 1990. Being a member of a black female-headed family gave a person a 50–50 likelihood of being in poverty in 1993 (when the overall poverty rate was 15.1 percent).

What are the causes of this increase in pathology in the inner city? Wilson considered and ruled out racial discrimination and migration. No one can suggest why there should have been an increase in racial discrimination during these years, in the aftermath of the civil rights movement and the outlawing of discrimination in employment and housing. And, as has been noted in this book, the Great Migration of blacks from the South to the Northeast ended roughly in 1970. One factor does play a role—an increase in the percentage of the black population that was young. However, this factor cannot explain very much of the increases in crime, female-headed families, inner-city poverty, and the rest.

Wilson believes that the shift in the composition of demand for labor away from workers with less education to those with more has been especially pronounced in major urban areas, and has left the black population with a larger mismatch between its education and the requirements of jobs. Wilson then went on to make the argument that the concentration of poverty in certain inner-city areas had created the urban underclass as a result of what he called "concentration effects" of having a highly disproportionate number of the most disadvantaged members of society (1987, p. 58). Those concentration effects include increased levels of crime, joblessness, births out of wedlock, female-headed families, and dependency on welfare. His illustration of the concentration of poverty was taken from Chicago, using data on the seventy-seven community areas of the city. He showed that, in 1970, there were eight community areas with poverty rates at 30 percent or higher, and one of these had a poverty rate of over 40 percent. These areas were over 90 percent black. During the 1970s these areas had a net migration (change in population minus the natural increase of births minus deaths) of negative 152,000, which was 42 percent of their total population in 1970. During this time the number of households in poverty in these areas remained constant, so poverty became much more heavily concentrated. All eight community areas had poverty rates in excess of 40 percent in 1980, and two had poverty rates in excess of 50 percent. In addition, six more community areas had poverty rates in excess of 30 percent in 1980, and one of those had a poverty rate over 40 percent. Wilson (1987) also showed that no community area had an unemployment rate in excess of 20 percent in 1970 but that ten did so in 1980. All ten of those community areas are located in the black residential areas on the west and south sides of the city.

As mentioned above, Wilson's book was highly influential and was largely responsible for creating a field of underclass studies. The research community responded rapidly to this challenge to understand the underclass phenomenon. An important conference was held at Northwestern University in October 1989 that brought together most of the prominent researchers of the underclass and produced a collection of work that was published by the Brookings Institution in 1991. The book, edited by Christopher Jencks and Paul Peterson (1991), was titled simply *The Urban Underclass,* and it does a good job of describing the state of knowledge as of the end of the 1980s.

The Urban Underclass documents the economic condition of the underclass. Two of the studies in the volume demonstrated that the residents of the high-poverty areas in Chicago worked, were seeking to work, or wished to work, but faced discrimination in that employers used social and racial indicators as predictors of performance on the job. Nevertheless, studies by Richard Freeman (1991) and Paul Osterman (1991) found that black poverty and unemployment were reduced sharply during the economic boom in the

Boston area in the 1980s. A study by Greg Duncan and Saul Hoffman (1991) showed that schooling and delayed childbearing were the conditions needed for females of any race to avoid poverty as adults, and another study by Robert Mare and Christopher Winship (1991) concluded that these were precisely the conditions that underclass females are not meeting.

The Urban Underclass also included research on the causes and consequences of concentrated poverty. An important contribution by Paul Jargowsky and Mary Jo Bane (1991) defined high-poverty areas for all of the metropolitan areas in the nation as census tracts with poverty rates of 40 percent or more. They found that the amount of concentrated poverty in the nation so defined increased by 29.5 percent from 1970 to 1980, and that northern central cities had the largest increases. Four cities were studied in detail (Cleveland, Memphis, Philadelphia, and Milwaukee), and there the increase in the poverty rate in inner-city areas was coupled with an emptying out of the neighborhood. The methods employed by Jargowsky and Bane are used extensively in the remainder of this book. A study by Reynolds Farley (1991) challenged one of Wilson's propositions by arguing that the increase in the amount of concentrated poverty among blacks in Chicago was a result of a general increase in poverty among blacks during the 1970s, and not a result of an increase in economic segregation among the black population. Two studies, by Jonathan Crane (1991) and Susan Mayer (1991), reported findings showing the existence of neighborhood effects on whether females drop out of high school or give birth. On the other side of the coin, the chapter by James Rosenbaum and Susan Popkin (1991) reported on the program that gave black female residents of public housing in Chicago the opportunity to move to the suburbs or to another location in the inner city. The study showed that moving to the suburbs had positive effects—on whether the family head was employed (but not on hours worked or wages) and on school achievement and college attendance of the children. This finding, which has been widely cited and publicized, in effect demonstrated the negative effects of living in public housing—a place of highly concentrated poverty and pathology—by showing the positive effects of moving away from the inner city to the suburbs.

Wilson (1991) got the last word in *The Urban Underclass*. He concluded that there was essentially nothing in the research that would dissuade him from his views about the urban underclass. The studies that reached conclusions different from his used definitions of the underclass that omitted an important feature, such as the high geographic concentration of poverty in the inner city. He concluded by noting that the political climate of the day had a negative view of the inner-city poor, and argued for policies that are neutral with respect to race and capable of expanding opportunity for all who are disadvantaged.

Urban Economists, Urban Sociologists, and the Urban Crisis

Scholars from the fields of economics and sociology devoted a great deal of attention to the various aspects of the urban crisis starting in the 1960s. This chapter has provided a brief and selective review of this research. The field of urban economics was founded with a theoretical framework that was to be refined and expanded upon in the subsequent years. Some scholars are notable for their attempts to gain a more comprehensive understanding of the urban crisis, but most concentrated on one or two aspects of the problem. The late economist John Kain (1968) attempted to link housing segregation, metropolitan decentralization, transportation policy, and employment for blacks. His efforts were highly influential in both research and policy circles. While his work was criticized by scholars, the basic sense of his argument remained intact. His later efforts to construct large-scale computerized models of urban areas were less successful and less influential. Economists Bradbury, Downs, and Small (1981, 1982) developed an urban model based on Cleveland that permitted them to experiment with alternative policies designed to assist the central city. And Bradford and Kelejian (1973) actually found that the problem faced by central cities could be called a vicious circle.

Urban sociologists initially spent their time studying such topics as segregation, urban schools, and crime. Then William Wilson (1987) proposed that the term *urban underclass* could be a shorthand for the "tangle of pathology in the inner city." Sociologists and economists quickly responded to this assertion, and much was learned about those pathologies and some of their dynamics. However, *none* of these scholars offered the view that the urban crisis could turn around and get better. Instead, they offered some fairly weak policy suggestions that were not followed.

13
The Vicious Circle in Urban America

The 1980s ended with sociologists and some fellow-traveling economists debating the notion of the urban underclass. Is there an underclass? If so, how can it be measured? Is it growing? Measurement is important because we wish to know whether progress is being made, or if the problem is getting worse. Assessment of the effectiveness of public policies requires measurement. Furthermore, will the underclass respond to improved economic opportunity, or is the "culture of poverty" so ingrained that the basic problem is considerably less tractable? However, the detailed studies of the urban underclass discussed in the previous chapter devote little effort to understanding the larger picture of central cities in crisis, and largely fail to explore what William Wilson called the "tangle of pathology in the inner city" (1987, p. 21). The larger picture of the emerging urban crisis was explored in Chapters 10 and 11. In this chapter the term vicious circle is used instead of tangle of pathology, and the ongoing crisis of the major central cities is described.

Before we begin to look at the twenty-nine major central cities in some detail, an important research project must be described. Paul Jargowsky (1997) followed up on the underclass discussion of the late 1980s with an exhaustive examination of areas of high poverty in America's urban areas. He used census data for 1970, 1980, and 1990 to compute the number of census tracts (each with population about 4,000) with poverty rates of 40 percent or more in all of the 239 urban areas in American. He also computed the number of people who resided in these high-poverty areas. There was reasonable agreement (especially on the part of Wilson) that an area with a poverty rate of 40 percent or more qualifies as a place with serious social and economic problems—places that seem to have suffered from the tangle of pathology or the vicious circle. Jargowsky's results are pretty startling. He found that the number of people who lived in those areas increased from 4.15 million in 1970 to 5.17 million in 1980 and 7.97 million in 1990, an overall increase of 92 percent. The number of high-poverty census tracts had increased from 1,177 to 1,767 to 2,726 over those twenty years. Perhaps the "bottom line" is that the number of poor people who lived in those tracts almost doubled from 1.89 million to 2.38 million to 3.75 million. This is pretty good evidence that the urban underclass had been increasing—increasing pretty rapidly. The percentage of all poor people in the 239 metropolitan areas who lived in high-poverty tracts increased from 12.4 percent in 1970 to 13.6 percent in 1980 to 17.9 percent in 1990. While only a small minority of the urban poor lived in these high-poverty areas, that fraction was growing. The following sections include data from Jargowsky (1997) on the twenty-nine urban areas included in this study.

The Vicious Circle

As stated in the Introduction, a major assertion in this book is that, once a central city or a part of a central city starts downhill, the negative social and economic features of that downhill slide reinforce each other. The start of the downhill slide can be caused by a variety of external forces, including deindustrialization, building an expressway system leading to suburbanization of both jobs and people with decent incomes, rising incomes for the middle class that prompt a move to the suburbs, and so on. These forces act on the central city, but typically the worst outcomes are confined to particular portions of the central city such as those census tracts identified by Jargowsky (1997). Those particular areas are populated by black people (and Hispanic people in some urban areas) and often contain an older housing stock that is vulnerable to deterioration. Most old houses are eventually retired from service, of course, but the proposition is that negative neighborhood effects hasten that process and housing units are lost "before their time." First among those negative neighborhood effects is crime, in my judgment. Poor schools increasingly dominated by students with disadvantaged backgrounds also play an important role. Those who are able to leave and move to a better neighborhood do so.

What are the characteristics of the people who live in the high-poverty areas. And are negative, socially and economically dysfunctional behaviors "contagious"? A considerable amount of underclass research has investigated these questions. One line of research points out that females of otherwise equal characteristics in high schools dominated by a student body of lower socioeconomic status (SES, in the sociologists' parlance) have higher dropout rates and pregnancy and childbirth rates. One researcher, Jonathan Crane, called it an epidemic theory of ghettos, and concluded that, "Neighborhood effects on dropping out and teenage childbearing among both blacks and whites in 1970 were extremely large in very bad neighborhoods, particularly in urban ghettos" (1991, p. 317). Another line of research posits that the decline in marriage is self-reinforcing as children who grow up in one-parent families tend to repeat the experience. The decline in marriage has occurred in the entire society, but the trend among black people in the inner city is particularly strong. And then there is crime. A great deal of the truly serious crime has been perpetrated by members of urban street gangs that battle for control of territory and the market for illegal drugs, especially crack cocaine. In this case violence begets violence directly. Street gangs come in all races, but the ones that have garnered recent attention are black or Hispanic. The study of street gangs is a field of its own. One prominent study was conducted by Sudhir Venkatesh and Steven Levitt and is described in the popular book *Freakonomics* by Levitt and Dubner (2005). They concluded that being a member of a street gang does not pay well and is very dangerous, but that it does provide a (slight) chance at a brass ring. The murder rate in some inner-city areas shot up (puns intended). Protesting normal citizens and local clergy sometimes were shown on television after an innocent bystander, such as young child sitting on the front porch, was killed by gang gunfire. The crime wave in America's inner cities has motivated some to believe that permitting ordinary citizens to carry concealed guns can help to control crime. This group includes the economist John Lott, whose controversial book *More Guns, Less Crime* (2000) purports to demonstrate that states with such "right-to-carry" laws have less crime.

So let us now turn to the central cities in the seventeen major metropolitan areas of the Northeast.

The Central Cities of the Northeast

This section describes the crisis of the inner cities of the Northeast in succinct terms. The inner cities of the Sunbelt are examined in the next section. Here we look at a short list of variables for 1970, 1980, and 1990, including:

- murders per 100,000 in the central city;
- percentage of adults (age twenty-five and over) living in the central city who dropped out of high school;
- percentage of families with children with one parent present (typically the mother);
- number of people residing in a high-poverty area, as defined by Jargowsky (1997);
- the change in the median family real income in the central city.

The data on these variables are shown for the seventeen central cities in Tables 13.1 and 13.2.

Table 13.1

Northeastern Central Cities: 1970–1990

	Murders per 100,000	High-school dropouts (percent)	One-parent families with children (percent)	Population in high-poverty areas (1,000s)*
New York				
1970	14	53	22	310
1980	26	40	38	1,002
1990	31	32	38	960
Chicago				
1970	24	56	22	144
1980	29	44	40	323
1990	31	34	41	328
Philadelphia				
1970	18	60	22	112
1980	26	46	39	267
1990	32	36	41	242
Detroit				
1970	33	58	23	56
1980	46	36	48	120
1990	57	38	61	419
Boston				
1970	18	46	25	40
1980	16	32	42	23
1990	25	24	44	32
Pittsburgh				
1970	12	54	20	31
1980	12	39	36	38
1990	10	28	40	75
St. Louis				
1970	43	67	27	86
1980	50	52	46	88
1990	45	37	51	110
Cleveland				
1970	36	63	24	62
1980	46	49	41	72
1990	33	41	50	100
Washington, D.C.				
1970	29	45	32	36
1980	32	33	53	36
1990	78	27	53	21
Baltimore				
1970	25	66	27	96
1980	28	52	47	122
1990	41	39	53	107
Minneapolis				
1970	6	42	19	11
1980	10	25	34	24
1990	17	17	39	79

(continued)

Table 13.1 *(continued)*

	Murders per 100,000	High-school dropouts (percent)	One-parent families with children (percent)	Population in high-poverty areas (1,000s)*
Buffalo				
1970	12	61	21	6
1980	17	46	41	33
1990	11	33	48	72
Cincinnati				
1970	13	56	23	55
1980	13	42	39	57
1990	14	30	47	74
Milwaukee				
1970	7	51	17	17
1980	8	36	36	32
1990	25	28	45	141
Kansas City				
1970	24	44	16	16
1980	30	30	31	18
1990	28	21	34	32
Indianapolis				
1970	8	45	14	12
1980	15	33	28	15
1990	12	24	31	22
Columbus				
1970	9	44	17	27
1980	15	31	31	64
1990	14	21	34	87
Means				
1970	20	54	22	66
1980	25	40	39	140
1990	30	30	44	175

* Number of residents in census tracts with poverty rate of 40 percent or greater, as computed by Jargowsky (1997).
Sources: HUD State of the Cities Data, and Jargowksy (1997).

The mean values for these variables show the following trends:

- The average murder rate increased from 20 per 100,000 to 30 per 100,000.
- The percentage of central city adults who had not graduated from high school fell from 54 percent to 30 percent (as the older people in 1970 passed away and were replaced by cohorts who had higher graduation rates). The question is whether this sizable increase in schooling was enough to keep up with the changing demand for workers.
- The percentage of single-parent families with children increased dra-

Table 13.2

Northeastern Central Cities: Changes in Income, 1970–1990 (in percent)

	Change in median family real income: 1970–1980	Change in median family real income: 1980–1990
New York	−12.3	19.7
Chicago	−6.9	−4.2
Philadelphia	−11.5	7.7
Detroit	−11.1	−21.5
Boston	6.7	36.6
Pittsburgh	0.8	−8.2
St. Louis	−5.7	−8.6
Cleveland	−11.1	−17.7
Washington, D.C.	0.7	11.2
Baltimore	−9.8	5.0
Minneapolis	−0.2	−2.2
Buffalo	−10.7	−6.8
Cincinnati	−4.4	−6.7
Milwaukee	−2.2	−11.7
Kansas City	2.2	−3.7
Indianapolis	−1.7	−1.3
Columbus	−3.4	3.5
Mean	−4.7	−0.5

Source: HUD State of the Cities Data.

matically in the 1970s from 22 percent to 39 percent, and then increased further to 44 percent in 1990.

- The average number of residents of high-poverty areas in these central cities increased from 66,000 to 140,000 to 175,000 over these twenty years, a dramatic illustration of Jargowsky's (1997) findings for the entire nation of 239 urban areas. The percentage of the population of the seventeen central cities that lived in high-poverty areas tripled from 5.6 percent in 1970 to 10.0 percent in 1980 to 16.8 percent in 1990.
- Median family real incomes declined on average by 4.7 percent in the seventeen central cities from 1969 to 1979, but fell by just 0.5 percent from 1979 to 1989.

It is useful to review the seventeen cities. The murder rate in New York, at 14 per 100,000, was below average for the seventeen cities in 1970, but it increased to be close to the average of 30 per 100,000 in 1990. New York's record on high-school dropouts consistently was average for these cities, as was its percentage of one-parent families in 1970 and 1980. The percentage of one-parent families for New York did not increase in the 1980s, a relatively favorable outcome given that the average for the seventeen central cities did increase by 5 percentage points. The number of residents of high-poverty areas jumped from 301,000 to 1.0 million from 1970 to 1980, but then declined slightly to 960,000 in 1990. The overall poverty rate in New York City had declined slightly from 20.0 to 19.3 percent in the 1980s. Median family real income fell by 12.3 percent in the 1970s, but increased by a very strong 19.7 percent in the 1980s. These outcomes for the 1980s were hopeful signs and, as we shall see, indicate that urban rebirth took place in New York City in that decade.

Chicago's murder rate of 24 per 100,000 was somewhat above average for these cities in 1970. The subsequent increases in Chicago's murder rate only brought the city to the average for the seventeen in 1990. It was bad, but perhaps it could have been worse. Although it dropped sharply, Chicago's percentage of high-school dropouts was above the average for these cities in all three census years. Chicago's record with single-parent families with children similarly was about average for these central cities. The number of residents of high-poverty areas increased sharply from 156,000 in 1970 to 370,000 in 1980, and then increased again slightly to 396,000 in 1990. This last figure represents 14.2 percent of the city's population. Median family real income fell in both decades.

The murder rate in Philadelphia followed the trend for the seventeen cities, rising from 18 in 1970 to 32 per 100,000 in 1990. However, Philadelphia began the period with a high percentage of high-school dropouts; 60 percent of all adults age twenty-five and over had not graduated from high school. This percentage fell dramatically to 36 percent in 1990, but remained well above the seventeen-city average of 30 percent. Philadelphia's record on single-parent families started close to the average for these cities in 1970, and increased to 41 percent in 1990 (which is somewhat below average for the seventeen cities). The number of residents of high-poverty areas more than doubled from 1970 to 1980 (112,000 to 267,000), but then declined to 242,000 in 1990. Recall that the overall poverty rate in Philadelphia declined from 20.6 percent in 1980 to 20.3 percent in 1990. Median family real income declined by 11.5 percent in the 1970s, but rebounded by 7.7 percent in the 1980s. While Philadelphia's record on murders, high-school dropouts, and single-parent families was not particularly good, the slight shrinkage of the population living in high-poverty areas and the increase in median income in the 1980s were hopeful signs.

Now we come to Detroit. The murder rate in Detroit is shocking. It was 33 per 100,000 in 1970 (well above the average of twenty for the seventeen cities), and then proceeded to increase to 57 per 100,000 in 1990. (Be prepared, however, as the murder rates in Washington, D.C., Atlanta, and New Orleans were even more shocking than that in 1990.) The high-school dropout percentage in Detroit started relatively high at 58 percent and declined substantially to 38 percent, but still exceeded the seventeen-city average by eight percentage points. Detroit's record on single-parent families is also shocking. This figure was 23 percent in 1970, which was very close to the average of twenty-two for these cities. However, by 1990, Detroit's figure had jumped to 61 percent, compared to the average for the seventeen of 44 percent. And while the number of residents of high-poverty areas was a relatively modest 56,000 in 1970, there is nothing modest, relatively or otherwise, about the figure of 419,000 residents of such areas in 1990. This is 40.8 percent of the entire (declining) population of the city of Detroit. Median family real income in the city of Detroit fell by 11.5 percent in the 1970s, and then plummeted by 21.5 percent in the 1980s. This author is tempted to say, "I rest my case."

The case of Boston is quite different from that of Detroit. The murder rate was relatively low, and the high-school dropout rate and single-parent family percentage roughly tracked the average for the seventeen cities. The number of people living in high-poverty areas actually was lower in 1990 than in 1970, although the overall city poverty rate increased from 15.5 percent to 18.7 percent. Median family real income increased in both decades—by 6.7 percent in the 1970s and by a remarkable 36.6 percent in the 1980s. Recall that Boston was the case study used in *The Urban Underclass* volume to illustrate the positive impact of economic growth of the urban area on poverty and unemployment of the underclass. It is suggested below that Boston did not really experience the urban crisis that hit all of the other sixteen major urban areas of the Northeast included in this study.

Next, consider the other cities that were already identified in Chapter 10 as having had the worst experiences in the 1970s and 1980s. These include Pittsburgh, Cleveland, Buffalo, Cincinnati, and Milwaukee. The city of Pittsburgh had a low murder rate that actually fell from 12 in 1970 to 10 per 100,000 in 1990, and its record on high-school dropouts and single-parent families tracked the averages for the seventeen cities. The number of people living in high-poverty areas did more than double there from 31,000 to 75,000 (20.3 percent of the city's population), and this is roughly consistent with the increase in the city's poverty rate from 15.0 percent in 1970 to 21.4 percent in 1990. Median family real income in the central city was stable in the 1970s, but declined in the 1980s by 8.2 percent. So in this case, deindustrialization and the increase in central city poverty did not translate otherwise into additional extraordinary problems. In contrast, Cleveland experienced a high murder rate of 36 per 100,000 in 1970, which grew to 46 in 1980 (followed by a decline to 33 in 1990). Cleveland had a relatively bad record on high-school dropouts and single-parent families as well. By 1990, some 100,000 Cleveland residents were living in high-poverty areas (19.8 percent of the population of the city). Median family real income fell sharply in both decades (11.1 percent and 17.7 percent). The Cleveland case appears to fit the vicious circle scenario. Buffalo also had a low murder rate compared to the other sixteen cities. Also, its record on single-parent families was average for the seventeen cities. However, its high-school dropout rates were above average, and the number of people living in high-poverty areas was a mere 5,500 in 1970, which jumped to 72,000 in 1990 (22.0 percent of the city's population). Median family real income fell in the both decades. Like Pittsburgh and Buffalo, Cincinnati had a low murder rate throughout the period. Also, its record on high-school dropouts and single-parent families was no worse than the average for the seventeen central cities. However, the increase in poverty in the city from 17.1 percent in 1970 to 24.3 percent in 1990 brought the number of people living in high-poverty areas to 74,000 (20.4 percent of the population of the city). Median family real income declined in both decades. The last member of this group, Milwaukee, started with a very low murder rate of 7 per 100,000, but it increased to 24 in 1990—still below the average of 31 for the seventeen central cities. Milwaukee's record on high-school dropouts and single-parent families was at or below the record for the seventeen cities, but its number of people living in high-poverty areas jumped from 17,000 in 1970 to 141,000 in 1990 as the city's poverty rate almost doubled from 11.2 percent to 22.2 percent. Median family real income fell by 2.2 percent in the 1970s, but plunged by 11.7 percent in the 1980s. In essence, four out of five of these cities experienced deindustrialization and large increases in poverty and declining median income, but did not exhibit extraordinarily bad outcomes for murders, high-school dropouts (with the exception of Buffalo), and single-parent families. Cleveland is the exception in this group.

The remaining seven cities in the Northeast are St. Louis, Washington, D.C., Baltimore, Minneapolis, Kansas City, Indianapolis, and Columbus. St. Louis, Washington, D.C., and Baltimore are notable partly for their high murder rates. Indeed, the murder rate in the nation's capital was 78 per 100,000 in 1990, by far the highest murder rate among the twenty-nine cities studied in this book. Washington, D.C., is the one northeastern urban area that did not suffer from deindustrialization—because it had little manufacturing to lose, and benefited from population and employment growth. The poverty and median income figures for Washington, D.C., are among the best in the group. Its extraordinary rate of murders therefore is much out of line with the other cities. The other four cities—Minneapolis, Kansas City, Indianapolis, and Columbus—had low murder rates, did suffer increases in poverty and small declines in median family real incomes, but did not experience the urban

Table 13.3

Northeastern Central Cities: Correlations

	Murder rate	High-school dropouts	One-parent families	Percent living in high-poverty areas	Central city poverty rate
Murder rate					
1970	1	.56*	.65*	.54*	.71*
1980	1	.60*	.58*	.46*	.60*
1990	1	.37	.67*	.07	.22
High-school dropouts					
1970	—	1	.44*	.59*	.72*
1980	—	1	.54*	.77*	.81*
1990	—	1	.60*	.42*	.70*
One-parent families					
1970	—	—	1	.56*	.83*
1980	—	—	1	.76*	.76*
1990	—	—	1	.58*	.78*
Percentage in high-poverty areas					
1970	—	—	—	1	.84*
1980	—	—	—	1	.73*
1990	—	—	—	1	.86*

* Statistically significant at the 95 percent level for a one-tail test.
Source: Data from Table 13.1.

crisis as much as did others. The data shown in Table 13.1 do not include the city of St. Paul because Jargowsky (1997) presented high-poverty area data only for Minneapolis.

Another question can be asked. To what extent are the social and economic problems listed in Table 13.1 related to each other? To provide an answer, I first computed the percentage of the city's population that resided in high-poverty areas and added the poverty rate of the central city to the data base. Then the correlations among five variables were computed for 1970, 1980, and 1990; the variables are the murder rate, the percentage of high-school dropouts, the percentage on one-parent families, the central city poverty rate, and the percentage living in high-poverty areas. The results are shown in Table 13.3. There are ten simple correlations for each year for the five variables (4 plus 3 plus 2 plus 1). All ten of these correlations are positive and statistically significant for 1970. The correlations range from .44 up to .84 (between the percentage of the population living in high-poverty areas and the central city poverty rate). All ten correlations for 1980 are positive, and nine are statistically significant. Only the correlation between one-parent families and the percentage of people residing in high-poverty areas falls slightly short of statistical significance (.36 compared to the benchmark correlation for statistical significance of .41). Lastly, all ten of the correlations for 1990 are positive, and seven are statistically significant. The correlations of the murder rate with the other variables are not statistically significant (except for the correlation with one-parent families). However, it is clear that the very high murder rate in Washington, D.C., is an "outlier" in a statistical sense (and in a social and economic sense, too). Removal of Washington, D.C., from the data results in all ten of the correlations attaining statistical significance. Another test involved correlating the percentage of the black population that resided in high-poverty areas. This variable is highly positively correlated with the percentage of the total population residing in high-poverty areas and with the central city poverty rate in all three years. Its correlations with the other variables are not statistically significant.

What is the message provided by Table 13.3? The correlations show that all of these indicators of social and economic crisis go together—murders, high-school dropouts, single-parent families, large fractions of the population living in high-poverty areas, and high poverty in the city as a whole. Indeed, the correlations are quite high. At this point it appears impossible to untangle Wilson's tangle of pathology of the inner city. This result is what one would expect if these various pathologies are all part of a vicious circle in which they all reinforce each other. Which variable in Table 13.3 causes the others to move? The answer is likely "all of the above."

Another approach is to examine the correlations of the changes in the variables listed in Table 13.3. The correlations were computed for the changes from 1970 to 1980 and from 1980 to 1990. Some of the correlations among the variables are statistically significant, as follows:

- The change in the murder rate is positively correlated with the change in the central city poverty rate for 1970 to 1980, but not for 1980 to 1990 (because of Washington, D.C.).
- The change in one-parent families is correlated negatively with the growth of population in the central city and positively correlated with the change in the central city poverty rate in both periods.
- The change in the central city poverty rate is negatively correlated with the population growth of the central city for 1980 to 1990.

The basic finding from this exercise is that there are relatively few statistically significant correlations among the changes in the urban crisis variables.

Various additional exploratory statistical tests were performed on the data in Table 13.1. The only result that is worth reporting is that the percentage of black population living in high-poverty areas in 1990 was highly correlated with the same variable for 1980, which in turn was highly correlated with its counterpart for 1970. Finally, the percentage of blacks living in high-poverty areas in 1970 was correlated with the poverty rate in the central city in 1970. Thus, a high concentration of blacks in high-poverty areas seems to perpetuate itself.

An Index of Central City Urban Crisis

Can a summary measure of central city urban crisis be developed? This section proposes a rough and ready urban crisis summary measure of the economic and social outcomes in the seventeen central cities for the 1970s and 1980s. The summary measure consists of seven variables, as follows:

- change in central city population,
- change in the central city poverty rate,
- change in the population living in high-poverty areas,
- change in the central city murder rate,
- change in the percentage of single-parent families,
- change in the percentage of high-school dropouts, and
- change in the median family real income in the central city.

Each of these variables measures a somewhat different aspect of the urban crisis. Decline in the central city population produces weakness in the housing market and housing abandonment. The overall poverty rate in the central city is an obvious choice and, as William Wilson (1987) and others have emphasized, concentrated poverty is another dimension of the urban crisis. The murder rate is a proxy for overall crime in the central city. Single-parent families and high-school dropouts are measures of social and economic disability. Lastly, the change in the median family real income is a measure of the overall economic health of the central city that may be distinct from the poverty rate.

The seventeen central cities are given plus, minus, or zero on each of these seven variables for the 1970s and the 1980s in Table 13.4. A plus means that the variable moved in a positive direction (e.g., central population increased, the poverty rate declined, and so on). A minus means that the variable moved in the unfavorable direction, and a zero means that the variable changed very little or not at all. In a few cases double plus or double minus is awarded for very large changes. For example, median family real income fell in New

York City by 12.3 percent in the 1970s (double minus), and increased by 19.7 percent in the 1980s (double plus). The final step is to add up the pluses and minuses to arrive at a net score for the central city, and these net scores are also shown in Table 13.4.

The results of this simple exercise for the 1970s are quite striking. Sixteen of the seventeen central cities have a net score of –2 or lower, and twelve of those sixteen have a score of –4 or lower. The city of Boston is the only one with a positive net score (of +1).

The index suggests that sixteen of the seventeen experienced the urban crisis in the 1970s, and that the worst cases were New York, Philadelphia, Detroit, Cleveland, and Buffalo (with net scores of –6).

The results for the 1980s are not as consistent as for the 1970s. The largest change is in New York City, where the net index went from –6 for the 1970s to +4 for the 1980s. As suggested above, New York City experienced an urban rebirth in the 1980s that included:

- an increase in the central city population,
- a reduction in the central city poverty rate,
- a reduction in high-school dropouts,
- a very strong increase in median family real income, and
- no changes in the population living in high-poverty areas and in single-parent families.

In short, it can be argued that urban rebirth came first to New York City among those northeastern central cities that experienced the urban crisis.

Four other central cities showed substantial improvement in the 1980s over the 1970s—Philadelphia, Washington, D.C., Baltimore, and Indianapolis. In the 1980s, Philadelphia had reductions in the poverty rate and the number of people living in high-poverty areas, coupled with a nice increase in median real family income of 7.7 percent to go from a net index of –6 for the 1970s to +1 for the 1980s. However, the central city continued to lose population, the murder rate continued to climb, and the percentage of single-parent families increased as well. While the 1980s were a large improvement over the 1970s, Philadelphia cannot be called a clear case of the virtuous circle of urban rebirth because not enough of the indicators were moving in the positive direction. Washington, D.C., improved from a –3 for the 1970s to a +2 index for the 1980s because of the decline in the central city poverty rate and the number of people living in high-poverty areas. However, the disastrous increase in the murder rate to 78 per 100,000 is too bad to call this a case of urban rebirth. Improvement in poverty, concentrated poverty, and median family real income brought Baltimore from an index of –5 in the 1970s to +1 for the

Table 13.4

Urban Crisis Index: Northeastern Central Cities

	Population	Median family income	Poverty	Murder	Poverty concentration	One parent	High-school dropout	Net index
New York								
1970s	−	− −	−	−	−	−	+	−6
1980s	+	++	+	−	0	0	+	+4
Chicago								
1970s	−	−	−	−	−	−	+	−5
1980s	−	−	−	−	0	0	+	−3
Philadelphia								
1970s	−	− −	−	−	−	−	+	−6
1980s	−	+	+	−	+	−	+	+1
Detroit								
1970s	−	−	−	−	−	−	+	−6
1980s	−	−	− −	−	− −	−	−	−10
Boston								
1970s	−	+	−	+	+	−	+	+1
1980s	+	++	+	−	−	−	+	+2
Pittsburgh								
1970s	−	0	−	0	−	−	+	−3
1980s	−	−	−	+	−	−	+	−3
St. Louis								
1970s	−	−	−	−	0	−	+	−4
1980s	−	−	−	+	−	−	+	−3
Cleveland								
1970s	−	− −	−	−	−	−	+	−6
1980s	−	− −	−	+	−	−	+	−4
Washington, D.C.								
1970s	−	0	−	−	0	−	+	−3
1980s	−	++	+	− −	+	0	+	+2
Baltimore								
1970s	−	−	−	−	−	−	+	−5
1980s	−	+	+	−	+	−	+	+1

(continued)

Table 13.4 *(continued)*

	Population	Median family income	Poverty	Murder	Poverty concen-tration	One parent	High-school dropout	Net index
Minneapolis								
1970s	–	0	–	–	–	–	+	–4
1980s	0	–	–	–	–	–	+	–4
Buffalo								
1970s	–	– –	–	–	–	–	+	–6
1980s	–	–	–	+	–	–	+	–3
Cincinnati								
1970s	–	–	–	0	0	–	+	–3
1980s	–	–	–	0	–	–	+	–4
Milwaukee								
1970s	–	–	–	0	–	–	+	–4
1980s	0	– –	–	–	–	–	+	–5
Kansas City								
1970s	–	+	–	–	0	–	+	–2
1980s	–	–	–	+	–	–	+	–3
Indianapolis								
1970s	–	–	–	–	–	–	+	–5
1980s	+	–	–	+	–	–	+	–1
Columbus								
1970s	0	–	–	–	–	–	+	–4
1980s	0	–	–	0	–	–	+	–1

Sources: Tables 13.1 and 13.2.

1980s. However, central city population, murders, and single-parent families continued to move in the wrong direction. In Indianapolis the improvements were in central city population and the murder rate, but the net score for the 1980s was still a negative number, –1.

On the negative side, the city of Detroit scored –10 for the 1980s (compared to –6 for the 1970s) because of the large increases in the poverty rate, the number of people living in high-poverty areas, and the murder rate. Also, the percentage of high-school dropouts increased in the 1980s—the only instance of an increase in this variable among the seventeen central cities of the Northeast included in this study.

The outcomes for the other eleven central cities in the 1980s are roughly consistent with the outcomes in the 1970s. In ten the urban crisis continued.

In Boston the avoidance of the urban crisis continued. Indeed, median family real income in Boston increased by 36.6 percent in the 1980s.

The Central Cities of the Sunbelt

The central cities of the Sunbelt present a picture that is much more mixed than the Northeast. Table 13.5 shows that the mean value of the murder rate for the twelve central cities increased from 20 in 1970 to 30 in 1980, and moved up slightly to 31 in 1990. These figures for 1970 and 1990 are virtually identical to those for the northeastern central cities. The mean high-school dropout rate for the twelve cities fell from 45 percent in 1970 to 28 percent in 1990. The Sunbelt cities actually had lower high-school dropout percentages than did the northeastern central cities in all three years. The mean for the percentage of one-parent families was 20 percent in 1970 (compared to 22 percent for the northeastern seventeen), and it increased to 36 percent in 1990 (less than the 44 percent recorded for the northeastern cities). The average for the twelve cities of the number of people living in high-poverty areas was about the same in 1980 (54,000) as in 1970 (52,000), but doubled to 103,000 in 1990. Table 13.6 shows that median family real income was, on average, quite stable in the twelve central cities. However, the change in median family income varied widely from city to city and over time for the same city.

First let us look at the central cities of the South, beginning with Dallas. Only the central city of Dallas is included because Jargowsky (1997) did not report the concentration of poverty figures for Fort Worth. The murder rate in Dallas was high in 1970 (at 29 per 100,000 population), and it increased to 44 per 100,000 in 1990. The record for Dallas on high-school dropouts and single-parent families followed the averages for the twelve cities fairly closely. But, after dropping slightly from 1970 to 1980, the number of people living in high-poverty areas more than doubled from 1980 to 1990 to reach 126,000. Median family real income was stable in the 1970s (declined by 0.7 percent), and fell by 5.1 percent in the 1980s. The murder rate in Houston was a little above average for the twelve cities at 23 per 100,000 population in 1970, but it jumped to 39 in 1980 and came down to 35 per 100,000 in 1990. The high-school dropout percentages were above average for the twelve cities, but the record on single-parent families is lower than the averages. The impact of the bust in the oil market in the 1980s is evident in the jump from 1980 to 1990 in the number of people living in high-poverty areas—up to 162,000. Median family real income increased strongly by 12.1 percent in the 1970s, but dropped sharply by 19.1 percent in the 1980s. In short, the two major cities in Texas did display some of the urban crisis features during the period, especially in

Table 13.5

Central Cities of the Sunbelt: 1970–1990

	Murders per 100,000	High-school dropouts (percent)	One-parent families with children (percent)	Population in high-poverty areas (1,000s)
Dallas				
1970	29	46	17	70
1980	35	32	30	54
1990	44	26	32	126
Houston				
1970	23	48	15	43
1980	39	32	27	47
1990	35	30	31	162
New Orleans				
1970	17	58	25	126
1980	39	41	42	96
1990	61	32	50	166
Atlanta				
1970	49	54	26	58
1980	48	40	51	94
1990	59	30	57	92
Birmingham				
1970	21	56	20	60
1980	31	40	38	45
1990	47	31	42	55
Miami				
1970	27	57	21	42
1980	65	50	36	67
1990	36	52	44	148
Los Angeles				
1970	14	38	21	97
1980	34	31	32	120
1990	28	33	30	268
San Francisco				
1970	16	38	23	32
1980	16	26	33	30
1990	14	22	27	42
Seattle				
1970	8	35	18	10
1980	13	20	32	5
1990	10	14	29	25
Denver				
1970	14	38	18	24
1980	20	25	31	18
1990	14	21	35	30

(continued)

Table 13.5 *(continued)*

	Murders per 100,000	High-school dropouts (percent)	One-parent families with children (percent)	Population in high-poverty areas (1,000s)
San Diego				
1970	5	34	19	19
1980	12	21	27	5
1990	12	18	26	39
Phoenix				
1970	11	41	14	41
1980	13	27	22	44
1990	13	21	26	79
Means				
1970	20	45	20	52
1980	30	32	33	54
1990	31	28	36	103

Sources: HUD State of the Cities Data, and Jargowsky (1997).

Table 13.6

Central Cities of the Sunbelt: Changes in Income, 1970–1990 (in percent)

	Change in median family real income: 1969–1979	Change in median family real income: 1979–1989
Dallas	−0.7	−5.1
Houston	12.1	−19.1
New Orleans	1.8	−13.4
Atlanta	−18.1	8.3
Birmingham	-0.6	−8.0
Miami	−7.8	−13.4
Los Angeles	−5.9	3.4
San Francisco	1.5	13.5
Seattle	2.2	5.7
Denver	2.2	−4.0
San Diego	0.4	14.3
Phoenix	3.3	−1.7
Mean	−0.8	−1.6

Source: HUD State of the Cities Data.

the murder rates, the increases in the number of people living in high-poverty areas, and the reductions in median family income in the 1980s.

Then there is New Orleans. The murder rate was "only" 17 per 100,000 in 1970, which was below average for the twelve Sunbelt cities. But then murders jumped to 39 in 1980 and 61 per 100,000 population in 1990. This murder rate for 1990 is greater than the murder rate in Detroit, but not as high as the one for Washington, D.C. The high-school dropout percentages and percentages of one-parent families were higher in New Orleans than the averages for the twelve cities in all three years. The number of people living in high-poverty areas was a low 13,000 in 1970, but it increased to 96,000 in 1980 and 166,000 in 1990. And median family real income dropped by 13.4 percent in the 1980s. New Orleans was experiencing the urban crisis in the 1980s.

Next we have the curious case of Atlanta. Atlanta had very high murder rates (48 to 59 per 100,000 population), a bad record on high-school dropouts, and a very bad record on single-parent families. In 1990, 57 percent of families with children had only one parent (compared to an average for the twelve of 36 percent). The number of people living in high-poverty areas increased from 58,000 in 1970 to 94,000 in 1980, and then declined slightly to 92,000 in 1990 (23.3 percent of the population of the city). Median family real income dropped by 18.1 percent in the 1970s, but recovered by 8.3 percent in the 1980s. The urban crisis was visiting Atlanta in a big way, primarily in the 1970s.

Birmingham is another city that had a murder rate that increased to a very high level. The murder rate of 21 per 100,000 in 1970 was about average for the twelve cities, but it increased sharply to 47 per 100,000 in 1990. Birmingham's record on high-school dropouts was well above average for the twelve cities, but the single-parent percentages followed the Sunbelt averages closely. Also, the number of people living in high-poverty areas did not increase, making Birmingham the only city of the six in the South to have a decrease in this variable. Median family real income was unchanged in the central city from 1969 to 1979, but fell by 8.0 percent in the 1980s.

The murder rate in Miami was 27 per 100,000 in 1970 (not good), but it then made a shocking increase to 65 per 100,000 in 1980. The fiction presented on the television show *Miami Vice* was perhaps more accurate than we knew. Fortunately, the murder rate in 1990 had dropped to 36 per 100,000. This rate is still quite high, but it is a vast improvement from 1980. The high-school dropout percentages for Miami were very high at 50 percent or more in all three years. These figures are the result of the increase in the Hispanic population, especially the increase in foreign-born migrants. The number of Miami residents who lived in high-poverty areas increased sharply from 42,000 in 1970 to 148,000 in 1990, reaching 41.2 percent of the population of the city. Median family real income declined in both decades. The urban crisis was visiting Miami as well.

The six central cities of the South thus displayed symptoms of the urban crisis as fully as did the central cities of the Northeast. It is incorrect to think that the urban crisis and the growth of the urban underclass took place only in the Northeast. Table 13.7 presents the central city urban crisis index introduced in the previous section. All six of the central cities of the South included in this study experienced the urban crisis in either the 1970s or the 1980s (or both). The 1980s were the worse decade for Dallas, Houston, New Orleans, and Birmingham (the first three because of the decline in the oil industry in the 1980s). The urban crisis was worse in Atlanta in the 1970s, and Miami displayed urban crisis symptoms in both decades. How do the central cities of the West compare to those in the South and the Northeast?

Los Angeles presents us with another picture of urban crisis. The murder rate was 14 per 100,000 in 1970—below average for the twelve Sunbelt cities. But murders increased to 34 per 100,000 in 1980 before declining somewhat to 28 per 100,000 in 1990. High-school dropouts were a relatively low 38 percent in 1970, but declined only to 33 percent in 1990 (above average for the twelve cities). On the other hand, the record for one-parent families was comparatively good and stood at 30 percent in 1990. Residents of high-poverty areas increased from a relatively small 97,000 in 1970 to 268,000 in 1990. Median family real income increased in the 1970s but declined in the 1980s. San Francisco's record is in sharp contrast to all of the Sunbelt cities discussed thus far. Only the city of San Francisco is included in Table 13.5 because Jargowsky (1997) did not include Oakland. San Francisco had low murder rates, high-school dropout rates, and percentages of single-parent families. It also had relatively small numbers of people living in high-poverty areas. Median family real income increased slightly in the 1970s and moved up 13.5 percent in the 1980s. If there is a picture of avoidance of the urban crisis, it may be the city of San Francisco.

Denver is another city that shows little evidence of serious urban crisis. The murder rate was low, as were the high-school dropout percentages. The single-parent family record followed the averages for the twelve Sunbelt cities, but the number of people living in high-poverty areas was relatively small, and median family real income increased by a small 2.2 percent in the 1970s and declined by 4.0 percent in the 1980s. The case of San Diego is even better—low murder rates, low percentages of high-school dropouts, and low percentages of single-parent families in 1980 and 1990. The high-poverty areas contained a relatively small number of people—only 39,000 in 1990 (3.5 percent of the population of the city). Median family real income increased 14.3 percent in the 1980s. Phoenix resembles San Diego on these measures (except for the large increase in median income in the 1980s) and is another case of urban crisis largely avoided.

Table 13.7 shows the urban crisis index for the six central cities of the West included in this study. Los Angeles shows evidence of urban crisis in the 1970s with a net score of –3, a result of increases in poverty, concentrated poverty, murder rate, and single-parent families, along with a decline in median family

Table 13.7

Urban Crisis Index: Sunbelt Central Cities

	Popu-lation	Median family income	Poverty	Murder	Poverty concen-tration	One parent	High-school dropout	Net score
Dallas								
1970s	0	0	−	−	+	−	+	−1
1980s	0	−	−	−	−	−	+	−4
Houston								
1970s	0	++	+	−	0	−	+	+2
1980s	0	− −	−	+	−	−	+	−3
New Orleans								
1970s	−	+	0	−	+	−	+	0
1980s	−	− −	−	− −	−	−	+	−7
Atlanta								
1970s	−	− −	−	0	−	—	+	−6
1980s	−	+	0	−	0	−	0	−2
Birmingham								
1970s	−	0	+	−	+	−	+	−1
1980s	−	−	−	−	−	−	0	−6
Miami								
1970s	+	−	−	—	−	−	+	−4
1980s	+	−	−	+	−	−	−	−4
Los Angeles								
1970s	+	−	−	−	−	−	+	−3
1980s	+	+	−	+	−	+	−	+1
San Francisco								
1970s	−	+	0	0	0	−	+	0
1980s	+	++	+	+	−	+	+	+6
Seattle								
1970s	−	+	−	−	+	−	+	−1
1980s	+	+	−	+	−	+	+	+3
Denver								
1970s	0	+	0	−	+	−	+	+1
1980s	0	−	−	+	−	−	+	−2
San Diego								
1970s	+	0	−	−	+	−	+	0
1980s	+	++	−	0	−	0	+	+2
Phoenix								
1970s	0	+	+	−	0	−	+	+1
1980s	0	−	−	0	−	−	+	−3

Note: Cities with substantial increases in land area are rated zero on population.

Table 13.8

Central Cities of the Sunbelt: Correlations

	Murder rate	High-school dropouts	One-parent families	Percent living in high-poverty areas	Central city poverty rate
Murder rate					
1970	1	.65*	.44	.38	.47
1980	1	.92*	.56*	.76*	.76*
1990	1	.56*	.85*	.73*	.85*
High-school dropouts					
1970	—	1	.42	.88*	.92*
1980	—	1	.61*	.90*	.87*
1990	—	1	.55*	.84*	.82*
One-parent families					
1970	—	—	1	.49	.63*
1980	—	—	1	.82*	.89*
1990	—	—	1	.80*	.88*
Percent in high-poverty areas					
1970	—	—	—	1	.95*
1980	—	—	—	1	.96*
1990	—	—	—	1	.94*

* Statistically significant at the 95 percent level for a one-tail test.

income. The 1980s were an improvement (net index of +1), as the murder rate, single-parent families, and median income improved. San Francisco displays mixed results for the 1970s (net score of zero), and then the variables moved together positively in the 1980s (net score of +6). Seattle had a neutral −1 net score for the 1970s, and then moved to +3 in the 1980s. San Diego has a similar pattern, with a net score of −1 in the 1970s and +2 in the 1980s. On the other hand, Denver and Phoenix changed from a neutral +1 in the 1970s to negative numbers in the 1980s. In both cases, the negative changes were in poverty, concentrated poverty, and median income.

Given the contrasts between the South and the West on the urban crisis variables shown in Tables 13.5 and 13.6, it should not be surprising to find that the correlations among these variables are very high. Indeed, such is the case, as shown in Table 13.8. The five variables for which correlations are computed (for 1970, 1980, and 1990) include:

- the murder rate,
- the percentage of adults who had not completed high school,

- the percentage of families with children with only one parent present,
- the percentage of residents of the central city who lived in high-poverty areas, and
- the poverty rate for the central city.

Five of the ten correlations for 1970 are statistically significant (and positive), but ten out of ten correlations are positive and statistically significant for both 1980 and 1990. As in the Northeast, these strong correlations among these variables suggest that the various aspects of the urban crisis reinforce each other. Furthermore, the results for the Sunbelt cities indicate that the vicious circle did not occur in the cities of the West nearly as severely as in the South and the Northeast.

A final exercise is to examine the correlations of the variables that measure the changes in the urban crisis variables óver 1970 to 1980 and 1980 to 1990. A few of these correlations are statistically significant, but only one correlation is consistently statistically significant over the two time periods. That one is the positive correlation between the change in the poverty rate in the central city and the change in the percentage of people who lived in high-poverty areas. As is the case for the northeastern central cities, these data are not able to show that the changes in the urban crisis variables moved in concert.

The Urban Crisis of the Central Cities: 1970 to 1990

This chapter presents a statistical picture of the urban crisis that was experienced in America's central cities in the 1970s and 1980s. The average murder rate for the twenty-nine central cities in the study increased from 20 per 100,000 in 1970 to 30 per 100,000 in 1990, and hit the shocking levels of 78 in Washington, D.C., 57 in Detroit, 61 in New Orleans, 59 in Atlanta, and 65 in Miami. The proportion of single-parent families with children jumped from an average for the twenty-nine cities of 21 percent in 1970 to 41 percent in 1990. And the percentage of the central population who lived in high-poverty areas increased from 7 percent to 16 percent. However, the twenty-nine central cities had very different experiences. Except for Boston, the central cities of the Northeast exhibit some level of urban crisis during these years, but clearly Detroit, Cleveland, and Buffalo had the worst of it. New York City is unique among the northeastern urban areas because it experienced urban rebirth in the 1980s. All six of the cities of the South show strong evidence of an increasing urban crisis during these two decades, but only Los Angeles, Denver, and Phoenix of the six cities in the West had a combination of outcomes that resembles urban crisis (and in only one decade of the two).

This chapter shall end on a personal note. My wife Glena and I arrived in

Chicago in 1971 as I assumed a faculty position at the University of Illinois at Chicago. She took the university courses required for teacher certification and was assigned to a Chicago public school on the West Side in 1973. The school, the Pfc. Milton Olive IV Child Parent Center, was located in North Lawndale, the same neighborhood to which Martin Luther King, Jr., and family moved in 1966. Glena McDonald taught in the Chicago public schools for thirty-one years. Her experience as a teacher and school counselor in the inner city informed us (mainly her) of the nature of the urban crisis at the ground level. The Olive Child Parent Center provided a half-day school program for children aged three and four, full-day kindergarten for five-year olds, and programs for parents—from whom some participation was required. The program of child parent centers in Chicago was begun as part of the Great Society initiatives, is funded by the federal government, and is successful for both the children and their parents.

North Lawndale had turned from white to black in the 1950s, and the population had increased from 100,000 to 125,000, 91 percent of whom were black. The area was the scene for some of the urban riots of 1968, and the population had begun to decline, reaching 95,000 in 1970. At this point the neighborhood was 96 percent black, with a poverty rate of 30 percent. The exodus from North Lawndale continued in the 1970s, and the population fell to 61,500 in 1980. The poverty rate reached Jargowsky's 40 percent benchmark in that year. The 1980s brought further decline and increase in the poverty rate—to a population of 47,000 and a poverty rate of 44 percent in 1990. Sixty percent of the families were headed by females in 1990. The number of housing units in North Lawndale fell from 25,300 in 1970 to 15,700 in 1990 (with the vacancy rate standing at 11 percent in both years). In short, the population dropped by half, the number of housing units declined by 38 percent, and the poverty rate increased by 14 percentage points over the twenty years from 1970 to 1990.

Glena watched the enrollment in the Olive Child Parent Center decline as many of the middle-class families moved away. The neighborhood became increasingly dangerous. The school was a "closed campus," meaning that the children who attended all day did not leave for lunch. The teachers were able to leave the school at 2:30 in the afternoon. Night meetings at the school were relatively infrequent, and I always accompanied her on such occasions. The declines in enrollment in the neighborhood eventually meant that the Olive Child Parent Center was moved into rooms that had become available in another nearby Chicago public school, and eventually it ceased to exist as a separate school. In short, North Lawndale is a prime example of the urban crisis and the urban underclass.

Part IV

The Rebirth of Urban America
After 1990

14

Rebirth in America's Cities

Urban Rebirth: A Catalog of Causes

The crisis in most of the America's central cities has been documented. This final section of the book is an extensive examination of the rebirth that has taken place in metropolitan areas and their central cities. As stated in my introduction, a new chapter in American urban history began sometime around 1990—a chapter that involves a virtuous circle in which many aspects of urban life improve together. The social and economic situation in most of American's major central cities is still far from what one would hope it to be, but the pattern of general improvement is undeniable. The improvements will be documented extensively in the chapters that follow. This chapter begins with a catalog of reasons for the general improvement. The causal factors are arranged roughly in chronological order. Causes of urban rebirth fall into three categories: forces that were part of the evolution of urban areas, actions taken in response to the urban crisis, and factors exogenous to the urban condition that just happened.

First, the urban areas underwent major transitions in the 1960s and 1970s that were largely completed. Freeway systems were completed primarily in the 1960s (with little subsequent freeway construction), and the urban areas adjusted to this new transportation system by spreading out. The adjustment has taken several years (and may be still going on to some extent), but such an adjustment to a finite improvement in highways slows down and does not go on forever. Indeed, the failure to build enough freeways to keep up with the growth of traffic has increased travel times and provided some stimulus for the central city housing market. Another major transition was from a goods-producing economy to a service economy. While this transition still may be under way, it appears to have slowed in most urban areas. Central cities lost an enormous number of manufacturing jobs during the period of urban crisis, but once they are lost they cannot be lost again. Indeed, the transition to the service economy has been a stimulus for many of the downtowns of major urban areas.

Renovation of the central city housing stock in certain good locations started to pick up in the 1960s. Central cities have always contained high-income neighborhoods, but the conversion of neighborhoods from deteriorated condition to housing for higher-income households was something new. Von Hoffman (2003), in his detailed study of the rebirth of urban neighborhoods in New York, Chicago, Atlanta, Boston, and Los Angeles, states, "The recent wave of gentrification started during the 1960s and 1970s, came to a roaring climax during the economic boom of the 1980s, and consolidated its gains and spread further during the long prosperity of the 1990s."

These gentrifiers were attracted by the potential of the graceful older housing stock that had been built before 1920 and by locations near downtown. The incentive is strong for people who work downtown in the growing service economy to live in the central city, and this incentive has produced a boom in the construction of new condominium developments in and near downtown. New condominium developments are an alternative for those who do not wish to undertake the difficulties associated with renovating and maintaining an older home.

Central city governments, out of necessity, improved their abilities at fiscal management and planning (the latter with increased citizen participation). As part of these efforts, central cities became more adept at using local economic development tools. The old strategy that is known as "smokestack chasing" was seen as largely ineffective—mainly because there were few smokestacks to chase. Cities developed what is called the retention strategy in an attempt to prevent the loss of firms (especially manufacturing establishments), but this technique was often ineffective because it involved spending time and energy responding to emergency situations. A firm lets it be known that it is about to move, and there is really little that the city can do at that point. So cities eventually formulated more comprehensive strategies that built on the strengths of the local economy. One idea is to encourage the growth of the successful sectors of the local economy by supplying what they need from the public sector—for example, education and training programs in the local community colleges and universities. Central cities have also become adept at supplying amenities in and around the downtown area. Some observers believe that the desire to consume the amenities of urban living has been a chief factor in urban revitalization. One perhaps frivolous example is the fact that the city of Chicago sponsors some sort of downtown parade on almost every weekend in the summer.

Migration from abroad has revitalized many urban neighborhoods. That migration includes both legal and illegal immigration. A new immigration law that was passed in 1965 increased the number of immigrants to the United States permitted each year to 290,000, and included the feature that immigrants who had become citizens could bring in relatives as "non-quota" immigrants. By the 1990s, more than two-thirds of legal immigrants were entering as these non-quota relatives. According to scholars of migration, an important event was the decision by the federal government to grant an amnesty to many illegal immigrants in 1986, and approximately 1.7 million people took advantage of this amnesty. The 1986 law also included the requirement that employers check on eligibility of new employees to work in the United States, but provided no effective means to enforce the law. These policy decisions are said to have stimulated illegal immigration, particularly (but certainly not exclusively) from Mexico. Immigrants have come to America's cities in large numbers in search of the economic opportunity that was not available in their places of birth. They brought a work ethic and a desire to build successful lives for themselves—attitudes that surely help American's cities on balance. Indeed, the fact that America's cities have attracted large numbers of immigrants is eloquent testimony to their rebirth. Data on the increase in the Hispanic and foreign-born populations of New York, Los Angeles, and Chicago are provided in the last section of this chapter.

As discussed in Chapters 12 and 13, crime has been the scourge of America's central cities and has represented a very big deterrent to their rebirth. But crime has declined dramatically. Here are the basic facts of the decline in crime rates (per 100,000 population) from 1990 to 2000, by category of crime:

- Murder fell from 9.4 to 5.5.
- Rape dropped from 41.2 to 32.0.
- Robbery dropped by 43.6 percent from 257.0 to 144.9.
- Aggravated assault moved down from 424.1 to 323.6.
- Burglary fell by 41.1 percent from 1,236 to 728.4.
- Larceny-theft came down from 3,195 to 2,475.
- Auto theft dropped by 37.0 percent from 657.8 to 414.2.

These declines, especially the large declines in murder, robbery, burglary, and auto theft, were very good news for the entire society. As we shall see in Chapter 15, several central cities experienced large declines in crime.

There are several reasons for the decline in crime, conveniently laid out by Levitt and Dubner (2005) in their best-selling book *Freakonomics*. Their list of causes for the decline in crime includes:

- increased use of prisons and longer sentences;
- larger police forces and better policing strategies;
- tougher gun laws (especially increased prison time for someone caught with an illegal gun);
- the drop in the profits from dealing crack cocaine, starting in roughly 1991, which meant that the criminal gangs had less reason to kill each other;
- the aging of the population, which meant that there were fewer young men in their most crime-prone years;
- the legalization of abortion during the first two trimesters of pregnancy by the Supreme Court in *Roe v. Wade* in 1973, which, according to Levitt and Dubner (2005), was followed by the decline in crime eighteen years later.

This last reason is controversial, and the statisticians are continuing their argument about it. Levitt and Dubner (2005) also argue that some factors thought to be causes of the drop in crime are of little significance. These include increased use of capital punishment, right-to-carry gun laws, and the strong economy of the 1990s. The strong economy is good for many reasons, of course, but is not strongly related to declines in violent crime rates. Clearly, some of the factors behind the decline in crime were in response to the large increases in crime that started in the 1960s (more prisons and longer sentences, more police and better policing strategies, tougher gun laws). So it is reasonable to conclude that the urban crisis brought forth efforts to counter this social pathology—one era leads to the next. It is also true that other causes of the decline in crime were exogenous (decline in profits from selling crack, aging of the population, legalization of abortion), so some of the reasons for urban rebirth came from outside the urban "system."

Community-based organizations deserve some credit for the urban rebirth. They pressed city government for better services, organized crime watches, fixed up old houses and built new ones, put pressure on drug dealers, and established programs for a variety of good purposes such as drug rehabilitation and day care. Many of these organizations were funded by private foundations. For example, the Ford Foundation worked to establish the Local Initiative Support Corporation (LISC) in 1980. The LISC raises money from a variety of sources and provides funds to hundreds of local community organizations. These organizations also pressed for more home loans and residential insurance from the financial community. A local organization from Chicago, led by a woman named Gail Cincotta, was behind the passage of the Community Reinvestment Act (CRA) in 1977, which requires banks to report the details of their residential lending patterns, which are then taken into account by regulatory agencies. While John Yinger (1995), the leading scholar of housing discrimination, thinks that the CRA has had little effect on lending patterns, the publicity achieved by the local community organization is notable.

While the strong economy of the 1990s cannot be given credit for the decline in violent crime, economic growth surely is behind much of the rest of urban rebirth. The strong economy meant employment growth, low unemployment, low inflation, and strong productivity growth. Most of the employment growth took place in the suburbs of the major urban areas—some of it in newer suburban employment centers, which were dubbed "edge cities" in a popular book by Joel Garreau (1991). These centers began to emerge in the 1980s, and they provide firms with an agglomeration of economic activity that enhances all that locate there. Some of that employment growth took place downtown as well, but it would be fairly accurate to say that economic growth largely happened (and still happens) in the suburbs of American's major urban areas. However, as we have seen in previous chapters, both suburbs and central cities grow more rapidly together as parts of the same metropolitan area. Thanks to researchers such as Dale Jorgenson, Mun Ho, and Kevin Stiroh (2005), we now know that the resurgence of strong productivity growth in the American economy beginning in the early 1990s was associated with adoption of vastly improved information technology.

Extensive empirical research by Timothy Bartik (1991) has documented the favorable effects of employment growth in metropolitan areas. Bartik studied various impacts of employment growth in urban areas (including twenty-four of the twenty-nine urban areas examined in this book) on male workers over the 1979–86 period, and found that an increase in employment will increase labor force participation and reduce unemployment of the current residents. However, he found that most of the jobs were taken by migrants to the urban area. Bartik's summary is that, in the long run, 6 percent to 7 percent of new jobs will be filled by unemployed male residents, 16 percent will go to male residents who enter the labor force, and migrants will take 77 percent to 78 percent of the new jobs (1991, p. 95). These effects are estimated to be permanent. Furthermore, a 1 percent permanent increase in employment increased average earnings by 0.4 percent, but real wages per hour for a given occupation did not increase. The one-time increase in employment also permits some residents to move to better-paying occupations. This effect is strongest for black, less-educated, and younger workers. Not only that, the data show that the effects of an employment increase are highly progressive in that the largest gains in earnings are made by the lowest-income men. Bartik's results are that the men in the bottom 20 percent of earnings gained 4.64 percent in earnings when employment increased by 1 percent—compared to the average of 0.4 percent for all men (1991, p. 173). Bartik's findings suggest that poor people in an urban area benefit greatly from employment growth, regardless of the nature of the growth. He made no distinction between the different sources of employment growth, most of which was in the service sector. Bartik (1994) conducted a related study that shows that job growth from 1979 to 1988 in an urban area increased income for the *households* in the bottom 20 percent of income by more than for the average household. The increase in household income from a 1 percent increase in employment was 2.6 percent, compared to 0.9 percent for the top 80 percent of households.

Macroeconomic policy assisted the economy, and other federal policies made strong contributions to urban rebirth as well. Federal laws outlawing racial discrimination in employment and housing were passed during the Johnson administration. Numerous studies have documented the continued existence of racial discrimination in employment and housing, but surely there has been some improvement as more and more black and Hispanic people have joined the ranks of the middle class. Federal income tax rates were cut substantially during the early 1980s. The top rate was cut from 70 percent to 28 percent (and subsequently raised to 38 percent). Federal housing policy for low-income households changed in 1974 with the passage of the Housing and Community Development Act. This act provided community development block grants and created the rental assistance program. Over subsequent years, federal policy moved from providing funds for public housing to providing housing vouchers that are used in the private housing market. The Low Income Housing Tax Credit program was initiated in 1986 to stimulate housing investment in the inner city. More recently, federal policy has provided funds for the replacement of the aging public housing stock. The Earned Income Tax Credit (EITC) was enacted in 1975 and expanded in 1986, 1990, 1993, and 2001. This tax credit removes low-income households with children from the tax roles and supplements their incomes—thereby providing an incentive to work and thus to be a participant in the economy. In effect, the EITC acts as a wage subsidy for low-wage workers. And, after many years of debate and experimentation, welfare as we knew it ended. Under the Personal Responsibility and Work Opportunity Reconciliation Act (PRWORA) of 1996, welfare recipients have a lifetime limit of sixty months on Temporary Assistance to Needy Families (TANF) and must be employed or engaged in a job search, education, or job training. After this new policy was introduced, the welfare roles fell by over 50 percent. The strong economy was responsible for some of the decline in the roles, to be sure, but clearly the new TANF program provided yet another strong incentive for people to find work. The new system of TANF, coupled with education and training, is widely regarded as a success. While the new policy falls short of being ideal in the eyes of some observers, surely it is a sizable improvement over the old welfare system, which produced welfare dependency that often reached across generations. This new system has had a major impact in inner city areas.

In summary, urban rebirth is the result of several causal factors that came together at roughly the same time. Some of these forces were responses to the urban crisis itself—efforts to fight crime, increasing effectiveness of city governments, responses of community-based organizations and those foundations that provide funding, and changes in federal policy (EITC, welfare reform, community development funds, housing vouchers, transformation of public housing). Other forces were part of the evolution of the urban areas. The transition to the new freeway systems and the transition to the service economy occurred and then largely came to an end. As we shall see, some urban areas made a more successful transition to the service economy than did others. Housing renovation and gentrification grew out of the existence of the housing stock inherited from the early part of the twentieth century. Other forces appear to be essentially exogenous to urban systems—part of the decline in crime, immigration from abroad, and macroeconomic growth. No one could have expected that all of these forces would have converged at roughly the same time. The next task is to see how these forces played out in the urban areas and their central cities included in this study.

Global Cities: Something New?

The resurgence of a few major urban areas has been attributed to their increased participation in the global economy. What are the important dimensions of that participation, and which urban areas can claim to be "global cities"?

The volume of international trade in the world has increased by leaps and bounds, and the U.S. economy has been a full participant in that increase. U.S. exports of goods were 3.7 percent of gross domestic product (GDP) in 1960, and imports equaled just 2.8 percent of GDP. The U.S. economy was running a sizable surplus in its current international trade account. In 1970, the volume of trade in goods had increased slightly more rapidly than GDP, so that exports of goods were 4.1 percent of GDP. Goods imports were equal to 3.8 percent of GDP in that year. After 1970, the volume of international trade took off. In 1980, the share of goods exports in GDP had doubled to 8.0 percent, while goods imports increased at even a faster rate—to equal 9.0 percent of GDP. The United States had begun consistently to run a sizable deficit in the current international trade account in 1976. GDP grew more rapidly during the 1980s than did trade in goods, so exports were 6.7 percent of GDP and imports were equal to 8.6 percent of GDP in 1990. Exports grew again to 7.9 percent of GDP in 2000, but imports jumped to equal 12.5 percent of GDP in that year. Real GDP increased by 2.6 times from 1970 to 2000, and goods exports had increased by almost double that amount (while goods imports had increased by more than triple that amount). Furthermore, the volume of international financial transactions multiplied. Foreign investment in the United States has boomed. The businesses involved in handling the huge increase in the volume of international trade and financial transactions are located in urban areas. A variety of services are needed to handle foreign trade and investment—financial services, legal services, consulting services, and so on. All of this is good news for the urban areas positioned to supply those services, and clearly some of the major urban areas in the United States have participated in this growth.

The notion of "global cities" goes beyond the idea that cities supply the services needed to handle the growth in international trade and financial transactions. Saskia Sassen, currently a professor of sociology at the University of Chicago, is the most prominent scholar who argues that global cities are something rather new. Her definition of a global city (2004, pp. 17–18) starts with the proposition that large corporations have expanded around the world and have created elaborate supply chains in which the components of a final product are produced in far-flung places. This kind of enterprise requires sophisticated coordination and a variety of business services in accounting, law, communications, public relations and marketing, and other areas. These services are best delivered by specialists, who find it best to locate together in major cities so that they can communicate easily with each other. Given that these specialized services are supplied by separate firms, the corporations are free to locate their headquarters outside of the downtowns of major cities. As Sassen puts it, "For global cities, it is the high-level agglomeration of state-of-the-art specialists—the global law firms, accounting firms, and the like—that create the core" (2004, p. 17). Some of these specialists live in or near the downtowns of the global city, thereby creating a new agglomeration of downtown housing, hotels, shops, restaurants, and entertainment. The specialists have high incomes, but the people who serve them in the shops, hotels, and restaurants do not. Sassen (2004, p. 18) asserts that income inequality in global cities has increased as their economic bases have shifted from goods production to the production of high-level business services: "At the same time, the global economy runs on large numbers of poorly paid employees at the bottom—store clerks, dishwashers, dog walkers, parking valets—to serve this new global class" (2004, p. 18). The class of global cities is small—perhaps numbering no more than forty. However, Sassen asserts that the same kind of effects can be seen in smaller urban areas that serve as regional economic capitals.

As we saw in Chapter 12, sociologists use the concept of social class to understand society. That urban underclass was examined in that chapter. Now we have two more classes—identified by Sassen as the new global class and the class of poorly paid employees who serve its members. These new classes have emerged as the size of the American "working class" created by the industrial economy has declined. But Sassen (2000) pushes the point even further. She acknowledges that the middle class in the United States remains the large majority of the population, but argues that they have abandoned the central cities for the suburbs. The groups that remain in the major central cities are two: the highly paid professionals and specialists (who directly serve the major corporations) and the low-income nonprofessionals who serve them. Sassen states, "We see here an interesting correspondence between great concentrations of corporate power and large concentrations of 'others'" (2000, p. 143). However, Sassen avoids using the term underclass. She goes on to write that:

> We can then think of cities also as the place where the contradictions of the internationalization of capital either come to rest or conflict. If we consider, further, that large cities also concentrate a large share of disadvantaged populations—immigrants in both Europe and the United States, African Americans and Latinos in the United States—then we can see that cities have become a strategic terrain for a whole series of conflicts and contradictions. (2000, p. 143)

So there we have it. Under global capitalism, the central cities of the major urban areas have become dominated by two classes that depend upon each other, but that are also in conflict over resources and space in the city. Does this line of argument sound familiar? While Sassen (2000) does not suggest that the solution for the "others" is to rise up in revolution against the capitalist system, the basic framework of two dominant classes that are in conflict in the central city is influential among some urban scholars and activists.

One concrete example of the influence of this framework is a book about the transformation of public housing in Chicago whose title asks, *Where Are Poor People to Live?* (Bennett, Smith, and Wright 2006). Recall that public housing in Chicago has a bad reputation that began by building projects in existing poor areas of the inner city, thus segregating low-income black people in those areas. All of this was done before Chicago became a global city. Some of those housing projects were located near the downtown area. The problems of public housing had long been recognized and were behind the passage of the Housing and Community Development Act of 1974 that created the housing voucher and community development block grant programs. The idea that existing public housing projects should be transformed into something else, such as low-rise developments with mixed-income populations, started with a congressional study of distressed public housing in 1989, and a program was created in 1992 that would provide funds for local public housing agencies to rehabilitate or replace the worst public housing projects. The idea that public housing should be transformed was pursued in the early years of the Clinton administration and then, after the Republicans had taken control of the House of Representatives in 1994, Congress passed the Quality Housing and Work Responsibility Act of 1998. This act enabled local public housing agencies to close buildings more easily by using a viability test, coupled with Housing Choice vouchers. The act also provides funds for the development of mixed-income projects to be undertaken by private developers. The act in effect turned the Chicago Housing Authority into a publicly funded partner in the housing development business. As Bennett, Smith, and Wright (2006) note, federal policy regarding housing for low-income people has shifted largely from a supply-side policy to a demand-side policy. It is fair to say that most housing economists are cheered by this change.

Much of the book edited by Bennett, Smith, and Wright (2006) raises legitimate concerns about the details of the plan for the transformation of Chicago's public housing and its short-term and longer-term impacts on the public housing tenants who must adapt to the new programs. The editors are also dubious about the idea that mixed-income housing developments can be successful for the poor, and look with favor upon a group that called itself the Coalition to Protect Public Housing. In fact, some of the work that the editors performed was at the request of this group. Smith's final statement on the matter is that public policy has, once again, not been designed to benefit the poor: "public housing reform is really no different from urban renewal efforts begun in the 1950s; it will do little to benefit the very poor and a lot to benefit the middle-class and private developers" (2006, p. 279).

Bennett's (2006) summary takes a broader perspective. He links Chicago's (i.e., Mayor Richard M. Daley's) use of the federal program as a means to expand the amount of upscale housing near the downtown area by moving most of the public housing residents to other locations. The title of Bennett's chapter is "Downtown Restructuring and Public Housing in Contemporary Chicago: Fashioning a Better World-Class City." Chicago's officials have consistently used William J. Wilson's (1978) argument that public policy should aim to reduce the social isolation of the very poor engendered by public housing. In Bennett's view, Chicago officials have seized upon this argument about the underclass simply as a rationale for pursuing another agenda—that of enhancing Chicago's ability to be a global city (although Bennett avoids using the term global city and instead refers to a world-class city). This global city agenda creates conflict between the professional specialists who are part of the global economy and the poor people who are expected to take the nonprofessional jobs needed to serve them. Bennett suggests that the agenda for Chicago is the creation of a European-style social geography in which high-income households live near downtown and the bulk of lower-income households live at "considerable distance" from the urban core (Bennett 2006, p. 296). Bennett dismisses the argument that is made by many (including Wilson, of course) that heavy concentrations of poor households headed by females tend to produce and reproduce social pathologies, and instead sees local policy as reflecting the conflict between social classes.

What are we to make of this theory of global cities and social classes in conflict? First, as this book has already demonstrated, the transformation of the American economy from goods production to services can be seen strongly in all of the major urban areas included in this study. Indeed, we have seen that an initial concentration on manufacturing was a negative factor in the subsequent history of a major urban area up to 1990. The composition of the demand for workers has changed. Wages for people with low levels of skill have declined in real terms, while the earnings of highly educated and trained people have increased. All of that is correct. However, these changes in the earnings picture are the result of many forces. The expansion of international trade and international financial markets is only a minor factor in the changing payoff to education and training in the American economy. For example, the sector of the modern economy that has grown the most is health care, with its high-income physicians and enormous number of other staff who earn much less. It is simplistic to link the decline of wages paid to people with low levels of education to global capitalism and international corporations. A better argument probably is to blame it on the huge increase in the demand for health care, which has been underwritten in considerable measure by the federal Medicare and Medicaid programs. Sassen and the others who use the theory of global cities and class conflict mainly see what they think is the dark side of the rebirth of urban areas. At the same time, they fail to provide more than circumstantial evidence in support of this theory. They eschew tests that are capable of rejecting the theory. What would we expect to see if the theory were not correct? This is not discussed. Lastly, suppose that some major cities are being driven primarily by the needs of the global capitalistic system and that social classes are in conflict in those cities as a result? What are we to do about it? Sassen and the others do not address "what is to be done." In my view, we should try to understand the factors that have brought about the urban rebirth that we see so that the virtuous circle can continue to operate.

America's Global Cities: New York, Los Angeles, and Chicago

Abu-Lughod's (1999) history of New York, Los Angeles, and Chicago has been cited frequently in this book. Abu-Lughod takes the notion of the global city seriously and refers in her book's title to New York, Los Angeles, and Chicago as "American's Global Cities." One of her goals is to demonstrate the variety of histories that America's three global cities experienced, and therefore to show the complexities of these major world-class urban areas. Each of the three has special features that make it unique among the world's cities. New York has Wall Street, Broadway, publishing, and, as Abu-Lughod enumerates, twice as many corporate headquarters as Los Angeles and Chicago combined (104 versus 23 in Los Angeles and 31 in Chicago as of 1991) (1999, p. 411). Los Angeles has the entertainment industry, and Chicago is home to several financial markets that offer new products for the mitigation of business risks. All three are centers of transportation and trade and the high-level services that facilitate international business. However, Abu-Lughod (1999) does not link growing income inequality within each urban area to its continuing development as a global city, and expresses skepticism of the idea that class-based conflict is a driving force in the life of each city. In short, as Abu-Lughod puts it, "they are much more than the products of globalization" (1999, p. 423).

It should be clear that I regard Abu-Lughod's book as an excellent source of information, but it has one major difficulty. The book essentially ends in 1990 (with a few bits of information from the early 1990s included). Because of the timing of the research, the book misses the urban rebirth. It ends on an ambiguous note for New York and with discouraging prognoses for Los Angeles and Chicago. Abu-Lughod notes that New York plays a very prominent role in the global economy, and that immigration has increased its vitality. However, its reliance on global economic forces and its political fragmentation make it potentially vulnerable. As for Chicago, Abu-Lughod states that, "In the short run, the picture looks dim indeed, as deindustrialization and international restructuring remove more and more of the city's traditional economic underpinnings" (1999, p. 356). Furthermore, she sees only "halting progress" in relationships among the races that may spell trouble. As she puts it, "If revival is confined to Edge City, as it has been thus far, fragmentation will at best undermine recovery, and at worst lead to revolt" (1999, p. 357). In the case of Los Angeles, the wave of migrants from Mexico and other nations has created a volatile mix. The outcome will depend upon whether there is a real redistribution of power, as opposed to cosmetic changes. Abu-Lughod (1999, p. 397) asserts, "Changes in policy may lead to improvements, but if they do not, the poor may again take to the streets, in the ever-repeating responses of 1965 and 1992."

As a prelude to the next two chapters on urban rebirth, consider the population data for New York, Chicago, and Los Angeles in Table 14.1. All three metropolitan areas gained population in the 1990s, and by remarkably similar percentages. Metropolitan New York gained 8.8 percent in population, while the Chicago urban area increased by 11.6 percent and the Los Angeles metropolitan area grew by 12.7 percent. For New York and Chicago this was a significant increase in growth from the 1980s, while metropolitan Los Angeles experienced a drop in population growth that had been 26.4 percent in the 1980s. All three central cities gained population in the 1990s. Remarkably, population growth in New York City of 9.4 percent exceeded the growth rate of the metropolitan area. As noted in an earlier chapter, the population of New York City had increased in the 1980s from its low point—one early sign of urban rebirth. The city of Chicago had its first population increase since the 1940s, a growth of 4.0 percent. It is significant that most of the areas of population decline in this central city stabilized in the 1990s while population was growing near the fringes of the central city and near downtown. The city of Los Angeles continued to grow, although the rate of growth dropped from 17.5 percent in the 1980s to 6.0 percent in the 1990s.

As Table 14.1 shows, the sources of population growth were the same for all three world-class urban areas—Hispanics and foreign-born people. Many Hispanic people are not foreign born, of course, but much of the *increase* in the foreign-born population is Hispanic. Consider first the case of New York. The population growth of the metropolitan area in the 1990s was 1.54 million, and the increase in the foreign-born population was 1.44 million. The Hispanic population increased by 983,000 to 3.63 million, so much of the increase in the foreign-born population (but by no means all) consisted of immigrants from Latin America. In 2000, 19.1 percent of the population of metropolitan New York and 27.0 percent of the population of New York City was Hispanic.

Population in metropolitan Chicago increased by 863,000 from 1990 to 2000, and 591,000 (68.5 percent) of that increase was in the Hispanic population. The foreign-born population increased by 541,000. The Hispanic population in the Chicago urban area had been 8.1 percent in 1980, and this percentage grew to 11.1 percent in 1990. But in 2000 Hispanics made up 17.1 percent of the metropolitan population, which was comparable to the black percentage of 18.6 percent and the Hispanic percentage for metropolitan New York of 19.1 percent. The Hispanic population in the city of Chicago increased from 435,000 in 1980 to 535,000 in 1990 and then jumped to 754,000 in 2000. The increase in the 1990s of 219,000 exceeds the total population growth in the central city by 107,000. The city of Chicago was 26.0 percent Hispanic in 2000.

As one would expect, the Hispanic population has its largest impact in Los Angeles, where Hispanics were 24.0 percent of the metropolitan population of 11.5 million in 1980, and their percentage increased to 32.4 percent in 1990

Table 14.1

Population of New York, Chicago, and Los Angeles: 1980–2000 (1,000s)

	1980	1990	2000
Metropolitan New York			
Total	16,952	17,504	19,047
Black	2,661	2,940	3,175
Hispanic	2,012	2,646	3,629
Foreign born	2,767	3,468	4,906
New York City			
Total	7,072	7,323	8,008
Black	1,694	1,875	1,962
Hispanic	1,406	1,738	2,161
Foreign born	1,670	2,082	2,871
Metropolitan Chicago			
Total	7,246	7,410	8,273
Black	1,418	1,410	1,541
Hispanic	584	820	1,411
Foreign born	749	885	1,426
City of Chicago			
Total	3,055	2,784	2,896
Black	1,188	1,076	1,054
Hispanic	422	535	754
Foreign born	435	469	629
Metropolitan Los Angeles			
Total	11,498	14,531	16,373
Black	1,038	1,171	1,200
Hispanic	2,755	4,714	6,599
Foreign born	2,124	3,945	5,067
City of Los Angeles			
Total	2,967	3,485	3,695
Black	495	461	402
Hispanic	816	1,370	1,719
Foreign born	805	1,337	1,513

Source: HUD State of the Cities Data.

and 40.3 percent in 2000. The increase in the Hispanic population in the 1980s accounted for 64.6 percent of the population growth of the metropolitan area during that decade. In the 1990s, the Hispanic population growth of 1.88 million accounts for all of the population growth in the Los Angeles urban area of 1.84 million. In the 1990s, the foreign-born population increased by 1.12 million, so a sizable amount of the Hispanic population growth was natural increase or migration from other locations within the United States. The Hispanic population of the city of Los Angeles increased from 27.5 percent in 1980 to 39.3 percent in 1990 and to 46.5 percent in 2000. It is likely that the Hispanic population will be in the majority in the central city at the time of the next general census in 2010.

New York, Chicago, and Los Angeles have participated in the emergence of the global economy since 1970, so there should be some evidence of their transition to global cities in the industry employment data. The basic nonagricultural employment data for the three metropolitan areas and for the nation are displayed in Table 14.2. Four broad industry categories are included—manufacturing, FIRE (finance, insurance, and real estate), business and repair services, and professional services.

The definitions of the manufacturing and FIRE sectors are obvious. Business and repair services include these industries:

- advertising, public relations, and related activities
- management consulting
- services to dwellings and buildings
- personnel supply services (i.e., temporary worker firms)
- computer and data-processing services
- detective/protective services
- automobile services

Employment in all of these industries has grown, but growth has been greatest in computer and data-processing services and personnel supply services. Employment in computer and data-processing services in the nation increased from 221,000 to 2.1 million from 1980 to 2000. Personnel supply services increased from 235,000 to 1.1 million over this same period. These are services that are used by businesses (and governments, too) of all types. Professional services include:

- health services
- elementary and secondary schools (private)
- colleges and universities (private)
- social services
- legal services

The professional services sector grew from 12.90 million in 1970 to 33.12 million in 2000, and its share of total employment increased from 17.2 percent to 24.8 percent over these three decades. Health services employment is the largest component of professional services, and grew from 4.47 million in 1970 to 12.65 million in 2000. Employment in legal services almost doubled from 1980 to 2000 (from 776,000 to 1.37 million).

Table 14.2

Nonagricultural Employment by Industry: 1970–2000
(employment in 1,000s)

	1970 Employment (share)	1980 Employment (share)	1990 Employment (share)	2000 Employment (share)
United States				
Total	75,111	95,939	115,570	133,509
Manufacturing	20,746	21,942	21,346	20,256
	(27.6%)	(22.9%)	(18.5%)	(15.2%)
FIRE	3,945	5,993	8,051	8,828
	(5.3)	(6.2)	(7.0)	(6.6)
Business and Repair Services	2,003	3,848	7,485	9,776
	(2.7)	(4.0)	(6.5)	(7.3)
Professional Services	12,904	19,853	25,351	33,123
	(17.2)	(20.7)	(21.9)	(24.8)
New York				
Total	7,064	7,410	8,425	8,492
Manufacturing	1,607	1,522	1,183	843
	(22.7%)	(20.5%)	(14.0%)	(10.1%)
FIRE	546	680	889	827
	(7.7)	(9.2)	(10.6)	(9.7)
Business and Repair Services	302	437	489	718
	(4.3)	(5.9)	(5.8)	(8.5)
Professional Services	1,196	1,629	2,212	2,246
	(16.9)	(22.0)	(26.3)	(26.4)
Chicago				
Total	2,939	3,328	3,635	3,894
Manufacturing	856	878	700	639
	(29.1%)	(26.4%)	(19.3%)	(16.4%)
FIRE	162	252	326	331
	(5.5)	(7.6)	(9.0)	(8.5)
Business and Repair Services	104	105	199	323
	(3.5)	(3.2)	(5.5)	(8.3)
Professional Services	422	632	818	878
	(14.4)	(19.0)	(22.5)	(22.5)
Los Angeles				
Total	3,959	5,345	6,977	6,933
Manufacturing	966	1,282	1,355	1,100
	(24.4%)	(24.0%)	(19.4%)	(15.9%)
FIRE	221	377	540	460
	(5.6)	(7.1)	(7.7)	(6.6)
Business and Repair Services	170	245	349	620
	(4.3)	(5.5)	(5.0)	(8.9)
Professional Services	638	1,011	1,424	1,509
	(16.1)	(18.9)	(20.4)	(21.8)

Source: HUD State of the Cities Data.

Table 14.2 shows how employment in the national economy has changed since 1970. The share of employment in manufacturing has declined steadily from 27.6 percent in 1970 to 15.2 percent in 2000. The share of employment in FIRE, business and repair services, and professional services increased from 25.2 percent to 38.7 percent over this same time, so the decline in the share of manufacturing of 12.4 percentage points was matched by the increase in the share of these three sectors of 13.5 percentage points. The share of employment in business and repair services increased from 2.7 percent to 7.3 percent, largely because of the computer and data-processing and personnel supply services industries. Professional services had the largest increase in share from 17.2 percent to 24.8 percent, and this was driven largely by health care. How do the three global cities compare to these national trends?

The composition of employment in New York differed from the nation in 1970. As shown in Table 14.2, manufacturing was 22.7 percent of its total (4.9 percentage points lower than the nation), and New York's share of employment in FIRE and business and repair services exceeded the national shares. Table 14.2 shows a dramatic decline in manufacturing employment in New York from 1.61 million jobs in 1970 to 843,000 jobs in 2000—a decline in share from 22.7 percent to just 10.1 percent. However, the decline in the share of manufacturing in New York just matches the decline at the national level of 12.4 percentage points. The FIRE sector in New York grew rapidly from 1970 to 1990 and increased its share from 7.7 percent to 10.6 percent, but then employment in this sector declined from 1990 to 2000, and its share fell to 9.7 percent. Nevertheless, the change in share of 2.0 percentage points exceeds the change in share at the national level of 1.3 percentage points, so here is evidence of New York's increasing participation in the financial operations of the global economy. The share of New York's employment in business and repair services increased by 4.2 percentage points from 1970 to 2000, but this increase is less than the change in share at the national level of 4.6 percentage points. Professional services in New York increased its share by 9.5 percentage points over the thirty years, and the change in share at the national level was 7.6 percentage points. One can conclude that the New York economy did indeed make a transition that differed from the nation as a whole—especially in professional services and FIRE. However, the largest component of professional services is health care, a service that is not part of the global economy's "command and control" system.

The economic transition in Chicago is displayed in Table 14.2 as well. Chicago also differed from the nation in 1970: its employment shares in manufacturing and business and repair services exceeded the national shares, and its share of employment in professional services was lower than the share at the national level. Employment in FIRE in Chicago was just 5.5 percent, which closely matched the national share of 5.3 percent, but this was to change. The share of manufacturing employment fell by 12.7 percentage points (matching the change in share at the national level of 12.4 percentage points). Total employment in this sector in metropolitan Chicago fell from 856,000 to 639,000 over thirty years as the city lost its basic steel industry (and others). Employment in FIRE increased from 5.5 percent to 8.5 percent of total employment, an increase that far exceeds the nation's change in share of 1.3 percent. The financial markets in Chicago are a success story, and include the Chicago Board of Trade (CBOT), the Chicago Mercantile Exchange (CME), and the Chicago Board Options Exchange (CBOE). The largest employment increases in this sector took place from 1970 to 1990. The business and repair services sector increased its employment share by 4.8 percentage points, which matches the change at the national level of 4.6 percentage points. Lastly, Chicago's employment share in professional services increased by 8.1 percentage points, which exceeds the increase in the nation of 7.6 percent. In short, the clearest evidence of Chicago's participation in the global economy is in the FIRE sector, as one would have expected.

The economy of the Los Angeles metropolitan area also did not match the national economy in 1970, but its pattern differed from those of New York and Chicago. Manufacturing employment was less than the national share (as in New York), but employment in FIRE of 5.6 percent was just barely greater than the national share of 5.3 percent (similar to Chicago). The share of employment in business and repair services of 4.3 percent matched New York (and exceeded the nation), and the share in professional services was less than the national share (as in New York). In other words, Los Angeles had (in relative terms) more manufacturing and less FIRE than did New York in 1970. Manufacturing employment in Los Angeles actually increased substantially from 1970 to 1990 along with its entire economy, but then declined in the 1990s. The share of manufacturing employment fell by 8.5 percentage points, which is much less than the decline in share at the national level of 12.4 percentage points. Manufacturing in Los Angeles has had some success compared to the rest of the nation (and compared to New York and Chicago). However, the decline in manufacturing employment in the 1990s appears to be a primary cause of the decline in total employment of 0.6 percent between 1990 and 2000. The share of employment for Los Angeles in FIRE increased by just 1.0 percentage point, which falls short of the increase in share at the national level of 1.3 percentage points. This fact therefore provides no evidence that Los Angeles is becoming a center of global finance. Also, the increase in the share of business and professional services of 4.6 percentage points just matches the change at the national level, and professional services had an increase in share of 5.7 percentage points, falling well short of the national change of 7.6 percentage points. These data provide no evidence that Los Angeles was becoming a "global city" similar to New York. However, the economy of Los Angeles has two features that make it a big part of the international economy—its port and its entertainment industry.

Summary

This first chapter on the period of urban rebirth accomplishes two objectives. A short catalog of reasons for urban rebirth is provided, and the notion of global cities is introduced. The basic reasons for urban rebirth are of three types—those that are logical extensions of the forces already at work in the urban areas, those that were responses to the urban crisis, and those forces that came from outside the urban area essentially in exogenous form. The global city is one idea of a force that is hypothesized to be a combination of an exogenous cause and then a logical extension of an internal dynamic. The globalization of the economy creates a demand for major urban areas to act as points from which the far-flung enterprises are managed by providing a variety of high-level financial, legal, communication, managerial, and other services. New York, Chicago, and Los Angeles are generally recognized as the chief global cities in the United States, and each plays particular roles on the global stage. However, it is not clear that one can conclude that the emergence of a city as a global city inexorably means that income inequality must increase and class conflicts emerge.

This chapter concluded with a short look at the population and employment trends in global cities of New York, Chicago, and Los Angeles in the 1980s and 1990s. All three metropolitan areas and central cities experienced population growth in the 1990s, the sources of which are the Hispanic and foreign-born populations. All three cities attracted large numbers of immigrants from abroad. The initial increases in immigration to these urban areas were probably due to changes in federal immigration policies in 1965 and 1986, but once the flow of immigrants reached some critical size, then more and more came in search of the economic opportunity that the previous immigrants had experienced. It seems reasonable to conclude that the recent immigration from abroad to America's global cities has become a virtuous circle in which successful immigrants beget more immigrants, who also have good chances of being successful. The employment data show that both New York and Chicago made economic transitions involving growth in finance, insurance, and real estate that are consistent with the global cities idea. In contrast, the economic transition in Los Angeles did not involve a major increase in FIRE employment. Rather, Los Angeles participates in the global economy as the major Pacific port and as the primary home of the entertainment industry.

15

Urban Rebirth in the Northeast: 1990–2000

This chapter is a detailed study of the northeastern urban areas in the decade of the 1990s that will show the dimensions of the urban rebirth. It follows the previous chapters in examining population, employment, household income, poverty, housing, and social pathologies. This chapter shows that the nature and extent of the urban rebirth varied among metropolitan areas. Some urban areas did much better than others, but all seventeen showed some signs of rebirth. Also, the chapter shows that progress was not made in all dimensions. For example, one discouraging outcome in all seventeen central cities is the continuing increase in single-parent families with children. The conclusion reached in this chapter is that ten of the seventeen urban areas and their central cities clearly displayed signs of urban rebirth in the 1990s.

An introductory version of the complete story from 1950 to 2000 can be seen in the population-change figures in Table 15.1. As we saw in Chapter 4, the seventeen major urban areas of the Northeast had an average population increase of 40 percent from 1950 to 1970. This figure of 40 percent average population growth exceeds the 27 percent population growth of the northeastern region by a sizable margin. Population growth was especially large in Washington, D.C. (93 percent), Minneapolis–St. Paul (81 percent), and Columbus (80 percent), but even metropolitan Pittsburgh (21 percent) and Buffalo (24 percent) recorded sizable population growth figures. Twelve of the central cities lost population during these decades, and the population of New York City did not change. The other four central cities (Milwaukee, Kansas City, Indianapolis, and Columbus) annexed territory, and central city population increased. The average population loss for the thirteen (excluding the four that annexed territory) was 13 percent as suburbanization was strongly under way, and this may well have been a signal of the urban crisis that was to come.

Table 15.1

Population Change in the Urban Areas of the Northeast: 1950–2000
(in percent)

	Urban area 1950–1970	Urban area 1970–1990	Urban area 1990–2000	Central city 1950–1970	Central city 1970–1990	Central city 1990–2000
New York	32	−3.3	8.8	0	−7.2	9.4
Chicago	28	5.7	11.6	−7	−17.2	4.0
Philadelphia	33	0.8	3.6	−6	−18.6	−4.3
Detroit	49	−1.1	4.1	−18	−32.0	−7.5
Boston	19	0.0	5.5	−20	−10.5	2.6
Pittsburgh	21	−10.8	−1.5	−23	−28.8	−9.5
St. Louis	34	1.5	4.5	−27	−36.2	−12.3
Cleveland	42	−9.0	2.2	−18	−32.6	−5.5
Washington, D.C.	93	31.9	16.6	−6	−19.8	−5.8
Baltimore	36	14.0	7.2	−5	−18.8	−11.5
Minneapolis– St. Paul	81	25.2	17.0	−11	−14.0	4.7
Buffalo	24	−11.9	−1.6	−20	−29.2	−11.0
Cincinnati	36	6.0	7.9	−10	−19.6	−9.1
Milwaukee	51	2.0	4.8	12*	−12.4	−4.7
Kansas City	54	14.5	12.2	11*	−8.3	1.6
Indianapolis	63	24.3	16.4	74*	−1.9	7.0
Columbus	80	18.6	14.5	44*	17.2*	12.3**
Mean	40	6.4	7.9	−2	−17.1	−2.3

*Central city annexed significant amount of territory during the period.
**Columbus expanded its area by 9.9 percent in the 1990s.
Sources: Census of Population and HUD State of the Cities Data.

As shown in Chapter 10, the population figures for the urban areas of the Northeast took a dramatic negative turn from 1970 to 1990. The average population growth for the seventeen urban areas was just 6.4 percent, which is roughly equal to the population growth for the northeastern region of 5.1 percent. Five of the seventeen—New York, Detroit, Pittsburgh, Cleveland, and Buffalo—lost population. These last three urban areas lost an average of 10.6 percent of their populations. As a result, the central cities lost population in large numbers. The average population loss for the seventeen central cities was 17.1 percent. Columbus was the only central city to annex territory and record a population gain. If Columbus is excluded from the computation, the average population loss for the central cites was 19.2 percent. The more complete story of the urban crisis in the Northeast has been examined in Chapters 10 and 13.

Now we come to the 1990s. Table 15.1 shows that the average population growth for the seventeen urban areas was 7.9 percent from 1990 to 2000, a figure that is close to the 7.0 percent population growth recorded for the northeastern region. The urban areas did not grow faster than did their region as a whole, but growth over one decade of 7.9 percent is a change from the 3.2 percent growth per decade that occurred from 1970 to 1990. The metropolitan areas with the largest population growth percentages are (in order) Minneapolis–St. Paul, Washington, D.C., Indianapolis, Columbus, Kansas City, and Chicago—all with growth in excess of 11 percent over the decade. At the other end of the list, Pittsburgh and Buffalo continued to lose population, but at much lower rates than before. Population loss in metropolitan Pittsburgh had been 10.8 percent from 1970 to 1990, and it lost 1.5 percent of its population in the 1990s. Buffalo's experience was virtually identical to that of Pittsburgh—losses of 11.9 percent from 1970 to 1990 and 1.6 percent from 1990 to 2000. The Detroit and Cleveland urban areas turned population losses in the 1970s and 1980s to modest population gains in the 1990s of 4.1 percent and 2.2 percent, respectively. All seventeen urban areas had an improvement in the population change figure for 1990–2000 compared to the change per decade for 1970–90 (i.e., divide the change figure for 1970–90 by two, and compare to the figure for 1990–2000).

Lastly, examine the population change figures for the central cities for 1990–2000 in Table 15.1. These are critical indicators of the state of the major central cities of the Northeast, the central points in the urban crisis. On average, the seventeen central cities lost 2.3 percent of their population during the decade. Seven of the seventeen central cities gained population in the 1990s, and this list includes New York City and the city of Chicago as well as Boston, Minneapolis–St. Paul, Kansas City, Indianapolis, and Columbus. Only Columbus had gained population from 1970 to 1990 (and annexed territory). The other ten central cities continued to lose population, but, except for Baltimore, the rate at which population declined was less than it had been during 1970 to 1990 (i.e., once again, divide the population figure for 1970–90 by two and compare to the change for 1990–2000). For example, the city of Detroit lost 16 percent of its population per decade from 1970 to 1990 but lost 7.5 percent in the 1990s. The population of the city of Cleveland fell by 16.3 percent per decade during 1970–90 but lost only 5.5 percent from 1990 to 2000.

The empirical relationship between central city population growth (or decline) and metropolitan population growth continued to hold in the 1990s. The estimated equation for the seventeen urban areas for 1990–2000 is:

$$CCPOPGRO = -8.79 + 0.77\ UAPOPGRO + 0.70\ AREA$$
$$(3.53)\ (3.34) \qquad\qquad (1.09)$$

The *R*-square for the equation is 0.388, and the *t* statistics in parentheses indicate that both the constant term and the coefficient of urban area population growth are highly statistically significant. The equation says that an urban area with no population growth would have had a central city that declined by 8.8 percent, and that each percentage point on urban area population growth would have boosted the central city population change by 0.77 percent. The coefficient of the change in the area of the central city (in percentage terms) is not statistically significant. Columbus was the only central city that annexed a significant amount of territory in the 1990s—an expansion of 9.9 percent. If the area variable is dropped from the equation, the coefficient of population growth of the urban area increases slightly to 0.85. The examination of the individual urban areas begins with an overview of the seventeen in the next section, which is followed by a discussion of each one in turn.

The Metropolitan Areas and Their Central Cities

The basic data for the overview of the metropolitan areas and their central cities are found in Tables 15.2, 15.3, and 15.4. As noted above, the average population growth for the seventeen urban areas was 7.9 percent from 1990 to 2000, and on average the central cities declined in population by only 2.3 percent. Both of these outcomes are distinct shifts from the previous two decades of urban crisis. However, Table 15.2 shows that average employment growth over the decade was a rather sluggish 7.2 percent compared to the average employment growth from 1970 to 1990 of 30.0 percent (i.e., about 15 percent per decade). Employment growth was relatively rapid (above 11 percent) in Minneapolis–St. Paul, Indianapolis, Columbus, Kansas City, and Cincinnati. Employment declined in the Buffalo metropolitan area by 2.0 percent, and increased by only a fraction of a percentage point in metropolitan New York and Philadelphia. The employment figures must be taken in context. During the 1990s (as reported by the decennial census), employment in the nation increased by only 12.1 percent (compared to the national employment growth from 1970 to 1990 of 50.9 percent). The population aged sixteen and over increased by 13.2 percent in the 1990s, and their labor force participation rate fell from 65.3 percent in 1990 to 63.9 percent in 2000. Therefore, sluggish employment growth in the 1990s was a national phenomenon, and not a feature just of the major metropolitan areas of the Northeast. The population of the Northeast grew by 7.0 percent in the 1990s, compared to 13.2 percent population growth for the nation (a difference of 6.2 percent), so it is not surprising that employment in the major urban areas of the Northeast grew more slowly than did employment in the nation by 4.9 percentage points. This is an important initial finding—urban rebirth in the Northeast was not necessarily tied to rapid employment growth.

Table 15.2

Northeastern Metropolitan Areas: 1990–2000

	Population growth	Employment growth	Median family income growth	Median family income $ 1999	Manufacturing employment 1990 (percent)	FIRE, prof., & business serv. 1990 (percent)	Segregation index	
							1990	2000
New York	8.8	0.8	-2.7	58,300	14.0	42.7	81	81
Chicago	11.6	7.1	6.6	61,200	19.3	36.9	84	80
Philadelphia	3.6	0.1	3.7	58,400	16.7	39.4	77	72
Detroit	4.1	6.7	6.7	49,200	23.8	34.3	87	85
Boston	5.5	2.5	2.2	55,200	11.3	44.5	69	66
Pittsburgh	-1.5	3.2	7.7	47,500	15.0	38.4	71	67
St. Louis	4.5	6.1	5.9	54,000	19.0	35.3	77	73
Cleveland	2.2	5.5	6.1	52,000	23.0	35.5	82	77
Washington, D.C.	16.6	8.2	2.0	72,200	6.0	29.0	65	62
Baltimore	7.2	2.7	4.6	59,300	12.1	37.0	67	64
Minneapolis–St. Paul	17.0	18.4	13.1	65,500	19.6	37.6	62	58
Buffalo	-1.6	-2.0	2.1	38,500	18.8	37.7	80	77
Cincinnati	7.9	11.2	11.2	54,700	19.9	34.1	76	74
Milwaukee	4.8	5.7	8.4	56,800	24.1	36.3	83	82
Kansas City	12.2	13.0	10.3	55,800	14.9	37.4	72	69
Indianapolis	16.4	16.7	10.4	55,200	18.7	37.3	75	70
Columbus	14.5	17.1	11.3	55,000	14.3	36.4	67	62
Mean	7.9	7.2	6.4	55,800	17.1	37.0	75	72

Sources: HUD State of the Cities Data and U.S. Bureau of the Census.

Median family incomes in real terms grew in all of the seventeen urban areas except for metropolitan New York. The average growth was 6.4 percent, and the average for the median incomes (in 1999 dollars) reached $55,800. The average for median family income growth for 1970 to 1990 was 7.6 percent (3.8 percent per decade), so families did somewhat better in the 1990s in terms of real income growth than they did in the previous two decades. Growth in median family income was driven by employment growth. The regression result is:

$$\text{MFIGRO} = 2.43 + 0.56\ \text{EMPGRO}$$
$$(2.58)\ (5.55)$$

The R-square for this estimated equation is 0.651 and, as the t statistic in parentheses indicates, the coefficient on employment growth is very highly statistically significant. The coefficient indicates that employment growth that was one percentage point greater was associated with median family real income growth that was 0.56 percentage point greater. So, while urban rebirth was not necessarily tied to rapid employment growth, faster employment growth was clearly associated with greater real income growth.

Median family incomes varied substantially around the average for the seventeen urban areas of $55,800. Those metropolitan areas with the highest median family incomes were Washington, D.C. ($72,000), Minneapolis–St. Paul ($65,000), and Chicago ($61,200), while those at the bottom were Buffalo ($38,500), Pittsburgh ($47,500), and Detroit ($49,200). The other eleven metropolitan areas had median family incomes that fell within the range of $52,000 (Cleveland) to $58,400 (Philadelphia). Recall from Chapter 10 that Buffalo, Pittsburgh, Detroit, and Cleveland are the four metropolitan areas that were hit hardest by the urban crisis. However, Pittsburgh and Detroit actually had median family income gains (of 7.7 percent and 6.7 percent, respectively) that were above average for the seventeen urban areas. The median family income increase in Buffalo was only 2.1 percent, while Cleveland recorded a respectable increase of 6.1 percent. Median family real income had actually declined in Detroit, Cleveland, and Buffalo from 1970 to 1990 (and increased by only 1.8 percent in Pittsburgh). In short, three of the four urban areas hit hardest by the urban crisis showed this one sign of recovery.

Table 15.2 includes a new variable for the metropolitan areas—the segregation index for black residents. The index for 1990 and 2000 has been computed at the metropolitan level, and it shows that in 1990 complete racial integration (at the census tract level) would be achieved in the seventeen metropolitan areas if an average of 75 percent of the black population were moved. This average for this index of segregation declined somewhat to 72 in 2000. The urban areas with the lowest levels of segregation in 2000 were Minneapolis–St. Paul (58), Columbus (62), Washington, D.C. (62), Baltimore (64), and Pittsburgh (67). The average segregation index for the seventeen urban areas was 78 in 1980. All seventeen urban areas recorded declines in the segregation index, so one can say that progress was made across the board (albeit at a slow pace in some urban areas).

This brief review of the major metropolitan areas of the Northeast reveals that population trends had shifted favorably in the 1990s, growth in median family real incomes had picked up, and racial segregation was falling. However, employment growth was sluggish in several urban areas, and employment growth was a critical factor in producing growth in median family incomes. Nevertheless, the four urban areas hit hardest by the urban crisis showed one sign of recovery—positive change in median family incomes. We now turn to the central cities for a more detailed look at the change from urban crisis to urban rebirth.

The basic population figures and their favorable trends for the central cities have already been discussed. In seven cases the population of the central city increased in the 1990s, and in nine out the other ten the rate of population decline was slower in the 1990s than in the 1970–90 period. An increase in the population of the central city can be both a consequence and a cause of urban rebirth. People decide to move in because conditions are improving, and people who move in may demand that conditions continue to improve. The dimensions of urban conditions that were examined in Chapter 13 are poverty, crime, concentrated poverty, single-parent families with children, and high-school dropouts. The data on these five variables for the central cities are shown in Table 15.3.

The average for the poverty rates in the central cities declined from 21.1 percent in 1990 to 20.6 percent in 2000. The average poverty rate had increased from 14.6 percent in 1970 to 21.1 percent in 1990, so the fact that this summary measure of central city poverty declined by even a small amount is welcome news. By this measure the vicious circle has stopped, but the virtuous circle is not clearly in evidence. The poverty rate declined in eight central cities, increased in another eight, and remained constant in St. Louis.

The overall decline in crime in the United States was discussed in Chapter 14, and the data on murder rates show that the average for the seventeen central cities fell from 30 murders to 20 murders per 100,000 people. Some of the individual central cities experienced remarkable drops in murders per 100,000: New York City from 31 to 9, Detroit from a terrible 57 to 41 (still awful, but better), Boston from 25 to 7, Cleveland from 33 to 14, Washington, D.C., from a horrendous 78 to 42, and Cincinnati from 14 to 4. Baltimore is the only central city with a high murder rate that did not decline significantly

Table 15.3

Central Cities of the Northeast: 1990–2000

	Population change (percent)	Poverty rate (percent)		Murder rate (per 100k)		Population in high-poverty areas (1,000s)		One-parent families w/children		High-school dropouts (percent)	
		1990	2000	1990	2000	1990	2000	1990	2000	1990	2000
New York	9.4	19.3	21.2	31	9	960	945	37.9	40.7	32	28
Chicago	4.0	21.6	19.6	31	22	413	235	40.8	41.5	34	28
Philadelphia	−4.3	20.3	22.9	32	22	242	241	41.3	51.0	36	29
Detroit	−7.5	21.9	26.1	57	41	421	108	61.0	63.1	38	30
Boston	2.6	18.7	19.5	25	7	32	33	48.7	48.0	24	21
Pittsburgh	−9.5	21.4	20.4	10	11	75	48	40.1	47.9	28	19
St. Louis	−12.3	24.6	24.6	45	36	110	71	50.9	57.4	37	29
Cleveland	−5.5	28.7	26.3	33	14	102	76	50.1	59.4	41	31
Washington, D.C.	−5.8	16.9	20.2	78	42	21	78	53.0	57.8	27	22
Baltimore	−11.5	21.9	22.9	41	40	107	76	52.9	60.9	39	32
Minneapolis–St. Paul	4.7	18.5	16.9	17	14	79	47	39.2	43.2	17	15
Buffalo	−11.0	25.6	26.6	11	13	72	51	48.2	58.1	33	25
Cincinnati	−9.1	24.3	21.2	14	4	74	51	47.2	56.6	30	23
Milwaukee	−4.7	22.2	21.3	25	21	141	77	45.3	53.0	28	25
Kansas City	1.6	15.3	14.3	28	25	32	17	35.0	42.4	21	18
Indianapolis	7.0	12.5	11.9	12	12	24	5	30.6	39.8	24	19
Columbus	12.3*	17.2	14.8	14	10	87	39	33.6	41.1	21	16
Mean	−2.3	21.2	20.6	30	20			44.2	50.7	30	26

Sources: HUD State of the Cities Data, FBI, and Jargowsky (2003).

(41 in 1990 and 40 in 2000). Other central cities, such as Pittsburgh, Minneapolis–St. Paul, Buffalo, Indianapolis, and Columbus, had relatively low murder rates (17 or under) in 1990 that did not change much. This strong decline in crime, especially in the central cities with high murder rates, is a primary aspect of the urban rebirth.

Next, Jargowsky (2003) has updated his computations of the number of people living in high-poverty areas (40 percent poverty or above) and has produced more remarkable results. Sizable declines in the number of people who lived in high-poverty areas were found for thirteen of the seventeen central cities. In three cases (New York City, Philadelphia, and Boston), the number of people who lived in these areas remained essentially unchanged, and the number increased in Washington, D.C. The declines are remarkable in two of the largest central cities—Chicago and Detroit. The decline in Chicago was from 413,000 to 235,000, a decline that was topped by Detroit's drop from 421,000 to 108,000. Recall that sociologists such as William J. Wilson and many others have argued that concentrated poverty is particularly harmful to the life chances of the people who live in these areas, so the deconcentration of poverty is good news—even if the overall poverty rate did not decline by very much.

The next variable, the percentage of families with children with only one parent present, is the one variable that went in the wrong direction. The average for the seventeen central cities was 44.2 percent in 1990, and it increased to 50.7 percent in 2000. Think about that. In nine of the central cities, more than half of the families with children had only one parent present in 2000. If the late Daniel Moynihan were still alive, he would surely say that this is a national disgrace. How can we expect the next generation to turn out well under such circumstances? Urban rebirth has not yet reached this critical aspect of the urban condition.

The last variable in Table 15.3 is the percentage of adults (age twenty-five and over) who had not graduated from high school. The overall average for the seventeen central cities fell from 30 to 26 percent in the 1990s, following a decline from 40 to 30 percent from 1970 to 1990. The decline of four percentage points in the 1990s is roughly in line with the drop of five percentage points per decade during the previous twenty years. The basic reason for this improvement is the fact that younger cohorts of people with higher levels of education are replacing older cohorts who had less education. Nevertheless, the trend is favorable because the life chances for people who do not graduate from high school are not good.

Table 15.4 shows that, on average, the number of occupied housing units in the central cities changed very little declining by 0.9 percent. This average masks the fact that some central cities gained occupied units (New York City,

Table 15.4

Central Cities of the Northeast: Various Changes, 1990–2000 (in percent)

	Change in occupied hous- ing units	Change in median family real income	Black population 1990	Black population 2000
New York	7.2	−2.7	25.6	24.5
Chicago	3.5	3.4	38.6	36.4
Philadelphia	−2.0	−8.6	39.5	42.6
Detroit	−11.1	17.1	75.5	81.2
Boston	4.3	1.0	24.0	23.8
Pittsburgh	−7.1	3.1	25.7	26.9
St. Louis	−10.9	0	47.4	50.9
Cleveland	−4.7	0.3	46.2	50.6
Washington, D.C.	−0.8	−4.9	65.2	59.4
Baltimore	−7.5	−6.6	59.0	64.1
Minneapolis– St. Paul	1.1	8.7	10.5	15.1
Buffalo	−10.3	−1.2	30.5	36.6
Cincinnati	−3.9	4.2	37.9	42.9
Milwaukee	−3.7	−0.3	30.3	36.9
Kansas City	3.4	3.8	29.4	31.0
Indianapolis	9.6	4.1	22.4	25.3
Columbus	17.5	−1.8	22.4	24.3
Mean	−0.9	1.3	37.1	39.6

Source: HUD State of the Cities Data.

Chicago, Boston, and four others), while others lost sizable numbers of occupied units (Detroit, Pittsburgh, St. Louis, Baltimore, and Buffalo), However, as one might have expected, the seven central cities that gained occupied units are also the seven that gained population. The other ten lost both occupied housing units and population. Table 15.4 also shows the percentage change in median family real income for 1990 to 2000. Nine central cities experienced an increase, seven declined, and one remained the same (St. Louis). The average for the seventeen central cities was a gain of 1.3 percent in median family real income. The last two columns in Table 15.4 display the percentage of the population of the central city that was black in 1990 and 2000. The average for the seventeen central cities increased modestly from 37.1 percent to 39.6 percent over the decade.

This examination of the data for the central cities in the 1990s has revealed that the urban rebirth indeed was under way. Central city poverty declined by a small amount and had become significantly deconcentrated, murder rates dropped (some by truly remarkable amounts), and the percentage of adults without a high-school diploma continued to fall. On the negative side, single-parent families became more prevalent in the central cities. So there we have it—clear improvement in four measures of social pathology, and change in the wrong direction in one (single-parent families). When combined with the basically favorable population trends in the central cities, it is reasonable to conclude that the virtuous circle has been at work. But has the virtuous circle been at work in all of the central cities? Perhaps not, so the next task is to examine each of the urban areas and their central cities.[1]

Urban Rebirth in New York?

The story of urban revitalization in New York is a most important story to tell. If there had not been some signs of urban rebirth in New York and strong rebirth in Chicago, then one might question my basic premise that urban history since 1950 has three acts.

As we saw in Chapter 10, New York in the 1980s was on its way back from the disastrous 1970s. The population of the metropolitan area had increased by 3.3 percent in the 1980s (compared to a decline of 3.6 percent in the 1970s), and the central city had gained 251,000 people (3.5 percent) instead of the 10.4 percent loss in the 1970s. But then came the 1990s. The metropolitan area population increased by 8.8 percent and, rather amazingly, the population of New York City increased by an even larger 9.4 percent. As we saw in Chapter 14, the population increase in New York was driven largely by Hispanic and foreign-born people. The increase in the foreign-born population accounts for 93.2 percent of the population increase of 1.54 million in the metropolitan area. Total employment in the metropolitan area increased by just 0.8 percent (from 8.42 million to 8.49 million). Employment in manufacturing declined by 28.7 percent, but employment in finance, insurance, and real estate (FIRE) also declined from 889,000 to 827,000 (a drop of 7.0 percent). The decline in FIRE employment was concentrated in New York City, which had a decline from 402,000 to 353,000. Employment in business services increased strongly from 418,000 to 718,000 (up 71.8 percent), but professional services employment was stagnant at 2.212 million in 1980 and 2.246 million in 2000. The sluggish performance in jobs translated into a decline in median family real income in the metropolitan area from $59,000 in 1990 to $58,300 in 2000—a decline of 2.7 percent.

The housing market was active. Housing units in the metropolitan area increased by 6.9 percent from 6.75 million to 7.22 million. The vacancy rate actually declined from 5.2 percent in 1990 to 3.9 percent in 2000, so there is no evidence of overbuilding. The number of housing units in New York City increased from 2.98 million to 3.17 million, an increase of 6.5 percent, and the vacancy rate declined from 5.4 percent to 4.8 percent. This means that the central city added 194,000 housing units in ten years, and the number of occupied units increased by 203,000. These numbers add up to the rebirth of several neighborhoods in New York City.

Measures of social pathologies in the central city, which were studied in detail in Chapter 13, show a dramatic reduction in crime and mixed results otherwise. The murder rate in New York City fell from 31 per 100,000 in 1990 to 9 per 100,000 in 2000—a stunning achievement that is good news for everyone. A detailed empirical study of housing prices in New York by Schwartz, Susin, and Voicu (2003) found that the decline in crime was responsible for about one-third of the increase in housing prices during 1988 to 1998. However, the poverty rate in the central city increased from 19.3 percent to 21.2 percent as a result of the sluggish job market and the wave of immigrants from abroad. There was no improvement in racial segregation. The index for the segregation of the black population at the metropolitan level was unchanged from 1980 to 1990 to 2000 at 81. (Note that this segregation index was computed for the metropolitan area, by the Census Bureau, in contrast to the indexes for just the central city that were discussed in the previous chapters.) Jargowsky (2003) reports that the number of people living in high-poverty areas (40 percent poverty or more) declined only slightly, from 960,000 to 945,000, over the decade. The percentage of families with children with only one parent present increased from 37.9 percent to 40.7 percent, but the number of adults who had dropped out of high school did decline from 32 percent to 28 percent. In summary, there were more New Yorkers in 2000 than in 1990, and they were much safer and somewhat better educated. However, in 2000 they were not more prosperous on average than they had been in 1990, and the index of racial segregation had not improved. A mixed bag, to be sure, but the population increase in the central city combined with the construction of new central city housing and the sharp decline in crime sound like good news. It is reasonable to expect that the wave of immigrants who came to New York during this time will find ways to have economic success as time goes on.

The urban rebirth in New York is exemplified by the revitalization of the South Bronx. This area was discussed in Chapter 10 as one of the worst examples of urban devastation in the nation in the 1960s and 1970s. The population of the area had dropped from 247,000 in 1970 to 91,800 in 1980 as block after block had been abandoned and victimized by arsonists. The South Bronx was and is a predominantly Hispanic area. The crisis in the South Bronx had stimulated the creation of a network of community organizations that are described in detail by von Hoffman (2003). These organizations had some success in housing renovation, albeit on a small scale, by combining federal and private foundation funding with their own entrepreneurial spirit until the federal funds were cut off during the Reagan administration in the early 1980s. The rebirth of the South Bronx started in earnest when Edward Koch, the newly reelected mayor, announced in 1986 a massive $5 billion rebuilding effort called the Ten Year Plan. The issues of housing, redevelopment, and homelessness had become prominent in the mayoral campaign. Of equal importance, the city had recovered from its near-bankruptcy of the 1970s and now had the financial ability to proceed with a large effort. The city's ability to borrow had been restored, and an urban redevelopment program was a good candidate.

The critical part of the rebuilding effort was the city's ownership of more than 40,000 vacant units acquired through tax delinquency proceedings. Most of these units were located in some of the worst neighborhoods, and could be renovated at reasonable cost. The city relied on small housing renovation firms (and their profit motive) and on a private, nonprofit organization called the Community Preservation Program to engage those firms and assist them through the process. It turned out that the small firms carried out their projects in a cost-effective manner—in order to make more money. The Vacant Building Program was the largest of the programs under Mayor Koch's initiative, and completed gut rehabs of 40,000 housing units in seven years. Another component of the Koch program involved the use of the new Low Income Housing Tax Credit program provided by the federal government. Under this program, New York is allocated a certain amount of housing tax credits each year, which are sold to major corporations to provide funds for low-income housing. The administration of the program partly was turned over to the New York office of the Local Initiatives Support Corporation, and another organization called the Enterprise Foundation played a role in selling the housing tax credits and obtaining other sources of funding for the local community organizations that were undertaking the renovation and construction projects. Another program provided homes that could be purchased by households with lower incomes. This program used land provided by the city for free and funding from the federal and local governments so that the houses could be sold for "affordable" prices. As von Hoffman (2003) notes, none of these efforts to revitalize the South Bronx would have been successful if the high crime rate had not been reduced drastically. The reduction in crime is generally credited to two factors: the introduction of aggressive policing by the Rudy Giuliani administration after 1994 and the end of the crack cocaine epidemic at roughly the same time.

The combined effects of these housing programs can be measured. Von Hoffman (2003) recounts that ten years after the programs were initiated by Mayor Koch, over 10,000 units had been created, of which 3,000 were new homes for sale. The number of abandoned buildings had been reduced, and thousands of apartment units had been renovated. The population of the South Bronx area that was mentioned above increased from 91,800 in 1980 to 121,100 in 2000, and those people can today be observed to be living in viable neighborhoods.

How does the experience of New York City relate to the underlying causes of urban rebirth discussed in Chapter 14, and to the notion of switching from a vicious circle to a virtuous circle? The underlying causes of revitalization in New York City clearly are those enumerated in Chapter 14—the increase in immigration to New York, the large decline in crime, more effective city government (with better financing and a flexible attitude), participation by nonprofit organizations, and federal programs (especially the Low Income Housing Tax Credit). The role of the strong economy of the 1990s is less clear in the New York case. As noted above, the New York job market in the 1990s was sluggish, and poverty in the city increased by 1.9 percentage points. Furthermore, except for the dramatic decline in crime, progress on the other elements of the underclass social pathologies was mixed. In short, urban rebirth in New York was a work in progress as of 2000. The vicious circle had ended in the 1980s and a virtuous circle had begun, but it was not clear that a virtuous circle was continuing in the 1990s.

Chicago

In contrast to New York, Chicago presents an unambiguous case of urban rebirth in the 1990s. The basic facts are shown in Tables 15.1, 15.2 and 15.3. Population growth at both the metropolitan and central city levels, primarily among the Hispanic and foreign-born groups, provided the underlying strength, but virtually all of the other signs are positive. Employment growth in the metropolitan area was a solid 7.1 percent, and median family real income advanced by 6.6 percent during the 1990s to reach $61,200—well above average for the seventeen metropolitan areas. The racial segregation index at the metropolitan level declined from 84 to 80. The urban rebirth can be seen most clearly in the central city, which saw its population increase (by 4.0 percent) for the first time since the 1940s. The central city poverty rate declined from 21.6 percent to 19.6 percent from 1989 to 1999, and the number of people living in high-poverty areas fell from 413,000 to 235,000. Median family real income in the city increased by 3.4 percent. The murder rate fell from 31 to 22 per 100,000 population—in line with the decline in the average for the seventeen central cities. The percentage of adults who had not graduated from high school declined from 34 to 28, a larger decline than average for the seventeen central cities. And the percentage of single-parent families increased only marginally, from 40.8 percent to 41.5 percent.

The housing market responded in a restrained manner. Total housing units increased by 11.2 percent from 1990 to 2000, and the vacancy rate declined from 6.1 percent to 4.8 percent. Housing in the central city increased by 17,000 units, an increase of 1.5 percent. The vacancy rate moved down from 9.3 percent to 7.5 percent, leading to some concerns about the supply of "affordable" housing. In any event, the central city housing market was not suffering from the negative effects of filtering that have occurred in previous decades.

Chapter 7 includes an examination of racial change and population trends in the community areas in the city of Chicago from 1950 to 1970. McDonald (2004) provides a detailed analysis of these community areas from 1970 to 2000. Of the 77 community areas in the city of Chicago, 8 had poverty rates of 30 percent of greater in 1970 (one of which had a poverty rate over 40 percent). In 1980, the number of community areas with poverty in excess of 30 percent had increased to 13, and 9 areas had poverty rates in excess of 40 percent (and 2 of these were above 50 percent). The number of community areas with poverty above 30 percent reached 17 in 1990, 11 of these had poverty above 40 percent, and 6 were above 50 percent. An aggregation of the data for the seventeen community areas with poverty of 30 percent or more in 1990 reveals the following. The number of families living in these 17 community areas declined from 199,995 in 1970 to 149,288 in 1980 to 119,664 in 1990—an overall decline of 40.2 percent. However, the number of families in poverty in these community areas increased from 51,054 in 1970 to 53,823 in 1980, and declined to 49,499 in 1990. The percentage of families in poverty in the seventeen community areas increased from 26 percent to 36 percent to 41 percent from 1970 to 1980 to 1990. The 1990s provide a strong reversal of these trends. While the total number of families in the seventeen community areas continued to fall—by 10,675 to 108,989—the number of families in poverty dropped by an even larger amount of 14,271 to 35,228. The percentage of families in poverty in these areas declined from 41 percent to 32 percent.

What accounts for the decline in families in poverty in the seventeen community areas? The 1990s were a time of changes in public policy, including the change from the old welfare system to the Personal Responsibility and Work Opportunity Reconciliation Act of 1996 and Temporary Assistance for Needy Families (TANF). Also, there was a large expansion of the Earned Income Tax Credit in 1993. Together these changes in public policy provide a strong incentive to work. Statistical tests performed by McDonald (2004) show that the variable that is most strongly associated with the decline in the poverty rate among families in the seventeen community areas is the percentage of females who were employed. The results show that an increase in the female employment rate of one percentage point was associated with a decline in the family poverty rate of 0.69 percent. The percentage of families on public assistance declined by an average of 19.5 percent in these seventeen community areas. Another statistical result showed that the change in the male employment rate in these areas was not associated with the decline in the family poverty rate. The McDonald (2004) study is the first to suggest empirically that the change in the welfare system is associated with both a reduction in poverty and the deconcentration of poverty within an urban area. In summary, the Chicago example is one of strong urban rebirth and the virtuous circle at work.

Philadelphia and Detroit

Philadelphia and Detroit represent contrasting cases. Philadelphia was never really a manufacturing town, and Detroit definitely was (and still is, but to a reduced degree). Detroit is virtually synonymous with the urban crisis, but Philadelphia is not. It therefore comes as something of a surprise that Detroit experienced the urban rebirth in the 1990s more fully than did Philadelphia. Here are the details.

Recall from Chapter 10 that the decade of the 1970s was a very bad one for Philadelphia, but that the 1980s brought some hopeful signs. The 1970s brought population decline for the metropolitan area, little employment growth, large declines in the central city population and in employment for city residents, and increasing central city poverty and housing vacancies. The 1980s were a rather different story. Employment in the metropolitan area grew by a solid 15.7 percent as Philadelphia was making the transition to the "new" service economy. Metropolitan population increased, and the loss of population in the central city slowed down. Did the 1990s bring further improvement that could be called a virtuous circle?

As shown in Table 15.1, population growth at the metropolitan level continued in the 1990s, but at the relatively slow pace of 3.6 percent. The central city population declined once again, this time by 4.3 percent (compared to 13.4 percent in the 1970s and 6.0 percent in the 1980s). The Philadelphia urban area was not a major destination for immigrants in the 1990s. The Hispanic population increased from 166,000 in 1990 to 259,000 in 2000 (3.4 percent in 1990 and 5.1 percent in 2000). The foreign-born population did increase from 253,000 to 357,000, which accounts for 58.1 percent of the population growth in the metropolitan area of 179,000. A particularly discouraging outcome is the failure of total employment to grow in the metropolitan area (an increase of only 0.1 percent in ten years). Median family real income did increase by 3.7 percent from 1989 to 1999, but this is well below the 16.3 percent median family income growth for 1970–90 (8.1 percent per decade). In short, the

Philadelphia economy did not do well in the 1990s. On a more positive note, residential segregation was lower in the Philadelphia urban area than in the New York and Chicago metropolitan areas. The index of segregation for the black population declined from 77 in 1990 to 72 in 2000.

The outcomes for the city of Philadelphia reflect the relatively low amount of immigration and the poor performance of the local economy. The central city poverty rate increased from 20.3 percent to 22.9 percent, and the number of people living in high-poverty areas did not decline (242,000 in 1990 and 241,000 in 2000). The percentage of one-parent families increased from 41.3 percent to 51.0 percent, an increase that exceeds the average for the seventeen central cities. On the plus side, the murder rate fell from 32 to 22 per 100,000. Also, the percentage of adults who had not graduated from high school declined from 36 to 29 percent, a relatively large decline. Median family real income in the central city declined from $40,500 to $37,000—a sizable drop of 8.6 percent. A more positive note is the stability of the (relatively high) housing vacancy rate in the central city: 10.5 percent in 1990 and 10.6 percent in 2000. The racial composition of the central city changed, but not by a great deal. The percentage black increased from 39.5 percent in 1990 to 42.6 percent in 2000 (an increase in the central city black population of 19,000). In summary, the failure of the Philadelphia urban area to attract people and jobs translated into a decade that is not an endorsement of the urban rebirth story.

In Chapter 10 it was concluded that the 1970s was a disastrous decade for the Detroit metropolitan area, and that the 1980s were no better. Recall that metropolitan Detroit lost population in both the decades of the 1970s and 1980s, placing it in select company (with Cleveland and Pittsburgh). The population of the central city fell by 32.0 percent in twenty years and was 75.5 percent black in 1990. The central city poverty rate increased from 14.7 percent in 1970 to 32.4 percent in 1990. In short, Detroit was the poster child of the urban crisis. What did the 1990s bring?

Well, the metropolitan population increased by 4.1 percent, employment grew by 6.7 percent, and median family real incomes advanced by 6.7 percent. Given the racial separation between central city and suburbs, it is not surprising that the segregation level was high and did not change very much. The index of racial segregation for the black population was 87 in 1990 and 85 in 2000. Like Philadelphia, Detroit was not a major destination for immigrants. The Hispanic population increased from 78,000 to 128,000 over the decade. The foreign-born population did increase by 101,000 (from 234,000 to 335,000), but was just 7.5 percent of the total population in 2000 (compared to 17.2 percent in the Chicago urban area).

How did the central city fare, given the positive economic trends? The central city population decline continued, but at a reduced rate of 7.5 percent.

The central city poverty rate fell from 32.6 percent to 26.1 percent, and the number of people living in high-poverty areas declined sharply from 421,000 to 108,000, the largest absolute decline among the seventeen northeastern central cities in this study. Median family real income in the city increased from a low $25,200 in 1990 to $29,500 in 2000, which is a robust increase of 17.1 percent. The number of employed residents of the city remained stable (336,000 in 1990 and 332,000 in 2000) as the population declined by 7.5 percent. The murder rate fell from (the truly alarming) 57 to (the almost as alarming) 41 per 100,000. But that is progress. High-school dropouts fell from 38 percent to 30 percent of the adult population. The percentage of single-parent families was 61.0 in 1990—by far the highest among the seventeen central cities. This percentage did increase in the 1990s to 63.1 percent, but the increase is relatively small. The central city increasingly became a black city—the black percentage increased from 75.5 percent to 81.2 percent as the population fell below 1 million (to 951,000) for the first time since 1920. The weakness of the central city housing market continued. The number of housing units in the central city continued to decline, this time from 410,000 units to 374,000 units, and the vacancy rate increased from 8.7 percent to 10.2 percent, so the number of occupied units fell by 10.2 percent. But altogether the Detroit story is one of urban rebirth that involves coming back from the deepest of depths. It is apparent that the underlying force is the strength of the local economy, and it is probable that the decline in crime and the new federal welfare policy and the Earned Income Tax Credit played supporting roles.

Boston and Pittsburgh

The urban crisis dealt Boston only a glancing blow. As shown in Chapter 10, the 1970s was a bad decade, but both the metropolitan area and the central city did relatively well in the 1980s. Boston had become a successful participant in the "new" service economy. Metropolitan population growth was a decent 5.5 percent in the 1990s, but employment grew by only 2.5 percent and median family real incomes advanced by a relatively weak 2.2 percent. The foreign-born population in the metropolitan area increased from 365,000 to 508,000, which accounts for 79.9 percent of the total population growth. Racial segregation is relatively low in the Boston urban area; the index of segregation for the black population was 76 in 1980, 69 in 1990, and 66 in 2000.

The population of the city of Boston increased by 2.6 percent in the 1990s, building on the 2.0 percent increase in the 1980s. The population increase was combined with no change in the number of housing units in the central city, so the vacancy rate declined from 8.6 percent in 1990 to 4.3 percent in 2000. This is a relatively tight central city housing market, and is consistent with rising housing prices. The poverty rate in the central city increased marginally from 18.7 percent in 1989 to 19.5 percent in 1999, and median family real income moved up slightly from $39,200 to $39,600 (a 1.0 percent increase). The number of people living in high-poverty areas was small in 1990 (just 32,000 people), and this number increased slightly (to 33,000). In short, the economy of the central city was moving sideways in the 1990s, in contrast to the solid gains that were made in the 1980s. However, one variable stands out. The murder rate in the city of Boston dropped sharply from 25 to 7 per 100,000. The murder rate of 25 per 100,000 in 1990 was somewhat less than the average for the seventeen central cities of 30 per 100,000, but a murder rate of 7 places Boston in second place among the seventeen in 2000 (behind Cincinnati with 4 per 100,000). Population growth in the central city and reduced crime would appear to go hand in hand. Another positive feature of the city of Boston is its low number of high-school dropouts, which fell from 24 percent to 21 percent of adults. Boston's record on single-parent families is typical for northeastern central cities: 43.7 percent in 1990 and 48.0 percent in 2000.

The case of Boston in the 1990s is thus one of a rather weak economic performance combined with a huge drop in crime and a continuation of the increase in the population of the central city. The tightness of the housing market is notable. The vacancy rate in the metropolitan area was only 2.7 percent in 2000 (down from 5.2 percent in 1990). In some ways Boston and New York produced similar results—weak economic performance combined with a huge drop in crime and some population growth in the central city (although substantially more population growth in New York City than in the city of Boston). This may or may not be called urban rebirth, given the lack of economic strength in this decade.

As we have already seen, Pittsburgh was another poster child for the urban crisis. Pittsburgh made progress in the 1990s, but was it enough to call it urban rebirth? The decline in the metropolitan population was 10.5 percent from 1970 to 1980, and the decline continued in the 1990s at the slow rate of 1.5 percent. Employment in the urban area had actually declined in the 1980s (by 0.8 percent), so the increase in employment in the 1990s of 3.2 percent came as welcome news. Manufacturing employment had dropped from 272,000 in 1980 to 156,000 in 1990, so the further decline in this sector to 141,000 was relatively minor. Manufacturing jobs that were lost thankfully cannot be lost again. This is an example of the economic transition that eventually plays itself out (one hopes). Median family real income dropped by 7.7 percent in the 1980s, but turned around to increase by 7.7 percent in the 1990s.

The city of Pittsburgh did continue to lose population in the 1990s—down another 9.5 percent following the declines of 12.7 percent in the 1980s and

18.5 percent in the 1970s. The positive view of this is that the rate of decline is slowing down, and eventually the decline probably will stop. The social and economic indicators tell a story of progress. The poverty rate in the central city declined from 21.4 percent to 20.4 percent, and the number of people who lived in high-poverty areas fell from 75,000 to 48,000 (a solid decline of 36.0 percent). Median family real income in the central city increased by a respectable 5.1 percent. The murder rate in Pittsburgh was low in 1990 and remained low in 2000 (10 and 11 per 100,000, respectively). High-school dropouts declined from 28 percent to 19 percent. On the negative side, single-parent families in the central city increased from 40.1 percent to 47.9 percent over the decade. The housing market in the central city continued to be soft: the vacancy rate increased from 9.6 percent in 1990 to 11.5 percent in 2000. This result is not surprising, given the 9.5 percent decline in the population.

Like Detroit, Pittsburgh appears to be a case of an urban area that had hit bottom sometime around 1990 (but with a very low crime rate for a major central city) and then started to come back in the 1990s. The negatives are the continued population decline (with the resulting softness in the housing market) and the increase in single-parent families in the central city. But overall the Pittsburgh case certainly resembles urban rebirth to this author.

St. Louis, Cleveland, and Buffalo

The next three urban areas include one (St. Louis) that did not do well in the 1970s and the 1980s, and two (Cleveland and Buffalo) for which these decades were disastrous. The St. Louis experience in the urban crisis was summarized in Chapter 10 and consisted of an absence of population growth at the metropolitan level, rapid decline of the central city population, decent employment growth, but slow growth in median family real income in the metropolitan area (and decline in the central city) and an increase in central city poverty. Metropolitan St. Louis came back in the 1990s. Metropolitan population grew by 4.5 percent, total employment rose by 6.1 percent, and median family real incomes advanced by 5.9 percent. The foreign-born population increased from 49,000 to 81,000, accounting for 28.8 percent of the population growth in the urban area. What about the central city?

The population of the city of St. Louis continued its decline in the 1990s. The decrease of 12.3 percent was the largest among the seventeen central cities included in this study. This decline matches the decline of 12.4 percent in the 1980s, so no progress was made on this front. The vacancy rate in the central city housing market increased from 15.3 percent to 16.4 percent as a result. These are very high vacancy rates that spell trouble. The number of employed residents of the central city declined by 11.1 percent, a figure that roughly matches the population decline. The central city poverty rate remained constant at 24.6 percent, but the number of people living in high-poverty areas declined from 110,000 to 71,000. Median family real income in the central city remained constant at $32,600. The murder rate fell from a high 45 to 36 per 100,000. The city of St. Louis is still a high-crime place, but progress was made. The black population continued to move to the suburbs. The central city black population fell from 188,000 to 177,000, and the suburban black population increased from 234,000 to 298,000. Nevertheless, the central city became a majority black city in 2000 with a black population of 50.8 percent (up from 47.4 percent in 1990). The high-school dropouts in the central city fell from 37 percent to 29 percent, but single-parent families increased from 50.9 percent to 57.4 percent.

The picture that emerges is one of suburban areas that were doing nicely while the central city continued to experience much of the urban crisis. The concentration of poverty in the central city did decline and crime also fell, but the continued large decline of population in the central city and its stubbornly high poverty rate are signs that the city of St. Louis had not yet turned the corner. Employment growth in the urban area prevented the situation from getting worse. St. Louis thus presents an ambiguous picture.

Next we come to Cleveland, an urban area at the center of the Buffalo-Detroit-Pittsburgh geographic triangle that is a primary locus of the urban crisis. The Cleveland metropolitan area experienced population loss, little job growth, and a decline in median family real income. Then there is the central city and the pathologies described in Chapters 10 and 13. Thankfully, the 1990s were much kinder to Cleveland. Metropolitan population growth was only 2.2 percent, but that is in sharp contrast to the 9.0 percent decline from 1970 to 1990. Cleveland was not a major destination for immigrants—the foreign-born population increased from just 100,000 in 1990 to 115,000 in 2000. Employment recorded a tidy increase of 5.5 percent instead of the 4.3 percent recorded over the previous two decades, and median family real income advanced by 6.1 percent from 1989 to 1999. The segregation of the black population in the metropolitan area declined from an index of 82 in 1990 to 77 in 2000. This much better performance at the metropolitan level was translated into some improvement in the central city as well. Central city population continued to decline, this time by 5.5 percent, but the rate of population loss clearly had slowed down. The central city housing market remained weak. The vacancy rate increased from 10.9 percent in 1990 to 11.4 percent in 2000, and the number of units declined from 224,000 to 215,000, so the number of occupied units fell by 4.7 percent. On the positive side, the poverty rate in the central city fell from a high 28.7 percent in 1990 to 26.3 percent in 2000, and the number of people living in high-poverty areas declined from 102,000 to 76,000. Median family real income was essentially unchanged (up 0.3 percent). The number of central city residents who were employed held steady (183,000 in 1990 and 181,000 in 2000) as the population declined by 5.5 percent. Even better was the decline in murders—from 33 to 14 per 100,000. The decline in the percentage of adults who had dropped out of high school was particularly large—from 41 to 31 percent. As elsewhere, the percentage of single-parent families increased in the central city, from 50.1 percent to 59.4 percent. The municipal authorities were promoting downtown development aggressively, with some success. The disastrous decline of the Cleveland urban area seems to have played out, and the several positive signs add up to a hope that a virtuous circle had begun.

Buffalo is the fourth member of the Buffalo-Cleveland-Pittsburgh-Detroit club. The Buffalo metropolitan area joined Pittsburgh as the only two urban major urban areas to lose population in all three decades—the 1970s, 1980s, and 1990s. However, the rate of population decline slowed from 11.9 percent from 1970 to 1990 to 1.6 percent in the 1990s. Employment also declined, by 2.0 percent, reversing the increase during the 1980s of 5.2 percent. Median family real income inched up by 2.2 percent in the 1990s. The central city produced a poor record. Population declined by 11.0 percent, and the central city poverty rate increased from an already relatively high 25.6 percent to 26.6 percent. Poverty did become less concentrated as the number of people living in high-poverty areas declined from 72,000 to 51,000. The vacancy rate in the central city housing market increased from 10.2 percent to 15.6 percent. The number of residents of the central city who were employed fell by 13.0 percent from 131,000 to 114,000. The median family real income in the central city declined slightly from an already low $24,800 to $24,500. The murder rate was a relatively low 11 per 100,000 in 1990 and increased slightly to 13 in 2000. However, it remained comparatively low (for a central city). High-school dropouts declined and single-parent families increased, as they did in the other central cities. The weakness of the Buffalo economy meant that, by most measures, the urban crisis in Buffalo continued.

The Other Northeastern Metropolitan Areas

The remaining eight urban areas fall into two groups—those that clearly had a virtuous circle at work in the 1990s, and those that were experiencing a more tenuous urban rebirth. This first group includes Minneapolis–St. Paul, Cincinnati, Milwaukee, Kansas City, Indianapolis, and Columbus, while the latter group consists of Washington, D.C., and Baltimore.

As Table 15.1 shows, with the exception of Milwaukee, the metropolitan areas in the first group had population and employment growth well in excess of 10 percent in the 1990s. Metropolitan Milwaukee added 4.8 percent to population and 5.7 percent to employment over the decade. All six urban areas saw median family real income advance by at least 8.4 percent (Milwaukee) from 1989 to 1999 (Table 15.2). As shown in Tables 15.3 and 15.4, all six central cities did well. Four of the six central cities gained population, while Cincinnati declined by 9.1 percent and the city of Milwaukee lost 4.7 percent of its population. However, the poverty rate declined in all six, and all six recorded sizable declines in the number of people who lived in high-poverty areas. Median family real incomes increased in four of the central cities, held steady in Milwaukee (at $38,000), and declined by $800 (1.8 percent) in Columbus (from $43,200 to $42,400). Central city murder rates were relatively low in all six in 1990, and declined in five of the six (and remained constant in Indianapolis). Indeed, the murder rate in the central city of Cincinnati fell to 4 per 100,000—a rate that is below the murder rate for the nation in 2000. High-school dropouts declined in all six. The negative outcome is the increase in single-parent families in all six central cities. This group of six clearly is experiencing urban rebirth. The only negative signs are the population declines in the cities of Cincinnati and Milwaukee and the continued increase in single-parent families.

Washington, D.C., and Baltimore present a mixture of outcomes. Population growth at the metropolitan level was quite strong in Washington, D.C. (16.6 percent), and positive in Baltimore (7.2 percent). However, employment growth fell below population growth in Washington, D.C., and Baltimore (8.2 percent and just 2.7 percent, respectively). This combination resulted in below-average increases in median family real incomes (2.0 in Washington, D.C., and 4.6 percent in Baltimore). The problems show up in the central city. Both central cities lost population and experienced increases in the poverty rate (Table 15.3). And, while the number of residents of high-poverty areas declined in Baltimore, the number increased in Washington, D.C. Median family real incomes declined noticeably in both central cities—by 4.9 percent in Washington, D.C., and 6.6 percent in Baltimore. The murder rate in Washington, D.C., fell from the war-zone level of 78 to 42 per 100,000, but the murder rate in Baltimore moved only slightly from 41 to 40 per 100,000. Housing vacancies in Baltimore increased from 8.9 percent in 1990 to 13.7 percent in 2000, although vacancies in Washington, D.C., moved downward from 9.7 percent to 9.2 percent. In short, the population growth in these metropolitan areas did not produce positive outcomes in the central cities. The continuing high murder rates in both central cities were particularly depressing. These two central cities provide little evidence of urban rebirth in the 1990s.

Table 15.5

Central Cities of the Northeast: Correlations for 2000

	Murder rate	High-school dropouts	One-parent families	Percent living in high-poverty areas	Central city poverty rate
Murder rate	1	.31	.85*	.81*	.79*
High-school dropouts		1	.23	.53*	.45*
One-parent families			1	.71*	.59*
Percent in high-poverty areas				1	.61*

*Statistically significant at the 95 percent level for a one-tail test.

Statistical Analysis of Urban Crisis Variables

Correlations among the urban crisis variables were examined in Chapter 13 for 1970, 1980, and 1990. These results show that the central city poverty rate, the high concentration of poverty, the murder rate, one-parent families, and high-school dropouts are all highly correlated. The correlations among these variables are shown in Table 15.5 for 2000, and all ten correlations are positive and eight are statistically significant. These variables remained highly intercorrelated.

Further tests were done to determine whether the urban crisis variables in 2000 are related to population growth at the metropolitan and central city levels and employment growth at the metropolitan level. Indeed they are. All five of the urban crisis variables are negatively correlated with the central city population growth rate for 1990 to 2000. And four of the five are negatively related to both the population and employment growth rates for the metropolitan area. Only the murder rate was not related to the metropolitan population and employment growth rates—because of the high population and employment growth and high murder rate in Washington, D.C.

Finally, correlations were computed between the changes in the five urban crisis variables: change in the poverty rate, change in the percentage living in high-poverty areas, change in the murder rate, change in the percentage of single-parent families, and change in the high-school dropout rate. Only two of the ten correlations are statistically significant. There is a strong positive correlation between the change in the central city poverty rate and the change in the percentage of people living in high-poverty areas. They are not necessarily measuring the same phenomenon, but their changes are highly correlated during the decade of the 1990s (however, they were not correlated for 1970–80 and 1980–90). Also, there is a positive correlation of the change in the murder rate and the change in single-parent families. However, these results are similar to those obtained in Chapter 13 for 1970 to 1980 and 1980 to 1990 in that few of the changes in the urban crisis variables are correlated.

Urban Rebirth in Central Cities: A Quick Summary

The above review of the seventeen major urban areas of the Northeast can be summarized. As in Chapter 13, I propose a rough-and-ready method for assessing the changes that took place in the 1990s in the seventeen central cities, which is shown in Table 15.6. The central cities are given a plus, a minus, or a zero on seven variables—central city population change (plus for growth, minus for decline), median family real income change, change in the poverty rate, change in the murder rate, change in the population in high-poverty areas, change in one-parent families (all minus), and change in high-school dropouts (all plus). In a few cases there was no change, hence a zero was given. In the case of the murder rate, cities with a low murder rate and no change are noted, and one with a very high murder rate that declined but remained high (Washington, D.C.) is also noted. Detroit is awarded two pluses for the increase in median family real income of 17.1 percent. Lastly, three cities had increases in single-parent families that were comparatively small. The change in the number of occupied housing units is not included as a separate variable because, as noted above, the change in the population is measuring the same phenomenon. An increase in population means an increase in occupied housing units.

The net scores for each central city were then computed. For example, New York City has three pluses, three minuses, and one zero for a net score of zero. Chicago has six pluses and one small minus for a net score of six minus, and so on. The last column in Table 15.6 awards a "yes" for rebirth if the net score is two or more. The urban areas that can be regarded as experiencing the virtuous circle of urban rebirth during the 1990s are ten: Chicago, Detroit, Pittsburgh, Cleveland, Minneapolis–St. Paul, Cincinnati, Milwaukee, Kansas City, Indianapolis, and Columbus. Population increased in five of the ten central cities (Chicago, Minneapolis–St. Paul, Kansas City, Indianapolis, and Columbus), but declined in the other five. Detroit, Cleveland, and Pittsburgh were coming back from very low depths, but they are coming back. Four urban areas showed some positive signs, but had net scores of zero or one and were not clearly in a virtuous circle. Those in this category are New York, Boston, St. Louis, and Baltimore. And finally, by virtue of their negative net scores, the urban crisis continued in three central cities—Philadelphia, Washington,

Table 15.6

Urban Rebirth Rankings: Northeastern Central Cities

	Population	Median family income	Poverty	Murder	Poverty concentration	One parent	High school dropouts	Net score	Rebirth?
New York	+	–	–	+	0	–	+	0	?
Chicago	+	+	+	+	+	–(low)	+	6–	Yes
Philadelphia	–	–	–	+	0	–	+	–2	No
Detroit	–	++	+	+	+	–(low)	+	5–	Yes
Boston	+	0	–	+	0	–	+	1	?
Pittsburgh	–	+	0	0 (low)	+	–	+	2+	Yes
St. Louis	–	0	0	+	+	–	+	1	?
Cleveland	–	0	+	+	+	–	+	2	Yes
Washington, D.C.	–	–	–	+ (high)	–	–	+	–3	No
Baltimore	–	–	+	0	+	–	+	0	?
Minneapolis–St. Paul	+	+	+	+ (low)	+	–(low)	+	6–	Yes
Buffalo	–	–	–	0 (low)	+	–	+	–2	No
Cincinnati	–	0	+	+	+	–	+	3	Yes
Milwaukee	–	+	+	+	+	–	+	2	Yes
Kansas City	+	+	+	+	+	–	+	5	Yes
Indianapolis	+	+	+	0 (low)	+	–	+	5+	Yes

D.C., and Buffalo. But ten out of seventeen is 59 percent—a pretty strong trend—and two were just one point away from my cutoff point.

Is there anything that distinguished the ten cases of urban rebirth from the other seven for which the data are mixed? The answer is pretty clear—metropolitan growth. We already know that central city population growth depends upon metropolitan population growth. The ten metropolitan areas with central cities in the urban rebirth category in the 1990s had an average population growth of 8.9 percent over the decade, and the other seven metropolitan areas had population growth of 6.4 percent. However, the more telling statistic is employment growth at the metropolitan level. The ten metropolitan areas with central cities that experienced urban rebirth had an average employment gain of 10.5 percent from 1990 to 2000, compared to just 2.6 percent employment growth for the other seven metropolitan areas. Not all of these ten had large employment gains (Pittsburgh with 3.2 percent and Cleveland with 5.5 percent), and two of the other seven had their own sizable employment increases (Washington, D.C., with 8.2 percent and St. Louis with 6.1 percent), but otherwise the distinction is clear. As noted above, New York City experienced rebirth in the 1980s but was held back in the 1990s by a lack of employment growth. This basic finding regarding employment growth and urban rebirth as defined here is confirmation of the earlier findings by Bartik (1991, 1994) of the favorable effects of employment growth in an urban area. Indeed, Bartik concentrated on the economic effects of employment growth, but the results in this chapter suggest favorable social effects as well.

Conclusion

This chapter has presented evidence that ten of the seventeen northeastern urban areas experienced an urban rebirth in the 1990s. Urban rebirth is defined as general improvement in the central city in several of the variables that measure the urban crisis—central city population growth, median family real income, poverty, crime, concentration of poverty, single-parent families, and high-school dropouts. Urban rebirth sometimes was accompanied by strong population growth in the metropolitan area and some population growth in the central city. However, population growth and urban rebirth are not the same thing. New York City had remarkably high population growth in the 1990s of 9.4 percent, and the murder rate dropped sharply, but the other urban crisis variables did not improve very much. New York thus falls into "maybe" category in the 1990s after clear signs of rebirth in the 1980s. Washington, D.C., had high population growth in the metropolitan area, but its central city languished. On the other hand, population in the cities of Detroit, Cleveland, Cincinnati, and Milwaukee declined in the 1990s, but most of the urban crisis variables improved. Rather, it is employment growth that better distinguishes the metropolitan areas with central cities in the urban rebirth category. The ten metropolitan areas in this category had an average employment growth in the 1990s of 10.5 percent compared to just 2.6 percent for the other seven metropolitan areas. Chapter 17 updates the story to early 2006 to determine whether the positive momentum has been maintained in spite of the recession of 2001, and whether any of the six urban areas joined the urban rebirth.

Note

1. A recent research project by Jargowsky and Yang (2006) used the 1990 and 2000 census data to define underclass census tracts. The definition is that a tract was one standard deviation above the national mean simultaneously on four variables: proportion of teenagers who had dropped out of high school, proportion of women heading a family, proportion of households on public assistance, and proportion of prime-age men not in the labor force. Based on this definition, the number of people living in underclass census tracts declined from 3.39 million to 2.16 million from 1990 to 2000, a decline of 36.4 percent. The decline was greatest among black Americans—from 2.12 million to 1.27 million, a drop of 40.1 percent. Whites in underclass census tracts fell from 604,000 to 359,000, and the number of Hispanics in underclass tracts dropped from 580,000 to 422,000. The number of underclass census tracts in some of the major urban areas of the Northeast is shown in Table 15.7. Large declines took place in New York, Chicago, Philadelphia, and Detroit. Washington, D.C., and Baltimore recorded smaller declines in the number of underclass tracts, while the existence of such tracts almost disappeared in Minneapolis and Boston. St. Louis experienced a small increase in the number of underclass tracts, from 20 to 23.

Table 15.7

Underclass Census Tracts: 1990–2000

	1990	2000
New York	125	60
Chicago	87	57
Philadelphia	51	28
Detroit	99	38
Boston	9	4
St. Louis	20	23
Washington, D.C.	12	7
Baltimore	37	29
Minneapolis–St. Paul	10	3

Source: Jargowsky and Yang (2006).

16

Urban Growth and Rebirth in the Sunbelt

When we last visited the Sunbelt metropolitan areas in Chapters 11 and 13, it was concluded that three had not really experienced the urban crisis in the manner that would be recognized in the Northeast. These three are San Francisco, Seattle, and San Diego. The three western urban areas that qualified as a locus of urban crisis were Los Angeles, Denver, and Phoenix, but only during one decade in each case. In contrast, the six urban areas of the South certainly had their own versions of urban crisis in the 1970s and 1980s. Did the nine that experienced the urban crisis come back in the 1990s? And did the three fortunate ones avoid an urban crisis in the 1990s? These are the questions for this chapter. The basic data are displayed in Tables 16.1, 16.2, 16.3, and 16.4.

This chapter shows that four of the six southern urban areas pulled out of the urban crisis and qualify as examples of urban rebirth. These four are Houston, New Orleans, Atlanta, and Miami. Dallas–Fort Worth and Birmingham did not perform as well as the other four, and had a combination of positive and negative outcomes in their central cities. In the West, San Francisco and Seattle continued to do extremely well, and Denver turned a mild form of urban crisis in the 1980s into urban rebirth in the 1990s. San Diego and Phoenix experienced mixed results in the 1990s, but their outcomes cannot be considered to be examples of urban crisis by the standards set in earlier decades. The (very) big problem was Los Angeles. The urban crisis that began in the 1970s continued there, fueled by job losses in the early 1990s, increasing central city poverty and concentrated poverty, and a discouraging drop in median family real income in the central city.

Southern Urban Areas in the 1990s

As Table 16.1 shows, the population of the six urban areas of the South increased by an average of 21.5 percent in the 1990s, which matches the average growth from 1970 to 1990 of 22.3 percent per decade. Population in the New Orleans and Birmingham urban areas grew by just 4.1 and 9.6 percent in the 1990s, but the other four each grew by more than 20 percent. Employment growth was robust in these urban areas as well. The average growth for the six urban areas was 17.6 percent. Median family real incomes advanced in five of the six urban areas (with Miami the exception). The average increase was 6.2 percent. The economic growth and prosperity of the 1990s is in evidence in the South. Central city population increased in four of the six cities (with New Orleans and Birmingham the exceptions). The average increase in the central city populations was 5.6 percent. The land area of Houston increased by 7.3 percent during the 1990s, but otherwise there were no significant territorial additions to these central cities.

Population growth was fueled by migration. In the Dallas–Fort Worth metropolitan area the Hispanic population grew from 511,000 in 1990 to 1,109,000 in 2000, and the foreign-born population increased from 319,000 to 784,000. The increase in the Hispanic population accounts for 50.5 percent of the total population growth of 1,185,000. The trend in metropolitan Houston was similar: the Hispanic population increased from 697,000 to 1,249,000 and accounted for 64.5 percent of the urban area's population growth. Miami continued to see an influx of migrants. The Hispanic population of the urban area increased from 1,056,000 to 1,564,000, and the foreign-born population grew from 1,073,000 to 1,558,000—to account for 71.0 percent of the total population growth of 683,000 during the 1990s. Growth of the Hispanic and foreign-born populations was a smaller factor for metropolitan Atlanta. The Hispanic population was just 55,000 in 1990, and it increased to 269,000 in 2000. The foreign-born population grew from 117,000 to 423,000 during the decade, accounting for 26.7 percent of the urban area's population growth. The growth of the black population was the larger component of population growth in metropolitan Atlanta. This group increased from 743,000 to 1,179,000 (up 58.7 percent) over the decade, and accounted for 37.8 percent of the total population growth. The Atlanta urban area was a destination for black migrants from both the North and the South.

New Orleans and Birmingham did not have large Hispanic or foreign-born populations in 1990, and these groups did not increase very much in the 1990s. The Hispanic population of the New Orleans urban area increased from 53,000 to 59,000, and the foreign-born group grew from 53,000 to 64,000 over the

Table 16.1

Population Growth in Sunbelt Urban Areas: 1950–2000 (in percent)

	Urban area population growth 1950–1970	Urban area population growth 1970–1990	Urban area population growth 1990–2000	Central city population growth 1950–1970	Central city population growth 1970–90	Central city population growth 1990–2000*
Dallas–Fort Worth	149	66.0	29.4	73	17.6	18.5
Houston	136	74.6	25.8	107	32.3	19.8
New Orleans	46	12.3	4.1	4	−16.2	−2.4
Atlanta	131	32.6	38.9	50	−20.7	5.8
Birmingham	32	13.8	9.6	−8	−11.6	−8.6
Miami	226	69.1	21.4	35	7.2	0.8
Los Angeles	102	45.7	12.7	43	19.2	6.0
San Francisco–Oakland	60	18.6	11.9	−7	1.9	−1.7
Seattle	97	40.3	18.8	14	−2.8	9.1
Denver	110	48.5	30.0	24	−9.2	18.6
San Diego	144	83.9	12.7	108	57.8	10.1
Phoenix	192	116.2	45.3	444	68.9	34.4

*Land area increases for 1990–2000: Dallas–Fort Worth, 2 percent; Houston, 7 percent; Birmingham, 1 percent; Phoenix, 13 percent; others, zero.

Sources: Census of Population and HUD State of the Cities Data.

Table 16.2

Sunbelt Metropolitan Areas: 1990–2000

	Population growth (percent)	Employment growth (percent)	Median family income growth	Median family income ($ 1999)	Segregation index	
					1990	2000
Dallas– Fort Worth	29.4	23.8	6.6	55,000	62	59
Houston	25.8	17.8	3.2	49,600	66	66
New Orleans	4.1	7.8	8.7	42,600	68	68
Atlanta	38.9	33.6	7.6	59,300	67	64
Birmingham	9.6	11.0	11.9	48,100	n.a.	n.a.
Miami	21.4	11.7	−0.6	44,600	69	69
Los Angeles	12.7	−0.6	−8.5	50,700	73	66
San Francisco– Oakland	11.9	7.0	6.3	68,900	64	60
Seattle	18.8	17.0	10.2	63,800	56	49
Denver	30.0	30.1	13.3	61,300	64	60
San Diego	12.7	5.8	−0.2	53,400	58	54
Phoenix	45.3	41.7	7.4	51,100	50	43
Means	21.7	17.2	5.5	50,500	63	60

Sources: HUD State of the Cities Data, and U.S. Bureau of the Census.

decade. The Hispanic population of metropolitan Birmingham was just 4,000 in 1990 and 17,000 in 2000, and the foreign-born population grew from 9,000 to 21,000 at the same time.

The level of segregation of the black population of the South continued in the 1990s. Table 16.2 shows that the segregation indexes for five metropolitan areas averaged 66.6 in 1990 (Birmingham not reported). This average was 65.5 in 2000. However, the highest segregation index of the five (69.4 in Miami) was lower than in ten of the seventeen metropolitan areas of the Northeast in 2000.

The measures of urban crisis in Table 16.3 show improvement. The poverty rate in the central city declined in all six central cities (but just by 0.1 percent in Birmingham). The average poverty rate for the six central cities was 25.9 percent in 1990 and declined to an average of 23.6 percent in 2000. The population living in high-poverty areas fell in five of the six cities (Atlanta being the exception). The murder rate fell substantially in all six central cities—from an average of a very bad 47 to 26 per 100,000 population, an average decline of 44.7 percent. The murder rates fell by more than 50 percent in Dallas–Fort Worth, Houston (by 65.7 percent), and Miami. These cities deserve credit for this major drop in crime. The percentage of adults who had dropped out of high school declined in four of the six central cities. High-school dropouts

Table 16.3

Measures of Urban Crisis in Central Cities of the Sunbelt: 1990–2000

	Population change (percent)	Poverty rate		Murder rate (per 100k)		Population in high-poverty areas		One-parent families (percent)		High-school dropouts (percent)	
		1990	2000	1990	2000	1990	2000	1990	2000	1990	2000
Dallas–Fort Worth	18.5	19.8	17.2	44	21	124	68	30.2	34.5	26	30
Houston	19.8	19.8	20.7	35	12	162	85	31.1	33.0	30	30
New Orleans	-2.4	31.6	27.9	61	43	166	108	50.0	54.7	32	25
Atlanta	5.8	27.3	24.4	59	32	92	92	57.4	59.0	30	23
Birmingham	-8.6	24.8	24.7	47	31	55	34	42.1	54.7	31	24
Miami	0.8	31.2	28.5	36	17	148	122	44.0	44.0	52	47
Los Angeles	6.0	18.9	22.1	28	15	268	560	29.9	32.4	33	33
San Francisco–Oakland	-1.7	16.1	14.1	14	8	42	39	32.8	31.8	22	19
Seattle	9.1	12.4	11.8	10	7	25	15	29.4	30.1	14	10
Denver	18.6	17.1	14.3	14	6	24	5	34.6	35.4	21	21
San Diego	10.1	13.4	14.6	12	4	39	72	26.3	27.9	18	17
Phoenix	34.4	14.2	15.8	13	12	93	92	26.4	32.0	21	23
Means	9.2	20.6	19.6	31	17	103*	108*	36.2	39.1	28	25

* Without Los Angeles the means are 88,000 for 1990 and 66,000 for 2000.
Sources: HUD State of the Cities Data, FBI, and Jargowsky (2003).

Table 16.4

Central Cities of the Sunbelt: 1990–2000

			(in percent)		
	Change in area	Change in occupied housing units	Change in median family real income	Black population 1990	Black population 2000
Dallas–Fort Worth	2.0	13.3	−2.4	26.9	23.9
Houston	7.3	16.6	−0.5	27.7	25.0
New Orleans	0	0	8.4	61.6	66.6
Atlanta	0	8.4	10.1	66.8	60.9
Birmingham	1.0	−5.7	−0.6	63.2	73.3
Miami	0	3.2	−0.3	24.8	19.9
Los Angeles	0	4.3	−13.6	13.2	10.9
San Francisco–Oakland	0	3.8	13.1	21.8	16.9
Seattle	0	9.7	16.0	9.9	8.3
Denver	0	13.3	12.1	12.4	10.8
San Diego	0	11.1	0.6	9.0	7.6
Phoenix	13.1	25.7	1.3	5.1	4.8
Mean	1.9	8.6	3.7	28.5	27.4

Sources: Statistical Abstract of the U.S. and HUD State of the Cities Data.

increased in Dallas–Fort Worth and did not change in Houston. As in the Northeast, the percentage of single-parent families increased in five of the six central cities (and remained constant in Miami). While these trends are positive, the record on median family real incomes in the central cities is mixed. Four of the central cities (Dallas–Fort Worth, Houston, Birmingham, and Miami) had small declines in median family incomes, but New Orleans and Atlanta experienced strong increases of 8.4 percent and 10.1 percent. Also, Table 16.4 shows that the change in occupied housing units in the central city was strongly positive for the four central cities with population growth, and zero (New Orleans) or negative (Birmingham) for the two central cities that lost population.

In short, it is not surprising that the urban areas of the South did well in the booming 1990s. Recall the method used in Chapters 13 and 15 to score the extent to which a central city experienced urban rebirth in the 1990s: the net sum of the positive and negative changes on seven crucial variables—central city population change, change in poverty, change in population in high-poverty areas, change in the murder rate, change in single-parent families, change in high-school dropouts, and change in median family real income. The scores for the six central cities of the South are:

Dallas–Fort Worth	+1
Houston	+3
New Orleans	+3
Atlanta	+4
Birmingham	+1
Miami	+4

By the standard used in Chapter 15 that a score of plus two or more means urban rebirth was under way, four of the six qualify. Indeed, Houston, New Orleans, Atlanta, and Miami scored three or four on this rough-and-ready index. Dallas–Fort Worth and Birmingham had net scores of only one. Dallas–Fort Worth had positive results for central city population growth, central city poverty, population in high-poverty areas, and murders, but the results for single-parent families, high-school dropouts, and median family incomes were negative. This mixed picture means that the medal for urban rebirth cannot be awarded. Birmingham had negative results for only central city population change and single-parent families, but scored positive results for just three variables—population in high-poverty areas, murders, and high-school dropouts. The fact that the central city poverty rate and central city median family income remained unchanged prevents Birmingham from being a clear case of urban rebirth. A positive result for either of these last two variables would have changed the conclusion.

This brief examination of the southern urban areas shows that four of the six did well in the 1990s—well enough to be classified as places of urban rebirth. And recall that all six clearly were cases of urban crisis in the 1970s and 1980s. Furthermore, the other two (Dallas–Fort Worth and Birmingham) came close to the urban rebirth standard that is being used.

Los Angeles

Metropolitan Los Angeles experienced some difficult times in the 1990s. The population of the metropolitan area increased by 12.7 percent during the decade, a very low number for Los Angeles. Employment declined from 1990 to 1994, and then rebounded from 1995 to 2000, but the net change over the decade was a decline of 0.6 percent comparing 2000 to 1990. The recession of the early 1990s and the end of the Cold War, with its resultant decline in defense expenditures, were among the causes of the dip in employment. The result of population growth coupled with no increase in employment produced a decline in median family real income in the metropolitan area of 8.5 percent. Recall from Chapter 14 that population growth was accounted for entirely by the growth of the Hispanic population from 4.71 million to 6.60 million.

The implications for the central city of these metropolitan area trends are not good. Central city population continued to increase—by 6.0 percent. But central city poverty increased from 18.9 percent in 1990 to 22.1 percent in 2000, and the number of people living in high-poverty areas almost doubled from 268,000 to 560,000. The murder rate fell from 28 to 15 per 100,000, a result that is reason to cheer. As elsewhere, the percentage of single-parent families increased (from 29.9 percent to 32.4 percent), but the percentage of high-school dropouts did not decline, instead remaining at 33 percent. Lastly, and damagingly, median family real income in the central city fell by 13.6 percent. Two negatives are awarded for this discouraging outcome for families in Los Angeles. All of this adds up to a net score of minus three. The poor economic performance of the early 1990s could not be overcome, and so Los Angeles struggled through a continuation of the urban crisis.

On March 3, 1991, Los Angeles police officers stopped a car driven by one Rodney King on a charge of speeding. The officers claimed that King acted in an aggressive manner and may have been under the influence of drugs. They administered a brutal beating of kicks, blows, and shocks from a stun gun. The beating was recorded on videotape by a bystander. Four officers were charged and tried in a middle-class suburb. The officers claimed they were acting in self-defense. On April 29, 1992, an all-white jury acquitted the officers—in spite of the videotape that had been shown on television to the entire nation. The timing of this verdict could not have been worse. Within three hours a crowd of protesters had gathered in south central Los Angeles, and rioting exploded over an area of fifty square miles for the next two days.

The rioting ended on May 1, but by then fifty people had been killed, almost 400 had been injured, and approximately 17,000 had been arrested. Property damage was estimated at $1 billion. Looting was extensive, and many black-owned businesses were targeted (as were many businesses owned by Asian-American shopkeepers). The Los Angeles riot of 1992 came as a shock to many Americans, who had thought that the days of urban riots had passed twenty years before. Some observers interpreted the riot as much more than a reaction to police brutality. The riot apparently was fueled by lack of economic opportunity in the early 1990s and by ethnic antagonism. However, while smaller disturbances did occur in San Francisco, Seattle, Atlanta, and Pittsburgh, the Los Angeles riot did not set off rioting on a national scale. In the 1990s, rioting on a national scale, such as occurred in the aftermath of the murder of Martin Luther King, Jr., in 1968, could have set urban America on a very different course. It was fortunate that, as bad as it was, the Los Angeles riot of 1992 did not initiate another self-destructive period for central cities in general. In the aftermath of the rioting, the Los Angeles police department underwent some significant changes in top leadership and in standing policies and procedures.

Other Western Metropolitan Areas

The other five urban areas of the West present a story that differs from the Los Angeles saga. Just as the urban crisis landed only a glancing blow on the metropolitan areas of San Francisco–Oakland, Seattle, Denver, San Diego, and Phoenix, the decade of the 1990s was generally a decade of growth for these urban areas. However, San Diego and Phoenix did not perform as well as the other three. San Diego had an influx of migrants and relatively low job growth, and Phoenix had very rapid growth of population and employment that evidently produced some problems in the central city. However, the social and economic conditions in the central cities of San Diego and Phoenix remained relatively good, so one cannot conclude that the urban crisis as we have known it landed in these two cities in the 1990s.

Table 16.1 shows that the average population growth for these five metropolitan areas was 23.7 percent, and the data in Table 16.2 indicate that average employment growth was 20.3 percent over the decade. Among the five, growth was the most rapid in Phoenix and Denver and least in the California urban areas of San Francisco–Oakland and San Diego. Median family real income advanced nicely in five of the six urban areas but was static in San Diego. The average increase in median family income for the six urban areas was 7.4 percent. In San Diego employment growth of just 5.8 percent fell short of the population growth of 12.7 percent, and median family income inched downward by 0.2 percent. Table 16.2 shows one particularly hopeful aspect of these five western urban areas. While the black population of each metropolitan is relatively small, the indexes of segregation of this group are also relatively low. The average segregation index for the five urban areas was 58 in 1990, and declined to 53 in 2000.

Migration of Hispanic and foreign-born people was a major factor in population growth in each of the five urban areas, but the impact varied. The Hispanic population of metropolitan San Francisco–Oakland increased from 495,000 in 1990 to 734,000 in 2000, and the foreign-born group grew from 778,000 to 1,128,000 over the decade. The increase in the foreign-born population accounts for 80.1 percent of the population growth of 457,000. The Hispanic population of the San Diego urban area increased from 499,000 to 751,000 and accounted for 79.7 percent of the total population growth. Given the relatively slow employment growth, it is apparent that the San Diego area had some difficulty absorbing this growing population. The migration of Hispanic and foreign-born groups had a smaller impact on the Seattle urban area. There the Hispanic population increased from 53,000 to 127,000, and the foreign-born population grew from 170,000 to 332,000 to account for 42.4 percent of the total population growth of 382,000. Total population growth in metropolitan Denver was 492,000, and 38.6 percent of that growth was the increase in the Hispanic population from 209,000 to 399,000. The foreign-born population grew from 82,000 to 234,000. Lastly, population growth in the Phoenix urban area was 1,014,000—over 1 million people on a base of 2.24 million. The Hispanic population increased from 374,000 to 817,000 and accounted for 43.7 percent of the total population growth.

The five central cities did not perform equally well. Table 16.1 shows that four of the five central cities had increases in population, with San Francisco–Oakland the exception (1.7 percent decline). Other data for the central cities are contained in Tables 16.3 and 16.4. These data show that the poverty rate fell in three central cities (San Francisco–Oakland, Seattle, and Denver), but increased in the cities of San Diego and Phoenix. Likewise, the number of people living in high-poverty areas declined in San Francisco–Oakland, Seattle, and Denver, increased in San Diego, and was unchanged in Phoenix. Median family real income increased by over 12 percent in the same three central cities—San Francisco–Oakland, Seattle, and Denver—and was static in San Diego and Phoenix (up 0.6 percent and 1.3 percent). Only 5,000 people in the city of Denver were living in high-poverty areas in 2000, a remarkable finding. The murder rates in all five central cities were relatively low in 1990, and declined in all five during the 1990s. The murder rate of 4 per 100,000 population in the city of San Diego was below the national average of 5.5 for 2000.

Four of the five central cities had a good record on single-parent families. This percentage declined in San Francisco–Oakland and increased only by a small amount in Seattle, Denver, and San Diego. However, the percentage of single-parent families in the city of Phoenix increased from 26.4 to 32.0. Also, while the percentages of high-school dropouts in 1990 were relatively low in the five central cities (ranging from 14 percent in Seattle to 22 percent in San Francisco–Oakland), these figures did not improve very much in the 1990s. The average percentage of high-school dropouts declined from 19 percent in 1990 to 18 percent in 2000 (and increased in Phoenix from 21 percent to 23 percent).

How do these five central cities score on the urban rebirth index? San Francisco–Oakland, Seattle, and Denver do extremely well. Seattle gets a score of 7 out of 7 because I award two pluses for the increase in median family real income of 16.0 percent to offset the zero for the failure of the percentage of single-parent families to decline. San Francisco–Oakland scores 5 out of 7 (with double plus for median family real income growth of 13.1 percent, a negative for central city population decline, and a zero for no change in the number of people living in high-poverty areas). Denver also scores 5 out of 7 (with zeroes for no change in single-parent families and high-school dropouts).

In contrast, San Diego and Phoenix did not do well. The city of San Diego gets a net score of −1. Positive scores for central city population growth and the decline in murders were offset by the increases in the poverty rate, the number of people living in high-poverty areas, and the increase in single-parent families. Phoenix scores a net of −1 also, as the positives for central city population growth and the small increase in median family real income were more than offset by the increases in the poverty rate, the percentage of single-parent families, and the percentage of high-school dropouts.

Did some version of the urban crisis arrive in the cities of San Diego and Phoenix in the 1990s? This is not a reasonable inference because the conditions in these two cities were better than in many of the central cities of the Northeast and all of the six central cities of the South. Poverty rates were relatively low in 2000—just 14.6 percent in San Diego and 15.8 percent in Phoenix, which are lower than in all but three of the seventeen central cities of the Northeast and all six of the southern central cities. The murder rates were a remarkable 4 per 100,000 in San Diego and 12 per 100,000 in Phoenix. The percentages of single-parent families of 27.9 and 32.0 for San Diego and Phoenix were lower than every one of the seventeen northeastern central cities and every one of the six southern central cities included in this study. The percentages of high-school dropouts of 17 for San Diego and 23 for Phoenix were also quite low compared to the other central cities.

Conclusion

The twelve urban areas of the Sunbelt included in this study produced a rather diverse record in the 1990s. Houston, Atlanta, and Miami in the South, and San Francisco–Oakland, Seattle, and Denver in the West, all did extremely well. Indeed, the four central cities of Houston, Atlanta, Birmingham, and Miami reversed the negatives of the earlier two decades and had urban rebirth. The central cities of Dallas–Fort Worth, Birmingham, San Diego, and Phoenix experienced some difficulties that have been discussed in this chapter. Dallas–Fort Worth and Birmingham did not really turn urban crisis into urban rebirth in the 1990s. The cities of San Diego and Phoenix grew, but poverty increased and median family real incomes failed to grow. However, conditions in these two cities remained relatively good, so one cannot place the urban crisis tag on them.

Los Angeles is another story. The nation's second-largest metropolitan area suffered through the 1990s with job losses that were not fully recouped by 2000, coupled with population growth, an increase in central city poverty, and a very discouraging drop in central city median family real income of 13.6 percent. Los Angeles had a major urban riot in 1992 that harked back to the 1960s.[1]

Note

1. However, the study by Jargowsky and Yang (2006) of underclass census tracts shows that the number of such tracts fell in Los Angeles from 45 in 1990 to just 16 in 2000. Recall from Chapter 15 (note 1) that the definition of an underclass tract is based on relatively high levels of high-school dropouts, female-headed families, households on public assistance, and prime-age males not in the labor force. Underclass census tracts for some of the major urban areas of the Sunbelt are shown in Table 16.5. Underclass tracts fell in Dallas, Houston, and Atlanta (by just two tracts in the case of Atlanta) and increased in Phoenix. Underclass tracts basically did not exist in Seattle or San Diego.

Table 16.5

Underclass Census Tracts: 1990–2000

	1990	2000
Dallas	10	5
Houston	16	7
Atlanta	12	10
Los Angeles	45	16
Seattle	1	2
San Diego	2	0
Phoenix	8	13

Source: Jargowsky and Yang (2006).

17

Trends After 2000: What Is Next for Urban America?

America's urban areas have taken a beating since 2000. We've had recession and initial "jobless" recovery, 9/11, and Katrina. One hopes that nothing else will go wrong. On the positive side, the recession of 2001 stimulated the Federal Reserve to orchestrate a drop in interest rates to historically low levels that produced a boom in housing. Our concern is whether the first half-decade of the new millennium has brought a return to the days of urban crisis, or whether the cities weathered the storm. Clearly the literal answer for New Orleans is that it did not weather the storm, but what about the other twenty-eight metropolitan areas included in this study? In this chapter we take a look at the available data on our metropolitan areas from 2000 to early 2006. Finally, the book ends with a short review of recent opinion on urban rebirth and attempts to assess where the cities go from here.

Recession and Recovery

According to the National Bureau of Economic Research (NBER), the booming economy of the 1990s reached its peak in March 2001. Signs of economic trouble had already been seen in the stock market averages. The NASDAQ composite index had a significant drop in April 2000 as the dot-com bust was beginning, and the Dow Jones Industrial Average also showed signs of weakness during 2000. Real gross domestic product (GDP) declined by 0.5 percent (annual rate) during the first quarter of 2001, increased by a relatively weak 1.2 percent in the second quarter, and fell again by 1.4 percent in the third quarter. NBER dates the recession of 2001 as March to November. The recovery is dated from November 2001, but NBER reminds us that the initial recovery phase can be long and (as in this case) largely jobless. GDP increased by 1.6 percent (annual rate) in the fourth quarter of 2001, and began a strong record of growth with a 2.7 percent increase in the first quarter of 2002. The national unemployment rate stood at a low 4.3 percent in March 2001 and increased to 5.5 percent in November. But unemployment continued to rise throughout 2002 and peaked at 6.3 percent in June 2003.

Total employment in the nation peaked in November 2000 at 133.37 million. The annual average for total employment was 131.8 million in both 2000 and 2001, and fell to 130.3 million in 2002 and 130.0 million in 2003, then reached 131.5 million in 2004. This was the "jobless" recovery. GDP started to advance in the fourth quarter of 2000, but employment was below its previous peak throughout 2003 and 2004. Employment did not come back to its previous peak until the last quarter of 2004. Annual average employment in 2005 was 133.6 million, an increase of just 1.4 percent over its level in 2000 and 2001. This sort of record for national employment is not good for the major urban areas, as we shall see. Total (nonagricultural) employment in the nation increased from 109.5 million in 1990 to 131.5 million in 2000, an increase of 20.1 percent. This is the environment of economic growth that helped the major urban areas and their central cities.

The Federal Reserve moved aggressively to lower interest rates in 2001. The intended federal funds rate was lowered from 6.5 percent to 6.00 percent on January 3, 2001, and was reduced in every month, reaching 1.75 percent on December 11, 2001. Further reductions brought the federal funds rate down to 1.00 percent on June 25, 2003. The Fed did not move to bring the rate up until June 30, 2004, when it was increased to 1.25 percent.

The unemployment rate did eventually decline from its peak of 6.3 percent in June 2003. The average unemployment rate was 6.0 percent for 2003, falling to 5.5 percent in 2004 and 5.1 percent in 2005. During this time the Fed moved steadily to bring the intended federal funds rate up, reaching 5.25 percent in June 2006. Monetary policy had a dramatic effect on mortgage interest rates, which in turn stimulated the housing market. Mortgage interest rates averaged 8.06 percent in 2000, and dropped to 5.8 percent in 2005, a decline of 28 percent.

The national poverty rate was also affected by the recession and jobless recovery. The nation's poverty rate stood at 13.5 percent of the population in 1990, increased to 15.1 percent in 1993, and then fell steadily to 11.3 percent in 2000. The poverty rate started up in 2001 to 11.7 percent, and reached 12.7 percent in 2004—which is the same poverty rate as in 1998. The poverty rate made a small move downward in 2005 to 12.6 percent. The poverty rate for black Americans was 31.7 percent in 1990 and increased to a peak of 33.4 percent in 1992. From this point, poverty declined continuously to reach 22.5 percent in 2000. Since then the poverty rate among blacks has increased to

Table 17.1

Northeastern Metropolitan Areas: 2000–2006

	Urban area population change	Urban area employment change 3/00–3/05	Urban area employment change 3/05–3/06	Urban rebirth in the 1990s
	(in percent)			
New York	1.3	−0.6	1.2	Yes (1980s)
Chicago	2.6	−3.8	1.2	Yes
Philadelphia	1.9	0.6	1.3	
Detroit	0.3	−7.2	−0.8	Yes
Boston	−0.4	−5.6	0.9	
Pittsburgh	−1.4	−1.3	1.2	Yes
St. Louis	2.1	−0.2	0.8	
Cleveland	−0.9	−6.0	−0.1	Yes
Washington, D.C.	6.2	9.5	2.7	
Baltimore	3.0	2.6	2.0	
Minneapolis– St. Paul	4.0	0.3	1.6	Yes
Buffalo	−1.4	−2.2	0.6	
Cincinnati	2.2	0.9	1.3	Yes
Milwaukee	0.5	−3.6	−0.7	Yes
Kansas City	4.5	−0.4	1.4	Yes
Indianapolis	5.6	3.2	0.9	Yes
Columbus	4.3	0.8	0.9	Yes
Mean	2.0	−0.8	1.0	

Sources: U.S. Bureau of the Census, Bureau of Labor Statistics, and FBI.

24.7 percent in 2004, and it remained at 24.7 percent in 2005. However, this poverty rate for 2004 and 2005 is still lower than the 26.1 percent rate recorded in 1998. The poverty rate among Hispanic Americans fell from a high point of 30.7 percent in 1994 to 21.5 percent in 2000 and 21.4 percent in 2001. The poverty rate for this group moved up to 22.5 percent in 2003, but has since declined to 21.8 percent in 2005. In short, poverty increased after 2000, but the increase was relatively small.

How did the major metropolitan areas fare during this time of recession and mixed recovery?

Metropolitan Areas of the Northeast

The U.S. Bureau of the Census estimates that thirteen of the seventeen metropolitan areas of the Northeast gained population from 2000 to 2005. As shown in Table 17.1, Boston, Pittsburgh, Cleveland, and Buffalo are estimated to have lost population during these five years. The population of the Boston urban area had declined during the 1970s, but had grown by 8.2 percent from 1980 to 2000. Population decline in this metropolitan area was unexpected (but small in magnitude). Population losses in Pittsburgh, Cleveland, and Buffalo are not new experiences, of course. In the cases of Pittsburgh and Buffalo, population decline is simply a continuation of the trend that has been in place since 1970. Population had increased in metropolitan Cleveland by 2.2 percent in the 1990s, but gave back 0.9 percent in the first five years of the new century. Five of the urban areas (Washington, D.C., Minneapolis–St. Paul, Columbus, Indianapolis, and Kansas City) gained 4.0 percent in just five years. As Table 17.1 shows, the average population gain for the seventeen metropolitan areas was 2.0 percent, but this is a sizable drop from the average increase of 7.9 percent recorded for the 1990s (3.9 percent increase for each five-year period). For example, the New York metropolitan area added 1.1 percent to population during 2000–05 compared to a gain of 8.8 percent in the 1990s. And metropolitan Chicago increased by 11.6 percent in the 1990s, but grew by 2.6 percent during 2000–05, less than half the rate of increase during the previous decade.

The record for employment is much worse, as one would have expected given the recession and jobless recovery. The data in Table 17.1 show the change in total employment from March 2000 (the month of the 2000 Census) to March 2005 and March 2006. National employment was 130.5 million in March 2000 and increased by 1.2 percent to 132.0 percent in March 2005. This net change is the result of a decline in employment during 2001 and 2002, followed by employment growth. Table 17.1 shows that the average change in employment for the seventeen urban areas was a decline of 0.8 percent from March 2000 to March 2005. In other words, employment in these major metropolitan areas on average performed somewhat worse than the nation as a whole. The problem was the slow employment growth in the entire nation. However, some of the urban areas were hit hard by the recession and jobless recovery. Employment declines exceeded 3.0 percent in Chicago (off 3.8 percent), Detroit (down 7.2 percent), Boston (loss of 5.6 percent), Cleveland (down 6.0 percent), and Milwaukee (minus 3.6 percent). Employment was also down (by smaller amounts) in the Pittsburgh, St. Louis, Buffalo, and Kansas City urban areas. As we have seen, an urban area struggles when it loses jobs.

However, the hopeful sign is the employment growth that has taken place from March 2005 to March 2006. During this single year the nation's employment increased by an additional 1.6 percent, and most of the northeastern urban areas followed suit. Detroit, Cleveland, and Milwaukee recorded small job losses in this year, but the other fourteen gained employment—some in sizable numbers. The average employment gain for the seventeen urban areas was 1.0 percent for the year, in effect erasing the 0.8 percent job loss from 2000 to 2005.

As shown in Table 17.2, twelve of the central cities are estimated to have lost population during 2000–05. Population growth in the 1990s turned to estimated population losses for the central cities of Chicago and Boston. The central cities that gained population during 2000–05 are New York City, St. Louis, Columbus, Indianapolis, and Kansas City. The population increases were 1.6 percent for New York City and 2.4 percent for Columbus, but were less than 1.0 percent for the other three cities. The other ten central cities lost population, as they had in the 1990s and previously. The average population change for the seventeen central cities was negative 2.6 percent. Continuation of urban rebirth of the central cities of the Northeast is not evident in these population estimates.

The other variables that are available for 2000 and 2005 for the central cities are the poverty rate, the murder rate, the percentage of single-parent families, and the percentage of high-school dropouts. These figures show some discouraging outcomes for the first half of the new decade. The average poverty rate for the seventeen central cities increased from 20.6 percent in 2000 to 22.6 percent in 2005., The poverty rate increased in fourteen and declined in only three central cities. The average poverty rate for the seventeen cities was 21.2 percent in 1990, so on this measure central cities have done worse. The average murder rate for the seventeen central cities increased from 20 to 23 per 100,000 population, and increased in eleven. The increase in this average was driven by sizable increases in a few central cities—7 to 13 in Boston, 14 to 24 in Cleveland, 4 to 25 in Cincinnati, and 13 to 20 in Buffalo. These are central cities with low murder rates in 2000, so their murder rates for 2005 are not out of line with the other central cities, but these outcomes are discouraging nonetheless. On the positive side, the murder rate in New York City continued to decline from 9 per 100,000 in 2000 to 7 per 100,000 in 2005 to become the lowest murder rate among these major central cities. Murders also declined in Chicago and Washington, D.C., and changed very little in the other ten central cities. The hopeful interpretation of the murder rates in 2005 is that the average for the seventeen central cities of 23 is well below the average of 30 for 1990. The percentage of single-parent families in the central cities continued to increase—from an average of 50.7 percent in 2000 to 53.7 percent in 2005. At the same time, the percentage of high-school dropouts continued to decline from an average of 26 for 2000 to 19 for 2005. The net scores on these five indexes shown in Table 17.2 are –2 or –3 for nine of the seventeen central cities, which suggests that cities such as Philadelphia, Detroit, Pittsburgh, St. Louis, Cleveland, Baltimore, Buffalo, and Cincinnati

Table 17.2

Central Cities of the Northeast: 2000–2005

	Population change (percent)	Poverty rate (percent)		Murder rate per 100,000		Single-parent families (percent)		High-school dropouts (percent)		Net score 2000–2005 5 indexes
		2000	2005	2000	2005	2000	2005	2000	2005	
New York	1.6	21.2	19.1	9	7	40.7	43.3	28	21	+3
Chicago	−1.8	19.6	21.3	22	16	41.5	44.6	28	22	−1
Philadelphia	−3.4	22.9	24.5	22	26	51.0	58.5	29	22	−3
Detroit	−6.9	26.1	27.0	41	40	63.1	64.5	30	24	−2
Boston	−5.1	19.5	22.3	7	13	48.0	52.2	21	16	−3
Pittsburgh	−5.2	20.4	23.2	11	20	47.9	49.6	19	13	−3
St. Louis	−6.6	24.6	25.4	36	38	57.4	63.3	29	22	−3
Cleveland	−5.1	26.3	32.4	14	24	59.4	63.1	31	26	−3
Washington, D.C.	0.9	20.2	19.0	42	35	57.8	59.7	22	16	+3
Baltimore	−3.7	22.9	22.6	40	42	60.9	65.1	32	24	−2
Minneapolis–St. Paul	−2.0	16.9	19.9	14	11	43.2	39.8	15	13	+1
Buffalo	−3.7	26.6	26.9	13	20	58.1	63.8	25	20	−2
Cincinnati	−4.1	21.2	25.0	4	25	56.6	60.1	23	19	−3
Milwaukee	−2.9	21.3	24.9	21	21	53.0	59.3	25	20	−2
Kansas City	2.4	14.3	16.5	25	28	42.4	40.8	18	14	+1
Indianapolis	0.3	11.9	15.1	12	14	39.8	41.5	19	16	+1
Columbus	0.7	14.8	18.5	10	14	41.1	47.2	16	14	−1
Mean	−2.6	20.6	22.6	20	23	50.7	53.7	26	19	

Sources: American Community Survey (2005) and FBI.

may have slipped back into urban crisis mode during this period of recession and weak recovery for employment. Boston also recorded a net score of –3, and could be experiencing urban crisis as defined here for the first time.

The empirical relationship between population change in the metropolitan area and in the central city remains intact for the first five years of the new century. The estimated relationship is:

$$CCPOPGRO = -3.88 + 0.62 \ UAPOPGRO$$
$$(4.66) \quad (2.29)$$

where CCPOPGRO is the percentage change in the central city population, and UAPOPGRO is the percentage change in the population of the metropolitan area. The R-squared for this estimated equation is 0.209, and the t value of 2.29 indicates that the coefficient of urban area population growth is statistically significant. The equation states that an urban area with no population growth would have had a central city that declined by 3.9 percent, and that each percentage point of growth for the metropolitan area would have added 0.62 to the population growth of the central city. As one would expect, population and employment change at the metropolitan level are correlated (simple correlation of 0.601), but no causation is implied because they depend upon each other. However, one additional test shows that population change in the central city was not highly correlated with employment change in the metropolitan area.

In Chapter 15 it was concluded that the ten central cities of Chicago, Detroit, Pittsburgh, Cleveland, Minneapolis–St. Paul, Cincinnati, Milwaukee, Kansas City, Indianapolis, and Columbus all experienced urban rebirth in the 1990s. (And New York City has been given credit for urban rebirth in the 1980s.) Eight of the ten urban areas in which these ten central cities are located gained population in the 2000–05 period. The two urban areas that lost population are Cleveland and Pittsburgh. However, six of these ten metropolitan areas lost employment during these five years, and three of the others gained employment by less than 1.0 percent. Only Indianapolis did well, with employment growth of 3.2 percent from March 2000 to March 2005. Seven of the ten central cities are estimated to have lost population. Only Indianapolis, Kansas City, and Columbus gained population during 2000–05. Whether or not urban rebirth continued in these ten central cities will not be known until a more complete set of data is available, but the weak employment figures for the first half of the decade and the other data in Table 17.2 clearly are problematic. From the data in Table 15.2, these ten urban areas gained an average of 10.5 percent in employment from 1990 to 2000, compared to an average of 2.6 percent for the other seven—the urban areas that did not have urban rebirth in the central city. Metropolitan employment growth can make a difference. As noted above, the hopeful sign is the employment growth from March 2005 to March 2006.

The data for the other seven metropolitan areas suggest a mixed picture for urban rebirth in the central cities. The small increases in population and employment (the latter only from March 2005 to March 2006) in the New York metropolitan area, and the population increase and decline in poverty, murders, and high-school dropouts in New York City, suggest that the urban rebirth from the 1980s may have been rekindled there. Population and employment growth for metropolitan Philadelphia, coupled with a strong property tax incentive for housing renovation and construction in the central city, may have sparked urban rebirth, but the increases in poverty, murders, and single-parent families suggest otherwise. In contrast, population and employment decline in the Boston urban area, along with central city population loss and increases in poverty, the murder rate, and single-parent families, suggest that Boston should be watched for additional signs of urban crisis. The lack of employment growth in the St. Louis urban area is not a good sign. This urban area has yet to show clear signs of urban rebirth. On the other hand, both Washington, D.C., and Baltimore had sizable increases in population and employment at the metropolitan level, suggesting that urban rebirth may have commenced. The other signs for Washington, D.C., are positive, but Baltimore presents a mixed picture in Table 17.2.

The short conclusion is that the recession and jobless recovery have placed in jeopardy the continuation of the urban rebirth of the 1990s and hampered the ability of other central cities to turn the corner. The U.S. Department of Labor (2005) projects that employment in the nation will increase by 13 percent from 2004 to 2014 (in contrast to the zero employment growth from 2000 to 2004). Continuation of the employment growth that is taking place in 2005 and 2006 will enhance (but not guarantee) the ability of central cities to experience urban rebirth.

Major Urban Areas of the Sunbelt

The major urban areas of the Sunbelt had more population and employment growth than did the northeastern urban areas from 2000 to 2005. Table 17.3 shows that the average population growth for the twelve urban areas was 5.7 percent, and Table 17.4 shows that the central city population increased by an average of 2.8 percent over these five years. Total employment in these metropolitan areas increased by 2.3 percent on average, which exceeds the national employment growth figure. Table 17.4 shows that the central city poverty rate increased from an average of 19.6 percent in 2000 to 20.4 percent

Table 17.3

Metropolitan Areas of the Sunbelt: 2000–2006 (in percent)

	Urban area population change	Urban area employment change: 3/00–3/05	Urban area employment change: 3/05–3/06
Dallas–Fort Worth	8.8	0	3.5
Houston	9.0	3.9	3.1
New Orleans	0.5	−1.3	n.a.
Atlanta	11.1	1.1	3.2
Birmingham	2.7	0	1.5
Miami	6.0	9.7	3.1
Los Angeles	5.6	4.4	1.6
San Francisco–Oakland	−0.6	−6.4	1.9
Seattle	2.4	−1.9	4.2
Denver	3.1	−1.4	2.0
San Diego	5.2	7.3	1.7
Phoenix	14.2	11.9	6.3
Mean	5.7	2.3	2.9

Sources: U.S. Bureau of the Census, Bureau of Labor Statistics, and FBI.

in 2005 (a smaller increase than in the Northeast). As in the Northeast, the average murder rate increased in the twelve Sunbelt central cities from 17 to 19 per 100,000 population. But it is important to remember that the average murder rate for these central cities was 31 in 1990. The percentage of single-parent families continued to increase (except in New Orleans and Seattle), and the percentage of high-school dropouts continued to decline in every one of the twelve central cities.

The six metropolitan areas of the South included in this study had varied experiences. Dallas–Fort Worth, Houston, and Atlanta all had population growth figures at the metropolitan level of 8.8 percent or more—in just five years. Metropolitan Miami's population increased by 6.0 percent, and Birmingham added 2.7 percent. The New Orleans urban area increased by only 0.5 percent. The central city populations of Birmingham and New Orleans are estimated to have declined, and the other four are estimated to have increased. However, employment in three of the urban areas failed to grow from March 2000 to March 2005; those were Dallas–Fort Worth, New Orleans, and Birmingham. Houston and Miami added sizable numbers of jobs in these five years: 3.9 percent in Houston and 9.7 percent for Miami. Employment growth in Atlanta was a weaker 1.1 percent. Leaving aside New Orleans, the other five recorded significant employment gains from

Table 17.4

Central Cities of the Sunbelt: 2000–2005

	Population change (percent)	Poverty rate (percent)		Murder rate (per 100,000)		Single-parent families (percent)		High-school dropouts (percent)		Net score 2000–2005 5 indexes
		2000	2005	2000	2005	2000	2005	2000	2005	
Dallas–Fort Worth	6.0	17.2	21.0	21	14	34.5	38.1	30	27	+1
Houston	2.9	19.2	22.9	12	17	33.0	36.1	30	28	−1
New Orleans	−4.8	27.9	24.5	43	57	54.7	54.8	25	18	0
Atlanta	12.9	24.4	26.9	32	19	59.0	66.1	23	17	+1
Birmingham	−4.6	24.7	28.9	31	45	54.7	63.5	24	19	−3
Miami	6.3	28.5	28.3	17	14	44.0	55.8	47	37	+2
Los Angeles	3.8	22.1	20.1	15	13	32.4	36.5	33	28	+3
San Francisco—Oakland	−3.7	14.1	14.3	8	17	31.8	32.9	19	18	−3
Seattle	2.3	11.8	12.3	7	4	30.1	29.8	10	8	+3
Denver	1.8	14.3	15.3	6	11	35.4	38.4	21	18	−1
San Diego	0.5	14.6	13.5	4	4	27.9	30.3	17	13	+1
Phoenix	10.3	15.8	16.4	12	15	32.0	36.8	23	21	−1
Means	2.8	19.6	20.4	17	19	39.1	43.3	25	21	

Sources: American Community Survey (2005) and FBI.

March 2005 to March 2006. The average gain for the five urban areas is 2.9 percent in just one year, exceeding the national employment growth rate of 1.6 percent. The Bureau of Labor Statistics recorded an employment level of 426,000 for New Orleans in March 2006, down 30.5 percent from 613,000 in March 2005. This is one reasonably accurate estimate of the devastating impact of Hurricane Katrina.

The poverty rate in the central cities increased in four (Dallas–Fort Worth, Houston, Atlanta, and Birmingham) and declined in New Orleans and Miami. Central city murder rates also present a mixed picture. The murder rate declined in Dallas–Fort Worth, Atlanta, and Miami, but increased in Houston, New Orleans, and Birmingham. The murder rate in New Orleans of 57 per 100,000 population (an increase from 43 in 2000) was the highest among the twenty-nine central cities included in this study. Single-parent families increased in all but New Orleans, but high-school dropouts declined in all six central cities. The net scores shown in Table 17.4 for the six central cities on these five indexes suggest that Birmingham may have returned to urban crisis status in the first half of the new decade.

Recall from Chapter 16 that four of the southern central cities experienced urban rebirth in the 1990s (Houston, New Orleans, Atlanta, and Miami). The data in Tables 17.3 and 17.4 suggest that urban rebirth has been put on hold in Houston, New Orleans, and Atlanta, but Miami has continued after 2000 (although it is too early to reach a firm conclusion). Miami has a net score of +2 on the five indexes displayed in Table 17.4, but the other three are at –1, 0, or +1. These considerations are no longer relevant for New Orleans as it struggles to come back from one of the nation's worst natural disasters. It was also concluded in Chapter 16 that Dallas–Fort Worth and Birmingham did not provide clear evidence of urban rebirth in the 1990s. Dallas–Fort Worth had strong population growth from 2000 to 2005, but no employment growth. The murder rate declined (from 21 to 14 per 100,000 population), but poverty and single-parent families increased. Whether the two central cities of Dallas and Fort Worth have moved in urban rebirth status since 2000 cannot be determined as of this writing, although the employment growth of 3.5 percent from March 2005 to March 2006 is a hopeful sign. Birmingham had some population growth at the metropolitan level, but employment did not grow until after March 2005, and central city population fell. Poverty and single-parent families both increased. And the murder rate increased from 31 to 45 per 100,000, a very high rate. With a net score of –3, these data suggest that Birmingham has reentered urban crisis.

Now we head to the West. As shown in Table 17.3, five of the six metropolitan areas gained population. San Francisco–Oakland was the exception, with a slight decline of 0.6 percent. This population decline for an urban area in the West is not just unusual, it is unique. The Phoenix urban area led the group with a population increase of 14.2 percent, and the average population growth for the six urban areas was 5.0 percent. And five of the six central cities gained population as well. Table 17.4 indicates that the central cities of San Francisco and Oakland lost 3.7 percent of their combined populations, while population grew in the other five central cities. However, three of the six urban areas experienced declines in total employment from March 2000 to March 2005 (San Francisco–Oakland, Seattle, and Denver). The Los Angeles, San Diego, and Phoenix metropolitan areas added jobs from 2000 to 2005 (by 4.4 percent, 7.3 percent, and 11.9 percent, respectively). Employment in all six urban areas increased from March 2005 to March 2006 by an average of 3.0 percent (with a remarkable increase of 6.3 percent in the Phoenix urban area in this single year). The poverty rates in the six central cities remained relatively low, but did increase by more than a small fraction in three (Seattle, Denver, and Phoenix). The murder rates in the central cities of the West also remained relatively low, but increased in three cases—San Francisco–Oakland, Denver, and Phoenix. Single-parent families increased in five central cities (excepting Seattle), and high-school dropouts continued to decline marginally in all six.

In Chapter 16 it was concluded that the city of Los Angeles was experiencing its version of the urban crisis in the 1990s. The data in Tables 17.3 and 17.4 suggest that Los Angeles may have turned the corner and moved into the urban rebirth category. Population increased at both the metropolitan and central city levels, employment increased in the metropolitan area, and the poverty, murder, and high-school dropout rates in the central city show positive trends. The city of Los Angeles thus earns a net score of +3 for 2000 to 2005. All of this is good news for Los Angeles. San Francisco–Oakland, Seattle, and Denver turned in very strong performances in the 1990s, but as we have seen, San Francisco–Oakland encountered problems after 2000. Population and employment fell, and the murder rate in the central city increased. Given the strength that this urban area has displayed in the past, it is not likely that an urban crisis of northeastern standards has arrived in San Francisco–Oakland, but the record for the five years from 2000 to 2005 is worrisome. Seattle and Denver had population growth (at both metropolitan and central city levels) coupled with employment decline from 2000 to 2005—not a good combination. The hopeful sign is the employment growth in both urban areas since March 2005. Further, the city of Seattle recorded an additional decline in the murder rate, a decline in single-parent families, and reached a very low high-school dropout figure of 8 percent to earn a strong +3 score on the index in Table 17.4. The net score for Denver, on the other hand, is –1 because of the increase in poverty, murders, and single-parent families during 2000–05. San Diego, which had a mixed record in the 1990s, has turned in an excellent record since 2000. Population and employment have increased, poverty has declined, and San Diego has the remarkably low murder rate of 4 per 100,000 population. San Diego may well have entered the urban rebirth category, but a net score of just +1 on the index in Table 17.4 leaves this open to question at this time. Phoenix also had strong population and employment growth and maintained a relatively low murder rate. However, poverty, murders, and single-parent families increased in Phoenix.

The good news in the Sunbelt consists of the some strongly positive data for the central cities of Miami, Los Angeles, Seattle, and San Diego (especially Los Angeles). The other eight central cities present a mixed picture, largely because of the weak employment performance that occurred at the metropolitan level from 2000 to 2005. As in the Northeast, the urban areas of the Sunbelt that lost jobs in the first half of the new decade are cause for concern. Also, the general increase in poverty, murders, and single-parent families during these years is worrisome. But the job growth since March 2005 is reason to be optimistic.

Urban Rebirth: A Sampling of Opinion

The positive trends in some major urban areas in the 1990s caught the attention of several observers. This section provides a sampling of the thoughts that have been offered. The terms "comeback cities, resurgent cities, urban renaissance, and decline of the underclass" have been used by some researchers to describe "it." There is little agreement about what "it" is, how "it" should be measured, and what caused "it."

An early contribution is the book by Grogan and Proscio (2000) that was published before the final results of the 2000 Census of Population had been posted. Grogan and Proscio base their book *Comeback Cities* on four positive trends that are "quite different from one another but nevertheless linked" (2000, p. 3). They are:

- the expanding community development movement;
- the rebirth of market demand in the inner city, resulting from immigration, increasing flows of credit, and retail growth;
- the decline in crime; and
- more effective, less bureaucratic public policy such as welfare reform, the transformation of public housing, and initial steps to improve public schools.

The book provides a wealth of anecdotal evidence on each of these points, with special reference to the rebirth of the South Bronx in New York City. Grogan and Proscio conclude, "Individually small and uneven, when these changes are seen together, they add up to something coherent and phenomenal" (2000, p. 242). They argue that cities need continuation of all four forces listed above: "neighborhood-based development, private capital, public order, and deregulated or decentralized service systems" (2000, p. 243). Pragmatism is needed, not dogma. Based on the data presented in this book, these prescriptions certainly appear to be reasonable. However, one hastens to add that a strong national economy is what provides the underlying engine for urban rebirth.

A very recent contribution is the special issue of *Urban Studies* for July 2006, which is entitled "Resurgent Cities?" Note the question mark that is part of the title of the issue. The issue includes an article by Glaeser and Gottlieb (2006) that is a study of the top ten central cities in the United States from 1950 to 2000. The title of the article is "Urban Resurgence and the Consumer City." The authors conclude that cities have rebounded since the 1980s, but that the rebound has come primarily in the form of higher housing prices. Higher housing prices reflect the increasing attractiveness of cities as places to live, which depends upon the decline in crime and the increase in urban amenities such as museums, restaurants, and other forms of entertainment. For Glaeser and Gottlieb, "resurgent city" refers to increased attractiveness to the upper-middle class. This book has concentrated on the urban crisis that gripped the urban underclass, and rebirth is seen in that context.

Others have sought to explain why some northeastern cities thrive while others languish. A short piece by Julia Vitullo-Martin (2006) argues that cities have different cultures. Some cities have more "combativeness and cunning" than do others. New York City fought back from the disastrous 1970s, but Philadelphia has not been as effective. In Chicago Mayor Richard Daley and his administration have turned the city into what Vitullo-Martin calls "probably the most beautiful of post-industrial cities" (2006, p. W13). One might add that Chicago, with the assistance of the federal government, is aggressively transforming its public housing from the high-rise disasters to more benign low-rise, mixed-income neighborhoods. Indeed, Philadelphia decided to take aggressive action by providing a ten-year property tax holiday for new or substantially renovated housing. A walk around Philadelphia confirms the effect of this policy.

This survey of opinion would be incomplete without the argument by Joel Kotkin (2006) that the urban renaissance is "the ersatz urban renaissance." Kotkin cites some of the population data for 2000 to 2005 presented in this chapter to conclude, "This gives considerable lie to the notion, popularized over a decade, that cities are enjoying a historic rebound." Central cities, he argues, continue to decline even though they are attracting some upper-middle class residents—who drive up housing prices in some locations. Kotkin ignores the extensive data on urban rebirth presented in Chapter 15. Nevertheless, he is correct to point out that the data for the first five years of the twenty-first century are cause for concern.

Whither Urban America?

One good decade, followed by a period of recession and tepid recovery of employment and one year of strong employment growth, perhaps does not make a permanent trend. We simply will not know whether the urban rebirth that was clearly evident in the 1990s has continued until the full story of the current decade is told. The data for the northeastern central cities in Table 17.2 paint a negative picture for the 2000–05 years. But the history of urban America recounted in this book has indeed consisted of three acts—growth, crisis, and rebirth. Whether Act 3 continues or has become Act 4 is a question that must be answered later in another book.

One indicator of where urban America is headed is implied in the urban areas that were not included in this study. The seventeen urban areas of the Northeast included in the study are the largest urban areas in this region as of 2000. The next-largest one is Providence, Rhode Island, with a population of 1.19 million in 2000—considerably less than the population of Columbus of 1.64 million. Providence is an urban area that is not growing rapidly (with population growth of 4.9 percent in the 1990s). The future for the urban Northeast largely will be in the seventeen urban areas included in this study. The six urban areas of the West that are included in this study are also the largest six in this region. The next-largest is Portland, Oregon, with a population of 1.92 million in 2000—less than the population of the Denver urban area of 2.13 million. However, Portland, San Jose, Sacramento, and Las Vegas are all growing rapidly and clearly represent important parts of the future of urban America.

The six urban areas of the South that were chosen for this study were the largest in the region in 1950, but this picture has changed dramatically. The recent past, and foreseeable future, for urban America includes rapid development of several urban areas in the South. Birmingham is the smallest urban area included in this study as of 2000, with a population of 921,000, and there are now eleven other urban areas in the South with populations of 1.0 million or more (in addition to Dallas–Fort Worth, Houston, Altanta, and Miami). These are (with the population in 2000):

Tampa	2.40 million
San Antonio	1.59 million
Norfolk	1.57 million
Charlotte	1.50 million
Austin	1.25 million
Nashville	1.23 million
Memphis	1.14 million
Jacksonville	1.10 million
Oklahoma City	1.08 million
Louisville	1.03 million
Richmond	997,000

Tampa is the largest omission from this book. It has grown from a population of 409,000 in 1950 to 2.40 million and is a new center for international commerce as well as retirement. Indeed, given that the baby boomers are starting to retire in large numbers, these and other Sunbelt locations are likely to continue to grow briskly. A comprehensive study of the emerging urban areas of the Sunbelt, especially those in the South, would be an excellent topic for another book. Recall that the South had no urban area with a population of one million or more in 1950. Now there are fifteen.

This book about the ongoing drama of urban America shall end on the hopeful note with which it began. Act 1, the period of urban growth, was followed by Act 2, the period of urban crisis. But Act 2 ended and American's urban areas demonstrated an ability to rebound. We are now living in a time of urban rebirth, but it is also clear that the positive trends can be interrupted (and perhaps reversed). I think that Americans should increase their efforts to understand the reasons behind urban rebirth, and to take actions that will promote the continuation of the virtuous circle.

Bibliography

Abu-Lughod, Janet. *New York, Chicago, Los Angeles: American's Global Cities.* Minneapolis: University of Minnesota Press, 1999.

Alexander, Bevin. *How Great Generals Win.* New York: W.W. Norton, 1993.

Alonso, William. *Location and Land Use.* Cambridge, MA: Harvard University Press, 1964.

Ambrose, Stephen. *Nothing Like It in the World: The Men Who Built the Transcontinental Railroad.* New York: Simon & Schuster, 2000.

Auletta, Ken. *The Underclass.* New York: Random House, 1982.

Bartik, Timothy. *Who Benefits from State and Local Economic Development Policies?* Kalamazoo, MI: W.E. Upjohn Institute, 1991.

_____. "The Effects of Metropolitan Job Growth on the Size Distribution of Family Income." *Journal of Regional Science* 34 (1994): 483–501.

Becker, Gary. "Crime and Punishment: An Economic Approach." *Journal of Political Economy* 76 (1968): 169–217.

_____. *The Economics of Discrimination.* 2d ed. Chicago: University of Chicago Press, 1971.

Bennett, Larry. "Downtown Restructuring and Public Housing in Contemporary Chicago: Fashioning a Better World-Class City." In *Where Are Poor People To Live?* ed. L. Bennett, J. Smith, and P. Wright. Armonk, NY: M.E. Sharpe, 2006.

Bennett, Larry, Janet Smith, and Patricia Wright, eds. *Where Are Poor People To Live?* Armonk, NY: M.E. Sharpe, 2006.

Berry, Brian. "Ghetto Expansion and Single-Family Housing Prices: Chicago, 1968–1972." *Journal of Urban Economics* 3 (1976): 297–323.

Bevin, Alexander. *How Great Generals Win.* New York: W.W. Norton, 1993.

Blumstein, Alfred, and Joel Wallman, eds. *The Crime Drop in America.* New York: Cambridge University Press, 2000.

Bradbury, Katharine, Anthony Downs, and Kenneth Small. *Futures for a Declining City: Simulations for the Cleveland Area.* New York: Academic Press, 1981.

_____. *Urban Decline and the Future of American Cities.* Washington, DC: Brookings Institution, 1982.

Bradford, David, and Harry Kelejian. "An Econometric Model of Flight to the Suburbs." *Journal of Political Economy* 82 (May/June 1973): 566–589.

Branch, Taylor. *At Canaan's Edge: America in the King Years, 1965–68.* New York: Simon & Schuster, 2006.

Capeci, Dominic, Jr. *The Harlem Riot of 1943*. Philadelphia: Temple University Press, 1977.

Caplovitz, David. *The Poor Pay More*. New York: Free Press, 1963.

Center for Public Policy, University of Houston. *Databook Houston*. Houston: Institute for Regional Forecasting, Center for Public Policy, University of Houston, 2004.

Centers for Disease Control and Prevention. "Urban Community Intervention to Prevent Halloween Arson—Detroit, Michigan, 1985–1996." *Morbidity and Mortality Weekly Report* 46, no. 14 (1997): 299–304

Chicago Fact Book Consortium. *Local Community Fact Book: Chicago Metropolitan Area 1990*. Chicago: Academy Chicago Publishers, 1995.

Clark, Kenneth B. *Dark Ghetto: Dilemmas of Social Power*. New York: Harper & Row, 1965.

Collins, William, and Robert Margo. "The Labor Market Effects of the 1960s Riots." Working Paper, Department of Economics, Vanderbilt University, March 2004.

———. "The Economic Aftermath of the 1960s Riots in American Cities: Evidence from Property Markets." Working Paper, Department of Economics, Vanderbilt University, April 2005.

Community Renewal Program. *Local Community Fact Book: Chicago Metropolitan Area 1960*. Chicago: University of Chicago, Chicago Community Inventory, 1963.

Crane, Jonathan. "Effects of Neighborhoods on Dropping Out of School and Teenage Childbearing." In *The Urban Underclass*, ed. Christopher Jencks and Paul Peterson. Washington, DC: Brookings Institution, 1991.

Drake, St. Clair, and Horace Cayton. *Black Metropolis: A Study of Negro Life in a Northern City*. New York: Harcourt Brace, 1945.

Duncan, Greg, and Saul Hoffman. "Teenage Underclass Behavior and Subsequent Poverty: Have the Rules Changed?" In *The Urban Underclass*, ed. Christopher Jencks and Paul Peterson. Washington, DC: Brookings Institution, 1991.

Edel, Matthew, and Jerome Rothenberg, eds. *Readings in Urban Economics*. New York: Macmillan, 1972.

Farley, Reynolds. "Residential Segregation of Social and Economic Groups Among Blacks, 1970–1980." In *The Urban Underclass*, ed. Christopher Jencks and Paul Peterson. Washington, DC: Brookings Institution, 1991.

Fite, Gilbert. "Recent Progress in the Mechanization of Cotton Production." *Agricultural History* 24 (1950): 28.

Forrester, Jay. *Urban Dynamics*. Cambridge, MA: MIT Press, 1969.

Frazier, E. Franklin. "Negro Harlem: An Ecological Study." *American Journal of Sociology* 43 (1937): 72–88.

———. *The Negro Family in the United States*. Chicago: University of Chicago Press, 1939.

Freeman, Richard. "Employment and Earnings of Disadvantaged Young Men in a Labor Shortage Economy." In *The Urban Underclass*, ed. Christopher Jencks and Paul Peterson. Washington, DC: Brookings Institution, 1991.

Gaddis, John. *The Cold War: A New History*. New York: Penguin Press, 2005.

Garreau, Joel. *Edge City: Life on the New Frontier*. New York: Doubleday, 1991.

Glaeser, Edward, and Joshua Gottlieb. "Urban Resurgence and the Consumer City." *Urban Studies* 43 (2006): 1275–1299.

Glaeser, Edward, and Janet Kohlhase. "Cities, Regions, and the Decline of Transport Costs." *Papers in Regional Science* 83 (2004): 197–228.

Governor's Commission on the Los Angeles Riots. *Report of the Governor's Commission on the Los Angeles Riots*. Sacramento: State of California, 1965.

Grogan, Paul, and Tony Proscio. *Comeback Cities*. Boulder, CO: Westview Press, 2000.

Halberstam, David. *The Reckoning.* New York: William Morrow, 1986.

Haugen, Robert, and A. James Heins. "A Market Separation Theory of Rent Differentials in Urban Areas." *Quarterly Journal of Economics* (1969): 660–672.

Hirsch, Arnold. *Making the Second Ghetto: Race and Housing in Chicago, 1940–1960.* New York: Cambridge University Press, 1983.

Hoover, Edgar, and Raymond Vernon. *Anatomy of a Metropolis.* Cambridge, MA: Harvard University Press, 1959.

Iceland, John. *Poverty in America: A Handbook.* 2d ed. Berkeley: University of California Press, 2006.

Jackson, Kenneth. *Crabgrass Frontier: The Suburbanization of the United States.* New York: Oxford University Press, 1985.

Jargowsky, Paul. *Poverty and Place: Ghettos, Barrios, and the American City.* New York: Russell Sage Foundation, 1997.

_____. "Stunning Progress, Hidden Problems: The Dramatic Decline in Concentrated Poverty in the 1990s." Washington, DC: Center on Urban and Metropolitan Policy, Brookings Institution, 2003.

Jargowsky, Paul, and Mary Jo Bane. "Ghetto Poverty in the United States, 1970–1980." In *The Urban Underclass*, ed. Christopher Jencks and Paul Peterson. Washington, DC: Brookings Institution, 1991.

Jargowsky, Paul, and Rebecca Yang. "The 'Underclass' Revisited: A Social Problem in Decline." *Journal of Urban Affairs* 28 (2006): 55–70.

Jencks, Christopher, and Paul Peterson, eds. *The Urban Underclass.* Washington, DC: Brookings Institution, 1991.

Johnson, Lyndon. *Public Papers of the Presidents of the United States: Lyndon Johnson, 1963–64.* Washington, DC: U.S. Government Printing Office, 1965.

Johnson, Paul. *A History of the American People.* New York: HarperCollins, 1997.

Jorgenson, Dale, Mun Ho, and Kevin Stiroh. *Productivity: Information Technology and the American Growth Resurgence.* Cambridge, MA: MIT Press, 2005.

Kain, John. "Housing Segregation, Negro Employment, and Metropolitan Decentralization." *Quarterly Journal of Economics* 82 (1968): 175–197.

Kain, John, and John Quigley. "Housing Market Discrimination, Homeownership, and Savings Behavior." *American Economic Review* 62 (1972): 263–277.

_____. *Housing Markets and Racial Discrimination.* New York: National Bureau of Economic Research, 1975.

King, A. Thomas, and Peter Mieszkowski. "Racial Discrimination, Segregation, and the Price of Housing." *Journal of Political Economy* 81 (1973): 590–606.

Kotkin, Joel, "The Ersatz Urban Renaissance." *Wall Street Journal*, May 15, 2006, A14.

Lee, Alfred, and Norman Humphrey. *Race Riot.* New York: Dryden Press, 1943.

Levitt, Steven, and Stephen Dubner. *Freakonomics: A Rogue Economist Explores the Hidden Side of Everything.* New York: HarperCollins, 2005.

Lott, John. *More Guns, Less Crime: Understanding Crime and Gun Control Laws.* Chicago: University of Chicago Press, 2000.

Madden, Janice, and William Stull. *Work, Wages, and Poverty: Income Distribution in Post-Industrial Philadelphia.* Philadelphia: University of Pennsylvania Press, 1991.

Mare, Robert, and Christopher Winship. "Socioeconomic Change and the Decline of Marriage for Blacks and Whites." In *The Urban Underclass*, ed. Christopher Jencks and Paul Peterson. Washington, DC: Brookings Institution, 1991.

Massey, Douglas, and Nancy Denton. *American Apartheid.* Cambridge, MA: Harvard University Press, 1993.

Masters, Stanley. *Black-White Income Differentials: Empirical Studies and Policy Implications.* New York: Academic Press, 1975.

Mayer, Susan. "How Much Does a High School's Racial and Socioeconomic Mix Affect Graduation and Teenage Fertility Rates?" In *The Urban Underclass*, ed. Christopher Jencks and Paul Peterson. Washington, DC: Brookings Institution, 1991.

McDonald, John. "Housing Market Discrimination, Homeownership, and Savings Behavior: Comment." *American Economic Review* 64 (1974): 225–229.

_____. *Employment Location and Industrial Land Use in Metropolitan Chicago.* Champaign, IL: Stipes Publishing, 1984.

_____. "The First Chicago Area Transportation Study Projections and Plans for Metropolitan Chicago in Retrospect." *Planning Perspectives* (1988): 245–268.

_____. *Fundamentals of Urban Economics.* Upper Saddle River, NJ: Prentice-Hall, 1997.

_____. "The Deconcentration of Poverty in Chicago, 1990–2000." *Urban Studies* 41 (2004): 2119–2137.

McDonald, John, and Daniel McMillen. *Urban Economics and Real Estate.* Malden, MA: Blackwell Publishing, 2007.

McPherson, James. *Battle Cry of Freedom.* New York: Oxford University Press, 1988.

Meyer, John, John Kain, and Martin Wohl. *The Urban Transportation Problem.* Cambridge, MA: Harvard University Press, 1965.

Mills, Edwin. *Urban Economics.* Glenview, Il: Scott-Foresman, 1972.

Mosteller, Frederick, and Daniel Moynihan, eds. *On Equality of Educational Opportunity.* New York: Random House, 1972.

Murray, Michael. "Subsidized and Unsubsidized Housing Starts, 1961–1977." *Review of Economics and Statistics* 65 (1983): 590–597.

_____. "Subsidized and Unsubsidized Housing Stocks 1935 to 1987: Crowding Out and Cointegration." *Journal of Real Estate Finance and Economics* 18 (1999): 107–124.

Muth, Richard. *Cities and Housing.* Chicago: University of Chicago Press, 1969.

Myrdal, Gunnar. *An American Dilemma: The Negro Problem and Modern Democracy.* New York: Harper & Row, 1944 (original edition). Brunswick, NJ: Transaction Publishers, 1996.

National Advisory Commission on Civil Disorders. *Report of the National Advisory Commission on Civil Disorders.* Washington, DC: U.S. Government Printing Office, 1968.

National Advisory Commission on Urban Problems. *Building the American City.* Washington, DC: U.S. Government Printing Office, 1968.

Norton, R.D. *City Life-Cycles and American Urban Policy.* New York: Academic Press, 1979.

Osterman, Paul. "Gains from Growth? The Impact of Full Employment on Poverty in Boston." In *The Urban Underclass*, ed. Christopher Jencks and Paul Peterson. Washington, DC: Brookings Institution, 1991.

Patterson, James T. *Grand Expectations: The United States, 1945–1974.* New York: Oxford University Press, 1996.

Rosenbaum, James, and Susan Popkin. "Employment and Earnings of Low-Income Blacks Who Move to the Suburbs." In *The Urban Underclass*, ed. Christopher Jencks and Paul Peterson. Washington, DC: Brookings Institution, 1991.

Rothenberg, Jerome. "Problems in the Modeling of Urban Development: A Review Article On *Urban Dynamics* by Jay W. Forrester." *Journal of Urban Economics* 1 (January 1974): 1–20.

Sassen, Saskia. *Cities in a World Economy.* Thousand Oaks, CA: Pine Forge Press, 2000.

_____. "A Global City." In *Global Chicago*, ed. C. Madigan. Chicago: University of Illinois Press, 2004.

Schwartz, Amy, Scott Susin, and Ioan Voicu. "Has Falling Crime Driven New York City's Real Estate Boom?" *Journal of Housing Research* 14, no. 1 (2003): 101–125.

Sears, Stephen. *Gettysburg.* Boston/New York: Houghton Mifflin, 2003.

Seligman, Amanda. *Block by Block: Neighborhoods and Public Policy on Chicago's West Side.* Chicago: University of Chicago Press, 2005.

Spilerman, Seymour. "The Causes of Racial Disturbances: A Comparison of Alternative Explanations." *American Sociological Review* 35 (1970): 627–649.

Stanback, Thomas. *The New Suburbanization: Challenge to the Central City.* Boulder, CO: Westview Press, 1991.

Stull, William, and Janice Madden. *Post-Industrial Philadelphia: Structural Changes in the Metropolitan Economy.* Philadelphia: University of Pennsylvania Press, 1990.

Stull, William, and Judith Stull. "Housing in the Philadelphia Metropolitan Area, 1950–1990." In *Work, Wages, and Poverty,* ed. Janice Madden and William Stull. Philadelphia: University of Pennsylvania Press, 1991.

Sugrue, Thomas. *The Origins of the Urban Crisis: Race and Inequality in Postwar Detroit.* Princeton, NJ: Princeton University Press, 1996.

Summers, Anita, and Thomas Luce. *Economic Report on the Philadelphia Metropolitan Area 1985.* Philadelphia: University of Pennsylvania Press, 1985.

Taeuber, Karl, and Alma Taeuber. *Negroes in Cities: Residential Segregation and Neighborhood Change.* Chicago: Aldine Publishing, 1965.

Tomlinson, T.M., and David Sears. "Los Angeles Riot Study: Negro Attitudes Toward the Riot." UCLA Institute of Government and Public Affairs, Report MR-97, 1967.

U.S. Bureau of the Census. *Statistical Abstract of the United States: 1951 and 1971.* Available at www.census.gov, 2006.

U.S. Bureau of the Census. *American Community Survey: 2005.* Available at www.census.gov, 2006.

U.S. Department of Labor. *The Negro Family: The Case for National Action.* Washington, DC: Government Printing Office, 1965.

U.S. Department of Labor, Bureau of Labor Statistics. "Employment Projections." Available at www.bls.gov, 2005.

U.S. Office of Education. *Equality of Educational Opportunity.* Washington, DC: Government Printing Office, 1967.

Vernon, Raymond. *Metropolis 1985.* Cambridge, MA: Harvard University Press, 1960.

Vitullo-Martin, Julia. "A Tale of Several Cities." *Wall Street Journal,* October 20, 2006, W13.

von Hoffman, Alexander. *House by House, Block by Block: The Rebirth of America's Urban Neighborhoods.* New York: Oxford University Press, 2003.

Wilson, Franklin. *Residential Consumption, Economic Opportunity, and Race.* New York: Academic Press, 1979.

Wilson, James, Q., ed. *Crime and Public Policy.* San Francisco: ICS Press, 1983.

Wilson, William J. *The Declining Significance of Race: Blacks and Changing American Institutions.* Chicago: University of Chicago Press, 1978.

———. *The Truly Disadvantaged: The Inner City, the Underclass, and Public Policy.* Chicago: University of Chicago Press, 1987.

———. "Public Policy Research and 'The Truly Disadvantaged.'" In *The Urban Underclass,* ed. Christopher Jencks and Paul Peterson. Washington, DC: Brookings Institution, 1991.

Wright, Gavin. *Old South, New South: Revolutions in the Southern Economy Since the Civil War.* New York: Basic Books, 1986.

Yinger, John. *Closed Doors, Opportunities Lost: The Continuing Costs of Housing Discrimination.* New York: Russell Sage Foundation, 1995.

Index

About the Author

John F. McDonald is Emeritus Professor of Economics and Finance, the University of Illinois at Chicago (UIC). He received the Ph.D. in economics from Yale University in 1971 and joined the UIC faculty in that same year. He is the author of *Economic Analysis of an Urban Housing Market* (1979), *Employment Location and Industrial Land Use in Metropolitan Chicago* (1984), *Fundamentals of Urban Economics* (1997), *Economics of Urban Highway Congestion and Pricing,* with Edmond d'Ouville and L.N. Liu (1999), and *Urban Economics and Real Estate,* with Daniel McMillen (2007). He served as North American editor of *Urban Studies* from 2000 to 2005, and currently is editor of the *Journal of Real Estate Literature.*